I0147878

IROQUOIAN ARCHAEOLOGY
AND ANALYTIC SCALE

IROQUOIAN ARCHAEOLOGY AND ANALYTIC SCALE

EDITED BY LAURIE E. MIROFF
AND TIMOTHY D. KNAPP

The University of Tennessee Press / Knoxville

Copyright © 2009 by
The University of Tennessee Press / Knoxville.
All Rights Reserved.
Manufactured in the United States of America.
First Edition.

The paper in this book meets the requirements of American
National Standards Institute / National Information Standards
Organization specification Z39.48-1992 (Permanence of Paper).
It contains 30 percent post-consumer waste and is certified by
the Forest Stewardship Council.

Library of Congress Cataloging-in-Publication Data

Iroquoian archaeology and analytic scale /
edited by Laurie E. Miroff and Timothy D. Knapp.
    p. cm.
"The essays collected in this volume are adapted from
symposium presentations given at the 2002 Society for
American Archaeology annual meetings in Denver"—
Introd. Includes bibliographical references and index.

ISBN-13: 978-1-57233-573-8 (hardcover: alk. paper)
ISBN-10: 1-57233-573-4

    1. Iroquois Indians—Antiquities—Congresses.
    2. Excavations (Archaeology)—New York (State)—Congresses.
    3. Excavations (Archaeology)—Ontario—Congresses.
    4. Archaeology—Methodology—Congresses.
    5. New York (State)—Antiquities—Congresses.
    6. Ontario—Antiquities—Congresses.
    I. Miroff, Laurie E., 1969–
    II. Knapp, Timothy D., 1962–
    III. Society for American Archaeology.
        Meeting (2002: Denver, Colo.)

E99.I7I65 2008
974.7004'9755—dc22
2008000380

Contents

Illustrations

Figures

Tables

Acknowledgments

We would like to thank the authors who contributed to this volume. Their dedication and patience to this endeavor are greatly appreciated. We would also like to thank the reviewers of the volume. Their comments strengthened the introduction as well as the individual chapters. Nina Versaggi and the Public Archaeology Facility provided institutional support. Justin Miller and Mike Jacobson supplied technical assistance. Finally, we thank Thomas Wells, Scot Danforth, Gene Adair, and the staff of the University of Tennessee Press for their support and enthusiasm for this project.

Introduction
Scale and Iroquoian Archaeology

Timothy D. Knapp and Laurie E. Miroff

The essays collected in this volume are adapted from symposium presentations given at the 2002 Society for American Archaeology annual meetings in Denver.[1] The inspiration for a session devoted to scale and Iroquoian research sprang from our separate investigations at a single site (Thomas/Luckey). As we worked through our respective data, we each began to focus on different analytic scales. It was while discussing our preliminary interpretations that we came to appreciate how varying the scale at which we view our data can produce a richer and more dynamic understanding of the past. With this as an inspiration, we organized a symposium designed to initiate a dialogue among Iroquoianists about the role scale plays in their studies. We targeted fellow Iroquoianists because we believed that bringing together researchers focused on a single region and time period would maximize the synergistic effects of varying analytic scale and would more clearly highlight the role of scale in archaeological research. If scale matters, and we believe it does, then uniting researchers in a focused discussion facilitates the synthesis of research conducted at different scales. The chapters that follow are the outcome of this challenge. Each of these essays presents Iroquoian research with a specific emphasis on scale. Although these essays center on a specific region and time, the lessons drawn from paying critical attention to scale are applicable to any research.

Iroquoian archaeology covers the period after A.D. 900 and includes a wide geographical range centered on New York and southern Ontario (Figure 0.1). Seventeenth-century Northern Iroquoian speakers included the Five Nations Iroquois (Haudenosaunee)—Mohawk, Oneida,

Onondaga, Cayuga, and Seneca (the Tuscarora joined in the eighteenth century)—as well as the Huron, Neutral, Petun, Wenro, Erie, and Susquehannock. Northern Iroquoian speakers were sedentary farmers living in compact semipermanent to permanent villages that were periodically relocated. Iroquoian fields were dominated by the Three Sisters: maize, beans, and squash. By the sixteenth century most villages were palisaded and located on defensible hilltops, indicating the presence of warfare or significant boundary marking prior to the arrival of Europeans. At this time the longhouse had assumed its classic cigar-shaped form, with a central aisle containing evenly spaced hearths, flanked by living compartments equipped with sleeping benches. Each longhouse was occupied by several nuclear families, generally thought to have been related through the female line of descent (Morgan 1962 [1851]; Ritchie and Funk 1973:361–363).

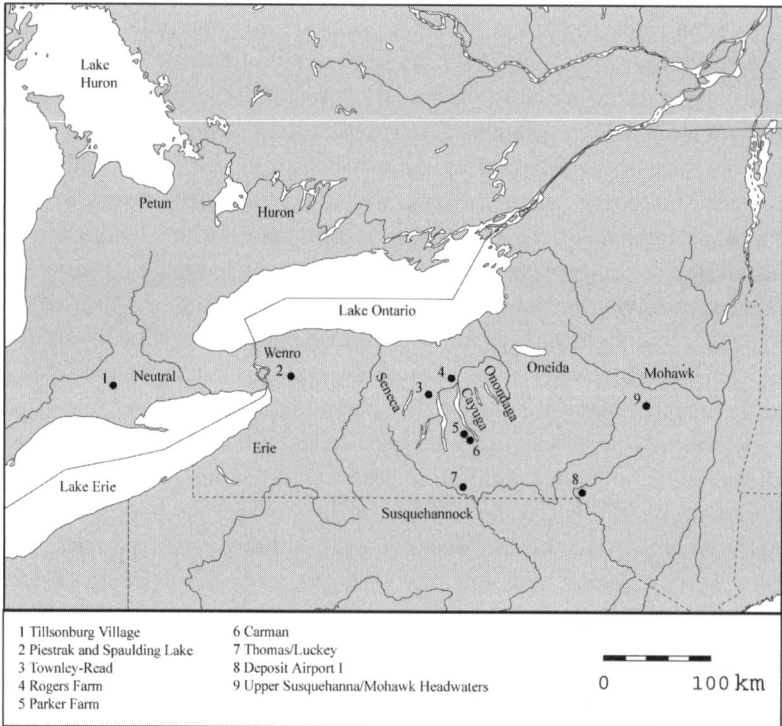

1 Tillsonburg Village	6 Carman
2 Piestrak and Spaulding Lake	7 Thomas/Luckey
3 Townley-Read	8 Deposit Airport 1
4 Rogers Farm	9 Upper Susquehanna/Mohawk Headwaters
5 Parker Farm	

Fig. 0.1. Location of historic Nations and case-study sites

Tipping the Scale

The title of the original symposium, "Tipping the Scale: Levels of Analysis in Iroquoian Archaeology," was intended as both pun and metaphor. As a pun, it plays off two homonyms of "scale," each with distinct etymologies derived from separate languages. One homonym, meaning "a progressive classification, as of size, amount, importance, or rank," arises from the Latin *scalae* meaning ladder (*Webster's II New Collegiate Dictionary* 1999). Explicit in this definition is a form of directional (progressive) measurement (area, time, etc.). Specific "rungs" along the classificatory ladder are also referred to as a "scale" and can be defined as a relative level or degree. It is, of course, this meaning of scale as specific levels along a "progressive classification" that is typically intended when we talk about "scale of analysis." Analytic scale is often defined as the spatial and/or temporal size of the analytic unit under study (e.g., Stein 1993:2). Despite the ladder model, the range of analytic scales available to a researcher is not limited to a predefined set of scales or rungs. Rather, potential analytic scales are best viewed as continuous, ranging from local to global and from short-term to long-term, with a theoretically infinite number of scales between each pole. Although the range of analytic scales is theoretically limitless, in practice archaeologists have tended to emphasize a limited number of discrete scales that they believed to be culturally meaningful (e.g., village or nation). In part this volume is about manipulating scale by stepping on new rungs to see how these might generate novel insights into past social life.

A second definition of scale is "a weighing instrument or machine." This meaning ultimately derives from the Old Norse *skál*, which translates as bowl and likely arose from the use of bowls as part of balance weighing devices (*Webster's II New Collegiate Dictionary* 1999). It is this sense of the word that provides both pun and metaphor in the phrase "tipping the scale." When used as a verb, "to tip the scale" can be defined as "to offset the balance of a situation" (*American Heritage Dictionary of the English Language* 2000), which is precisely how this volume was conceived, as a first step in shaking up the status quo and suggesting that a more explicit focus on scale needs to be applied to Iroquoian research, and by extension to all archaeological studies. Continuing with this metaphor, we would suggest that while different analytic scales balance and complement each other, it might be better to conceive of scale as constantly tipping in a seesaw-like motion, reflecting the dialectic relationship between and among scales, with a more complete understanding accomplished by the movement back and forth between different analytic scales.

Inspiration for a multiscalar approach has its origin in a series of essays by William Marquardt and Carole Crumley published in the late 1980s and early 1990s that drew attention to the critical role of scale in archaeological research (Marquardt 1985, 1992; Marquardt and Crumley 1987). One of the key insights offered by these authors was that more robust archaeological interpretations can be produced if a multiscalar approach is brought to bear on the study of the past. The strengths of a multiscalar approach are manifold. However, as we see it, there are three aspects of scale that are particularly germane: the way in which variability in data is cloaked by the analytic scale we choose; the dialectic or interactive nature of scales; and the multiscalar nature of human experience.

Analytic Scale

The models we construct to explain the past are channeled by our research strategies. Every research project involves selecting a scale of analysis at which to make observations. Typically selection of analytic scale flows from our research questions. However, once a scale is adopted, it directs our investigations in ways that may cloak significant variability. This filtering of data, inherent in all scales of analysis, can profoundly affect our interpretations of the past. Apparently random variation, or what might otherwise be labeled as outliers, observed at one analytic scale may be treated as insignificant noise and ignored. However, when viewed using a different scalar referent, this "noise" may highlight meaningful social practices. Therefore it is critical to consider the impacts of analytic scales on our interpretations of the past.

Within the geographical, geophysical, and biological sciences—where engagement with the concept of scale has had a relatively long tradition—two primary components of scale are commonly recognized: extent and grain (Dungan et al. 2002; Pereira 2002; Turner et al. 1989; Weins 1989; Wu and Li 2006). Ecologists Wu and Li (2006:8) provide succinct definitions of these two aspects of scale: "*grain* is the finest resolution of a phenomenon or a data set in space or time within which homogeneity is assumed, whereas extent is the total spatial or temporal expanse of a study." Adapting these concepts of extent and grain to archaeology, we propose that analytic scale consists of three primary components: spatial, temporal, and methodological. The first two, spatial and temporal, are in themselves distinct components of extent. Given the importance of time in archaeological research, it is productive to decouple time and space and consider them as separate components of scale. The third, the methodological component, is closely related to the concept of grain.

The spatial component of scale refers to the areal extent of data collection for any given study and can range from as small as a single feature to as large as the entire continent. Figure 0.2 lists examples of increasingly more inclusive spatial scales. As can be seen from this list, a number of spatial scales can be defined socially (e.g., tribal, confederacy) or physically (e.g., Eastern Woodlands, drainage basin). However, for many spatial scales the distinction between social and physical is blurred. In part this reflects the mapping of social relations onto the physical world.

The temporal component of scale can range from as short as a single event to as long as the entire breadth of prehistory. Figure 0.3 charts examples of increasingly encompassing temporal scales. Items lower on the spatial scale would have been within the experience of people in the past, while those higher on the scale are largely the constructs of archaeologists.

We have opted to use methodological scale instead of grain because we feel that it more precisely reflects the aspect of scale that we are attempting to isolate, while at the same time moves away from the connotations of two-dimensional grid space sometimes associated with the concept of grain. According to the geographer Pereira (2002:22), "grain is the fundamental unit by which a phenomenon is measured or described." It is this emphasis on the scale of measurement that leads us to refer to this as the methodological component of scale. In an analogy that hits close to home for archaeologists, Weins (1989), an ecologist, uses a screen analogy to explain the relationship between grain and extent. According to Weins, grain is like mesh size, while extent is like the overall size of the screen. While this is a useful analogy, it presents a flat two-dimensional image of grain that is avoided by the term "methodological component."

The key to methodological scale lies in Wu and Li's emphasis on the minimal unit of observation for which homogeneity is assumed; that is the level at which data is recorded. All studies impose a methodological scale for collecting data. Common methodological scales include, but are by no means limited to, type, attribute, and microscopic approaches. As is readily apparent to anyone who has ever observed and recorded data, the very act of recording filters out variability by implicitly or explicitly

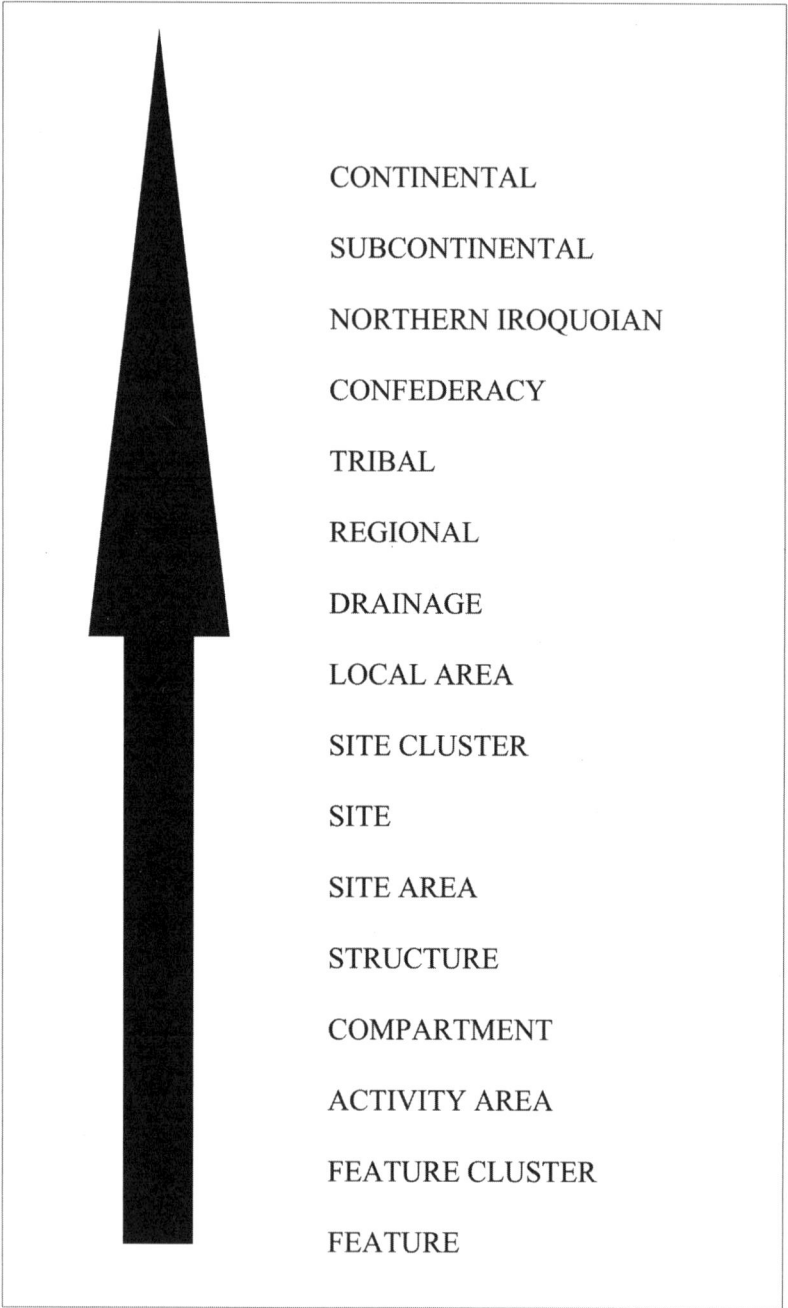

CONTINENTAL

SUBCONTINENTAL

NORTHERN IROQUOIAN

CONFEDERACY

TRIBAL

REGIONAL

DRAINAGE

LOCAL AREA

SITE CLUSTER

SITE

SITE AREA

STRUCTURE

COMPARTMENT

ACTIVITY AREA

FEATURE CLUSTER

FEATURE

Fig. 0.2. Examples of increasingly inclusive spatial scales

ENTIRE SPAN OF PREHISTORY

MULTIPLE TIME PERIODS (e.g., Woodland)

TIME PERIODS (e.g., Late Woodland or Late
Prehistoric)

"PHASE"

LIFE CYCLE

GENERATION

VILLAGE CYCLE

YEAR

SEASON

ACTIVITY DURATION (e.g., length of use
of a hunting camp;
midwinter ceremony)

EVENT (e.g., potting episode, tool-making
episode)

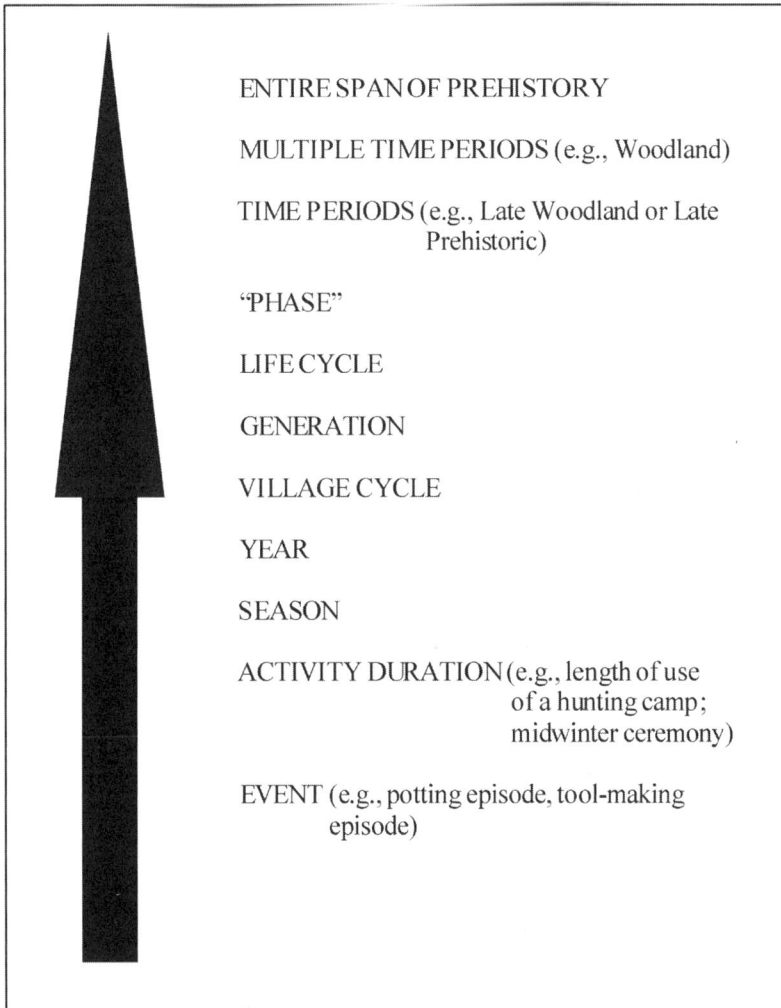

Fig. 0.3. Examples of increasingly inclusive temporal scales

assuming homogeneity at some level. This homogeneity is imposed by the researcher in order to explore patterns of past behaviors. For example, an attribute analysis of prehistoric pottery may include decorative technique as an attribute. Within this attribute there may be a variety of attribute states, such as incised, punctated, or cord-impressed. For each of these attribute states, homogeneity is assumed, with any potential variation ignored. But in fact it would not be hard to demonstrate that there was considerable variation within each attribute state. Cord impressing as a decorative technique is at one level an attribute; however, cord impressing could easily be broken down into a number of microattributes, some of which might include twist pattern, number of strands, strand diameter, or cord diameter. Therefore what is conceptually a single attribute state at one methodological scale itself can be divided into a number of micro-attributes when viewed at a finer methodological scale. Theoretically attributes could be continually subdivided into microattributes while, conversely, co-occurring attributes can be used to identify macroattributes or what we more typically would call types. This suggests that the distinction between an attribute and a typological analysis is largely a false dichotomy, primarily a difference of degree rather than kind, and that in fact there are a limitless number of methodological scales that may be brought to be bear on a given research problem. However, once a methodological scale is selected, variations that might be observable at finer methodological scales are lost, while simultaneously connections that might be discernable at grosser methodological scales are missed. The bottom line is that different methodological scales are likely to provide different insights into past social life, making it important to critically examine the filtering effect of methodological scale and whenever possible employ multiple methodological scales.

Each of these scalar components, spatial, temporal, and methodological, are independent of one another and yet can be combined in any number of meaningful ways. For instance, research on formal bifaces could employ a point type, point attribute, or trace element methodological scale at virtually any temporal or spatial scale. As one example, archaeologists could examine the distribution of Madison points within a longhouse, village, river valley, or physiographic province. Alternatively a study might track the frequency of basal point grinding by season, village relocation cycle, phase, or longer time period. At a microscopic level, one could use concentrations of trace elements to reconstruct raw material procurement strategies for any temporal or spatial scale.

Graphically, spatial, temporal, and methodological scales can be modeled as Cartesian vectors that describe a three-dimensional theoretical scalar space (Figure 0.4). For any given archaeological study, all three of these components are either explicitly or implicitly operative; intersecting at a unique point. Varying the scale along any of these three axes, places a study at a distinct position in this three-dimensional space. Because variability can be masked by selection of each of these scalar components, varying any of the components of scale may highlight distinctive patterns not visible at other scalar combinations. It is this engagement

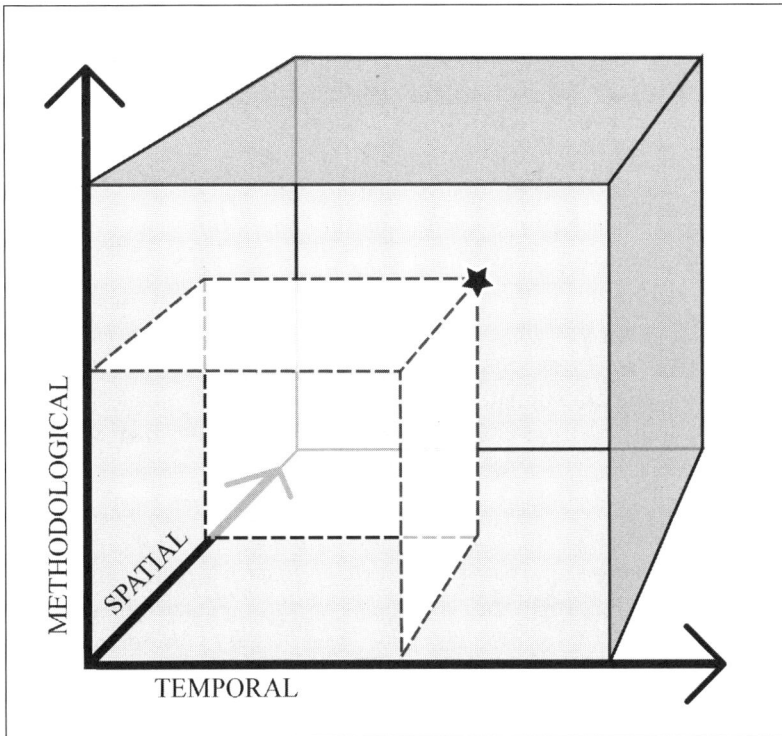

Fig. 0.4. A model of the intersection of the principal components of analytic scale

with scale, by varying one or more of these scalar components, which is at the heart of multiscalar analyses.

The authors in this volume employ a variety of spatial, temporal, and methodological scales, finding creative ways to reveal patterns that might otherwise be missed by other scalar approaches. Although all of the essays demonstrate the relevance of one or more of these components of analytic scale, in this introduction we highlight those which we believe most clearly support this premise. Laurie E. Miroff, Kurt A. Jordan, and Kimberly Williams-Shuker critique a solely regional perspective that tends to overlook microregional variation. In each case they work through local or subregional data sets to highlight important variability, which in turn informs on cultural, social, and economic differences within large regions. Peter A. Timmins, Christina B. Rieth, and Tracy S. Michaud-Stutzman demonstrate how even if the spatial scale of analysis is reduced to the subregion or to the level of a single site, relevant spatial variation can still be masked. In contrast to the above case studies, which demonstrate how narrowing the spatial focus can expose variability masked at larger scales, Timothy D. Knapp's essay shows how an exclusive focus on the local level obscures larger-scale processes operating across a region. Turning to the temporal scale of analysis, several contributors explicitly explore how temporal scale masks variability. Rieth breaks down the monolithic category of the early Late Prehistoric, while Douglas J. Perrelli examines the life history of a site, and Kathleen M. Sydoriak Allen explores short-term activities; in each case these authors bring to the surface patterns buried in longer temporal spans. Several contributions highlight how selection of methodological scale can influence pattern visibility. William Engelbrecht and Timmins apply methodological approaches that allow them to reveal variation in village defensive constructions and population densities that would be overlooked if standard methods and assumptions were applied. Through creative applications of landscape, household, and task differentiation approaches, respectively, Rieth, Miroff, and Perrelli demonstrate how care in the selection of methodological scale provides unique insights into past practices. The essays in this volume demonstrate the ways in which varying analytic scales reveal otherwise hidden patterns, by highlighting how regional perspectives overlook local variation and vice versa, how the selection of methodological scale can influence visible patterns, and how choice of temporal scale may hide important chronological trends.

Dialectic or Interactive Nature of Scales

While selection of analytic scale can obscure patterns, it is also critical given that scalar processes are inextricably linked in a dialectic or interactive relationship. This is most clearly visible in the intersection of local and regional processes. Over the past 20 years, anthropologists have challenged studies that isolate cultures from their larger regional context—studies that treated cultures as bounded phenomena—what Wolf (1982) has aptly characterized as a "billiard ball" model, where cultures bump into one another with minimal interaction, while retaining their bounded integrity in the face of outside forces (Champion 1989; Chase-Dunn and Hall 1991; Cobb 1991, 1993; Kohl 1987; Rowlands et al. 1987; Schneider 1977). These studies stress the importance of examining connections between groups. External relationships dynamically affect internal relations, and vice-versa. It is these interrelationships with which we must concern ourselves as they may influence the reproduction or transformation of a given practice (Pauketat 2001:2; see also Lightfoot 2001:238). Most researchers stress the importance of interaction work with stratified or "complex" groups that are connected in some form of world or miniworld system. However, these concepts are equally valid among nonstratified, small-scale late prehistoric horticultural peoples of the Northeast. Unfortunately we have not always recognized interaction among these farming communities, particularly when interactions cross "cultural boundaries." As Sassaman (1998:94) has cogently argued, "the normative view of culture has had such a lasting effect in Americanist archaeology that the recognition of cultural boundaries still invokes thoughts of isolationism." Rather than assume that Iroquoian horticultural communities were isolated, we must seek data that specifically address how communities, or, more precisely, how individuals within communities, articulated with one another, sometimes across our taxonomic boundaries. It is the recognition that local- and regional-scale processes are inextricably linked that dictates a multiscalar approach for modeling social changes in the past.

A number of essays in this collection highlight the linkages between local- and regional-scale processes. Engelbrecht and Timmins's contributions demonstrate how the degree of intraregional hostilities can affect local-level decisions on village configuration. Jordan's comparison of eighteenth-century Seneca and Mohawk political economies shows that each of these groups responded differently as they were increasingly drawn into the world system. Miroff interprets cultural conservatism within the Chemung Valley as a partial response to regional-scale coalescence of Iroquoian groups in the heartland area. Knapp proposes that co-occurring local and nonlocal pottery styles at sites in southern New York and northern Pennsylvania are the result of the intersection of regional and local processes. And finally Rieth considers her microregional research within the larger regional context of shifting horticultural reliance, changing configuration of households, and increasing concern with defense.

As this brief discussion indicates, and the volume contributors make evident, processes operating at different scales are often intimately linked. As a number of authors show, local and regional processes can not be understood in isolation from one another. By recognizing these scalar linkages, these writers underscore the importance of engaging scale in archaeological research.

Multiscalar Nature of Human Experience

In addition to the recognition of the dialectic or interactive relationship between scalar processes, examining the past at multiple scales is also important because it reflects the multiscalar nature of human experience. Individuals operate simultaneously at different scales—e.g., individuals identify themselves as members of a household, as part of a village community, as clan members, as trading partners, etc. At each of these scales, an individual's role is situational, and one's interests are likely to vary depending on the situational scale. These varying interests may produce conflicts and tensions. At times the mediation of these situational contradictions will result in social transformations. Therefore the intersection of multiple scales in an individual's lived experience is an important locus for change, which requires that we conduct a multiscalar analysis of the past.

Iroquoian ethnohistoric research has often centered on the common theme of Iroquoian factionalism (e.g., Aquila 1997; Berkhofer 1965; Campisi 1980; Fenton 1955, 1978, 1998; Quain 1961; Reid 2004; Richter 1983, 1985, 1989, 1992; Snow 1994b; Trigger 1976, 1985). Building on this literature, Bruce Trigger (1976, 1985) introduced the concept of interest group to Iroquoian studies. Trigger (1985:169) defines interest groups as "specific groupings that emerge within societies as a result of common interests shared by people in concrete historical situations." He further elaborates that "within individual Indian tribes, various groupings based on clan membership, sex, age, trade, waging war, communities, and political factions had opposing interests in dealing with one another, with other tribes, and with Europeans" (Trigger 1985:169). Important for a volume focused on scale, Trigger (1985:170) argues that "the kinds of groups that the historian [or prehistorian] will choose to study are strongly influenced by the scale of the social networks he is investigating." A corollary of this point is that the choice of scale can conflate distinct interest groups and consequently may obscure important social dynamics operating in the past. Therefore careful attention must be given to how scale colors our interpretations.

Individuals simultaneously experience life at a number of scalar roles. Interest groups form around these roles, linking individuals with common needs and goals. Consideration of the multiple, and at times conflicting, interest groups within an Iroquoian community is a crucial scalar issue given that the varying needs and goals of these groups may give rise to structural contradictions, the resolution of which must be a daily negotiated practice. Awareness of these scalar tensions and realities leads to richer interpretations of Iroquoian social life.

Several contributors to this volume highlight the diversity of interest groups that are present within Iroquoian communities. One of the most fundamental and universal ways in which roles are culturally defined is along gender lines, giving rise to gendered interest groups. Perrelli and Allen's contributions directly tackle the presence of gendered segments of Iroquoian society. Michaud-Stutzman's discussion of the integrative function of sweat bathing points out that even within a single gender category (men), interests may be fractured along other lines. Essays by Williams-Shuker and Knapp explicitly deal with the presence of foreign peoples within Iroquoian communities. At times these foreign-born people may have shared interests in common with their adoptive village, while at other times their allegiances may have lain with their natal communities.

To demonstrate that a multiscalar approach provides a richer interpretation of the past, we have highlighted three aspects of scale—the way in which the analytic scale we choose masks variability in data; the dialectic or interactive nature of scales; and the multiscalar nature of human experience. It is our belief that conscious attention to scale and varying scales in our research allows new insights into the past. Thus we have pinpointed where volume essays deal with these three aspects of scale.

Overview

The work here covers a wide scope, encompassing much of the temporal and spatial range covered by Iroquoian archaeology. The research reported covers nearly a millennium (ca. A.D. 900–1800) and is organized in a roughly chronological fashion. Rieth and Knapp investigate the early Late Prehistoric period (ca. A.D. 900–1400). Contributions by Perrelli, Timmins, and Miroff focus on the fifteenth century. Research by Allen and Michaud-Stutzman concentrates on sixteenth-century Iroquoian groups, while Williams-Shuker examines the seventeenth century, and Jordan tackles the eighteenth century. The temporal diversity is nearly matched by areal coverage, although there is a clear New York State focus apparent, with the exception being Timmins's research on the Tillsonburg village site in Ontario. The New York State contributions cover a wide geographic range, including, from west to east, the Lake Erie–Ontario Plain (Perrelli), the Finger Lakes (Jordan, Allen,

Michaud-Stutzman, and Williams-Shuker), the Chemung Valley (Miroff and Knapp), the Upper Susquehanna/Mohawk headwaters (Rieth), and the Delaware Valley (Knapp). A variety of topographic settings and a diversity of site types are also covered, including major river floodplains, terraces/plateaus along tributary creeks, terraces associated with a large wetland marsh, and upland headwater areas. The sites (or nonsites *sensu* Rieth this volume) covered in these essays range from isolated finds to large villages. It is important to note that several of these pieces directly address smaller sites, including campsites and limited-use loci, which have been historically overlooked by Iroquoian archaeologists.

In her contribution Rieth tackles the supposed early Late Prehistoric abandonment of a small area at the northeastern edge of the Allegheny Plateau, as populations purportedly coalesced in neighboring areas. Although her spatial scale is centered on the drainage divide between the Susquehanna and Mohawk rivers, Rieth's contribution reveals how breaking a microregion down into even smaller spatial components (backcountry and major waterways) can reveal important variability, ultimately leading to dramatic reinterpretations of land use histories. Rieth questions the notion of "site" as traditionally defined by archaeologists and instead applies a landscape methodological approach that treats the distribution of cultural materials as continuous, providing a more nuanced interpretation of shifting land use. Her study divides the early Late Prehistoric period (A.D. 700–1300) into two smaller temporal frames of A.D. 700–900 and A.D. 900–1300, which allows her to track land use patterns that are not apparent when the period is considered as a whole. By varying the temporal scales, she is able to identify continued use of this microregion, while at the same time demonstrating a clear shift in land use patterns. Rather than abandonment, Rieth notes that groups concentrate their residential loci along waterways, while they continue to use the entire region for limited-activity loci. As she demonstrates, these shifting patterns can be understood only if considered within the larger regional context.

Seasonal camps are seldom studied by Iroquoianists, who tend to target data-rich village sites. Recently researchers have recognized that nonvillage sites, such as camps and workshops, were an important part of Iroquoian social and economic life. Perrelli examines two multifunctional seasonal camps (Piestrak and Spaulding Lake) in Erie County, western New York, and demonstrates the critical data they provide for understanding the role of gender in organizing daily activities. Adopting a task differentiation methodological approach for organizing his data allows him to group artifacts and features into gendered categories that provide important insights unlikely to have been visible with traditional methodological approaches. Perrelli is able to define meaningful differences between the two sites that are related to gendered Iroquoian subsistence and ceremonial practices. Bringing a life history approach to the analysis facilitates teasing apart the sites' use history, thereby avoiding conflating gendered microtemporal differences in the uses of these sites. His research reveals how the gender domains of "village" and "forest," rather than representing fixed spatial entities, were in fact in flux, with shifting boundaries that undoubtedly involved negotiations between women and men. This local-level analysis provides data for examining regional variation in lifeways and worldview within and between Iroquoian and other Late Woodland groups.

Timmins's analysis highlights how even within a region (southwestern Ontario) there can be significant variation in community patterning, thereby exposing the dangers of uncritically projecting regional or subregional patterns. Timmins critiques village population estimates that rely solely on village size, effectively masking any internal population density differences between sites. His case study concentrates on the Middle Ontario Iroquoian Tillsonburg village site located north of Lake Erie. The site was completely excavated during a salvage archaeology project, and at least 10 contemporaneously occupied structures were identified. The completeness of excavation and the unusual size of the village (8 ha) allow Timmins to consider how researchers have described the village scale in terms of size and population. Employing existing methods for calculating village population at Tillsonburg proves misleading, given the dispersed, rather than tightly packed, nature of the site. His analysis demonstrates that Tillsonburg may represent an atypical community pattern that was consciously designed to include abundant open space. Timmins considers his findings in terms of regional dynamics, by suggesting that relatively peaceful regional conditions allowed the Tillsonburg residents to experiment with a new form of community organization that incorporated open space. Timmins's work highlights the dangers of assuming a fixed, pan-Iroquoian relationship between village size and population size.

Miroff demonstrates the value of a local-level approach for fleshing out regional diversity by applying an explicit household approach to her research at the Thomas/Luckey site in the Chemung Valley. In particular she challenges the homogenizing effect that named cultures (e.g., Owasco or Iroquois) and phases (e.g., Carpenter Brook or Chance) have had on our perceptions of Late Prehistoric societies. Miroff points out that these cultural-historic taxons mask potential spatial and temporal variability. In a two-pronged approach she challenges both traditional spatial and temporal constructs used to characterize Iroquoian groups. Implementing spatial analysis within a household framework, Miroff documents that a single household occupied one of the structures at the Thomas/Luckey site. Through intensive AMS dating, Miroff establishes that the primary occupation dates to the fifteenth century, coeval with the Chance phase. However, Miroff's detailed comparisons reveal that Thomas/Luckey is strikingly different from Chance phase sites in the Five Nations' heartland. Miroff argues that the continuance of traditional practices within the Chemung Valley was a form of resistance to dominant groups coalescing in the heartland area. Identity markers materially signal connections with groups to the south. Through deconstructing existing cultural taxonomies and a local-level household approach, Miroff highlights the temporal and spatial diversity characteristic of the Late Woodland period.

Knapp also confronts the problem of cultural taxa, noting that these taxa are often conflated with cultural groups. Never the intent of these schemas, these taxa have now been reified to the point that they have artificially imposed seemingly impenetrable cultural boundaries, consequently inhibiting how researchers perceive cultural interaction at a regional scale. Knapp examines one form of regional interaction across supposed social boundaries by detailing two local-level Late Prehistoric contexts where "foreign pottery" was recovered in higher than expected quantities. Although the presence of foreign pottery has often been interpreted as evidence of captured women, or "captive brides," even when data for warfare is absent, Knapp offers an alternate interpretation. Instead of wife capture, Knapp examines the possibility that the presence of foreign pottery is evidence for interregional interaction across cultural boundaries. Knapp suggests a more peaceful form of interaction, one in which women actively fostered and maintained ties between communities.

The value of a multiscalar analysis of the local level itself is effectively demonstrated by Michaud-Stutzman. Using data from multiple contexts at the Parker Farm site, an early sixteenth-century Cayuga village on the west side of Cayuga Lake, Michaud-Stutzman is able to weave together data from two spatial contexts—the broad community represented by village-level data and the microhousehold, manifested by a single longhouse compartment—to present a more complete and nuanced picture of domestic life. By examining economic, socio-political, and ritual practices from multiple scales, Michaud-Stutzman illustrates that the types and intensity of domestic activities varied between the community and the microhousehold. Her detailed analysis of a single longhouse compartment reveals how data relevant to a micro-household can be masked by analyses conducted at a village scale. One interesting point highlighted by examining the microhousehold is the presence of a ritualized integrative feature, hinting at tensions between distinct interest groups, in this case men from unrelated lineages or different villages.

The crux of Allen's contribution is the interrelationship between the temporal and spatial scales of analysis. Allen notes that while the temporal scale is at the heart of archaeology, we tend to focus on the macrotemporal scale, given the difficulty of identifying and resolving smaller scales of time. However, Allen argues that in order to interpret archaeological remains, we must pay attention to the contributions of short-term activities. Allen uses practice theory to examine the microtemporal scale at the local, household level as a means to access the gendered division of labor in Iroquois society. To examine microtemporal and microspatial activities, Allen focuses on a single refuse pit at the Carman site, a sixteenth-century Cayuga village, west of Cayuga Lake. Allen's analysis employs a very fine temporal scale, which allows her to compare and contrast individual strata, each of which represents distinct temporal acts. Broader issues of time, labor, and space are illuminated by examining the feature in detail. The size, shape, and contents reveal daily, and possibly seasonal, activities, most likely conducted by women. Allen's focus on the microtemporal scale of a single feature provides a window into village-level activities that is relevant for understanding the practices of the Cayuga as a whole and their relationship to other Iroquoian groups.

Engelbrecht takes a unique approach to the concept of scale by starting with the theme of defense and examining it at multiple spatial scales. Intraregional hostilities were often a prevalent concern among the Iroquois that in part influenced the structure of their living space. Engelbrecht defines several defensive strategies employed by the Iroquois, including the palisade, overlapping palisade entryways, the arrangement of longhouses within villages, and the construction and layout of the longhouse itself. Although the palisade is recognized as defensive in nature, the longhouse is generally described as having social and economic advantages and not ones related to defense. This defense interpretation is strengthened by Engelbrecht's use of multiple lines of evidence, including the ethnohistorical record, cross-cultural data, oral tradition, and archaeological site plans. Engelbrecht uses his data sets to demonstrate how varying the analytic scale allows longhouses to be seen as defensive, revealing insights not apparent when analysis of hostilities stops at the palisade.

Williams-Shuker employs a household perspective to explore effects of European encroachment at the seventeenth-century Cayuga Rogers Farm site. In particular she is interested in which households remained the same or changed during the Contact period. While ethnohistoric/ ethnographic research, focused on broad-scale processes, has been uncritically used by some archaeologists to define traditional prehistoric domestic organization and activities, Williams-Shuker takes a critical approach to the use of these documents. Instead of mapping ethnohistoric/ethnographic accounts onto archaeological data obtained from the Rogers Farm site, she compares the site with the prehistoric archaeological record, with other historic sites, and with the ethnohistoric/ethnographic model to present an account of what occurred at the local level of Rogers Farm. Through a detailed analysis of structural attributes (e.g., bench width), functional differentiation of space (e.g, storage areas), and the distribution of historic artifacts grouped by function (e.g., warfare/ hunting), Williams-Shuker demonstrates that for the Rogers Farm site, many traditional aspects of an Iroquois household endured in the face of European contact.

In the final contribution Jordan highlights the danger of uncritically extending a subregional pattern to an entire region. Specifically he critiques what he perceives as the uncritical projection of the relatively well-documented eighteenth-century Mohawk onto all eighteenth-century Iroquoian groups. Jordan's work seeks to remedy this situation by undertaking a detailed comparison of eighteenth-century Mohawk and Seneca lifeways as revealed in historic documents and the archaeological record. The centerpiece of his study is data from his local-level research at the Seneca Townly-Read site (ca. 1715–54). Regional variation is explored through a detail comparison of housing, use of domesticated animals, participation in the fur trade, farming practices, and property definition. Jordan convincingly demonstrates that Seneca and Mohawk cultural practices had diverged by A.D. 1750. After documenting this, Jordan details the locally specific political-economic factors that framed the choices made by eighteenth-century Seneca and

Mohawk groups, arguing that the Seneca's contact with Europeans was fundamentally different from that experienced by the Mohawk.

As can be seen from the above discussion, a range of topics and innovative approaches characterize these works and indicate that Iroquoian research remains a dynamic and innovative field. Issues explored here include gender relations, regional diversity, changes in land use over time, the universality of village size as a measure of population size, differential responses to European contact, resistance to the forces driving coalescence in the heartland areas, interaction across supposed cultural boundaries, and the organization of village space as a defensive strategy. Approaches brought to bear on these issues include a landscape approach, a household perspective, practice theory, task differentiation, spatial analysis, and deconstruction of traditional cultural-historic frameworks.

Although these essays concentrate on Iroquoian archaeology, our intent is to demonstrate that attention to scale and a focus on multiple spatial and temporal scales result in a more dynamic understanding of the past and is therefore relevant to a wider archaeological audience. These writers present a compelling argument for the importance of scale in archaeological research. Distinct insights can be generated by varying analytic scale; the lived experiences of people in the past involved their participation in social networks at a large number of scales; and a dialectic relationship exists between these various scales. Given this, it is critical for archaeologists to approach their research using a multiscalar approach. As Sassaman (1999) has argued, if our goal is modeling the historical processes and social actions that led to "culture building" in the prehistoric past, we should adopt a strategy that allows us to tack back and forth between local and extralocal contexts (see also Cobb and Nassaney 1995; Crumley 1979; Crumley and Marquardt 1987; Marquardt 1985, 1992; Marquardt and Crumley 1987; Nassaney and Cobb 1991). The research presented in this volume attests to the strength of employing multiscalar approaches in archaeology.

Note

1. In this volume we use "Iroquoian" to refer generically to speakers of Northern Iroquoian languages. We acknowledge that Native Peoples prefer the use of Native names, such as Haudenosaunee, when specific groups are being referenced. We will use the term "Iroquoian" when referring to Northern Iroquoian speakers in general.

1

Reevaluating Scale in the Eastern Woodlands
The View from Eastern New York

Christina B. Rieth

Archaeological studies of Northern Iroquoians are often conducted at different spatial scales and units of analysis.[1] The units used in these studies are often of varying size and scope and include studies of specific artifact classes (Chapdelaine 1995; Kuhn and Sempowski 2001; Morin 2001; Rinehart 2000; Schulenberg 2002; Shen 2001; Stewart 1991), related households (Michaud-Stutzman, this volume; Miroff 2002b, this volume; Prezzano 1996; Williams-Shuker, this volume), individual sites (Hart 2000; Hayden 1973; Knapp 2002a; Lennox and Hagerty 1995; Warrick 1984; Wray et al. 1987), and larger regions (Needs-Howarth 1999; Rieth 2002a; Smith 1997; Snow 1995b; Tuck 1971). Although many archaeologists limit their analyses to one of these spatial units, archaeologists interested in reconstructing past land-use patterns often simultaneously juggle units operating at different scales. In her analysis of the relationship between scale and landscape studies, Wandsnider (1998:90) comments on the important role that multiple scales of analysis play in interpreting local land-use patterns, stating that "the operation of processes at one scale can be said to give rise to conditions perceived at a larger scale, and larger scale conditions set the stage for processes occurring at smaller scales."

A central concern of most landscape studies involves the relationship between site and nonsite units of analysis. As Dunnell (1992) notes, site-based approaches are often flawed since they fail to consider activities occurring beyond the boundaries of sites and ignore the role that smaller artifact assemblages play in reconstructing land-use patterns. Consequently many archaeologists have adopted a distributional or off-site approach to reconstructing prehistoric land use (Ebert 1992). Distributional approaches focus on individual artifacts as the primary units of analysis and seek to understand variation in these artifacts across the landscape.

A landscape approach is of benefit in examining Early Late Prehistoric (A.D. 700–1300) land use in eastern New York. The repeated recovery of isolated finds and small limited-activity loci contradict earlier assumptions that Native groups abandoned specific topographic features in eastern New York. In fact the recovery of these artifacts and their spatial arrangement across the landscape suggest that some areas served as important resource-procurement areas into the thirteenth century. Multiple occupations at several sites further suggest that some locations may have served as persistent places for Native groups.

Background

Landscape Studies in Archaeology

Northeast archaeologists often address research questions related to the settlement patterns of Iroquoian groups; much of their work highlights the important contributions that settlement studies play in reconstructing the activities of Native populations and document the activities of both households and larger communities. Unfortunately settlement studies, as carried out in American archaeology, often present a fragmented view of the settlement history of a population through their concentration on sites (Dunnell 1992:22–23; Wandsnider 1998; Willey and Phillips 2001).

According to Dunnell (1992:22–23), the site concept, as employed by most archaeologists, is problematic since sites are units constructed by modern archaeologists to define the spatial proximity of artifacts and features to each other. Often the historical connections between the depositional events that caused these artifacts to be associated with each other are not explored, causing a spatially related concentration of artifacts to be viewed as the "archaeological equivalent to an ethnographic community" (Dunnell 1995:42). Other problems, including the establishment of contemporaneity between sites (Dewar 1992) and defining the relationship between sites and larger settlement units, have also plagued site-based settlement studies (Teltser as cited in Wandsnider 1998:94). Although archaeologists have often sought solutions to these problems by altering the definition of "site" (Dewar and McBride 1992; Dunnell 1992) and the units used to define sites (Bintliff et al. 1999), the problem still remains that sites often represent inadequate units of analysis when reconstructing settlement behavior.

Dunnell (1992:33, 1995) and others (Ebert 1992; Zvelebil et al. 1992) suggest that smaller-scale observation units, such as individual artifacts, should be the primary units of analysis since they more accurately reflect the range of behaviors encountered by past populations, allow for more accurate delineations of artifact clusters by allowing the archaeological record to be viewed as a continuous distribution of artifacts, and allow activities located beyond the boundaries of sites to be investigated as part of the overall settlement system. Finally the use of artifacts as the primary units of analysis also allows for more systematic comparisons between societies whose sites may include clusters of artifacts of differing size and composition (Dancey 1981:18–19).

Landscape approaches address problems inherent in site-based settlement studies by focusing on individual artifacts as the primary units of analysis (Dunnell 1992, 1995; Ebert 1992; Volmar and Blancke 2002; see also Rossignol and Wandsnider 1992). According to Rossignol (1992:4), landscape studies seek to record "the distribution of archaeological artifacts and features relative to the elements of the landscape . . . [and] provide insight into social and economic organization in the past." As discussed below, the distribution of archaeological artifacts and features is often overlaid by units of time allowing changes in the use of the landscape to be recorded (Crumley and Marquardt 1990; Wandsnider 1992b).

Unlike settlement studies, landscape studies seek to understand the relationship between site and off-site materials (Bintliff et al. 1999:139–141; Dunnell 1992; Dunnell and Dancey 1983; Ebert 1992; Holl 1993; Wandsnider 1992a, 1998:92–95). According to Willey and Phillips (2001:18), sites are units of space marked by a continuous concentration of artifacts associated with a single unit of settlement. Following this definition, sites may range from small camps to larger multiacre communities but do not include smaller, noncontinuous artifact concentrations such as isolated finds (Dunnell 1992:24–25). In contrast off-site (or nonsite) materials usually do not fit into the neat packages and continuous artifact concentrations that characterize sites. Instead off-site studies often include isolated finds and other ephemeral traces found in the intervening spaces between sites (Cherry et al. 1991:21). These off-site materials often represent the locations of activities conducted beyond site boundaries and represent important components of past settlement systems.

In an attempt to bridge the gap between sites and off-site materials, archaeologists often refer to the locations where these materials are found as "places." Following Rossignol and Wandsnider (1992:62), places are locations where the conjunction of resources, topographic elements, and anthropogenic features combine to represent areas of land use. Places can vary in size and scale and may range from isolated find spots (Cherry et al. 1991; Schlanger 1992) to larger architectural features (Chang 1992) to multiacre settlements (Bintliff et al. 1999).

Habitation and limited-activity loci represent two types of places commonly identified in the archaeological record (Binford 1982; Schlanger 1992). Habitation or residential loci are places that are associated with residential activities and are characterized by both subsurface and above-ground evidence (or features) of past occupation. Features commonly found at habitation sites include architectural and residential remains, food- and resource-processing areas, small and large storage receptacles, and refuse middens, as well as more-specialized features such as palisades and earthen fortifications (Hayden 1973; Prezzano 1996; Ritchie and Funk 1973; Snow 1995b; Tuck 1971). Limited activity or short-term occupation loci are places that are created on an ad hoc or as-needed basis to support activities occurring at larger habitation loci or serve as temporary camping venues for travel beyond the foraging radius of the larger residential loci. The features found at these sites are usually not as pronounced as those found at residential loci and may often include the remains of temporary structures, small cooking or heating features, small clusters of artifacts, and a few resource-processing areas (Lennox 1995; Otto 1991; Rieth 2002a; Smith 1997; Stewart 1994).

Determining contemporaneity between places is often difficult and requires an examination of both cultural and noncultural formation processes. As discussed in Cherry et al. (1991), Jones and Beck (1992), and Sloma and Callum (2002), landscape approaches seek to record the distribution of places as a single unit across a continuous landscape. In this approach it is assumed that a group may have exploited different parts of the landscape during a seasonal round or during resource-procurement activities as described above. Since isolated finds and smaller surface scatters are often discovered during surface surveys, one challenge for archaeologists is linking these sites with the contemporaneous landscape that formed them. Compounding this problem are natural processes, such as erosion and alluviation, and cultural processes, such as building activities, which transform the landscape from its original state. Although the recovery of diagnostic artifacts and chronometric dating remain the most viable mechanisms for establishing contemporaneity between places, innovative techniques involving the dating of archaeological sediments (Chester and James 1999) and individual artifacts themselves (Jones and Beck 1992) represent potential solutions to this problem.

Places that form in areas with important resource and topographic features are often reoccupied and may serve as persistent places. Persistent places commonly form in areas that possess unique qualities that make it suitable for specific activities or under circumstances that serve to encourage reoccupation (Binford 1982; Chang 1992; Schlanger 1992:97; Wandsnider 1992b). Examples of the former include locations near waterways, needed resources, or abundant food supply, and the presence of extant features such as residences and storage pits, represent examples of the latter.

The systematic movement of groups also influences reoccupation. As demonstrated by Binford (1982:13–16) and Schlanger (1992), as a group moves laterally across the landscape, the function of a site may change to accommodate the movement of the residential base. Sites that were initially used as residential bases may change functions and be reoccupied as short-term logistical camps, or other seasonal loci. As the residential focus of the group shifts to a new location, former seasonal loci and logistical camps may either be maintained or reoccupied as a new residential base. According to Schlanger (1992), as the group moves further away from its initial residential base, some of these sites may no longer be reoccupied and may fall into permanent disuse.

Landscape Studies among Northern Iroquoians

Although landscape studies are regularly applied to northeastern hunter-gatherer populations (e.g., Carlson 1979; Dewar 1986:77–88; Dewar and McBride 1992:237–241; Leveillee and Harrison 1996; Stafford and Hajic 1992:137–161; Volmar and Blancke 2002), landscape studies among horticultural populations remain limited. Although the reasons for this may be related to the absence, until recently, of adequate technological systems (i.e., geographic positioning systems [GIS]) for mapping and recording the locations of isolated finds and smaller artifact clusters (Crumley and Marquardt 1990; Schlanger 1992:91; Wandsnider 1992a:287), Lennox (1995:6) argues that an additional problem may also lie in our conceptualization of Iroquoian settlement patterns.

Northeast archaeologists have long considered settled villages to be the focus of Iroquoian settlement studies because of the villages' large size, (comparatively) easy detection across the landscape, and potential for producing large data sets (Lennox 1995:6). Although villages were an important feature of early Iroquoian settlements, small and large camps, resource-processing stations, and horticultural hamlets were critical to the survival of these Native populations. According to Lennox (1995:6), "villages must have been a hive of activity . . . with the demands . . . on local resources being incredible. . . . Satellite communities as well as fishing and hunting camps and isolated activity areas must have diffused this environmental drain over a broader area . . . lessening the likelihood of failure." Descriptions of fishing, food processing/procurement, and cabin sites in ethnohistoric accounts of the Huron (Sagard 1939 [1632]; see also Tooker 1991:62–67; Trigger 1990) and Five Nations Iroquois (Van den Bogaert 1988) further highlight the importance of these sites among Native populations.

Early Late Prehistoric Occupation of New York

The Early Late Prehistoric populations of New York employed a mixed subsistence economy involving the use of both wild plants and tropical cultigens (Funk 1993; Rieth 2002a; Schulenberg 2002). The most important tropical cultigen grown by these groups was maize, which Schulenberg (2002) and others (Hart and Brumbach, personal communication 2004) have shown was present in New York as early as the seventh century A.D. Aquatic resources and fauna were also hunted and represent important components of Native diets (Rieth 2002a; Ritchie and Funk 1973; Snow 1995b).

Archaeological evidence from sites located in central and eastern New York suggest that the settlement patterns of these populations were diverse, with habitation, seasonal, and limited-activity loci identified in the archaeological record. Habitation loci are the best-documented facilities and are primarily represented by small villages located in lowland areas atop smaller knolls overlooking primary waterways (Prezzano and Rieth 2001). Unlike seasonal and limited-activity loci, habitation loci are often characterized by a range of settlement features, including circular storage and refuse pits, cooking and roasting hearths, oblong-shaped residences, and tool- and resource-processing stations (see Knapp 2002a; Prezzano 1996; Ritchie 1980:258–266, 280–281). Although many archaeologists have suggested that the Early Late Prehistoric occupants of New York occupied larger semipermanent villages (Ritchie 1980; Ritchie and Funk 1973), Hart (2000) suggests that these types of settlements are not evident in the archaeological record until the thirteenth century.

Limited-activity loci are also an important component of the Early Late Prehistoric settlement system. In the Northeast small resource-processing stations, temporary camps, quarry sites, fishing locales, and other specialized activity areas were occupied (Rieth 2002a; Ritchie et al. 1953; Smith 1997; Stewart 1991). These sites share similar characteristics, including their temporary use, small size, absence of formal residences and storage facilities, and limited concentrations of artifacts and features. In eastern New York limited-activity loci have been identified in both upland and lowland settings along primary and secondary waterways (Snow 1980).

Early Late Prehistoric groups also occupied seasonal loci, including small and large camps and horticultural hamlets. According to Funk (1993:281), these loci were often occupied as seasonal residences during the summer and fall and are commonly found in similar locations as larger habitation loci. Although seasonal loci often contain similar features as larger village sites, horticultural hamlets and small and large camps tend to be smaller in size and often do not display the number of activity areas found at larger sites (Funk 1993:281; Ritchie 1980; Ritchie and Funk 1973).

Finally it is important to remember that the kind of use that these "abandoned" features received on a long-term basis was partially dependent on the scale of residential relocation. Although little is known about the timing and distance movement of early Iroquoian villages, data from later groups suggest that Northern Iroquoians may have moved their villages 3 to 4 km every ten years to deal with the depletion of firewood and accumulating garbage (Sutton 1990). Assuming that Early Late Prehistoric groups moved more frequently, we can speculate that as the residential focus of the settlement system shifted across the landscape, places associated with the former residential locus may have changed roles in systematic ways.

Early Late Prehistoric Settlement Organization and Land Use in Eastern New York

Earlier arguments that the local landscape was abandoned after A.D. 900 as a result of the coalescence of groups in neighboring valleys can be challenged, as the evidence indicates that the study area continued to be occupied after A.D. 900 and served as an important resource-procurement area for Early Late Prehistoric populations residing in the adjacent river valleys.

Overview of Study Area and Local Landscape

A small stretch of land in eastern New York forms the study area. The landscape of interest measures approximately 30 km in length and is located along the northeastern edge of the Allegheny Plateau (Figure 1.1). The surrounding landscape comprises a mixed topography of sloping uplands, which predominate in the southwestern part of the region, and valley walls/floors, which are concentrated along the northern and eastern sections of the study area. Tributaries of the westerly Susquehanna, easterly Schoharie, and northerly Mohawk Rivers intersect the area, providing access to these adjacent river valleys. In addition several smaller microenvironments, such as Hudson and Otsego Lakes, are located west of the project area (Mitchell 1978) and would have allowed local populations to exploit a range of aquatic and aviary resources.

Although earlier occupations are well documented in the region, the occupation of the region by Early Late Prehistoric groups remains poorly understood (Funk 1993; Rieth 2002a; Versaggi 1987). The coalescence of habitation sites in the neighboring Susquehanna and Mohawk valleys

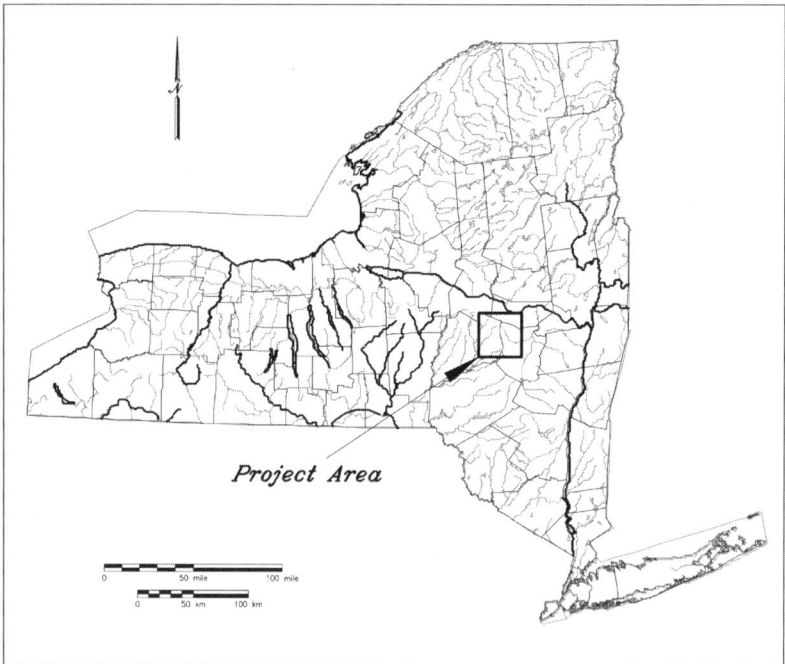

Project Area

Fig. 1.1. Map showing the location of the study area within eastern New York

and the reported absence of large habitation sites has led some archaeologists to suggest that the region was abandoned after the tenth century A.D. (Snethkamp 1975). Drawing on data from the adjacent Susquehanna Valley, Funk (1993:291) similarly argues that the region was not extensively occupied during the second half of the Early Late Prehistoric period, stating that although many sites can be found in adjacent areas, the uplands east of Oneonta have not produced an impressive number of Late Woodland sites.

Recent research completed during a series of highway salvage projects leads one to question this assumption (Rieth 1996, 1998, 2002b). During these projects, information about the number of archaeological assemblages and their settlement features was compiled and plotted on topographic maps to assess the spatial location of places in the region. The results of this work tend to indicate that the region's post–A.D. 900 occupants inhabited similar topographic features as pre–A.D. 900 groups with locations near waterways and known resource-procurement areas (i.e., quarries) being important. Differences in the types of artifacts recovered from these places further indicates that there was a shift in land use prior to and after A.D. 900.

Archaeological Database

Seventy Early Late Prehistoric assemblages have been identified within the study area (Figure 1.2; Table 1.1) and include both isolated finds and sites identified during academic and museum projects (e.g., Ritchie and Funk 1973; Snow 1995b), cultural resource management (CRM) projects (e.g., Rieth 1996, 1998, 2002b; Snethkamp 1975) and local archaeology society digs (e.g., Gette 2000; Schoharie Museum Project File 1999). Isolated finds and sites from academic and museum projects, as well as CRM excavations, were tested using a combination of shovel test pits, larger excavation units, and in two cases mechanical stripping of the sod layer. Excavations conducted by local archaeology society digs were carried out using larger excavation squares and trenches. Surface collections were made at all sites when surface visibility was possible. Sites that were tested simply using shovel test pits were not included in this study, thus ensuring that low numbers of artifacts were not a product of the limited testing carried out at the site.

The artifact assemblages identified in the study area were grouped into two categories: sites and nonsite assemblages. The decision to group artifacts into these two categories was partially influenced by the need to describe adequately the assemblage at hand and to provide a format

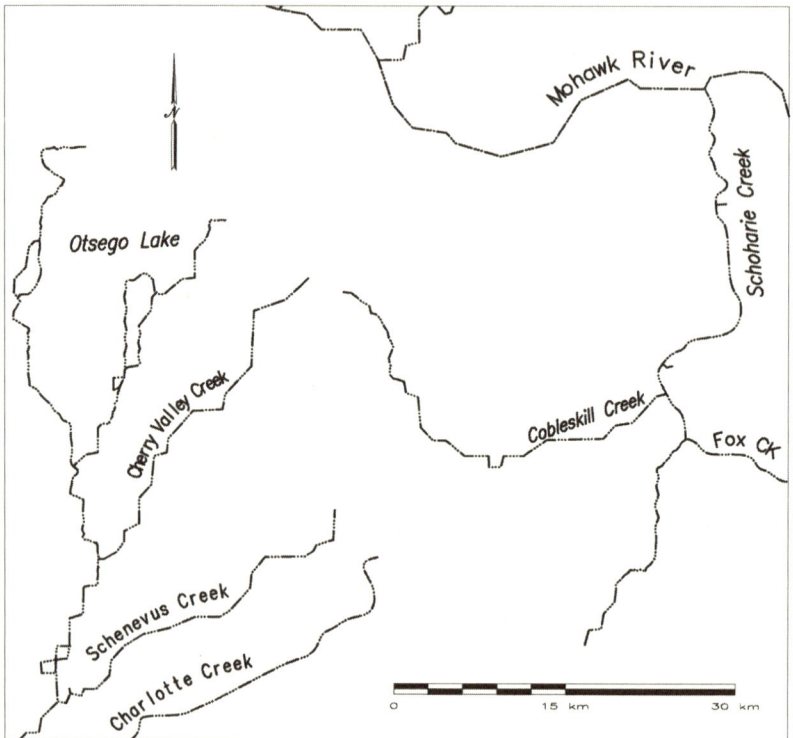

Fig. 1.2. Detail map of the study area

Table 1.1. Summary of Site and Nonsite Assemblages

Period	Sites	Nonsites	Total
Pre–A.D. 900 (c. A.D. 700–900)	14	17	31
Post–A.D. 900 (c. A.D. 900–1300)	8	27	35
Multicomponent pre–A.D. 900/ post–A.D. 900	4	—	4
Total	26	44	70

in which data sets collected by a diverse group of researchers and under different circumstances could be incorporated. For the purpose of this project, "sites" are identified as assemblages with at least 25 artifacts and three or more features. These assemblages largely include habitation and seasonal loci. Nonsite assemblages are characterized by less than 25

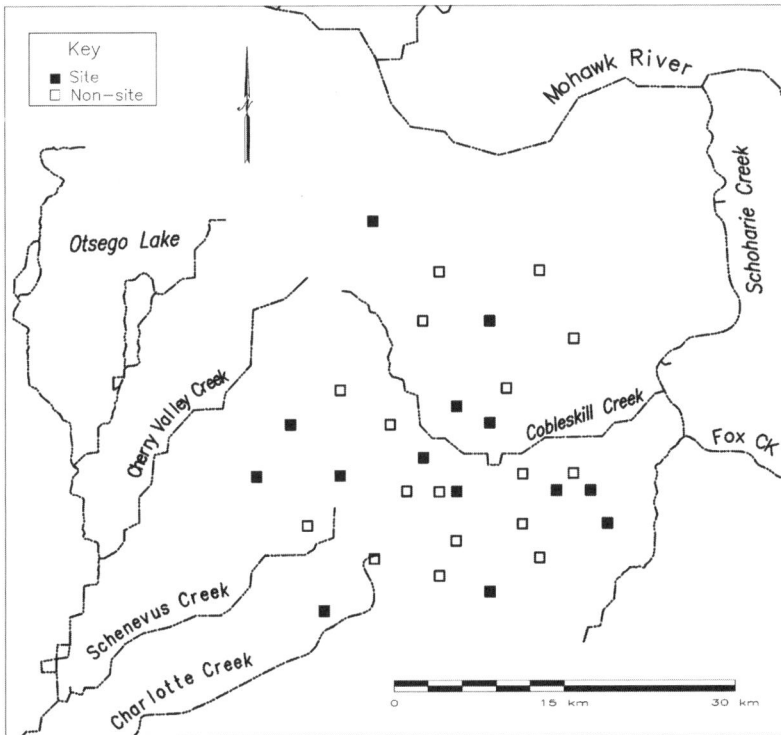

Fig. 1.3. Map showing the location of pre-A.D. 900 site and nonsite assemblages

artifacts and less than three features. Small camps, isolated finds, and resource-gathering areas (e.g., chert outcrops) make up these nonsite assemblages.

The Early Late Prehistoric assemblages identified within the study area were also grouped into two categories based on calibrated radiocarbon dates and diagnostic artifacts. The first group is associated with the occupation of the region prior to A.D. 900 and consists of assemblages that date between A.D. 700 and 900. Thirty-one assemblages dating prior to A.D. 900 were identified within the study area (Table 1.1; Figure 1.3). Fourteen assemblages were classified as sites, while the remaining 17 assemblages were nonsites. The second group postdates A.D. 900 and includes assemblages dating between A.D. 900 and 1300. Thirty-five assemblages were identified, including eight sites and 27 nonsites (Table 1.1; Figure 1.4). Four multicomponent sites were also identified and produced pre– and post–A.D. 900 deposits (Table 1.1; Figure 1.5).

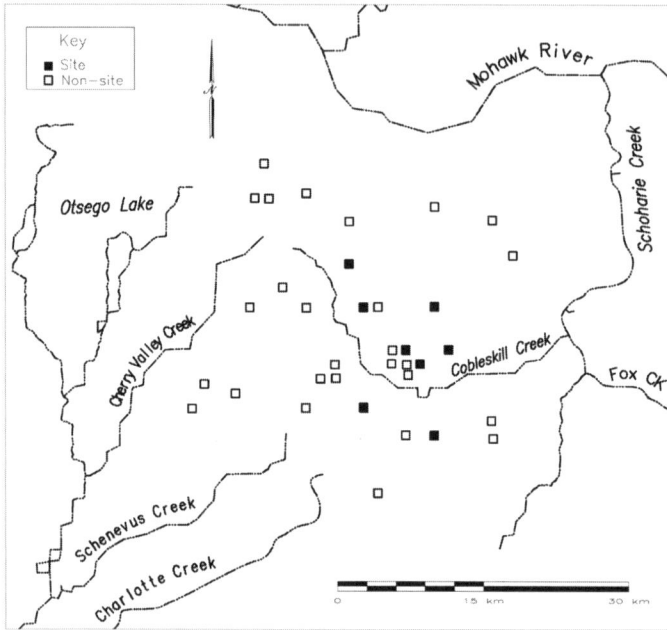

Fig. 1.4. Map showing the location of post-A.D. 900 site and nonsite assemblages

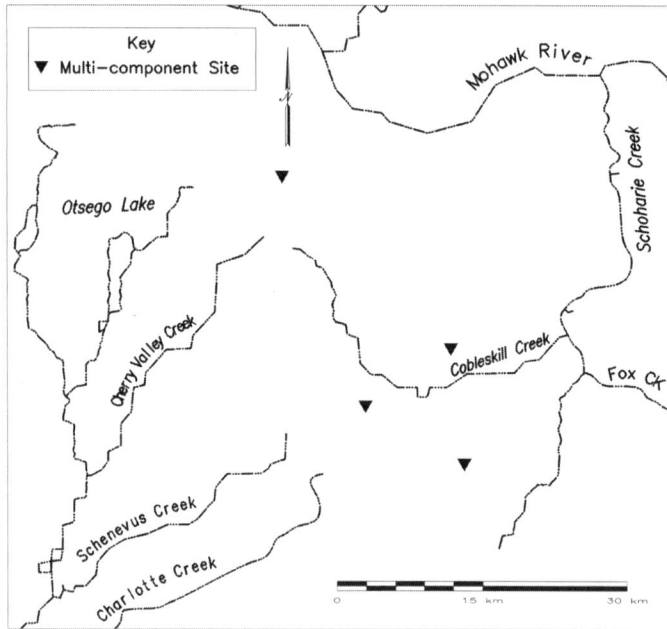

Fig. 1.5. Map showing the location of multicomponent sites in the study area

Early Late Prehistoric Land Use

Figures 1.3, 1.4, and 1.5 illustrate the locations of site and nonsite assemblages within the study area. As shown in these figures, Early Late Prehistoric assemblages were recovered from places located along the Cobleskill and Cherry Valley Creeks and along tributaries of these waterways. Overall, nonsite assemblages (44 or 63 percent) outnumber site assemblages (26 or 37 percent) and show a more dispersed pattern across the landscape. Within the study area, site assemblages tend to cluster along primary waterways and are usually not found in backcountry areas. Of the 26 site assemblages identified within the study area, only five (19.2 percent) assemblages were recovered from backcountry areas.

Nonsite assemblages, however, are predominantly found in backcountry areas away from major waterways. Of the 44 nonsite assemblages identified, 33 (or 75 percent) were located more than 2 km from the Cobleskill and Cherry Valley Creeks. The remaining assemblages were found in floodplain and terrace settings adjacent to these waterways.

When viewed in terms of pre– and post–A.D. 900 assemblages, the spatial arrangement of these places provides information about changes in land-use patterns through time. The distribution of pre–A.D. 900 assemblages is illustrated in Figure 1.3. Pre–A.D. 900 sites are concentrated in the eastern and western portions of the study area within a radius of 12 km of the Cobleskill Creek. Of the 14 pre–A.D. 900 sites identified, nine (64.3 percent) sites were situated on the floodplains and lower terraces of the creek, while five (35.7 percent) sites were found in backcountry locations. These sites range in size from 250 to 10,500 m^2 and largely consist of seasonal loci occupied during the summer and fall months. Charred floral and faunal remains were recovered from the Osterhout 57 (Schoharie Museum Project File 1999) and Smith Farm sites (Fort Plain Museum 2002) and document the seasonal use of these sites. Features, including circular hearths, middens, refuse pits, and post molds, were identified at these sites and document cooking, food-processing, and residential-construction activities.

Artifacts recovered from the Osterhout 57 (Schoharie Museum Project File 1999), NYSM Site 8702 (New York State Museum Site File 2002) and the Smith Farm sites (Fort Plain Museum 2002) include corner-notched projectile points, grit-tempered cord-marked and stamped pottery, side- and end-scrapers, and other miscellaneous chipped and ground stone tools. One projectile point, manufactured from Normanskill chert, was recovered from the Smith Farm site and suggests interaction with other groups in eastern New York (Fort Plain Museum 2002).

Nonsites, including those identified at NYSM Sites 1186, 1887, and 1888, are largely concentrated south and west of the Cobleskill Creek and range in size from 5 to 25 m². These sites are found in lowland and backcountry settings. Unlike the sites described above, features consist largely of small hearths, lithic scatters, and isolated charcoal concentrations. No post molds or refuse pits have been identified, supporting the belief that these sites were used on a temporary basis. A few charred *Rubus* sp. seeds were recovered from features at the Smith Farm II (Fort Plain Museum 2002) and Osterhout 54 sites (Fort Plain Museum 2002) and document the seasonal use of these sites. The artifacts recovered from these nonsites largely consist of projectile points, end-scrapers, expedient chipped stone tools, and lithic debitage. The absence of other artifacts, including ground stone and bone tools and pottery, suggests that many of these sites may have functioned as hunting camps.

The distribution of post–A.D. 900 site and nonsite assemblages shows a somewhat different land-use pattern (see Figure 1.4). Sites dating to this time period are concentrated along the eastern half of the study area on the north side of the Cobleskill Creek. Most of these sites are located within 2 km of the creek and are within its general view shed. Although Loder IV (Knoerl 1975; Weber 1973) and Osterhout 43 (Schoharie Museum Project File 1999) are located on small terraces above the creek and may have been occupied year-round, other habitation sites, including SUBi-508 (Knoerl 1975), Site 1 (Vaillancourt 1990), and NYSM Site 6590 (New York State Museum Site File 2002), probably represent seasonal loci.

Noticeably absent is the presence of residential loci in backcountry areas. As discussed, residential loci dating prior to A.D. 900 are found along the floodplains and terraces of the Cobleskill Creek and in backcountry areas. After A.D. 900, archaeological evidence suggests that there is a distinct shift in the location of these residential loci from backcountry areas to the floodplains and terraces of major waterways. This trend is not unique to the study area but seems to coincide with similar changes occurring elsewhere (Funk 1993; Ritchie and Funk 1973; Snow 1980).

More than half of the places dating after A.D. 900 are nonsite assemblages. As shown in Figure 1.4, many of these are located south and west of the Cobleskill Creek. Unlike sites these places are located within 15 km of the creek and can be found in backcountry areas away from the view shed of the waterway. Overall there does not appear to be any difference in the size of these sites when compared with those dating prior to A.D. 900. Nonsite assemblages dating after A.D. 900 range in size from 3 to 21 m² with the average size being approximately 10 m². The features recovered from these sites resemble those described for the pre–A.D. 900 assemblages and include small hearths and lithic scatters. Two post molds were identified at NYSM Site 4761 (New York State Museum Site File 2002) and may represent portions of a small lean-to structure.

The artifacts recovered from these places generally resemble those found at pre–A.D. 900 sites and largely consist of projectile points, scrapers, and lithic debitage. Although the use of these places seems to be oriented towards hunting, NYSM Site 4761 produced a small concentration of ceramics, suggesting that the location may have also been used for other activities besides hunting (New York State Museum Site File 2002).

Four multicomponent sites were also identified within the study area. Each was identified within 10 km of the Cobleskill Creek on gentle slopes and terraces. The location of these sites would have provided access to food, nonsubsistence resources, and an important transportation route to larger waterways in eastern New York. Although located along this waterway, three of the four sites are farther away from the floodplain and are not within the view shed of the creek. These sites are, however, located in areas sheltered from the wind and other weather elements, increasing the likelihood that each site was repeatedly used. The Sebold site is located closer to Cobleskill Creek and may have been visible from the waterway during certain times of the year (New York State Museum Site File 2002). The site's location near a chert outcrop may have also contributed to the site's repeated occupation.

Changes in the use of Early Late Prehistoric sites are also reflected in the size, number of features, and range of artifacts identified at these multicomponent sites. Components dating prior to A.D. 900 are best described as residential loci that range from 500 to 1780 m² in size. These components each contain three or more hearths, at least one refuse pit, and food- and resource-processing areas. The artifacts recovered from these earlier components include chipped (projectile points, knives, drills, scrapers) and ground (netsinkers, hammerstones, nutting stones) stone tools, cord- and dentate-stamped pottery sherds, and charred floral and faunal remains.

The post–A.D. 900 components are much smaller, which suggests that these sites were not reoccupied as habitation loci but were probably reoccupied as small limited-activity loci. Evidence of this is reflected in the reduced size of the later components from several hundred square meters to less than one hundred square meters. These later components are each characterized by less than two features with the most common feature being a small hearth. Finally the artifact assemblages from these components are largely composed of a single projectile point and a few pieces of debitage. The absence of more extensive tool kits suggests that these later components may have been used primarily for hunting activities.

In summary the results of this study suggest that the Early Late Prehistoric occupants of this region did not abandon the study area as previously thought. Instead the focus of the area seems to have shifted from one in which the region was occupied by small habitations to one in which the procurement of resources dominated. Evidence of this is not only reflected in the continued occupation of the region until A.D. 1300, but is also reflected in the reoccupation of several places by Native groups.

Discussion

Land-use studies are reliant on the interpretation of data at different scales and units of analysis. For the purpose of this project, temporal and spatial scales of analysis were employed to reconstruct Early Late Prehistoric land use in eastern New York. As discussed below, this landscape is dotted with a variety of site and nonsite assemblages located in both upland and lowland settings. The assemblages span a 600-year period ranging from A.D. 700 to 1300. Although chronometric dates for some of these sites are available, the vast majority of sites could only be dated using diagnostic artifacts requiring analyses to be completed at a much coarser time scale.

It seems likely that a small tract of land in eastern New York was not abandoned after A.D. 900 but continued to be used as an important resource-procurement area by pre-Iroquoian populations until A.D. 1300. The spatial arrangement of both smaller-scale site and nonsite assemblages (and their incorporation into land-use studies at the regional scale) provides a detailed picture of land use during the Early Late Prehistoric period. Documentation of these places across the landscape is important and not only contributes information about the types of sites that were occupied but also provides information about changes in land use over time. One interesting aspect of this research has been the documentation of changes in the location of residential loci after

A.D. 900. The results of this project suggest a shift in the location of residential loci from both lowland and backcountry settings prior to A.D. 900 to lowland settings after A.D. 900. While it is currently not known why these Early Late Prehistoric groups chose to occupy different land features, changes occurring at the larger regional scale—i.e., increased reliance on maize horticulture, changes in the structure of individual households, and defense—(Hart and Rieth 2002; Prezzano and Rieth 2001:169–170; Snow 1980) may have influenced land use in this region and in other parts of New York.

Despite the changing locations of residential loci, limited-activity loci appear to have been continuously occupied during this period. Comparisons of the site size, number of features, and overall location across the landscape show little or no change throughout the Early Late Prehistoric period. During this period small resource-procurement sites were occupied in both lowland settings adjacent to the Cobleskill Creek and in upland areas away from the floodplain. Although many of these small-scale sites functioned as hunting camps, the recovery of ceramic sherds and chipped stone debris suggests that these sites may have also been used for other activities. Archaeological evidence from later Iroquoian sites in central and southern New York (Abel 2002:181–197; Miroff 2002b) highlights the important role that these small sites played in the collection of plants, tubers, and other necessary resources.

The continued use of these sites until A.D. 1300 also highlights the risky environment in which Native populations lived. The increasing reliance on maize horticulture and sedentism during the second half of the Early Late Prehistoric period (Prezzano and Rieth 2001) probably increased the risk of starvation during periods of crop failure. Hunting of small and large fauna, fishing, and the collection of berries, nuts, and other plants probably lessened the group's risk of starvation and may have increased the group's survival during lean times (Lennox 1995).

The identification of four multicomponent sites within the study area provides evidence of the reoccupation of specific places during the Early Late Prehistoric period. As discussed, pre– and post–A.D. 900 groups appear to have occupied many of the same landscape features. However, later occupations formed at a much smaller scale than earlier occupations and suggest reoccupation as limited-activity loci rather than habitation loci. Given the movement of habitation loci from upland and lowland settings to primarily lowland settings, it seems likely that the reoccupation of these sites is a result of the lateral movement of groups across the landscape as described earlier.

Conclusion

Archaeological deposits from pre– and post–A.D. 900 assemblages suggest that the study area continued to be occupied as a persistent place between A.D. 700 and 1300. The use of both site and nonsite data has contributed to our understanding of prehistoric land use, making clearer the range of settlements utilized by these pre–Iroquoian populations and also providing information about the ways that these occupations changed over time.

The results of this study suggest that changes in land use during the Early Late Prehistoric period were largely associated with the movement of larger habitation loci from both lowland and upland locations to low-lying floodplains after A.D. 900. Limited-activity loci were continuously occupied during this period and are believed to represent an important component of these early settlement systems.

Note

1. Thanks are owed to Timothy D. Knapp and Laurie E. Miroff for the invitation to participate in this volume. Dean Snow, David Smith, and J. Scott Cardinal provided comments on an earlier version of this essay. Collections from these sites are currently curated at the following institutions: New York State Museum, Schoharie Iroquois Museum, Yager Museum at Hartwick College, Fort Plain Museum, Public Archaeology Facility at Binghamton University, and the Van Epps-Hartley Chapter of the New York State Archaeological Association. Lihua Whelan drafted all of the maps and figures. All errors and omissions are the sole responsibility of the author.

2

Iroquoian Social Organization in Practice

A Small-Scale Study of Gender Roles and Site Formation in Western New York

Douglas J. Perrelli

Archaeologists often consider subsistence, settlement patterns, and social organization at a regional scale. Many use such traits to define Iroquoian culture and differentiate it from other cultures in time and space. The adoption of a smaller scale of analysis helps to identify material patterns associated with a specific Iroquoian culture and time period. Considering different scales of analysis may allow us to understand relationships between local, microscale processes and regional material patterns. This particular study represents a small step towards the larger goal of recognizing variation within and between Iroquoian and other Late Woodland groups. It is possible to identify archaeological correlates of gender roles in subsistence and ritual production, in one case, through a comparison of two closely related prehistoric Iroquoian sites.

The Piestrak (UB 2581) and Spaulding Lake (UB 2497) sites are located in the Town of Clarence, Erie County, New York (Figure 2.1). Both are Iroquoian sites occupied around A.D. 1450. The small seasonal camps are located within about 300 m of one another. They appear contemporaneous, consisting of about ten cultural features each, and each covers less than 0.4 ha. Despite their outward similarity, there is significant variation in terms of artifact frequency, artifact diversity, and feature morphology between the two sites.

Using a practice approach and assumptions about Iroquoian gender roles as structuring elements of daily life, between-site differences are

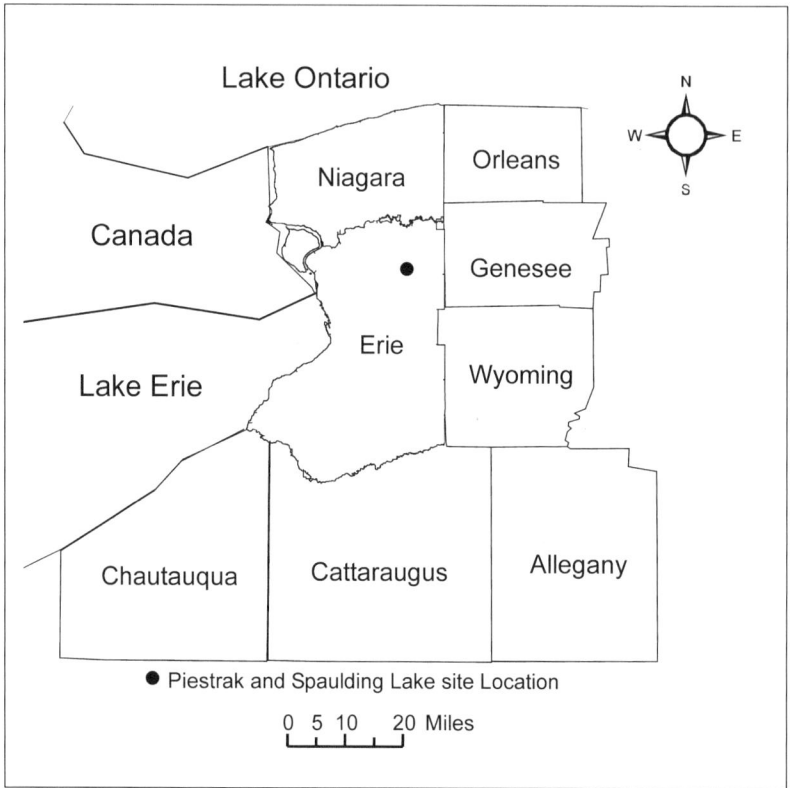

Fig. 2.1. General location of the Piestrak and Spaulding Lake sites in western New York State

shown to reflect variance in the social composition and nature of activities performed by individuals and work groups at the sites. Exploring the gender composition of work groups in association with specific subsistence and ceremonial activities greatly enhances interpretations of Piestrak and Spaulding Lake site function. Combining small- and large-scale studies, here and elsewhere in the Eastern Woodlands, may facilitate the identification of important subregional variation in worldviews and lifeways of diverse Late Woodland groups.

Employing a task-differentiation approach in a practice framework helps to associate material patterns with historically identified subsistence and ceremonial practices (Conkey and Spector 1984; Spector 1983, 1998). Task differentiation uses information from ethnohistoric accounts to model the operation of gender roles in historic context before seeking representative patterns in the archaeological record. The approach works by associating Iroquoian individuals with specific tools, activities, foods, and land-use patterns based on gender roles. Task differentiation has potential for connecting historical information and archaeological data if relevant contextual information is available and used with realistic expectations.

Practice theory provides a framework for combining the Iroquoian ethnohistorical and archaeological data to understand the social factors that influence material patterns. Practice is a social theory of technology and material production, as opposed to a biological theory of adaptation (Bourdieu 1977, 1984; Dobres 1995; Dobres and Hoffman 1994; Giddens 1979, 1984; Ortner 1984). The performance of daily activity is an arena where social relationships develop and persist. Material culture is a medium for the expression, maintenance, and negotiation of social relationships in a particular context (Dobres and Hoffman 1994:121; Ortner 1984:148). Material patterns in part reflect daily activities of individuals and small-scale social groups. In the Iroquoian case, the operation of gender roles appears to influence daily activity, creating a separation of land use and workspace and linking certain individuals with specific roles and material culture elements. This aspect of Iroquoian worldview and social organization forms a basis for comparing and contrasting Piestrak and Spaulding Lake site function.

Iroquoian Gender Roles in Historic Context

In identifying Iroquoian gender roles and land-use patterns from an ethnohistoric perspective, abundant ethnohistorical data pertaining to Iroquoian groups in Ontario and New York serves to aid in the interpretation of archaeological data (Perrelli 1994, 2001). A direct historical approach is used to connect task differentiation and engendered meaning in this Iroquoian case (Ascher 1961; Donley-Reid 1990:115; Fenton 1978; Gould and Watson 1982; Tringham 1991). Fenton (1978:296) refers to this process as up-streaming. Ethnohistoric models are appropriate and useful for identifying prehistoric archaeological correlates of gender-divided labor.

Although the Iroquoian ethnographic record is rich and detailed, the effects of colonization on Iroquoian worldviews and gender roles may limit or negate the utility of an historical model for understanding prehistory. Further, much information relates to the Huron in Ontario, Canada, or member nations of the Iroquois Confederacy in central New York. Information about these groups may not be directly applicable to groups in western New York or elsewhere in the Eastern Woodlands. Despite potential problems similar comparisons of data from throughout the region, employing a more generalized form of up-streaming, may be useful exercises. Such comparisons need not be limited to issues of gender-divided labor. The accumulation of information from throughout the Eastern Woodlands, and comparisons of different analytical scales, will increase our understanding of gender roles, among other things, and provide new insights into variation between and among Late Woodland groups.

Data Collection

Selected primary and secondary ethnographic and historical accounts dating from European contact through the eighteenth century provide data for modeling Iroquoian gender roles. Secondary sources, including ethnoarchaeological research and oral tradition, bring in the views of contemporary Iroquoians and other researchers. Primary sources include the *Jesuit Relations* (Thwaites 1896–1901) and the journal of Harmen Meyndertsz van den Bogaert, an employee of the Dutch West India Company who visited New York in 1634–1635 (Gehring and Starna 1988). Other primary sources include letters from early settlers in the New Amsterdam area (Albany, New York) from the seventeenth century (Snow et al. 1996).

Descriptions of subsistence, land use, technology, and ritual practices of individuals and small-scale social groups represent the specific ethnohistoric data used to model gender roles. References to the age, gender, sex, or sociopolitical status of individuals and social group members within Iroquoian communities and associations with specific tools, tasks, and space use are plentiful. Important information relates to whether individuals are members or captives within a given Iroquoian community and to locations where individuals performed particular activities with respect to the village/forest dichotomy.

One striking aspect of available ethnographic data is the subsistence and settlement variability described between different Iroquoian groups, including Seneca, Mohawk, Erie, Neutral, and Huron. Between-group differences in the use of staple foods, such as corn or deer meat, or in the size and number of villages are common (Thwaites 1896–1901:1:11–73; 29:145; Waugh 1916:5). These distinctions may represent seasonal or other fluctuations in population and resource availability or local variation in lifeways. Unfortunately, different groups can be difficult to distinguish and models based on these data are necessarily general and descriptive.

Waugh (1916) provides a summary of gender roles based on 12 months of ethnoarchaeological research concerning Iroquois foods and food preparation conducted by the author in Ontario, Quebec, and New York from 1912 to 1915. Archaeological data and previous historic literature concerning methods of obtaining, processing, and preparing maize and other foods are studied. He considers ethnohistorical data critically and maintains an awareness of tribal, geographic, and other cultural differences between Iroquoian and non-Iroquoian groups. Waugh (1916:5) describes differential dependence on corn horticulture among Algonquian, Huron, and Iroquoian tribes, observing the latter two groups depended on it more than the former. Cultivated fields are numerous around villages. Women did the planting and tended crops. Collective work groups, or "work bees," tended to the fields. Waugh (1916:6) describes seasonal aspects of food availability, including specific references to summer fruit collection and processing.

Men selected village locations and cleared them with axes and fire. They also cleared horticultural fields of timber and occasionally aided in planting and crop-tending activities but were, for the most part, interested in hunting and fishing (Waugh 1916:8–9). Women's work included care of all household affairs, such as the building and repair of small huts or wigwams, food preparation, and the transport of water and firewood. Captives were a separate social class that performed women's work, including horticulture. Children also represented a separate social and gender class and worked the fields. The elderly were another identified subgroup that contributed to domestic production.

Waugh (1916:12) describes the movement of work bees and the transport of coals and ash from one field camp to another in a circuit of field tending around villages. Women used a land-tortoise shell rattle to conduct a planting ritual. Other farming tools used by women include wood, stone and bone hoes, wood digging sticks, and containers of wood and bark (Waugh 1916:14). Women also built temporary shelters and containers of corn stalks, wood, and bark. They used pins of wood and bone for husking corn and ground corn with stone mano and metate. They struggled to keep villages and camps supplied with firewood and often cooked food by boiling with hot stones (Waugh 1916:39–58). Waugh (1916:21, 55, 131) indicates that women did not participate in agricultural, food preparation, and medicinal activities during menstruation.

Gender Roles: Subsistence and Land-Use Patterns

European observers and Iroquoians alike acknowledged gender roles as important elements of Iroquoian worldview practiced in daily life throughout Ontario and New York. Written records and oral tradition describe a clear dichotomy of gender roles in terms of subsistence production, including the use of different spatial domains, raw materials, and technologies. Men and women appear to have performed complimentary subsistence roles, alone and in small groups, in support of a village population. A spatial model of Iroquoian gender roles identifies a village domain in association with women's tasks and a forest domain with activities of men (Wallace 1969:24). This division is both symbolic and functional.

A semipermanent horticultural village community was the focal point around which domains were organized. The village area itself was a zone of intensive activity witnessing a variety of overlapping activities by individuals of every sex, age, and social status. This area corresponded with the land in and around the palisade of a typical Late Woodland village. The size of this area may have depended on village population, house size and placement or on relationships with neighboring communities.

The village domain was a much larger area surrounding a village, including all agricultural fields and a variety of gathering and activity areas exploited primarily by family groups and women's work groups. The need to transport food products and other processed or raw materials to the village limited the size of this area (Wallace 1969:24). Other factors included population size, ease of clearing and cultivation, soil fertility, distance to water sources, and duration of occupation. The forest domain extended beyond the village domain to cover the remainder of lands associated with a given community, including hunting, fishing, and other resource-collection locations and territories. The forest domain was symbolically associated with men. Family groups might have traveled quite far from villages during certain seasonal resource acquisition forays, such as fishing. Community and tribal boundaries possibly limited the size of the forest domain and the areas where families and work groups from a given community could obtain resources.

Iroquoian communities were complex arrays of individuals varying by age, sex, and social or political status. These variables combined to determine the gender association of an individual, thereby determining subsistence roles and domain association (Figure 2.2). This has implications for understanding the social composition of work groups and spatial distribution of subsistence tasks on the local landscape.

Children, the elderly, and captive noncommunity members lived and worked within the village domain under the direction of elder women and performed subsistence tasks associated with women. Adolescent members of the community were in transition and may have interacted in both domains for a time. Adult men from the community were spatially and symbolically isolated from other members as warriors and denizens of the forest domain.

Intermittent dashed lines in Figure 2.2 indicate that old age and adolescence were transitional periods for male community members. Adolescent males moved symbolically from the village to the forest

```
                    VILLAGE DOMAIN        FOREST DOMAIN
                    WOMEN'S ROLES         MEN'S ROLES

IROQUOIAN
COMMUNITY
MEMBERS

Adult:
      Female----------------X

      Male--------------------------------------------------------------X

Adolescent:
      Female----------------X

      Male-------------------X - - - - - - - - - - - - - - - - - - > X

Children:
      Female----------------X

      Male--------------------------------------------------------------X

Elderly:
      Female---------------X

      Male-------------------X < - - - - - - - - - - - - - - - - - - X


CAPTIVES/
NON-GROUP
MEMBERS

      Male--------------------X

      Female----------------X

      Children--------------X
```

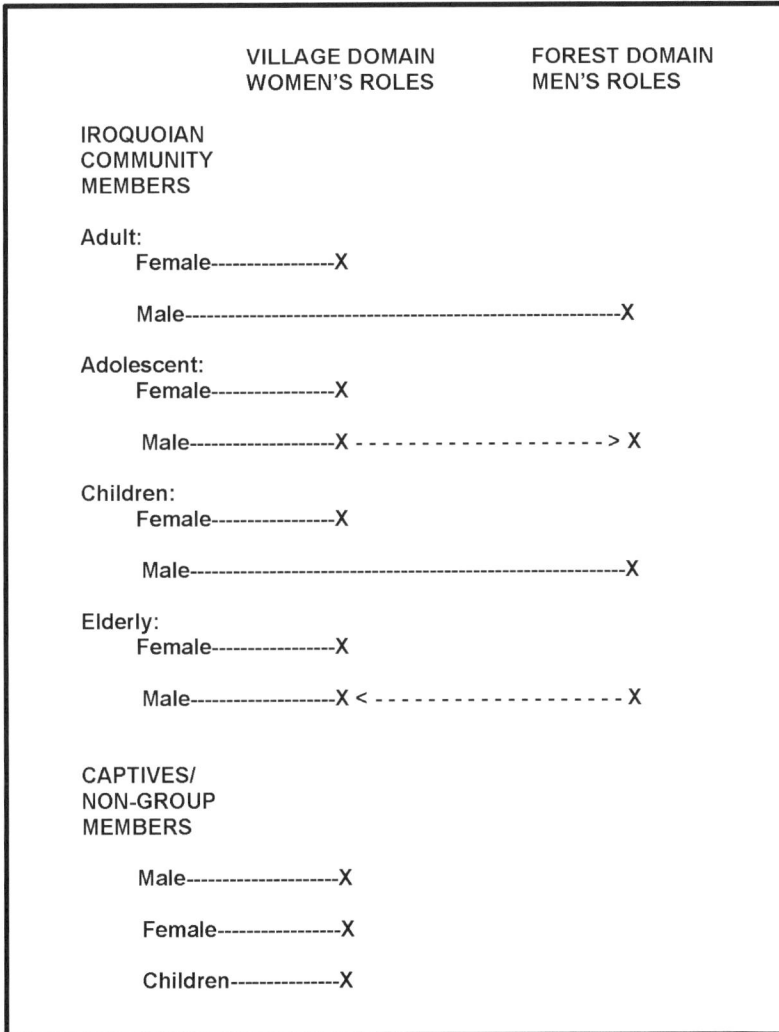

Fig. 2.2. Gender roles and domain associations of Iroquoian community inhabitants according to age, sex, and social status in ethnohistoric literature

domain. Older men experienced a decrease in mobility through time, becoming physically restricted to villages, hamlets, and seasonal camps in the village domain. Captive nonmembers of communities were restricted to the village domain and were under the supervision of women, regardless of sex and age. In the context of community-organized subsistence production, a large and diverse subset of the population included people overseen and associated with women. This group forms the various work parties that tended fields and produced most of the food consumed by the community, particularly vegetal resources (Beauchamp 1900:38-42; Morgan 1962 [1851]; Noon 1949:35; Parker 1968b [1916]; Shafer 1941:79; Thwaites 1896–1901:3:247; Waugh 1916:6–58).

A nonbiological, culturally constructed gender identity applies to the women's work group (Conkey and Gero 1997; Gero and Conkey 1991:8). References to women and women's work—cultivation, wood and water collection, food processing, and preparation—apply to a group regularly made up of men, women, and children (Thwaites 1896–1901:3:77, 248; Beauchamp 1900:38; Shafer 1941:79–82; Waugh 1916:6, 9, 54). The social identity and roles of men could shift symbolically and functionally in terms of domain residence and subsistence task performance, whereas the roles of women appear to have been more rigidly defined.

Adult male members of the community were a comparatively small group with less subsistence responsibility, greater mobility, and more sociopolitical freedom. Men, both individually and in work groups, had increased responsibility for village protection and social interaction with outside communities. One result of the operation of Iroquoian gender roles was the maintenance of a large core population that produced most of the food in close proximity to the village. A small subset of the community was free to exploit other resources and interact with distant people and environments (Wallace 1969:29).

Ethnohistoric accounts commonly refer to hunting and fishing expeditions taking families far from the village for days or weeks at a time (Gehring and Starna 1988). Family groups represent another common type of work party—a corporate group that moved about to perform specific tasks in support of a village. Many sources observed a separation of work along gender lines when family groups camped and worked together (e.g., Fenton 1951). Women were responsible for preparing and managing camps and processing foods, while men hunted away from camps (Noon 1949; Shafer 1941). Functional and symbolic gender distinctions were maintained within and between camps.

Gender Roles: Ritual Activity

Wallace (1969:49) describes Iroquoian ritual as a mechanism for strengthening group unity and interdependency and for ensuring the psychological well-being of individuals. Communal ceremonies in particular were closely associated with seasonal cycles, subsistence activities, and particular foods (Wallace 1969:17, 49–59, 344). Many ceremonial and ritual activities had strong gender associations, whereas others were more individualistic. Wallace (1969:59–75) and Heidenreich (1978:373) emphasize the importance of dreams for Iroquoian individuals.

Sources describe sweat baths and tobacco smoking as particularly important ritual elements in the lives of Iroquoian men (MacDonald 1988, 1992; Thwaites 1896–1901; Williamson 1983; Sagard 1939[1632]). Huron shaman used sweat bathing as a medium for communication with the spirit world. Sweat bathing induces altered states of consciousness amplified through fasting, dehydration, hyperventilation, and the use of tobacco (MacDonald 1988:18). Smoking, chanting, and singing were important elements of sweat bathing for these reasons (Thwaites 1896–1901:13:203, 14:65). This practice was reportedly widespread among North American Indian groups and was a seasonal activity, according to Van der Donck (1996:120).

Other ritual activities associated with sweat bathing, smoking, and dream ceremonies include body painting and tattooing (Fenton 1978:303). This was achieved by first pricking the skin with a needle, then rubbing charcoal or other pigments into the wound. White (1978:410) states that Neutral and Wenro Iroquoians from western New York were renowned for extensive body painting and tattooing. Petun Iroquoians, in contrast with Huron groups, also displayed heavily tattooed bodies—a practice they may have picked up by association with the Neutral (Garrad and Heidenreich 1978:395).

Archaeological Correlates of Gender Roles

Ethnohistoric sources present gender roles and seasonal resource collection as important aspects of Iroquoian subsistence and land-use patterns (Fenton 1978:300–302; Heidenreich 1978:378–383; Wallace 1969:50–59). Fenton (1951) characterizes the use of hunting, fishing, agricultural, and plant collection territories as engendered, seasonal, and spatially patterned land use, suggesting a pattern of local resource collection stations radiating outward from focal villages. Combining models of seasonal land use and gender role performance, a number of simple expectations emerge regarding potential archaeological site patterning at the scale of the community. For example, landscapes around Iroquoian villages should contain numerous small sites representing a range of functions with close seasonal resource and gender associations. By studying such sites, it may be possible to document archaeological correlates of engendered activities identified in historic context.

The most frequent and distinct example of engendered landscape use is the field-tending camp occupied by women's work bees. They likely occur in close proximity to villages and represent spring through fall occupations where plant food collection and processing are the main activity (Goldenweiser 1914; Shafer 1941; Waugh 1916). Groups of adult women accompanied by children, elderly, and captive males were the primary occupants of field-tending camps. Maize cultivation in particular was labor intensive and required group effort and movement to multiple fields in a circuit of cultivating, planting, weeding, harvesting, and processing maize; this occurred with a variety of other plant foods as well. Many such sites supported a given village. They were in use for days at a time, recurrently from spring through fall.

Field-tending camps experienced a buildup of similar kinds of refuse, reflecting the seasonal pattern of occupation. On-site facilities would have included storage features and hearths containing complex secondary disposal patterns and overlapping site use from recurrent occupations. The numbers of such camps, their apparent use intensity, and their distance from villages will provide archaeologists with important information regarding diet and resource exploitation and may provide estimates of village size and population.

In contrast hunting and warfare exemplify the roles performed in a forest domain. Both tasks rely on high mobility. Archaeologically the result may be less visible than field-tending camps and may appear in the form of small sites located far from villages with small hearths and limited secondary refuse disposal. The kinds of resources procured and the high use and breakage rate of arrow points may skew artifact and ecofact assemblages. The location and magnitude of such sites will depend on factors such as group size, game availability, and the proximity and disposition of neighboring groups.

The comparison between women's work bees in the village domain and men's hunting camps in the forest domain oversimplifies this issue. It provides a view of potential land-use patterns and artifact associations that relate to the performance of Iroquoian gender roles. It serves to illustrate the potential for spatially discrete, engendered archaeological features and sites to form a distinct settlement or land-use pattern at various scales.

Ritual activities, such as subsistence practices, are potential sources of engendered material patterning both within villages and at small sites around villages. The sweat lodge is one example of engendered ritual space with potential archaeological visibility. Huron sweat lodges displayed considerable variability in terms of size and design, accommodating from one to 12 men (MacDonald 1988:18–19). *The Jesuit Relations and Allied Documents* describes individual sweat lodges about one cubic meter in size, with a domed roof of bark and skins (Thwaites 1896–1901:26:175–177). Communal lodges were a place for curing ceremonies, recreation, ritual purification, health maintenance, and interaction and socializing (Thwaites 1896–1901:13:203, 14:65, 26:175–177). Sagard (1939:197–198[1632]) indicates that sweat lodges were a feature of villages as well as temporary camps.

Sweat lodges were loci of men's activity with clear material associations in terms of artifacts, ecofacts, and features (MacDonald 1988:17–26). These include the sweat lodge itself, a large basin surrounded by post molds capable of enclosing several men, and the hearths and fire-cracked rocks associated with its use. Other items include used pipes and may include needles, beads, and other objects.

In summary ethnohistoric sources and oral tradition characterize gender roles as important aspects of Iroquoian worldview and community social organization. Gender roles apply to daily, seasonal, and annual rounds of subsistence and ritual activity (Fenton 1978:309; Morgan 1962 [1851]; Parker 1968b [1916]; Thwaites 1896–1901; Trigger 1981; Waugh 1916; Wallace 1969). This worldview is manifest in a symbolic division of the landscape into village and forest domains and through the association of men and women with specific subsistence tasks and ritual practices. Women's work groups, men's work groups and families each represent a prominent social group in Iroquoian worldview with specific subsistence responsibilities, allowing for some overlap. Table 2.1 summarizes these data by differentiating tasks and materials associated with families and gender-specific work groups in Iroquoian ethnohistory (Conkey and Spector 1984; Spector 1983, 1998). Table 2.1 provides expectations regarding archaeological correlates of gender role performance in the Iroquoian case.

Table 2.1. Activities and Objects Associated with Gender Domains and the Roles of Family Groups, Men, and Women in Ethnohistoric and Archaeological Context

Ethnohistoric Activities/Objects	Family	Women	Men	Archaeological Correlates
Fishing	+		+	hooks, net weights, fish bones
Hunting	+		+	arrow points, flake tools, mammal bones
Build cabins	+	+	+	post molds, axes, adzes
Collect maple sap	+	+		hearths, broken pots
Hunt pigeon	+	+		passenger pigeon bones
Cultivate fields		+		seasonal camps, hoes
Harvest crops		+		seasonal camps, domesticates
Care of camp		+		camp sites
Collect/process fruit		+		seasonal camps, fruit seeds, grinding tools
Collect/process nuts		+		seasonal camps, nuts/shells, grinding tools
Prepare food		+		hearths, vessels, FCR, flora, fauna
Food storage		+		storage pits, containers, vessels
Collect water		+		vessels
Collect wood		+		wood charcoal
Prepare maize		+		husking pins, grinding tools, maize
Sew, weave		+		bone awls, needles, porcupine quill
Make cooking pots		+		firing hearth, wasters, fired clay blobs
Make baskets, mats		+		mat weaving needle
Turtle shell rattle		+		turtle carapace
Clear land			+	seasonal camps, axes, adzes, celts
Make arrow points			+	bifaces, points, debitage
Make pipes			+	unused pipes, wasters, firing hearth
Sweat bathing			+	sweat lodge, pipes, totems
Tattooing			+	abraders, bone needles
Tobacco smoking			+	used pipes, tobacco
Make necklaces			+	bone beads, bead blanks

Archaeology of the Piestrak (UB 2581) and Spaulding Lake (UB 2497) Sites

The Piestrak (UB 2581) and Spaulding Lake (UB 2497) sites are small Iroquoian sites located about 300 m apart. They are about 40 km south of Lake Ontario and 24 km east of Lake Erie in the Erie-Ontario Plain (Miller 1973; Owens et al. 1986). Their location is within the Town of Clarence, Erie County, New York (see Figure 2.1). The sites are in a slightly elevated setting 450 m south of the Onondaga Escarpment in chert-rich soils. They consist of few features and occupy small surface areas, clearly representing nonvillage sites. Each site was the subject of separate reconnaissance survey, site examination, and data-recovery investigations (Cowan and Perrelli 1991; Cowan et al. 1990; Perrelli 1995, 1997; Perrelli and Cowan 1990). Recovery techniques conform to modern standards established for New York State (New York Archaeological Council 1994). The objective is to collect and analyze data from cultural features and sample A-horizon soil and nonfeature contexts before land development.

Piestrak (UB 2581)

Combined with shovel test pit excavation and ground surface inspection, 73 m² of test unit excavation identified 11 cultural features (Figure 2.3; Table 2.2). Extensive soil sifting and flotation sampling resulted in the recovery of 2,708 lithic and ceramic artifacts along with 9,406 bone fragments and a diverse assemblage of carbonized floral material. The artifact assemblage includes 1,255 chipped stone pieces, 1,267 ceramic sherds, 41 utilized cobbles, and 145 fire-cracked rocks (Table 2.3). Three traditional pottery types occur, including Lawson Opposed, Durfee Underlined, and Onondaga Triangular (MacNeish 1952:14,60–61; Table 2.4). Five variants of the Lawson Opposed type are present (MacNeish 1952:14). Experienced potters made most of the vessels; however, children made two of the pots, based on the small size, crude shape, and small fingernail impressions. No radiocarbon dates have been obtained from Piestrak site carbonized floral material.

Moderate to high densities of wood charcoal in most feature strata suggest that features represent hearths. Wood species identified in order of priority include maple (*Acer* sp.), beech (*Fagus grandfolia*), elm (*Ulmus americana*), birch (*Betula* sp.), walnut (*Juglans* sp.), ironwood (*Ostrya virginiana*), hickory, oak (*Quercus* sp.), and aspen (*Populus* sp.). These data indicate that the site area was a climax beech-maple forest at the

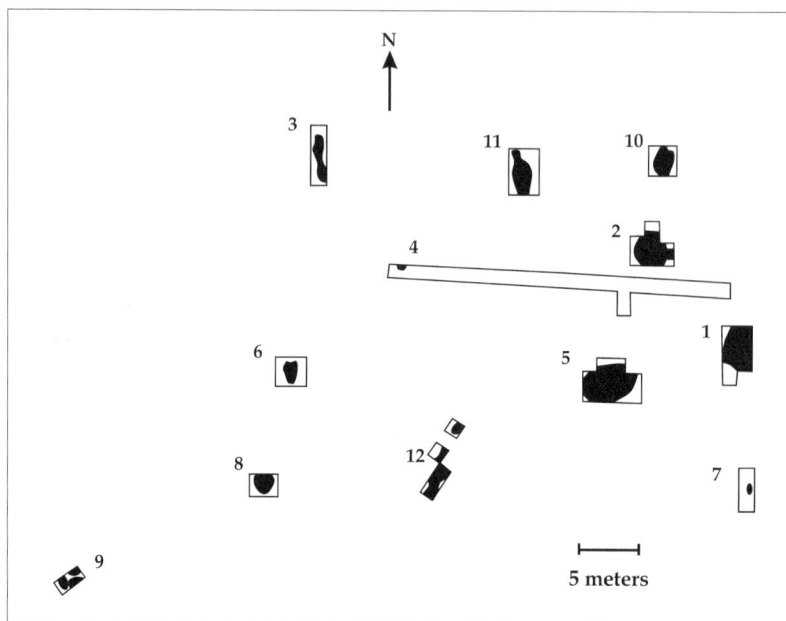

Fig. 2.3. Piestrak site (UB 2581) excavation areas and cultural features

time of occupation. Domesticates include maize (*Zea mays*), sunflower (*Helianthus annuus*), tobacco (*Nicotina rustica*), and squash (*Cucurbito pepo*). Butternut (*Juglans cinerea*), acorn (*Quercus* sp.), hickory (*Carya* sp.), black walnut (*Juglans nigra*), and hazelnut (*Corylus* sp.) account for about seven percent of the seed assemblage from the site, including corn.

A variety of summer-ripening fruits are abundant in site deposits, more so than maize, which represents about 24 percent of the seed sample. Tobacco and squash occur in low percentages. Nuts are ubiquitous in float samples, indicating that they are an important food source for site occupants; however, low nutshell density suggests opportunistic collection and use. The most common seeds are blackberry and/or raspberry seeds (*Rubus sensu lato*). Cattail (*Typha* sp.) and knotweed (*Polygonum* sp.) are also present, followed by elderberry (*Sambucus* sp.), cherry (*Prunus pennsylvanicus*), sumac (*Rhus* sp.), hawthorn (*Crategus* sp.), strawberry (*Frageria* sp.), and black nightshade (*Solanum nigrum*), in order of abundance.

Floral data suggest that Piestrak was a warm-weather seasonal camp. Fleshy fruits were the primary resource handled by site occupants. The diversity and quantity of crop plants was low in comparison to wild

Table 2.2. Piestrak and Spaulding Lake Site Investigation Methods Summary

Investigation Method	Piestrak	Spaulding Lake
Surface collection area	7,000 m²	4,000 m²
STP excavated on 5 m grid	77	149
Site perimeter STP	100	64
Total no. STP	177	213
1 by 1 m test units excavated	73	55
Total area excavated	90.7 m²	76.3 m²
Soil stripping	0	600 m²

Table 2.3. Piestrak and Spaulding Lake Site Feature and Artifact Summary

Site	Feature Count	Total Artifacts*	Chipped Stone Artifacts	Ceramic Sherds	Utilized Cobbles	Fire-Cracked Rocks	Bone Fragments
Piestrak	11	2,708	1,255	1,267	41	145	9,406
Spaulding Lake	8	18,743	13,594	2,728	69	2,352	13,051

*Excludes bone.

Table 2.4. Piestrak and Spaulding Lake Site Traditional Pottery Types

Cultural Association (MacNeish 1952)	Traditional Pottery Type	Number of Vessels Represented at Piestrak	Number of Vessels Represented at Spaulding Lake
Neutral-Wenro	Lawson Opposed	5	7
Neutral-Wenro	Lawson Incised		5
Neutral-Wenro	Ontario Horizontal		1
Onondaga	Onondaga Triangular	1	3
Onondaga	Durfee Underlined	1	2
Onondaga	Roebuck Low Collared		2
Onondaga	Syracuse Incised		1
Huron	Huron Incised		2
Huron	Warminster Horizontal		2
Huron	Black Necked		1
Total		7	26

plants. Crop plants may represent material brought to the site to sustain inhabitants while they collected and processed summer fruits. The low density and high diversity of nuts indicates a targeted, opportunistically collected fall resource and indicates recurrent site use from spring through fall.

Faunal material recovered from the site (n=9,406 bones weighing 193.5 g) corroborates a spring and summer occupation based on the absence of deer and bear and the presence of a wide array of birds, fish, and small mammals. Site occupants exploited spring- and fall-spawning fish along with amphibians, passenger pigeon, and migratory waterfowl available from spring through fall. Fish include large lake species not available from the site area. The transportation of dried fish to the site for consumption most likely accounts for their presence.

Spaulding Lake (UB 2497)

The Spaulding Lake site also underwent surface survey and shovel testing. In addition to mechanically stripping more than 600 m^2 of A-horizon surface soil, the excavation of 55 1 by 1 m test units resulted in the identification of eight cultural features (Figure 2.4; see Table 2.2). Excavations and flotation sampling recovered 18,743 artifacts, 13,051 bones, and a diverse assemblage of archaeobotanical material. Artifacts include

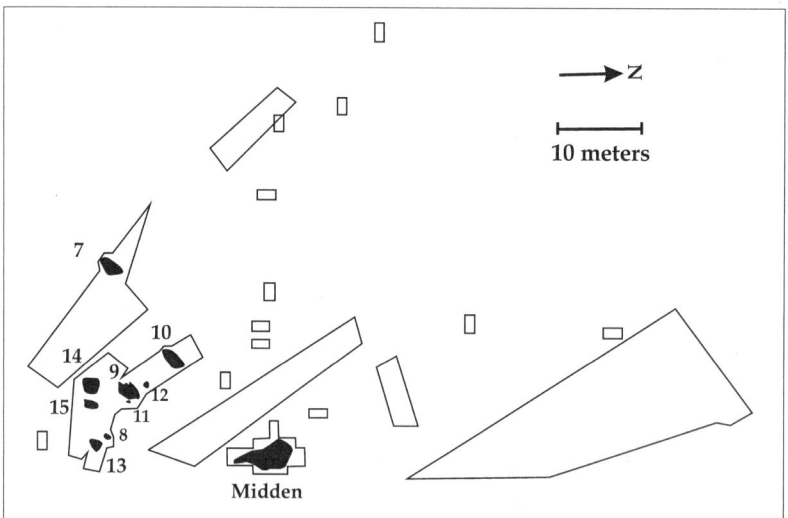

Fig. 2.4. Spaulding Lake site (UB 2497) excavation areas and cultural features

13,595 chipped stone pieces, 2,728 ceramic sherds including vessels and pipes, 69 cobble tools, and 2,352 fire-cracked rocks (see Table 2.3).

Ten traditional pottery types are identified among the 26 complete rim sections (Table 2.4). Like Piestrak, the assemblage suggests a mid-fifteenth-century prehistoric Iroquoian occupation of mixed groups from Ontario and New York, dominated by types associated with Neutral-Wenro groups (Dodd et al. 1990; Lennox and Fitzgerald 1990; MacNeish 1952; Wright 1966). About 60 percent of the vessels were made by experienced adults with some apparently made by children (n=8). Temporal associations of ceramic artifacts are supported by radiocarbon dates (Table 2.5).

Cultigens include only maize (*Zea mays*) and bean (*Phaseolus vulgaris*). Three nut species identified include butternut (*Juglans cinerea*), acorn (*Quercus* sp.), and hickory (*Carya* sp.). Blackberry (*Rubus sensu lato*), hawthorn, elderberry (*Sambucus* sp.), strawberry (*Fragaria* sp.), plum (*Prunus* sp.), cherry (*Prunus pennsylvanicus*), and grape (*Vitis* sp.) are also present.

Unlike the findings at Piestrak, here maize is the most important food plant, based on relative proportion, followed by fruits. Maize is present in 93 percent of float samples from the site. Maize kernels and plant parts comprise 88 percent of all edible foods from the site. Less than 1 percent of the identified plant remains are nuts. A spring and summer

Table 2.5. Spaulding Lake Site (UB 2497) Radiocarbon Dates, Clarence, New York

Provenience	Laboratory Number	Radio-carbon Age (B.P.)	Radio-carbon Age (A.D.)	Calibrated Date* (cal A.D.).	Material Dated
Midden	Beta-52668	340±70	1610	1430 (1516, 1599, 1618) 1952	corn
Feature 9	Beta-52669	320±60	1630	1440 (1525, 1563, 1628) 1952	wood charcoal
Feature 13	Beta-52670	460±70	1490	1324 (1435) 1631	wood charcoal
Feature 14	Beta-52671	460±70	1490	1324 (1435) 1631	wood charcoal

*Stuiver and Pearson (1986). One or more intercepts shown in parenthesis between 2σ age range based on intercepts (method A).

occupation of the site offers the best explanation for the paucity of nut remains and the dominance of corn and summer fruits.

Faunal material includes 13,051 bones weighing 972.2 g. The faunal assemblage represents exploitation of a broad spectrum of western New York habitats and includes a wide array of fish, birds, small mammals, and few large mammals. A minimum number of 52 individual (MNI) fish represents more than 50 percent of the meat found at the site. Species include walleye, sturgeon, sucker, pike, bass, and sunfish. In general fish species are not available from the immediate site area, and many fish species are available only from large streams and lakes located well away from the site. Mammals comprise most of the remaining meat (MNI=22). Ranked in order of meat mass are dog or coyote, a single deer, several squirrels, one black bear, a fox, and muskrat. Scott (Perrelli 1995) suggests that bear and muskrat bones represent pelts, not food remains, based on the presence of foot and skull bones only. Deer, fox, and squirrel bones appear to be food remains.

Gender Roles in Archaeological Context

As small camps occupied during the warm weather months, Piestrak and Spaulding Lake display outward similarities in terms of site size, in the number of features, and in some aspects of artifact and ecofact assemblages. Important quantitative and qualitative differences exist in terms of artifact frequency and diversity and feature size, shape, and layering. The Spaulding Lake site displays more use intensity and/or duration, and more diversity of activities are represented. These differences appear to stem from overlapping, recurrent site use by different kinds of work groups.

Artifacts

Spaulding Lake yielded about 10 times more chipped stone artifacts than Piestrak (see Table 2.3); however, the assemblages are similar in terms of technology. Formal chipped-stone tools are few, and unprepared cores and flake tools predominate at both sites. Each yielded a small number of Madison arrow points (Justice 1987:224–227; Ritchie 1971:33–34, 88)—tools most closely associated with men. Formal groundstone tools, such as axes and adzes, occur at Spaulding Lake only and are associated with men's corporate work groups and land clearing activities. The site produced manufacturing preforms and used tool fragments. Fire-cracked rock is more prevalent by a factor of 16 at Spaulding Lake. This material is associated with women and food preparation for the most part, but also with men and sweat lodges.

Piestrak produced 7 kg of pottery with fewer than 10 different vessels represented, two of which are children's pots. No pipes were found. This material is clearly associated with families and/or women's work groups in ethnohistoric accounts. In contrast, Spaulding Lake produced 11 kg of pottery, including 65–70 vessels and about 15–20 pipes. Spaulding Lake produced worked bone tools and accoutrements not present at Piestrak, including a turtle carapace, 15 bone beads, a shell bead, and several tooth beads. Bone beads, along with awls, needles, and pins, are made of dog, small mammal, avian, and fish bones.

Among the pins and needles are a variety of tools that appear functionally different, based on size, shape, and the sharpness of their points. Potential functional differences have strong gender associations. A smoothed-bone tool with tapered rather than pointed ends may be a mat-weaving needle. Griffin (1952, Figure 18:K and Figure 19:H) depicts similar objects for Owasco and Iroquoian sites; however, the Spaulding Lake tool lacks a perforation. Mat weaving is a task associated with women's work groups. Several awls are shaped like those in Griffin (1952, Figure 35:Q and Figure 36:M–O), having tapered rather than sharp ends (see also Griffin 1952, Figure 12:P). These appear to be husking pins associated with women's work bees and corn processing. Awls and needles like those already referenced, but with fine, sharp points (Griffin 1952, Figure 18:J, also Figure 12:U and Y), may be tattooing needles associated with male ritual. Evidence of on-site bead manufacture occurs in the form of scoring and cut marks on avian long bones, with bead blanks partially cut but not detached. Whole beads appear similar to those depicted by Griffin (1952, Figure 19:N), including a short columella bead (Griffin 1952, Figure 16:G). Bone beads are associated with men in the ethnohistoric literature.

Ecofacts

Spaulding Lake yielded a larger MNI in all animal classes and a greater diversity of species in most. The dominance of passenger pigeon and frog legs among the food remains suggests site occupation in early summer, though both sites most likely experienced spring through fall use. Maize is fragmentary and occurs in low density at Piestrak and moderate density at Spaulding Lake. The presence of cob sections and shank fragments suggests maize processing at Spaulding Lake only. The presence of husking pins supports this interpretation. Two bean fragments indicate corn and beans grew in tandem near the sites. Squash occurs at Piestrak only, along with traces of sunflower and tobacco. Tobacco use occurs at Spaulding Lake, based on the recovery of used pipe bowls and stem fragments.

Between-site artifact and ecofact similarities show that both sites were occupied by women's work bees and perhaps family groups during seasonal resource collecting and processing forays focused on wild plant foods. Differences appear to result from the use of Spaulding Lake for a specific set of male subsistence and ritual activities and more frequent or intensive use by women for processing corn (see Table 2.1). A feature analysis explores this variation in more detail.

Feature Analysis

Features are nonportable cultural units that occur in a soil matrix and denote areas of prehistoric activity (Barnes 1980:102; Stewart 1977:149). Variability in shape and artifact content can reflect feature function (Schiffer 1987:23). Barnes (1980:102, 108) suggests that features reflect site function, ecological, and cultural variables better than artifacts because they are made for specific reasons, despite their potential to become filled with secondary refuse. Combined with artifact and other material associations, they represent a rich source of data for reconstructing site function (Barnes 1980; Green and Sullivan 1997:2; Moeller 1992; Stewart 1977).

Differences between Piestrak and Spaulding Lake features are most notable in terms of depth, profile shape, internal layering, and artifact diversity. The average depth of Spaulding Lake features is 28.8 cm with 3.8 internal stratigraphic layers. Piestrak features average 19.2 cm in depth and only 1.6 stratigraphic layers. These characteristics result from the nature of feature function and subsequent refuse disposal and site abandonment patterns.

Piestrak features contain secondary and some primary refuse (Schiffer 1995:31). They occur in natural soil depressions such as tree-fall pits and suggest site use of limited duration and scope, showing little evidence of construction or improvement. Hearth locations are ephemeral and feature contents are variable across the site, suggesting different activity area functions. One large pit filled with secondary refuse is evident, along with two hearths that contain some primary refuse. Figure 2.5 shows a representative hearth feature plan and profile for Feature 11 at the Piestrak site.

Features from Spaulding Lake include three large basins with layered secondary refuse and three hearths with secondary and primary refuse. One feature, the Spaulding Lake midden, measures more than 3 by 6 m and contains several distinct soil layers (Figures 2.6 and 2.7). Differences between the sites relate to the increased magnitude of storage facilities and the presence of a sweat lodge at Spaulding Lake. Piestrak lacks large food storage facilities yet represents intensive plant collection and processing. Hearths are located on the ground surface, whereas Spaulding Lake hearths occupy subsurface basins, most likely former storage facilities. Widespread secondary deposits at both sites indicate recurrent, short-term occupations.

Piestrak Features 2, 5, and 12 appear to be hearths on the ground surface. They are associated with food processing and habitation areas. Features 3 and 11 at Piestrak and Features 7, 10, 13, and 14 at Spaulding Lake all represent hearths in basins or soil depressions of some kind. Piestrak Feature 5 is a hearth in a former storage basin. Based on high seed density and the large volume of soil moved to create the basin, it was probably a processing and storage area for summer fruits including raspberries, blackberries, and elderberries. Maize may have been processed, stored, and consumed here as well during recurrent seasonal occupations of the site. Women's work bees typically performed these activities.

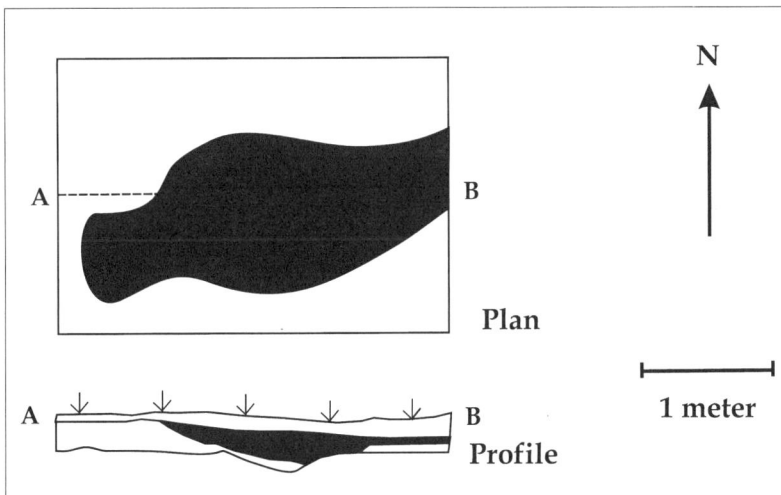

Fig. 2.5. Piestrak site (UB 2581) Feature 11 plan view and profile

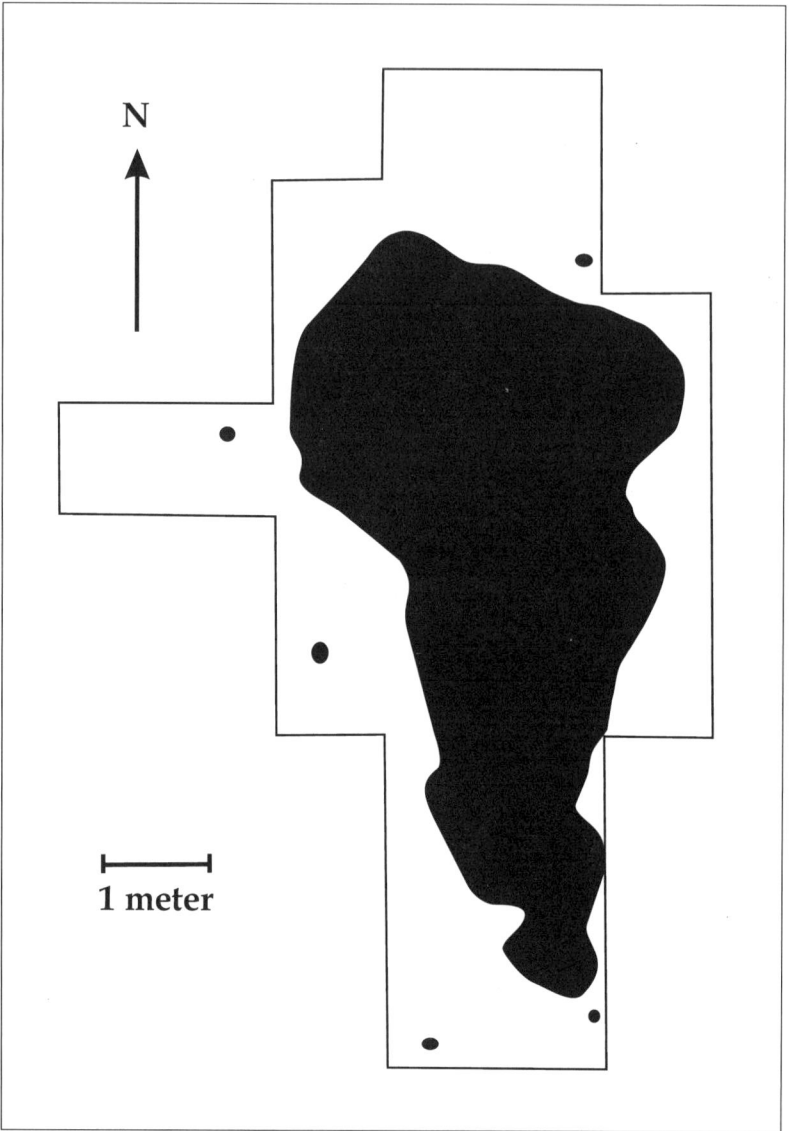

Fig. 2.6. Spaulding Lake site (UB 2497) midden plan view

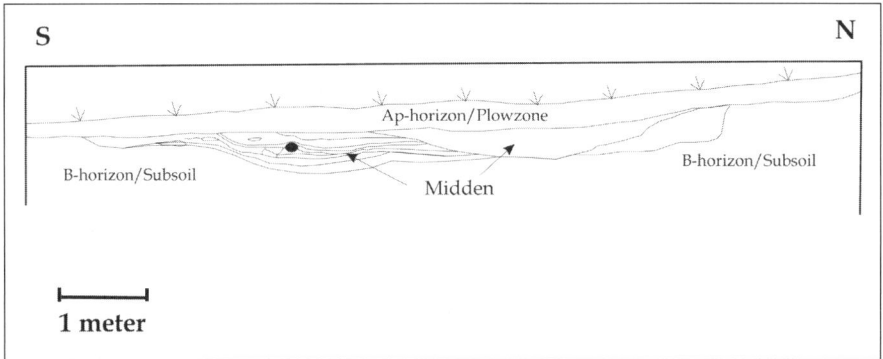

Fig. 2.7. Spaulding Lake site (UB 2497) midden long-axis profile

Spaulding Lake Features 7 and 10 are hearths that contain plant remains limited to maize and summer fruit seeds—mostly raspberries and blackberries. The features contain maize cob and shank fragments and are located away from storage pits and habitation areas. They also contain moderate amounts of chipped stone tools and cobble tools. They appear to be hearths with primary refuse and loci of summer plant food processing. Fenton (1968:95) and Parker (1968:94–99) indicate raspberries and blackberries were vital summer fruits that ripened just before the corn in mid-summer. They were eaten fresh or preserved by drying on rocks, on mats, and in baskets or by heat from hearths (Waugh 1916:119). This activity appears to be in evidence at Features 7 and 10.

Piestrak Feature 11 seems to represent the main food-processing hearth and the center of activity at the site. Hearth activity of some duration and intensity is apparent, based on continuous layers of ash and charcoal that appear to represent primary deposits. Abundant fire-cracked rock and food remains suggest stone boiling and roasting were important cooking methods at the site. Feature 11 displays some layering and may have served the same food processing function throughout the use life of the site. It represents repeated site use by women's work bees between April and October, based on faunal and flora associations.

Archaeobotanical analysis by Gardner (Perrelli 1995:259) indicates Spaulding Lake maize cobs are smaller than Fort Ancient Eastern Eight-row cobs (Cutler and Blake 1973) and taper at one end. They may be carbonized green corn, a favorite food of the Iroquois with ceremonial significance and various preparation techniques (Parker 1968b [1916]:66–68, 77; Sturtevant 1984:146). Green corn roasting occurs on rock platforms in basins such as Features 7 and 10 (Parker 1968b [1916]:60–61, 68, 77).

Following DeBoer (1988:8–13), Green and Sullivan (1997:3) suggest that subterranean food storage is a preservation and concealment strategy in the Northeast associated with seasonal site use and periodic abandonment. This concept may explain much about features and site function. Storage functions pertain to Piestrak Features 1, 5, and 10 and Spaulding Lake Features 9, 12, and 13. The latter are large, cylindrical pits that most likely served as storage containers for plant foods and later as hearths and refuse facilities.

Storage and refuse pits were often the same (Stewart 1977:149). Ritchie and Funk (1973:166–167) make clear that plant foods were commonly stored in subsurface pits and basins, and that such pits were later filled with secondary refuse. Piestrak Feature 10 and Spaulding Lake Features 8, 9, and 13 appear to be storage basins and pits filled with secondary refuse. The fact that storage facilities contain secondary trash indicates that the sites were reoccupied.

Ceramic Production

Kapches (1994b) describes information regarding ceramic manufacture in the Northeast as scant. She suggests ceramic manufacture may be difficult to discern in the archaeological record because individual and household production was generally small-scale and informal. This low-output activity overlaps with other domestic activities (Rice 1987:181; Warrick 1984:110). Most people assume that women made pots and men made pipes (Woolfrey et al. 1976) and that clay was collected and processed in the summer. Iroquoian vessels were shaped from a single mass of clay using the paddle-and-anvil technique. Vessels were air-dried and open-air fired in a hearth. Arnold (1991), Rice (1987), Rye (1981), and Sinopoli (1988) agree that cross-culturally, household ceramic production tended to be a seasonal activity involving open-air firing in hearths.

Warrick (1984:105) indicates women and young girls made vessels at villages or agricultural cabins surrounding villages. Evidence of Iroquoian vessel production occurs at the Hill site in Toronto (Kapches 1994b:91, 97–100). The site yielded poorly fired vessel fragments (wasters) and fired clay blobs in features. The Hill site material suggests that Ontario Iroquoian ceramic production occurred at small, nonvillage sites with atypical refuse patterns and a limited artifact assemblage, not unlike Spaulding Lake. Secondary refuse from the midden contains irregular blobs of fired clay and waster vessel sherds.

Spaulding Lake displays a specific set of material patterns attributable to men's ritual activity. The midden is interpreted as a former sweat lodge filled with primary and secondary refuse from alternating uses of the site area by families and different gender-specific work groups at different times of year. Feature 13 is important as a locus of smoking-pipe production—an activity closely associated with male ritual. Other artifact patterns support this interpretation.

Evidence of smoking-pipe production at Spaulding Lake occurs in Feature 8, Feature 13, and the midden. Feature 13 is similar to the vessel-firing hearth described by Kapches (1994b). Primary evidence of pipe manufacture occurs in stratigraphic layer five of this feature. A yellow brown (10YR 5/8) pocket of sand yielded conjoining fragments of two different pipes, including a large trumpet pipe and a much smaller simple elbow pipe. Feature 8 is a sand-borrow pit filled with secondary refuse. The pipes do not display black incrustations or residue on interior stem and bowl surfaces. Used pipes from the site display encrustations and residue.

Based on the morphology and stratigraphy of Features 8 and 13, pipe production appears to have involved covering formed clay pipes with a layer of sand. Sand may have dissipated heat and allowed pipes to fire slowly and evenly. In this instance firing occurred in a former cylindrical storage pit. Hearth refuse occurs over the sand layer containing the pipes. Presumably men recovered whole pipes after firing, and broken pipes or "wasters" (Kapches 1994b:95) remained with primary refuse in Feature 13.

Sweat Lodge

The Spaulding Lake midden appears to be a former sweat lodge filled with primary and secondary refuse. Based on the large size and basin shape, it may have served a storage function at one time, and secondary deposits dumped after lodge abandonment include material from diverse lithic production and food-processing activities. Multiple interpretations can explain the artifact and ecofact content, size, and stratigraphy of this unusual feature. Similarities with Late Woodland sweat lodges documented in Ontario, Canada (MacDonald 1988, 1992) and ethnohistoric accounts of sweat lodges support the sweat-bath interpretation.

The practice of sweat bathing was reportedly universal among North American Indian groups. MacDonald (1988:17–26) characterizes sweat lodges as poorly studied but important elements of Iroquoian culture.

Ontario Iroquoian sweat lodges were of two general types. Some occurred on the ground surface attached to longhouses. They appear as a cluster of small post molds along the central corridor or bunk line of houses containing concentrations of fire-cracked rock (MacDonald 1988:19; Williamson 1983:18–32). Semisubterranean sweat lodge remains occur as distinctive "keyhole-shaped" features with a ramped entrance profile (MacDonald 1988:19–24, 1992). They are oval, round, or subrectangular in plan view with a small oval extension at one end. Post molds are not always present and can occur beneath the feature or below the depth of primary deposits. This type of lodge is associated exclusively with longhouses in Ontario (MacDonald 1992:323). At the Coleman site, two semisubterranean sweat lodges protruded from longhouse walls, with access obtained from inside the longhouse (MacDonald 1988:21). The norm is for lodges to correspond with the central corridor or bunk-line of a longhouse.

Considerable variation exists in sweat lodge forms identified elsewhere in the Northeast. A similar shape and function has been attributed to "turtle pits" in western Pennsylvania by Dragoo (1976:79) and Dragoo and Lantz (1971; see also Macdonald 1992:326). The term turtle pit refers to the feature shape—a large oval basin with a protrusion at on end, not unlike the shape described as a keyhole. Similar lodges from the Late Woodland period occur in the Susquehanna River area of eastern Pennsylvania (Smith 1976). Algonquian groups in the Northeast also used sweat lodges (Butler 1945). Storage is an alternative function associated with features of this size and shape.

Sweat lodges are small enclosures by design and typically accommodate from one to 13 men. The small size and enclosed nature minimizes heat loss (MacDonald 1988:18–19; Sagard 1939:197–198 [1632]). Sagard (1939:197 [1632]) suggests that a sweat lodge occupying 3.5 m² could accommodate eight adult men. An external hearth supplying heated stones was a necessity for the operation of sweat bathing (MacDonald 1988:21).

Access to a lodge occurred through a short, ramped entranceway marked by the characteristic oval extension to the lodge itself (MacDonald 1992:323). This configuration is evident in the Spaulding Lake midden plan view (see Figure 2.6) and long axis profile (see Figure 2.7). Note the ramped profile with the proposed entrance on the left of the profile. The plan-view shape is similar to a keyhole or turtle pit. The size and shape of the Spaulding Lake midden suggests a communal, semisubterranean lodge accommodating eight to 12 people.

This is a large sweat lodge compared with other known examples from the Northeast. The presence of two distinct fill events in profile suggests two use episodes of similar scale. The continuous banded layers of ash, charcoal, and soil identified left of center in the long axis profile represent one use episode (see Figure 2.7). The large fill volume, shape, and stratigraphic relationship of the two thick layers on the right side may represent a second use episode, such as the construction of a new lodge with an alternative entrance. Both potential use episodes occupy 1.5 by 3 m in surface area and have a depth of 40 to 50 cm. This size is remarkably similar to that reported elsewhere (Dragoo 1976; Dragoo and Lantz 1971; MacDonald 1988, 1992).

Alternative interpretations of the Spaulding Lake midden are plausible. The continuous fill lenses of the midden may represent multiple episodes of secondary refuse disposal. These interpretations are not mutually exclusive in the context of recurrently occupied seasonal sites. If the sweat bath was in use before food-processing activities occurred at the site, a great deal of secondary refuse might have accumulated in the feature after lodge abandonment. Alternating layers of ash and charcoal-rich soil with quantities of fire-cracked rock and secondary refuse are common in Ontario Iroquoian lodges (MacDonald 1988:21, 1992: 324).

The nature of feature fill and artifact content supports a sweat-lodge interpretation. Most semisubterranean sweat lodges in Ontario display a thin, continuous black basal layer of charcoal and ash, along with primary fill lenses of ash and dark soil. Exterior and interior posts, evidence of rebuilding and abandonment, the presence of pipes, and faunal remains of totemic animals such as bear skull bones and bobcat teeth are common. All of these elements are present in the Spaulding Lake midden.

The main difference between Spaulding Lake and Ontario sweat lodges is that Ontario lodges typically occur in conjunction with longhouses (MacDonald 1992:324). MacDonald (1992:326) notes that outside Ontario, however, sweat lodges tend to be freestanding rather than attached to longhouses. This is particularly true in Pennsylvania, where isolated lodges are associated with various Late Woodland groups (Butler 1945; Dragoo 1976; Dragoo and Lantz 1971; Smith 1976).

Piestrak (UB 2581) and Spaulding Lake (UB 2497) Site Function

Engendered ritual and subsistence activities may be most easily identifiable at seasonal support sites around focal villages in the village and forest domains. The Piestrak and Spaulding Lake sites are two such multifunctional seasonal camps with different assemblages in terms of both quantity and quality. A number of different activities are attributable to the sites, based on the functional interpretation of features.

Family work groups appear to have used Piestrak and Spaulding Lake based on the presence of certain artifact and feature combinations; however, the efforts of families in general, and the activities of men in particular, are much better represented at Spaulding Lake. Small numbers of arrow points and the diversity of flora and fauna, along with hearths and storage pits, suggest opportunistic hunting, trapping, and collecting by family groups at both. The presence of children's pots supplies direct evidence of children at both as well. Children may be associated with women's work bees or family groups. Men were present at Spaulding Lake as well, based on arrow points, pipes, axes, and bone needles and beads. These objects relate more exclusively to male subsistence and ritual activities as opposed to family-organized subsistence production. Women's work bees appear to account for a majority of artifacts and features at the sites. In the absence of material associations with men, such as arrow points and pipes, most of the hearths and storage facilities at these sites are attributable to women's work groups exclusively.

Life Histories of Sites

A great deal can be surmised about the life history of the Piestrak and Spaulding Lake sites combining functional interpretations of features with models of gender-divided labor and seasonal site use. For example, the large volume of secondary refuse in the sweat lodge at Spaulding Lake suggests sweat bathing occurred before site use for food processing and storage. This pattern indicates sequential site use by corporate work groups with different gender compositions. Another possible scenario is site occupation by families or an extended family group with a mixed gender composition. In this case intrasite variation may result from the spatial separation of food-production and male ritual activities. In either case domestic and ritual activities occurred at different sites and in different areas within sites. At Piestrak the site deposits are more homogenous with less artifact diversity. Although there is no evidence of ritual activity, material patterns demonstrate some spatial separation of engendered subsistence activity.

Based on the sum total of functional interpretations of all identifiable activities, the Piestrak site appears to be a village domain site occupied by families or by corporate work groups dominated by women. Activities with clear ethnohistoric and archaeological correlates are associated with women, families, and the village domain. These include all aspects of camp maintenance and food production, opportunistic hunting and fishing, maple-sap collection and processing, pigeon harvesting, crop tending and harvesting, and wild fruit and nut collecting and processing. Activities associated with men and the forest domain are limited to opportunistic hunting.

The life history of the Piestrak site is one of repetitive use for domestic food production. The primary function of the site is seasonal plant resource acquisition and processing. Some temporary storage of foods occurred, but subsistence resources were most likely processed or consumed on-site and transported to a nearby village. Activities at Piestrak, in comparison to those of habitation sites and to the Spaulding Lake site, are small in scale as evidenced by moderate artifact density, low artifact diversity, and comparatively shallow, homogenous features. Features show few signs of modification or intensive use. Broken pots damaged by food processing and hundreds of flake tools dominate the artifact assemblage. A number of informal cobble tools are present, representing tool production and food processing. Piestrak site use probably occurred from spring through fall over the course of several years. Women's work groups returned to the site sporadically during warm-weather months, perhaps for as many as five to 20 years, or as long as the local community occupied a nearby village.

Many of the tasks and items cited in relation to the Piestrak site also occurred at Spaulding Lake. In this respect the sites are similar and represent seasonal resource-acquisition stations. A number of different activities occurred at Spaulding Lake and appear to represent ritual as opposed to domestic production, men rather than women, and potential forest-domain activities. Subsistence and ceremonial tasks specific to Spaulding Lake include sewing, weaving, and clothing production; ceramic production, including pipes and vessels; intensive and specialized corn processing; formal woodworking; land clearing; sweat bathing; tattooing; tobacco smoking; and bone-bead production.

The life history of the Spaulding Lake site may have begun when a work group composed of men occupied the site in early spring for field clearing, using axes and adzes to girdle trees and burn brush (Parker 1968b [1916]:21). Site selection reflects favorable conditions for cultivation, recurrent occupation, and food storage. Following one or more seasons of field clearing, men abandoned the site and a female-dominated work party occupied it in late spring, to begin the process of preparing fields for planting. A similar group returned to the site many times throughout the summer to tend crops and to collect and process other plant and animal foods available in the area. Food products were collected from the surrounding area and were processed and stored on-site during the summer season. Material is stored on-site and periodically moved to the village for consumption. Foods may have been transported from Piestrak to Spaulding Lake for storage and/or consumption. Women's work bees used the site for harvesting and food-processing activities again in late summer and fall before the site was abandoned. This cycle probably occurred over the course of many years.

Sometime after the initial site use for food production and storage, a group of men returned to the site to construct a sweat bath, using the location as a place of meditation. They also made pipes for smoking, which "soothes the mind and sobers thought" (Parker 1968b [1916]:37). Sweat bathing, smoking, and field preparation are closely linked male subsistence and ritual activities. Repeated site use for sweat bathing and men's ritual production may have occurred. Women's work bees and men's work groups returned to the site in subsequent years to conduct similar activities in a cyclical round of seasonal resource collection and ritual activity. The sweat lodge and storage facilities, like Features 9 and 13, experience reuse and abandonment.

An alternative interpretation for the Spaulding Lake site involves site use by family groups. The array of women's and men's activities portrayed by site deposits supports this interpretation. In this scenario the site can be seen as a hamlet or cabin site as defined archaeologically by Ritchie and Funk (1973:359–368) and ethnohistorically by Heidenreich (1971), Tooker (1991), and others. Mixed-gender family groups occupied such sites continually from spring through fall for one or more years, returning to villages for winter. They may have been self-sufficient and contributed food products to the larger village community.

Shifting Gender Domains

If Piestrak and Spaulding Lake were in fact contemporaneous, their close proximity would appear to situate them in the same gender domain; however, the sites differ in terms of function and gender-role identity. By comparing Piestrak and Spaulding Lake, we see that village and forest domains are not defined in real space, as concentric rings around focal villages; rather, they are mental constructs that exemplify an Iroquoian worldview.

The Spaulding Lake site in particular appears to have undergone a transformation from forest domain to village domain or vice versa. This assertion hinges on apparent sequential occupations by corporate work groups of different gender compositions. This pattern suggests that symbolic gender domains had shifting boundaries that changed through time. Symbolic domain boundaries may have shifted seasonally and may have depended on factors such as the length of time a focal village was occupied and local resource availability, including that of firewood, game, and plant resources. Variation in the perception and awareness of gender roles from person to person, between Iroquoian groups and through time can be expected.

Conclusions

Ethnohistoric literature depicts Iroquoian gender roles as a major influence on daily activity. The operation of gender roles results in distinct land-use patterns and associations of specific tools and tasks with men and women. Practice-based ethnoarchaeological research suggests that differences between Piestrak and Spaulding Lake relate to site use by individuals and social groups performing different gender-specific tasks. Identifying the gender composition of work groups in association with specific subsistence and ritual activities greatly enhances interpretations of these nonvillage sites. This study demonstrates the utility of small-scale analyses and the task differentiation approach for achieving a more subtle understanding of feature and site function. In doing so, the research approaches an understanding of material expressions of Iroquoian social organization and worldview. The findings have broad implications for studying Iroquoian subsistence, settlement patterns, social organization, and between-group variation. Conducting similar studies elsewhere in the Eastern Woodlands may facilitate the identification of subregional variation in the worldview and lifeways of diverse Late Woodland groups. Variation in the performance of gender roles may relate to or influence variation in subsistence and settlement patterns at the community level.

In some ways Iroquoian archaeology suffers from a focus on village sites and regional scales of analysis. By looking more closely at small-scale material patterns displayed by nonvillage sites, specific subsistence and ritual activities are more easily identified and the engendered nature of the landscape surrounding Iroquoian villages may be realized. Variation between and among Iroquoian groups in the Northeast may be better understood by studying nonvillage sites in conjunction with villages. A practice-based, task-differentiation approach allows for the recognition of individual and small-scale social group action as a source of variation within and between sites.

3

Don't Fence Me In
New Insights into Middle Iroquoian Village Organization from the Tillsonburg Village

Peter A. Timmins

Iroquoianists have had a longstanding interest in understanding Iroquoian village organization and its relationship to demography and social organization (Finlayson 1985, 1998; Heidenreich 1971; Noble 1969; Snow 1994b, 1995a, 1996b; Warrick 1984, 1990, 2000).[1] Following in that tradition, it is worth examining a large Middle Ontario Iroquoian site, dating to about A.D. 1400, that has been the subject of a recent salvage excavation (Archaeologix Inc. 2001, 2002). The excavation of the Tillsonburg village resulted in the documentation of ten widely dispersed longhouses. There is no evidence of a perimeter palisade, and although the precise limits of the village have not been determined, it is estimated that the site covered in excess of 8 ha. Such extremely large village size and dispersed community pattern has not, it would seem, been previously reported in Iroquoia. The Tillsonburg case challenges Iroquoianists to rethink notions concerning the relationship between site size and village population. It also contributes to an understanding of the development of Iroquoian village organization and sociopolitical development.

Background

The three-period chronological scheme for Ontario Iroquoian development was devised by J. V. Wright (1966), with minor revisions arising from subsequent research (Warrick 2000). Iroquoian origins in southern Ontario are traced to the Princess Point culture (A.D. 500–1000), which is followed by Early, Middle, and Late Precontact Iroquoian periods, between A.D. 1000 and 1534 (Warrick 2000:420). The Early Iroquoian period is generally aligned temporally and culturally with the Owasco culture in upper New York State (Ritchie 1980). Based on ceramic affinities, the Tillsonburg village is estimated to date late in the Middle Iroquoian period, ca. A.D. 1400 (Archaeologix Inc. 2002).

During the 1960s William Noble (1969:18) equated the archaeological longhouse with the "sociological lineage household" using historic Iroquoians as an analogue. Noble recognized "proto-longhouses" on Early Iroquoian sites (ca. A.D. 900–1300) and interpreted them as evidence of extended family households that were probably matrilineally organized. Noble also attempted to infer aspects of Early Iroquoian political organization by postulating a relationship between community organization and political structure. He concluded that Iroquoian houses prior to A.D. 1300 were randomly arranged through the village, implying that community planning was "either non-existent or unnecessary" (Noble 1969:19).

Following Noble's lead, in the early 1980s Gary Warrick (1984) investigated the relationship between Iroquoian sociopolitical organization and village organization. Drawing upon a range of ethnographic and ethnohistoric sources, Warrick suggested that internal sociopolitical forces were major determinants of village organization and proposed a series of trends in Iroquoian house size and village organization from Early to Late Iroquoian times. Early Iroquoian villages, with groups of small houses arranged haphazardly, indicated little development of village government, clans, or household cooperation (Warrick 1984:131). By Middle Iroquoian times, it was suggested, competition for arable lands, hunting territories, and chert sources led to overcrowded, fortified villages with extremely large longhouses led by powerful military leaders (Warrick 1984:131). After A.D. 1450 expanding alliance networks lead to the development of clan and tribal institutions, more long-distance exchange, more village planning, but smaller longhouses (Warrick 1984:131).

Study of the thirteenth-century Calvert site, located near London, Ontario, indicates that the confused nature of some Early Ontario Iroquoian villages was a product of overlapping structures resulting from multiple rebuilding of the village (Timmins 1997). At Calvert it was possible to recognize evidence of purposeful planning and village organization once site-formation processes were accounted for and the occupational history of the village was better understood (Timmins 1997). Drawing upon ethnographic analogues makes it possible to infer population size on a house-by-house basis. A shift to smaller houses in the final phase of the Calvert occupation was taken as supporting evidence for hunting parties rather than extended families occupying the houses, reflecting a change in village function that was supported by faunal data (Timmins 1997).

Several researchers have used house size and hearth numbers in a similar manner to estimate house and village populations (Finlayson 1985; Snow 1994b, 1996b; Warrick 1990). This method is based on analogy with historically documented Iroquoian households in which two families shared a hearth, thus the calculation of household population becomes a straightforward manner of counting or estimating the number of hearths and multiplying by an average nuclear-family size— usually five or six people per family. William Finlayson (1985) used this method to calculate population growth within the Late Iroquoian Draper village, which grew from a core of 400 people through five expansions to house eventually about 2,000 people.

As the results of large-scale village excavations accumulated during the 1970s and 1980s, regularities in community patterns were recognized, and some researchers began to infer village populations from village size alone. These studies assume that village sizes are accurately known and that longhouse densities and hearth numbers within villages can be accurately predicted. In a detailed study of Huron-Petun population history, Gary Warrick (1990) employed village size data to reconstruct population trends from A.D. 900 to 1650. In a similar manner Dean Snow (1994b, 1995a; see also Snow and Starna 1989) reconstructed Mohawk population trends based on estimates of village size and calculations of village area per person, grounded in data from a few totally excavated villages. While these studies have provided the best estimates of precontact Iroquoian populations in south-central Ontario and northeastern New York, they are predicated on the assumption that there is much regularity in Iroquoian community patterns. In view of the Tillsonburg data, it is appropriate to revisit briefly the theoretical basis for such population estimates.

Village Size, Population, and Problems of Scale

Archaeological studies of regional population trends have traditionally relied on site counts and site sizes to estimate population size, although artifact density, food remains, mortuary data, and ethnohistorical information have also been employed (Hassan 1981:63–82). It is not possible to rely only on excavation data in making regional population estimates because in most cases the majority of sites in a regional sample are unexcavated (Warrick 1990:209). Site size or area is normally estimated based on the distribution of artifacts on the site surface or, in the case of unplowed sites, on the distribution of positive test pits or test units.

In an ethnoarchaeological hunter-gatherer context involving the !Kung Bushmen, Yellen (1977), Wiessner (1974), and Casteel (1979) examined the relationship between camp size and population size. Yellen (1977:103) defined the spatial concept LNAT (limit of nuclear area, total) as the space occupied by huts, hearths, and associated debris and found that this area was highly correlated with population size. Wiessner (1974) noted a standard hut-hearth relation in !Kung camps and developed an equation, later refined by Casteel (1979), to estimate population size from site area. Warrick (1990:211) adopted the LNAT concept in his studies of Iroquoian demography and reasoned that "the LNAT of an Iroquoian village would include all longhouses and associated open areas and middens." However, given the differing spatial and population dynamics between hunter-gatherers and agriculturalists, the application of LNAT to population estimates of agricultural villages must be empirically grounded.

Most Iroquoian villages display a nucleated settlement pattern wherein clusters of similarly aligned longhouses are often surrounded by one or more rows of palisade. Palisades were usually constructed close to, or even abutting, the nucleated longhouses; however, in some excavated cases, an outer row of palisade extends far beyond the houses, creating significant open areas within the village that were not used as residential space. Examples include the Nodwell site (Wright 1974), the Uren site (Wright 1986), and the Calvert site (Timmins 1997). Other Iroquoian villages, such as Molson, were not palisaded and may display a more dispersed distribution of longhouses (Lennox 2000). Warrick (1990:210) has argued that it is possible to define the limits of such villages "by inscribing an arc that joins the outermost edges of middens and longhouses."

It is generally accepted that as Iroquoian villages grew in size, they also grew in population. However, rather than relying only on village size as a relative indicator of population size, archaeologists have sought to quantify population using site specific settlement data. As noted above, the most common tact has been to rely on hearth preservation and interpolation to derive the number of hearths in a house or village and then multiply the number of hearths in the village by the number of people estimated to have shared each hearth. The latter figure is usually derived from ethnohistoric accounts.

To derive regional population estimates for the Huron-Petun, Warrick's (1990:168) method involved: (1) acquiring a representative sample of village sites; (2) developing a regional chronology and assigning sites to specific time periods; (3) estimating site size for each site and total site area for each period; (4) estimating hearth density for each time period; (5) multiplying hearth density by total site area for each period; (6) estimating the number of persons per family and the number of families sharing a hearth in each time period; and (7) multiplying the number of hearths by the number of people per hearth to derive a regional population estimate for each time period. Separate calculations of average village size and average hearth density were made for each time period based on data from excavated sites (Warrick 1990). Once average hearth densities and village sizes were derived for each period, it was a straightforward matter to multiply the total site area per period by hearth density and number of people per hearth to derive population estimates.

Using this methodology and acknowledging several assumptions built into the analysis, Warrick was able to provide what is arguably the most complete account of population trends ever derived for the Huron-Petun. Among the most significant findings of this research is the revelation that the Huron underwent a veritable population explosion during Middleport times, ca. A.D. 1330 to 1420. According to Warrick's estimates, population increased from 11,000 to 29,000 in less than a century. However, such estimates will only be accurate insofar as the underlying assumptions of uniformity in village organization and hearth density are correct. The discovery of the large Middle Iroquoian Tillsonburg village with its dispersed settlement pattern indicates that there are hitherto unrecognized issues of scale and community organization that should be considered in constructing regional population models.

The Tillsonburg Village

The Tillsonburg village is located in the Town of Tillsonburg, 35 km southeast of the City of London and 25 km north of Lake Erie (Figure 3.1). It was discovered in the fall of 2000 during the grading of a large municipal soccer complex. Government authorities were notified of the presence of the site by an avocational archaeologist after substantial grading had already occurred. Archaeologix Inc. was contracted by the Town of Tillsonburg in the late fall of 2000 to salvage as much information as possible. The work plan approved by provincial authorities excluded areas at the northeast and south ends of the property where grading had been completed. Investigations subsequently determined that the site continued into both of those areas.

The site is located on an elevated plateau overlooking Stony Creek to the south and west. Stony Creek flows southeasterly and empties into Big Otter Creek within the Town of Tillsonburg. The local topography is gently rolling terrain. The northerly portion of the site is relatively flat, but there is a significant drop of 6 m from north to south, over a distance of about 300 m. Soils on the site are well-drained Fox loamy sand (Chapman and Putnam 1984:154).

The investigation proceeded by cleaning the exposed subsoil and recording and excavating subsurface cultural features. A gradall (excavator with ditching bucket) was employed to remove the loose soil and clear trenches between the houses to ensure that no structures were missed. In total five widely spaced longhouses were exposed and recorded in the fall of 2000. An additional five houses were exposed, in whole or in part, in the spring of 2001.

Significant portions of the property were heavily impacted prior to the discovery of the site and an unknown portion of the archaeological deposit was lost (Figure 3.2). The area of House 1 in the northwest part of the site was the least affected. In that area the topsoil had been stripped, and an estimated 10 cm of subsoil had also been removed, resulting in some impacts to the intact archaeological deposit below the plowzone. All of the other houses were more seriously impacted. In some areas the grading was so deep that only remnants of very deep posts and

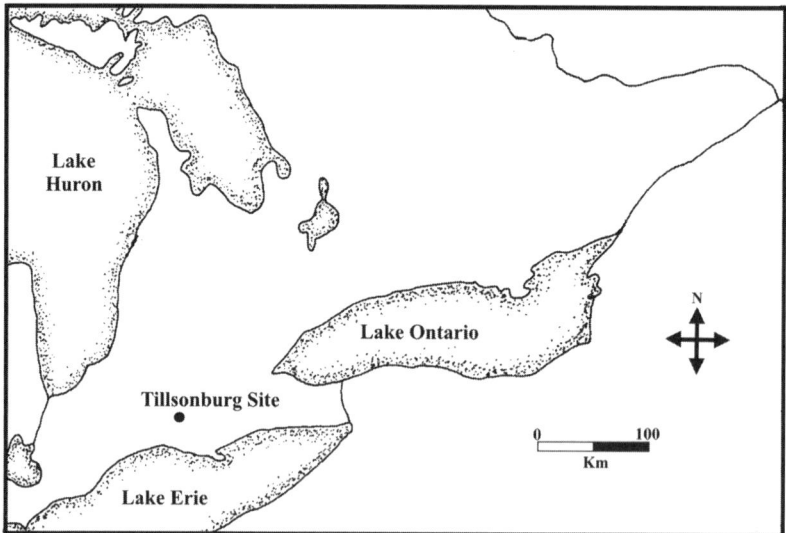

Fig. 3.1. Location of the Tillsonburg Village

features were preserved. Fortunately the site was located on very sandy soil, and post mold and feature definition was good.

In total 616 cultural features were excavated, yielding more than 11,000 artifacts. The majority of the features were small basin-shaped pits filled with ash or other debris. They cluster around hearths in the

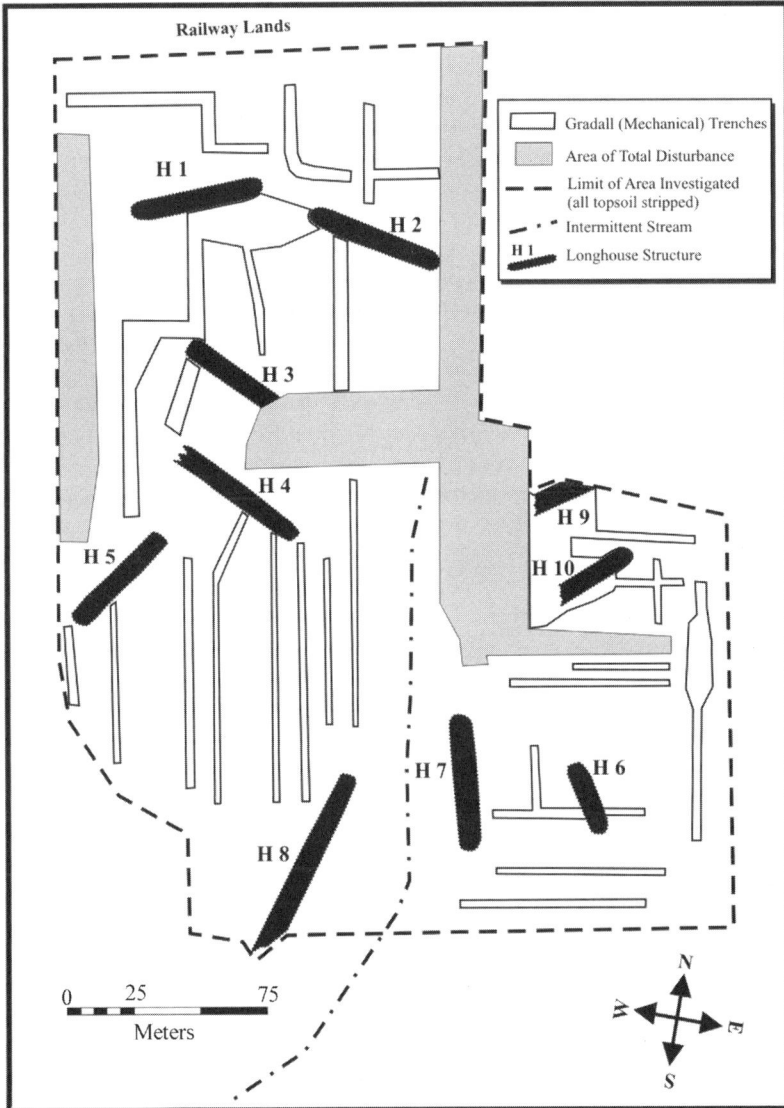

Fig. 3.2. Plan of the Tillsonburg Village

central corridors of the houses. In addition 11 large pits interpreted as semisubterranean sweat lodges were found (Figure 3.3). These features were rectangular in plan view with an entrance lobe at one end, and they are similar to those documented at other Middle and Late Ontario Iroquoian sites (MacDonald 1988). They contained artifact-rich living floors that yielded finely made bone awls and bodkins, chert knives of the "foliate biface" type, and large ceramic pipes (Figure 3.4).

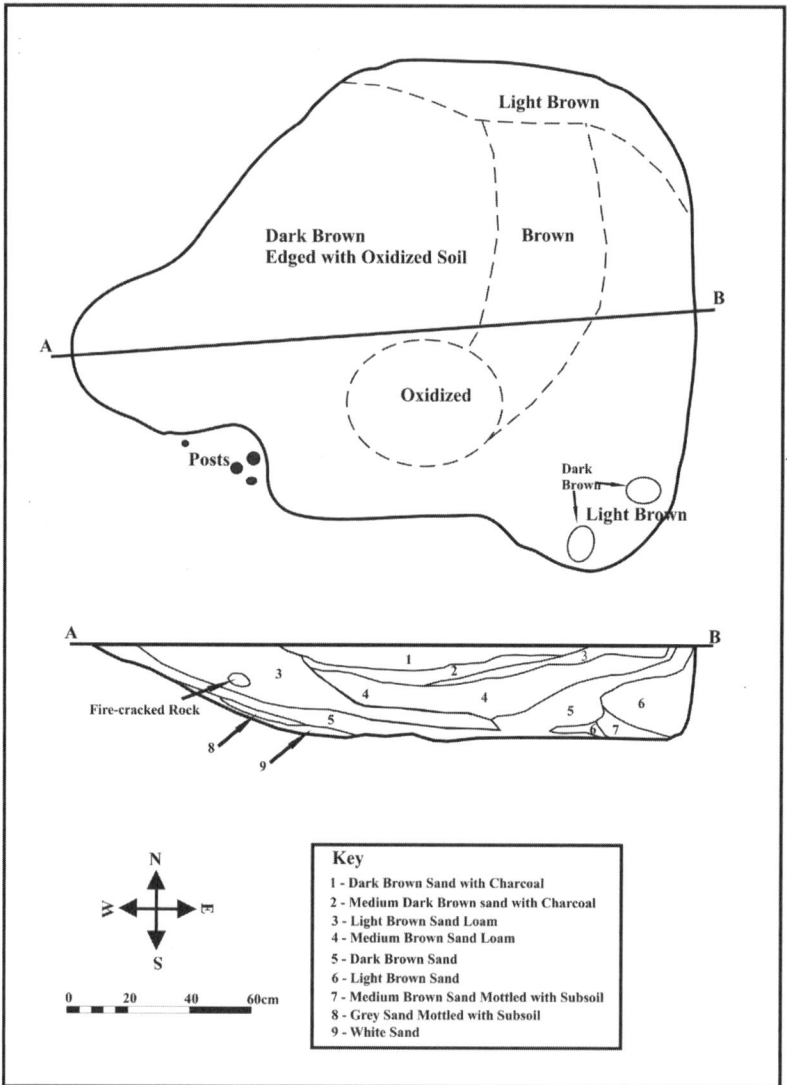

Key
1 - Dark Brown Sand with Charcoal
2 - Medium Dark Brown sand with Charcoal
3 - Light Brown Sand Loam
4 - Medium Brown Sand Loam
5 - Dark Brown Sand
6 - Light Brown Sand
7 - Medium Brown Sand Mottled with Subsoil
8 - Grey Sand Mottled with Subsoil
9 - White Sand

Fig. 3.3. Plan and profile of sweat lodge

The artifact collection, which includes only 53 analyzable ceramic vessels, is dominated by Middle and Late Iroquoian ceramic types, such as Middleport Oblique (26 percent), Pound Necked (19 percent), Ontario Horizontal (11 percent), and a simple stamped form consisting of a single row of stamped obliques over plain undecorated necks (23 percent) that does not fall within an established ceramic type (Figure 3.5; Table 3.1). The ceramic vessel data suggest that the site was occupied near the end

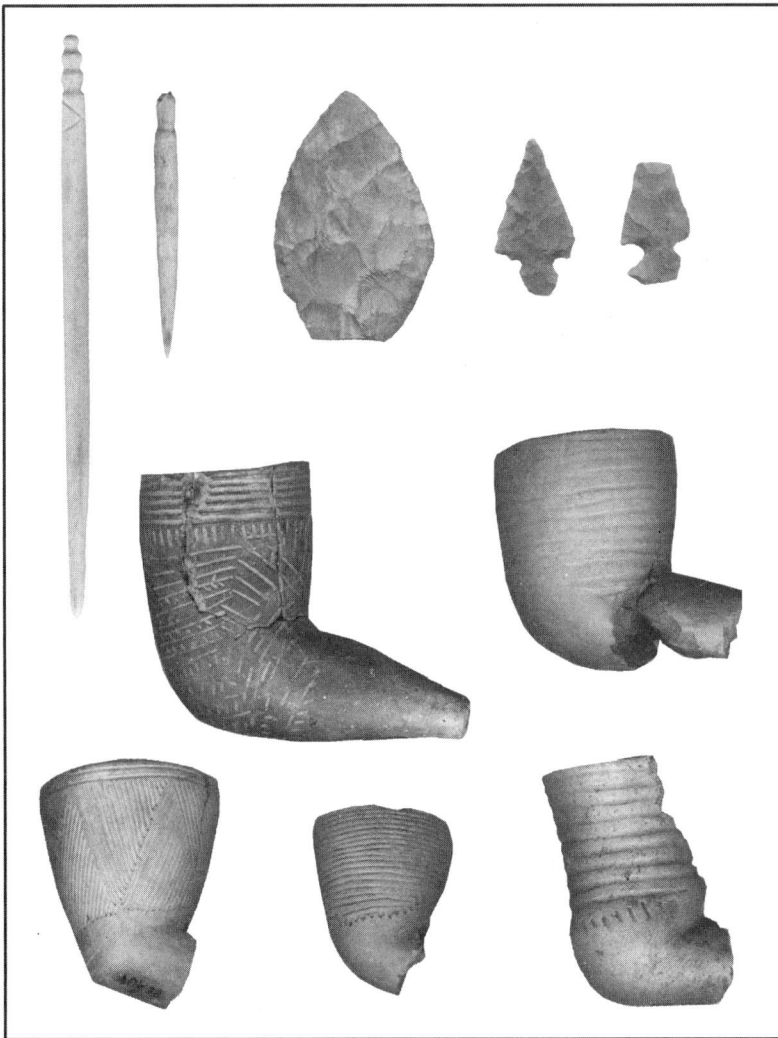

Fig. 3.4. Bone bodkins, foliate bifaces, projectile points, and ceramic pipes

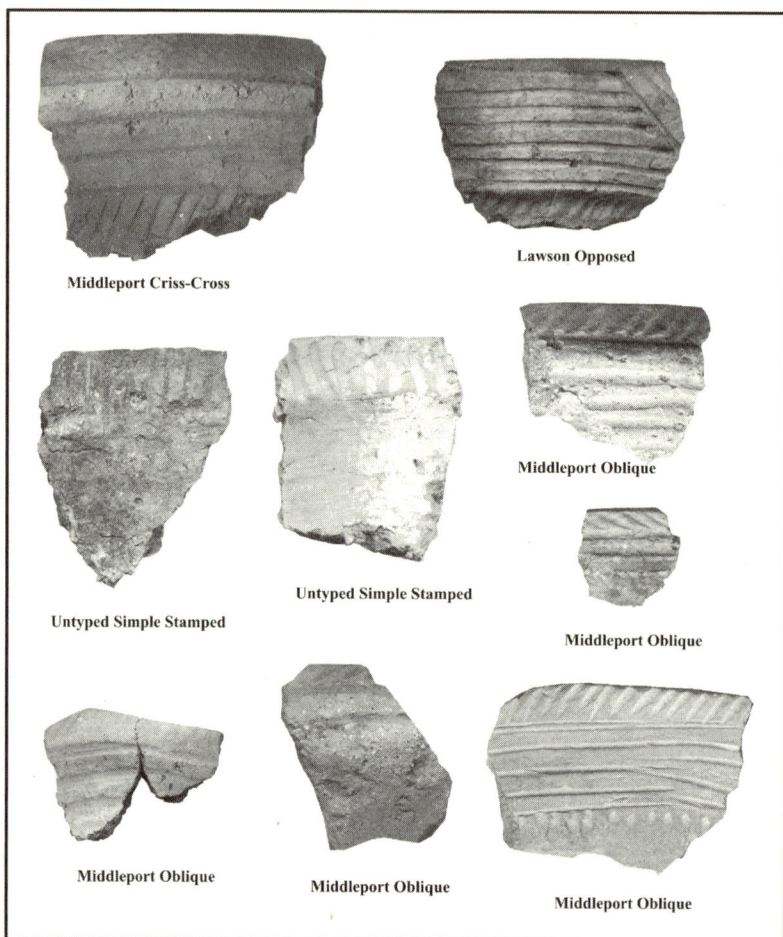

Fig. 3.5. Tillsonburg Village, representative ceramics

of the Middle Ontario Iroquoian period, ca. A.D. 1400 (Archaeologix Inc. 2002:73). The ceramic pipes support this temporal placement. Of the 15 analyzable pipe bowls in the collection, eight are conical, three are barrel-shaped, and four are vasiform. Conical pipe bowls are the most common bowl form on late Middle Ontario Iroquoian (Middleport) sites (Dodd et al. 1990:338).

Table 3.1 summarizes the ceramic data by house and ceramic type and shows that only three houses (Houses 1, 7, and 8) contained more than three ceramic vessels. The small number of vessels from each house

Table 3.1. Summary of Ceramic Types by House

Ceramic Type	H.1	H.2	H.3	H.4	H.5	H.6	H.7	H.8	H.9	H.10	Total
Middleport Criss-cross	1						3				4
Middleport Oblique	3			1	2		5	1	1	1	14
Pound Necked	5							1	2	2	10
Lawson Opposed	1										1
Ripley Plain		1					1				2
Untyped (simple stamped)	5	1	1	2		1		2			12
Ontario Horizontal							3	3			6
Black Necked							1	1			2
Pound Blank							1				1
Ontario Oblique								1			1
Total	15	2	1	3	2	1	13	10	3	3	53

makes it difficult to draw definitive conclusions about the temporal placement of individual houses based on ceramic data (Archaeologix Inc. 2002:73). However, the most popular ceramic type, Middleport Oblique, occurs in all but three houses; the second most frequent type, untyped simple stamped, occurs in all but four (Table 3.2). Taken together, all houses contain one or more of the Middleport Oblique or simple stamped vessels, which is taken as some, albeit limited, evidence for house contemporaneity. While we cannot rule out the possibility that some houses were occupied sequentially, sequential house occupation within a large open village area is not a recognized settlement pattern for Middle Ontario Iroquoian villages. Nonetheless, if some houses were occupied sequentially, this would obviously affect population estimates based on full contemporaneous occupation of all houses.

The Tillsonburg houses are widely distributed, and their layout appears to have been at least partially determined by topography, as there is significant topographic relief within the village. Houses 1 through 5 all lie on the upper terrace and are separated by distances ranging from 20 to 50 m. Houses 9 and 10 also lie on the upper terrace, about 50 m

Table 3.2. House Dimensions and Population Estimates for the Tillsonburg Village

House No.	Length (m)	Width (m)	Total End Cubicle Length	Living Space Length (m)	6 m Compartments		9 m Compartments	
					Estimated Number of Compartments	Population Estimate	Estimated Number of Compartments	Population Estimate
1	50.5	7.8	14	36.5	6	60	4	40
2	51.8	7.5	12	39.8	7	70	4	40
3	44+	8.0	14	30	5	50	3	30
4	68+	8.0	22	46	8	80	5	50
5	49.6	7.8	12	37.6	6	60	4	40
6	27.7	7.0	9	18.7	3	30	2	20
7	52.0	7.6	7	45	8	80	5	50
8	74+	8.0	10***	64	11	110	7	70
9*	21+	6.7+				68		43
10*	32+	7.4				68		43
Additional house**						68		43
Additional house**						68		43
Total pop.						812		512

* Average population based on Houses 1–8
** Inferred additional house—see text
*** Estimate—north cubicle length is 4 m; south cubicle length is unknown; average cubicle length of 6 m was used for the south cubicle

east of Houses 3 and 4 (Figure 3.2). An intermittent drainage channel oriented north-south runs between Houses 3 to 4 and Houses 9 to 10 and provided good natural drainage. Houses 6, 7, and 8 were all located on the southerly lower terrace of the site. Each of these houses was situated on the top of a well-drained north-south trending ridge (Figure 3.2).

The houses ranged from 27.7 to greater than 74 m in length, with a mean of 46.3 m for the completely exposed structures. They ranged between 7.0 and 8.0 m in width, with a mean of 7.7 m. Figures 3.6 and 3.7 provide examples of typical house patterns (Houses 1 and 7), and Table 3.2 summarizes the house dimensions.

The overall community pattern might best be described as a "dispersed radial" pattern, as several houses appear to radiate from the center of the site. Although this pattern may indicate a communal central plaza area, it is noted that the intermittent stream originates in the central site area as well. It is possible that there was a spring in this area that would have provided a source of fresh water at the time the site was occupied.

The entire subsoil surface of the site was intensively examined for evidence of other houses or exterior activity areas, but none was found. Trenches were excavated with the gradall to search for additional houses, with negative results. It is likely that there was at least one additional house located in the northeast part of the site (between Houses 2 and 9) in the area already cleared by provincial authorities. There may also have been an additional structure located west of Houses 1, 3, and 4. This is the highest point of land on the property and was deeply cut by the time the archaeologists arrived. The avocational archaeologist who found the site noted exposed features in this area. Thus we expect that there were at least two other longhouses on the Tillsonburg village, for a total of 12 houses within an area of 8 ha.

Despite trenching and subsurface examination at the northern, southern, and eastern limits of the site, no evidence of a palisade was found. Perhaps this is not surprising. Given the sprawling nature of the village, construction of a palisade around its perimeter would have been a monumental task. Moreover, if the Tillsonburg people were concerned with defense, it seems likely that they would have built a more tightly nucleated settlement.

Hearth preservation at Tillsonburg was not good enough to permit detailed population estimates using actual hearth numbers. However, if one adopts the approach used by Dean R. Snow (1994b) for calculating population estimates on Iroquoian sites at the same period, it is possible

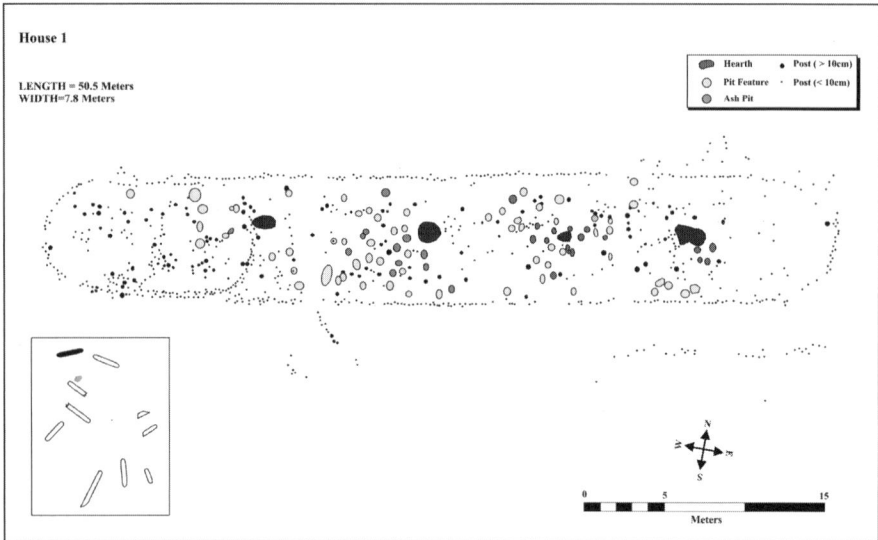

Fig. 3.6. Tillsonburg Village House 1

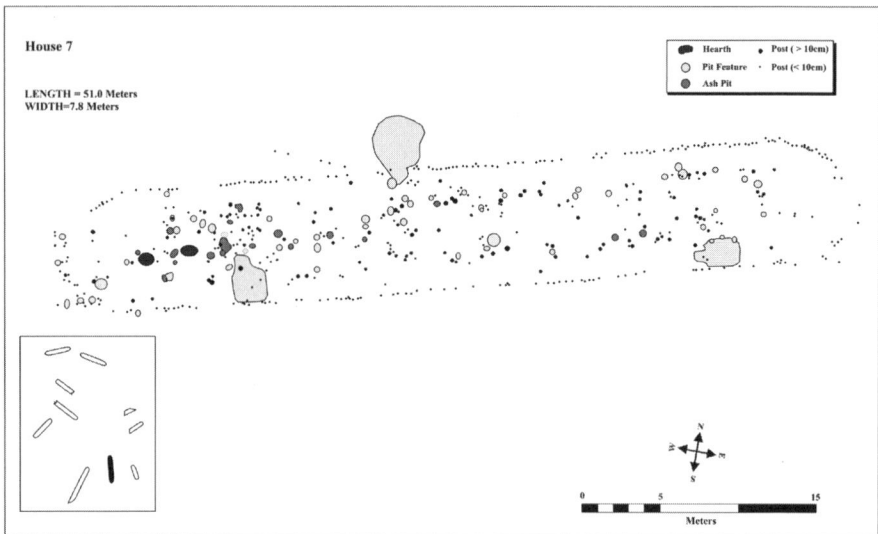

Fig. 3.7. Tillsonburg Village House 7

to derive some figures for comparative purposes. This method, based on a combination of ethnohistoric data and archaeological evidence, accounts for end storage areas and assumes that longhouse compartments were approximately 6 m long, with each compartment containing a single hearth and two family-occupied cubicles (Snow 1994b:41–44). Nuclear family size was, on average, estimated to be five individuals.

Since Houses 9 and 10 were only partially excavated, they were assigned an average population of 65 people based on the results for Houses 1 through 8. The resulting estimated population of Houses 1 through 10 is 676 people. If there were at least two more houses in the village, as discussed earlier, the population estimate for the entire village would be about 812 people, or one person per 98.5 m^2 (Table 3.2).

These population estimates assume that the houses were occupied at a similar population density as other historically and archaeologically documented Iroquoian longhouses. However, this may be an unfounded assumption, especially in view of the evidence that the Tillsonburg villagers seemed to prefer open spaces. An alternative approach would be to assume that House 1, which was the best preserved of the houses, can be taken as representative of the other houses for population calculation purposes. Although House 1 seems to have originated as a small structure, it was expanded to contain four regularly spaced hearths with a compartment size estimated at nine meters in length. If we apply a nine-meter compartment size to the Tillsonburg house data, it has the effect of reducing the population estimate by about one-third, to 512 people or one person per 156 m^2 (Table 3.2).

Discussion

At an estimated 8 ha in size, the Tillsonburg village dwarfs other known Iroquoian villages of the period. In southern Ontario the largest Middle Iroquoian villages known to date fall in the 2.8 to 3.2 ha range (Dodd et al. 1990:350). Thus the Tillsonburg village is "off the scale" in comparison to its contemporaries with respect to overall size.

With an estimated population of more than 500 people, this community would certainly have been governed by a village council, possibly composed of representatives from different clan segments (Trigger 1985:93; Warrick 2000:446). The wide spacing of the houses represents such a purposeful departure from other Iroquoian villages of the time that it is possible that its builders were seeking a new type of community organization, one in which abundant space was a key ingredient.

The Tillsonburg village certainly does not reflect the concern for defense that is characteristic of some nucleated and heavily palisaded Iroquoian settlements (Finlayson 1985). It seems likely then that Tillsonburg people either lived in times of relative peace or they were located far enough from frontiers with potentially hostile neighbors that warfare at home was not a concern.

An estimated population of 500 to 800 people for a site with 10 to 12 longhouses is not unusual. However, the distribution of the houses over such a large area is unprecedented for a precontact Iroquoian village. Village area per person on a sample of New York Iroquoian sites dating between A.D. 1325 and 1400 is estimated at 20 m² per person, and this drops to 12 m² per person between A.D. 1400 and 1525 (Snow 1994b:47). The wide open spaces of the Tillsonburg village provide 156 m² per person for 512 people and 98.5 m² per person if there was a population of 812.

However, problems emerge if we apply "village area per person" or "hearth density" estimates to derive the population of the Tillsonburg village (Snow 1994b, 1995a; Warrick 1990). For example, a population density value of 20 m² per person (Snow 1994b:46, 1995b:44), yields a population estimate of 4,000 people for the Tillsonburg village. Similarly a hearth density of 50 hearths per hectare with 11 people per hearth, as suggested by Warrick (1990:298–299, 315) for the late Middleport period, yields an estimated population of 4,400 people. Both estimates are at least five times higher than the estimate of 500 to 800 people based on house compartments, which is certainly more accurate.

It is unfortunate that we did not have the opportunity to view the surface of the Tillsonburg village and judge the extent of the site based on the surface artifact distribution. Given the large gaps between long-houses and the topographic variability, it is possible that the village may not have been recognized as a single site. Aside from Tillsonburg, experience indicates that virtually all precontact Iroquoian sites will be less than 6 hectares in size and that they will be marked by relatively dense artifact surface distributions. The surface artifact distribution at Tillsonburg probably included large areas with sparse surface remains (between houses). This may have led to several smaller sites being defined, a pattern that would better fit our normative "mental template" of Iroquoian settlement patterns. In this regard it may have been fortuitous that such a large area was exposed in the grading operation; otherwise the full extent of the site may never have been understood. The experience reminds us that the full range of variation in Iroquoian community patterns may not yet be known.

The full significance of the Tillsonburg village will only be determined as future research demonstrates whether the Tillsonburg community pattern is an isolated regional anomaly or a settlement type not previously recognized in other parts of Iroquoia. For now the Tillsonburg village presents a cautionary tale to archaeologists about the dangers of normative thinking. We are classifiers by profession, and we are trained to seek patterns and reduce our data into "types," whether artifact types or village types. We make bold interpretations about precontact populations, based on the assumption that most villages are organized in a similar manner and direct historic analogies are applicable. In southern Ontario recent cultural resource management research is suggesting that the reality may be far more complex than our demographic models suggest, stressing the continuing need for archaeologists to escape "the confines of normative thought" (Cordell and Plog 1979).

Note

1. The Tillsonburg village excavations were funded by the Town of Tillsonburg and conducted by Archaeologix Inc. Thanks are owed to Steven Lund of Tillsonburg and the Tillsonburg Soccer Club for facilitating the project and to Jim Wilson of Archaeologix Inc. for the opportunity to analyze the Tillsonburg data. The excavations were conducted under the supervision of Brent Wimmer with the assistance of Arthur Figura, Jaime Ginter, Jodie Blumenfeld, Adam Hossack, Kurt Kostick, David Riddell, Sheri Smith, Dori Rainey, Jackie Hoek, John Sheen, and Kris Dietrich. Thanks are also extended to Jack Rooney for his careful gradall work. The author's gratitude goes to Laurie E. Miroff and Timothy D. Knapp for bringing the volume to publication.

4

A Local-level Analysis of Social Reproduction and Transformation in the Chemung Valley
The Thomas/Luckey Site

Laurie E. Miroff

A great deal of research on the Late Woodland period in the region of Northern Iroquois speakers is focused on macroscales of analysis.[1] Although many Iroquoian scholars have concentrated on the regional scale and broad spans of time, a local-level analysis balances and complements the macroscale. Work at the Late Woodland Thomas/Luckey site in New York's Chemung drainage demonstrates the potential of a fine-grained local analysis for providing insights into social dynamics that are often overlooked at larger, regional scales. Household analysis combined with extensive dating provides new data with which to challenge the standard structural and temporal divisions of the Late Woodland into a simple scheme of broad, coextensive periods, each further divided into phases defined by cultural traits (Table 4.1; Hart and Brumbach 2003; see also Versaggi 1999b; Versaggi and Knapp 2000; and Versaggi and Miroff 2004 regarding similar arguments for earlier periods). Fifteen accelerator mass spectrometry dates, associated with a structure of Owasco design, place site occupation in the fifteenth century, the temporal equivalent of the Iroquoian period Chance phase. A local-level site analysis demonstrates that typical Chance phase characteristics are absent, revealing variability in the practices of individuals and groups who influenced and were influenced by regional cultural actions. A local-level analysis of household spatial patterning and associated activity areas addresses social organization in a specific temporal and spatial context.

The Local Scale

The majority of archaeological work in New York and Ontario has concentrated on the large, nucleated villages in the historic heartland of the Five Nations Iroquois (Seneca, Cayuga, Onondaga, Oneida, and Mohawk), located in the Finger Lakes Region, Mohawk Valley, and Ontario Lake Plain. These sites provided data for constructing a regional culture history and chronology (e.g., Dodd 1984; Hayden 1977; Kapches 1980, 1984, 1990; Knight 1987, 1989; Norcliffe and Heidenreich 1974; Parker 1916; Ritchie 1980; Ritchie and Funk 1973; Warrick 1988; Wright 1974). This culture history, based on typical artifact styles and the few radiocarbon dates obtained in the early to mid–twentieth century, created the framework for our understanding of Northern Iroquoian groups. Today these periods and phases tend to limit interpretations and constrain further understanding of Iroquoian groups (Parker 1916; Ritchie 1980; Ritchie and Funk 1973). New data are made to fit the interpretive paradigm, resulting in a diminished appreciation of regional variability. Those data that do not meet expectations, particularly new chronometric dates, are explained as the result of flawed association and are generally dismissed.

Although the heartland has been well researched, entire Late Woodland period (A.D. 900–1550) villages or structures outside this area have rarely been excavated, and, when they are exposed, it is generally at the expense of artifact provenience data and internal organization. Consequently much research in Iroquoia is focused primarily on macroscales of analysis (e.g., regional and interregional scales), and data on local-level patterns and artifact distributions are limited and almost absent from other areas, including south-central New York (exceptions include Prezzano 1992, 1996, 1997). Households and communities become invisible archaeologically, when they should be prominent. The present research narrows this gap in our knowledge of local-level patterning by making the social units of households visible.

To understand the household and community within a particular context, multiple scales of analysis are beneficial. Local and regional level analyses balance and complement one another and result in a richer, more complex understanding of cultural dynamics (Cobb 1993; Marquardt and Crumley 1987; Nassaney and Sassaman 1995). Since local-level actions affect regional processes and vice versa, researchers need to examine a cultural group from multiple temporal and spatial scales. It is only in this manner that we can understand the cultural dynamics that influenced individual and group actions and understand the spatial and temporal variations between regions (Cobb and Nassaney

Table 4.1. New York Late Woodland Period Phases and Associated Dates

Period	Phase	Approximate Date (A.D.)
Owasco	Carpenter Brook	900–1100
	Canandaigua	1100–1200
	Castle Creek	1200–1300
Iroquois	Oak Hill	1300–1400
	Chance	1400–1500
	Garoga	1500–1550

1995; Nassaney and Cobb 1991). Different scales of analysis result in different interpretations, and their relationship demands that analysis move back and forth between them (Crumley 1979; Crumley and Marquardt 1987; Marquardt 1985, 1992; Marquardt and Crumley 1987). Investigations of the Thomas/Luckey site aimed to illuminate variability and enrich our static interpretations of this period. A local-level analysis of village (and nonvillage) sites located outside the historic Iroquoian core can lead to new interpretations of cultural transformation.

Extensive dating and a household analysis at Thomas/Luckey provide new data to challenge the traditional cultural taxa of the Late Woodland. Spatial analysis illuminates the everyday actions of individuals who affected and were impacted by panregional Iroquoian cultural changes. Furthermore this research demonstrates the potential of a fine-grained local analysis for providing insights into social dynamics that are often overlooked at larger scales.

Data indicate that the Thomas/Luckey site does not possess traditionally expected fifteenth-century Iroquoian site characteristics in terms of structures, pottery, and site location. These deviations suggest that regional social organization deviated from expected patterns that are based largely on studies conducted in the Iroquois core. While occupants at Thomas/Luckey chose to adopt some new cultural traits, such as pottery styles, they also chose to maintain house patterns, reflecting persistence of social relations. Combining local-level analyses with those conducted at the regional scale highlights the variability in social relations that was present during the fifteenth century.

The Household

Investigations of social organization at the local level center on how people used and organized space at the Thomas/Luckey site. Unlike regional studies, local-level analyses are primarily concerned with variation within sites. The data typically consist of the distribution of artifacts and features and their relation to one another, frequently to delineate activity areas. In Iroquoian archaeology, local-level studies have generally focused on the site as a whole or the structure (the longhouse). The structure itself has been broken down as a unit of analysis into intrastructural units, including the compartment (Michaud-Stutzman, this volume), or a particular activity area or feature (Allen, this volume; see also Kapches 1980). The longhouse has long been recognized as a key element in Iroquoian village life, and thus it is believed that longhouse attributes examined over time and space contribute to an understanding of Iroquoian social, political, and economic organization (Dodd 1984). In recent years structural and substructural studies, as well as those at the level of the site, have been influenced by an archaeology of households and of communities (e.g., Allen 1992; Prezzano 1997; see Allen, Michaud-Stutzman, and Williams-Shuker, all this volume). Although recognizing the several scales at which relations of social and economic interaction can be analyzed, the approach here primarily examines these relations at the local or, more specifically, the household level to balance the more pervasive studies at the regional level.

With the concept of "household," researchers are investigating intrahousehold and intravillage social relations. In past Iroquoian studies, "individuals or households [were] rarely seen to promote change, nor [were] day-to-day interactions in villages at the microsocial level" perceived as affecting cultural development (Prezzano 1992:20). However, it is at this scale that social choices made by groups are perceptible (Cobb and Garrow 1996:25). These social dynamics are frequently overlooked when studies are conducted at the broader scale alone. To understand social reproduction and transformation, researchers are realizing the importance of a finer degree of resolution (Cobb 1993; Marquardt and Crumley 1987). The addition of a household perspective to Iroquoian archaeology has added richness to the interpretation of the local level. It has done this by focusing on the role of the household in larger-scale political and economic development, leading to a greater understanding of not just the local level, but also sociopolitical and economic factors at the macroscale (e.g., Allen 1992; Martelle 1999; Michaud-Stutzman, this volume; Prezzano 1996, 1997; Prezzano and Rieth 2001; Williams-Shuker, this volume). Research using a household perspective has directed attention to the discord between ethnographic and ethnohistoric documents and the archaeological record. In addition recent studies have identified variability in longhouse function, examined the spatial distribution of artifacts and features to identify activity patterns, examined village and longhouse structure to understand social organization and local-level production and consumption, and discussed gender relations (Allen 1992; Fogt and Ramsden 1996; Kapches 1990; Knight 1987, 1989; Martelle 1999; Prezzano 1992, 1996, 1997). A household focus has thus allowed patterns of daily life to emerge, and these are the most basic elements of social relations (Allen 1992; Byrd 1994; Hart 1995; Nass 1989).

One of the most frequently cited definitions of the household is an economically and socially cooperative unit whose functions include production, distribution, consumption, transmission, and reproduction or a combination of these (Wilk and Rathje 1982; for alternate definitions of the household, see Ashmore and Wilk 1988; Netting 1982; Rogers 1995). These functions were not merely mapped onto structures (or portions of structures), but provided a starting point from which to examine the usefulness of this definition for identifying households on Iroquoian sites.

In an archaeology of the household and of the community, it is important to remember that households and communities, and the people who comprise them, are active decision-making units and do not merely respond to external factors (Pauketat 1996:220; Yaeger and Canuto 2000). Households are often termed the "building blocks" of society, implying a permanent and unchanging entity. In contrast households (or the members of households) respond to and cause change in membership (birth, death, and illness), labor organization, production, and sociopolitics (both within and beyond the household or community) and initiate transformations that may be evident archaeologically by changes in structure size and organization (Allison 1999; Ashmore and Wilk 1988; Moore 1992; Nass 1995:84; Netting et al. 1984; Wilk and Rathje 1982:619). Thus households have a "developmental cycle": they expand and contract, changing in composition over the course of their lifetime (Roth 1989:45).

It follows then that while all households may have engaged in the same tasks and interacted with the same physical and social environment, they are not necessarily the same in terms of their actions and reactions to external conditions and their internal organization (Allison 1999; Cobb 2000; Hendon 1996:46; Moore 1992:131). Not all household units are identical at any one point in time or in any single community (Fogt and Ramsden 1996; Knight 1987, 1989; Prezzano 1992). Although it may appear at the outset that similar social structures and material culture exist between areas, individual histories of specific regions must be examined to understand community patterns within their particular context.

Many archaeologists, however, have tended to fit their data into existing models, generally those derived from ethnohistorical and ethnographic sources, instead of looking for and trying to explain discontinuities (Fenton 1949, 1952; Jamieson 1989). Historical descriptions of community and household patterns are highly normative and idealized models that can not be uncritically projected onto the past (Jamieson 1989:308; Ramsden 1977, 1996). Archaeological research in the heartland and the use of ethnohistoric records from this region have resulted in certain expectations regarding prehistoric community patterns for areas situated outside the Iroquoian "core." Archaeological research in areas outside this area and in earlier time periods is limited and is often colored by historical descriptions of the Five Nations Iroquois (Jamieson 1989:308). Instead we need to "expand our horizon beyond the tyranny of the ethnohistoric record" (Jamieson 1989:309). According to Stahl (1993:235), points of dissimilarity between the ethnographic and archaeological contexts, combined with those points that are similar, can lead to a more dynamic understanding of the past (see also Feinman 1997:372–374). Similarities between local-level patterns within and outside the heartland and between the historic and prehistoric periods cannot be assumed; they must be demonstrated (Chase-Dunn and Hall 1994; Cobb 1993; Roseberry 1989; Trigger 1981; Wolf 1982). Iroquoian communities and households are only beginning to be examined and interpreted independent of historic records (Prezzano 1992, 1996, 1997).

In summary an archaeology of households recognizes actors as active participants in their history. The choices made by individuals and the shifting relations between individuals lead to cultural reproduction or transformation. Therefore one productive approach to understanding social reproduction and transformation at the local level is household archaeology. Through the examination of structures and contextual data at Thomas/Luckey, we can see the remains of real actors. Analysis at the site began by studying the material correlates of households to understand what households do and the practices of their members. From there the social organization of a particular group in a specific temporal and spatial context was addressed through an analysis of spatial organization and associated activity areas.

Thomas/Luckey Site

The Thomas/Luckey site is located on the Chemung River's north bank in Chemung County, New York, and was the focus of the 1994–2001 Bing-

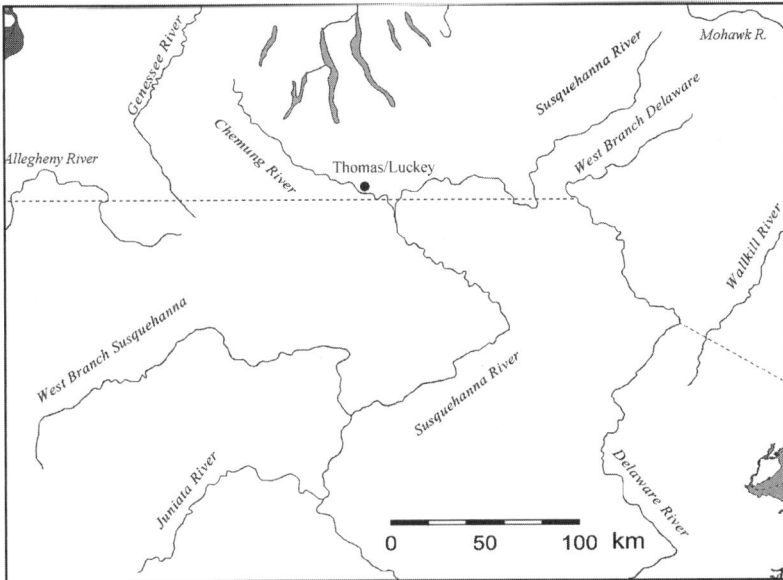

Fig. 4.1. Location of the Thomas/Luckey site

hamton University summer field school and Public Archaeology Facility Community Archaeology Program investigations (Figure 4.1). Thomas/ Luckey represented an excellent opportunity for examining intrasite variability and community organization, as excavation methods were designed to obtain a variety of data types, including structural patterns, spatially controlled artifact distributions, and feature data. Large-scale block excavations provided information on artifact patterning and the nature of occupation. Archaeologists excavated more than 1,700 m² at the site and identified numerous ceramic and lithic artifacts, two complete structures, and more than 140 features (Knapp 1996, 2002; Miroff 1997, 2002a). Data were collected on activities both within and outside of the structures. In addition screening and flotation samples produced data on microartifacts and floral and faunal remains.

The present research focuses on Structure 2, exposed during the 1997 and 1998 investigations (Figure 4.2). Structure 2 measured 16.5 m long and 6.3 m wide. Possible evidence for expansion (or contraction) existed in the western portion. The structure was oriented east-west, following a low, elevated portion of the Chemung River floodplain, and was approximately 21 m west of Structure 1, identified during the 1994 investigations (Knapp 1996, this volume).[2] Possible bench posts were located along the south wall of Structure 2, and two roughly circular clusters of small, shallow posts were located at the structure's center.

Associated with Structure 2 were 66 features, including hearths, earth ovens, storage pits, and small noncooking pits. Ceramic vessel fragments, ceramic pipes, chipped and ground/rough stone tools and their by-products, and fire-cracked rock were recovered from inside and adjacent to the structure. Although wood, bone, and antler tools were not recovered, microwear analysis on debitage, macroscopically identified utilized flakes, and formal tools revealed their use on wood,

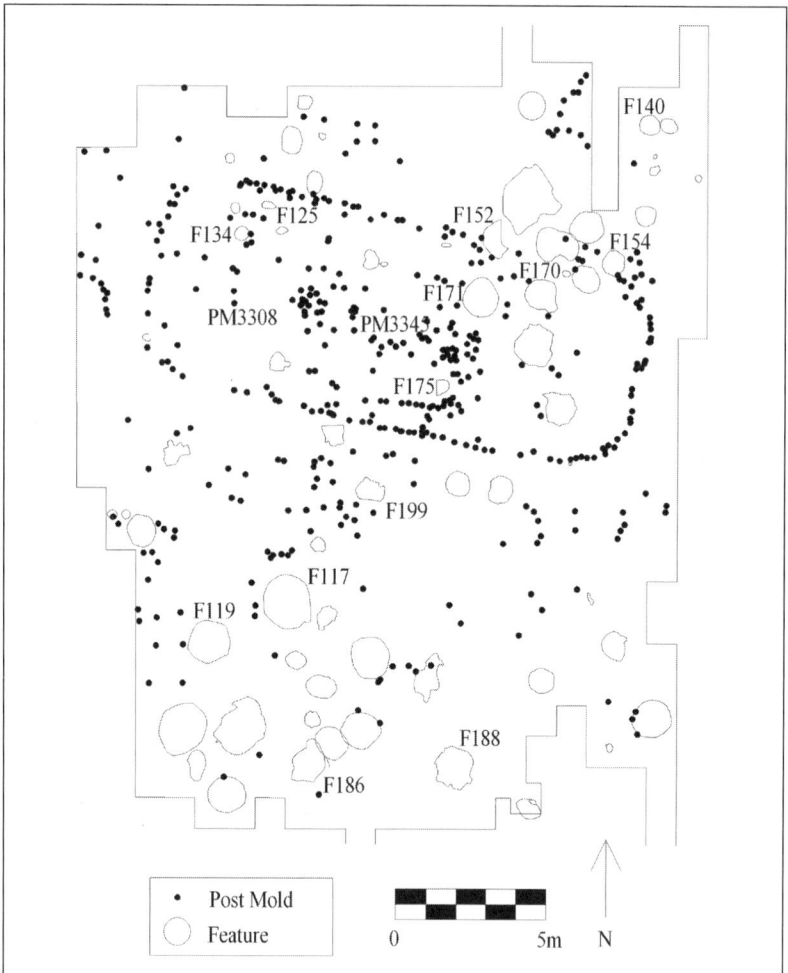

Fig. 4.2. Structure 2, Thomas/Luckey site (dated features labeled)

plant, hide, meat, bone, antler, and possibly fish (Pope 2002). Faunal remains included mammal, fish, and bird (Beisaw 1998), and archaeobotanical analysis of feature contents identified domesticated and wild plant remains, including maize (*Zea mays*), beans (*Phaseolus vulgaris*), sunflower (*Helianthus* spp.), nutshell, grass seeds, medicinal/beverage plants, fleshy fruits, and economic/weed seeds (Asch Sidell 2001b).[3]

Chronology

Understanding the actions of site occupants within their proper context required that traditional chronologies be thoroughly examined and cultural homogeneity across space and time questioned. Stylistic analysis of pottery rim sherds, accelerator mass spectrometry (AMS) dating of botanicals, and thermoluminescence (TL) dating of pottery provided three lines of evidence for establishing site chronology.

The Owasco and Iroquois periods are divided into phases marked by changes in site location and artifact types and styles, particularly ceramics. These phases, approximately 100 years in length, were defined by few radiocarbon dates, most of which have large standard deviations, some as large as 100 years themselves. Occasionally sites were placed into phases based only on ceramic types that are poor temporal markers, as several pottery types span more than the single phase for which they were initially defined (Niemczycki 1984; Snow 1994). Furthermore pottery sequences established for New York (MacNeish 1952; Ritchie and MacNeish 1949) are based upon sites located to the north in the Iroquoian core area. At the time these pottery sequences were established, no sites outside this region, including those in the Chemung Valley, had secure dates. Thus those sites did not contribute to the sequences' construction.[4] Recent work recognizes that the New York typologies are not always suitable for analyzing pottery across the region and even require revision for analyzing assemblages from within the heartland (Niemczycki 1984; 1986; Snow 1994).

Site chronology based on pottery typology alone is thus problematic given the meager number of radiocarbon-dated sites in New York, especially those in the south-central part of the state. Change defined within the Owasco and Iroquois periods in terms of 100-year-long phases must therefore be questioned. Favoring pottery typologies over radiocarbon dates may result in masking variability between sites and regions. Though the Owasco and Iroquois periods can not be characterized as two unified packages of traits that were the same across Iroquoia, neither can the phases. This temporal scale, characterized by phase names, does not capture the variability that existed over time and space. New dates from Iroquoian sites are constantly refining our understanding of chronology and may in the future convince researchers to abandon completely period and phase names (Hart 1999, 2000; Hart and Brumbach 2003; Hart and Scarry 1999; Hart et al. 2003; Schulenberg 2002).

Given this, pottery analysis of sherds provided only an initial temporal framework for the site. While pottery typologies from New York and Pennsylvania were employed, their usefulness for understanding the Thomas/Luckey assemblage was critically assessed. Archaeologists recovered 48 rim sherds representing 36 vessels from features in and adjacent to Structure 2. Removing those rims categorized as "indeterminate" and "untyped" resulted in a study sample of 30 typed pottery rim sherds representing 21 vessels (Table 4.2).

The most common vessel type in the feature assemblage, Sackett Corded (33.3 percent), mainly dates to the middle Owasco Canandaigua phase (A.D. 1100–1200), but significant percentages are identified on

Table 4.2. Pottery Types Associated with Structure 2, Feature Contexts

Early Owasco Period (vessel count, percentage)	Middle/Late Owasco Period (vessel count, percentage)	Late Owasco/Early Iroquois Period (vessel count, percentage)
Carpenter Brook Cord-on-Cord (2, 9.5)		
Levanna Cord-on-Cord (4, 19)		
Levanna Corded Collar* (1, 4.8)		Shenks Ferry Cord-Marked Collared*
	Sackett Corded (7, 33.3)	
	Kelso Corded (1, 4.8)	
	Oak Hill Corded (1, 4.8)	
	Shenks Ferry Incised (1, 4.8)	
		Richmond Incised/Cayuga Horizontal or Lawson Incised/Ripley Triangular (3, 14.3)
		Lawson Incised/Ripley Triangular (1, 4.8)

*Cannot distinguish between Levanna Corded Collar and Shenks Ferry Cord-Marked Collared.

early and late Owasco phase sites and into the early Iroquois period (Funk 1993; Niemczycki 1984; Prezzano 1992; Ritchie 1944, 1980; Ritchie and Funk 1973; Ritchie and MacNeish 1949).[5] Thus it is not particularly useful as a chronological marker. Comparing the remaining "early" and "late" types from feature contexts, uncollared early Owasco types (Levanna Cord-on-Cord, Carpenter Brook Cord-on-Cord[6]) represent at least 28 percent of the vessel assemblage; short-collared middle/late Owasco and the temporally equivalent Pennsylvania types (Kelso Corded, Oak Hill Corded, and Shenks Ferry Incised) represent more than 14 percent; and late Owasco/early Iroquois higher-collared types (Richmond Incised/Cayuga Horizontal and Lawson Incised/Ripley Triangular) represent 19 percent of the assemblage (Tables 4.2 and 4.3).

Elsewhere these types have been dated from approximately A.D. 900 to at least A.D. 1500. One possible explanation for this wide distribution at Thomas/Luckey is multiple occupations. Minimally an earlier occupation would be represented by Carpenter Brook Cord-on-Cord and Levanna Cord-on-Cord vessels and, in part, Sackett Corded vessels. The later occupation would include Kelso Corded, Oak Hill Corded, Shenks Ferry Incised, and, possibly, Sackett Corded vessels. Further it is possible that the high-collared types represent a third component postdating the fourteenth century; however, they date as early as A.D. 1250 and overlap the temporal span of several other types identified at the site, including Shenks Ferry Incised, Kelso Corded, Oak Hill Corded, Sackett Corded, Castle Creek Incised, and even Levanna Cord-on-Cord. An alternative explanation is that the types that have been generally recognized as early, namely Levanna Cord-on-Cord and Carpenter Brook Cord-on-Cord, had a greater temporal span than suggested. Their presence, then, would not indicate an earlier occupation of the site but would demonstrate that they were made beyond their typically cited ages. This interpretation is more compatible with the spatial analysis of co-occurring types in features and the AMS dates obtained.

Fifteen samples of maize or bean were AMS dated by the University of Arizona Accelerator Mass Spectrometry Laboratory. These constitute the largest suite of dates for a single site in the region and provide the best chronometrically dated site in the Chemung Valley (Table 4.4). Samples were chosen based on feature type, location, and pottery types present to achieve a representative sample. Samples from undisturbed feature contexts within and adjacent to Structure 2 were submitted for analysis. In addition wood charcoal from two posts within Structure 2 was submitted. These posts were part of the small central clusters of post molds within the structure and appeared to have been burned in place,

Table 4.3. Pottery and Associated AMS Dates, Area in and Adjacent to Structure 2

Feature Number	Lab Number	¹⁴C Age (B.P.)	Calibrated 2σ Range and Intercepts (A.D.)*	Diagnostic Pottery (number of sherds/vessels)	Expected Pottery Ages (A.D.)
117	AA41925	510±45	1326(1421) 1450	Levanna Cord-on-Cord (1)	900–1100
				Carpenter Brook Cord-on-Cord (1)	900–1100
125	AA41929	427±45	1415(1445) 1624	Richmond Incised/Cayuga Horizontal or Lawson Incised/Ripley Triangular (but very small sherd; 1)	1250/ 1350–1650
134	AA41926	418±44	1420(1449) 1627	untyped decorated collar (4/1)	
				Richmond Incised/Cayuga Horizontal or Lawson Incised/Ripley Triangular (3/1)	1250/ 1350–1650
				Lawson Incised/Ripley Triangular (4/1—same vessel as in Feature 152)	1250–1650
140	AA41923	483±58	1326(1433) 1489	indeterminate decorated rim (1)	
175	AA41932	381±45	1435(1481) 1640	Richmond Incised/Cayuga Horizontal or Lawson Incised/Ripley Triangular (2/1)	1250/ 1350–1650
170	AA41930	460±44	1405(1439) 1487	miniature incised vessel	
186	AA41936	393±45	1431(1475) 1637	Sackett Corded (1)	1100–1200
188	AA41935	616±72	1275(1318, 1352, 1388) 1437	Sackett Corded (but very small sherd; 1)	1100–1200
				Kelso Corded (1)	1200–1300
PM 3308	AA41934	430±51	1410(1445) 1628	none	

Table 4.3. continued

Feature Number	Lab Number	¹⁴C Age (B.P.)	Calibrated 2σ Range and Intercepts (A.D.)*	Diagnostic Pottery (number of sherds/vessels)	Expected Pottery Ages (A.D.)
PM 3345	AA41933	409±45	1424(1453) 1631	none	
119	AA41924	640±46	1281(1302, 1369, 1382) 1408	indeterminate undecorated rim (2/2)	
				Sackett Corded (2/1)	1100–1200
				Oak Hill Corded (1)	1200–1400
				Shenks Ferry Cord-Marked Collared or Levanna Corded Collar (1)	1250–1400 or 900–1100
152	AA41928	705±45	1256(1288) 1390	Lawson Incised/ Ripley Triangular (1; same vessel as in Feature 134)	1250–1650
				Shenks Ferry Incised (1)	1250–1400
171	AA41927	707±52	1223(1288) 1393	indeterminate undecorated rim (1)	
				Levanna Cord-on-Cord (1)	900–1100
199	AA41937	720±46	1222(1284) 1386	indeterminate decorated rim (possibly Sackett Corded; 1)	
154	AA41931	840±45	1042(1216) 1280	Sackett Corded (1; refits a sherd in undated Feature 180)	1100–1200

*Calibrated using CALIB 4.3, Stuiver and Reimer (1993).

unlike the structure's wall posts. One post from each cluster was dated in an attempt to directly date the structure.

Ten dates overlap into one grouping (Cluster 1; Figure 4.3).[7] These dates are not significantly different from each other (0.05 level; OxCal 3.3). The average of these ten dates is 441±15 B.P. (cal A.D. 1430–1476, 2σ). Of the remaining five samples, four are not significantly different (0.05 level) from one another (Cluster 2) and their average date is 693±24 B.P. (cal A.D. 1270–1390, 2σ). This second cluster of dates may represent an earlier occupation of the site. Two dates (from Features 188 and 119) connect the early and late clusters (0.05 level; average cal A.D. 1290–1410, 2σ). However, one has a large standard deviation that may explain why the dates are not significantly different.

Although at least two occupations may be represented, summing the probabilities of all 15 dates (3 standard deviations; Calib 4.1) does not clearly point to multiple occupations (Figure 4.4). It does, however, suggest the potential for continuous occupation, possibly interrupted by a brief hiatus (Nelson and Hegmon 2001). Thus the AMS dates obtained from Thomas/Luckey indicate continuous occupation over a long period with a possible interruption, and not clear separation into distinct components.

Comparing pottery types from dated features implies that the typical date ranges for several types extend beyond traditional chronologies. An AMS date on maize from a feature (Feature 117) with Carpenter Brook Cord-on-Cord and Levanna Cord-on-Cord vessels returned a date of cal A.D. 1326–1450 (calibrated at 2σ with OxCal 3.3), far later than the typical date range of A.D. 900 to 1100.[8] Similarly Sackett Corded, thought not to extend beyond A.D. 1350, was dated to cal A.D. 1431–1637 (calibrated at 2σ; Feature 186), based on an AMS date on bean. An AMS date on maize, cal A.D. 1223–1393 (calibrated at 2σ; Feature 171), supports the interpretation that Levanna Cord-on-Cord vessels date to all phases of the Owasco period. Further it demonstrates a co-occurrence of this "Owasco" type with the type Shenks Ferry Incised of the Susquehanna's West and Main Branches, Blue Rock phase (A.D. 1250–1400; Graybill 1989).

The temporal range represented by pottery types from dated features within Cluster 1, based on their expected ages, spans between A.D. 900 and at least 1500. However, the average age of the dated features is A.D. 1430–1476. Cluster 2 contained types that in the traditional culture history are also said to span in age between A.D. 900 and at least 1500, but the AMS dates averaged A.D. 1270–1390. The AMS dates obtained from features in and around Structure 2 and the associated pottery

Table 4.4. AMS Dates from the Thomas/Luckey Site, Area in and Adjacent to Structure 2

Cluster	Feature Number	Feature Type	Lab Number	Material	$\delta^{13}C$	^{14}C Age (B.P.)	Calibrated 2σ Range and Intercepts (A.D.)*	Location of Feature in Relation to Structure 2
1	117	storage	AA41925	maize	-10.2	510±45	1326(1421)1450	outside (2+ m south)
	125	earth oven	AA41929	maize	-9.2	427±45	1415(1445)1624	inside (west side)
	134	small noncooking pit	AA41926	maize	-9.5	418±44	1420(1449)1627	inside (west side)
	140	hearth	AA41923	maize	-8.3	483±58	1326(1433)1489	outside (2+ m north)
	175	hearth	AA41932	maize	-10.2	381±45	1435(1481)1640	inside (east side)
	170	small noncooking pit	AA41930	maize	-9.2	460±44	1405(1439)1487	inside (east side)
	186	storage	AA41936	bean	-26	393±45	1431(1475)1637	outside (2+ m south)
	188	storage	AA41935	maize	-9.8	616±72	1275(1318, 1352, 1388)1437	outside (2+ m south)

Table 4.4. continued

Cluster	Feature Number	Feature Type	Lab Number	Material	δ¹³C	¹⁴C Age (B.P.)	Calibrated 2σ Range and Intercepts (A.D.)*	Location of Feature in Relation to Structure 2
1	PM 3308	post mold	AA41934	wood	-25	430±51	1410(1445)1628	inside (west pm cluster)
	PM 3345	post mold	AA41933	wood	-27.6	409±45	1424(1453)1631	inside (east pm cluster)
2	119	storage	AA41924	bean	-26.6	640±46	1281(1302, 1369, 1382)1408	outside (2+ m south)
	152	storage	AA41928	maize	-9.5	705±45	1256(1288)1390	in wall (northeast)
	171	storage	AA41927	maize	-9.5	707±52	1223(1288)1393	inside (east side)
	199	small noncooking pit	AA41937	maize	-10.2	720±46	1222(1284)1386	outside (2m south)
None	154	small noncooking pit	AA41931	maize	-8.6	840±45	1042(1216) 1280	inside/in wall (northeast)

*Calibrated using CALIB 4.3, Stuiver and Reimer (1993).

types suggest that the expected dates associated with the types are not applicable for the Thomas/Luckey site, which brings into question their applicability for the entire Chemung drainage and possibly for the entire region of Northern Iroquoian speakers. These analyses force Iroquoian researchers to rethink the temporal placement of certain pottery types and perhaps the use of types (versus attributes) in general.

Given that so much of Iroquoian chronology is associated with decorated pottery and sites are frequently dated based on pottery types alone, thermoluminescence dating of sherds was also conducted (Table 4.5; Luminescence Dating Laboratory at the University of Washington; Feathers 2002). Six samples from AMS-dated features were chosen for analysis. These samples represent sherds that traditionally date to the early Owasco period (Carpenter Brook Cord-on-Cord, Levanna Cord-on-Cord), the middle/late Owasco period (Kelso Corded, Oak Hill Corded), and late Owasco/early Iroquois period (Richmond Incised/Cayuga Horizontal or Lawson Incised/Ripley Triangular, Lawson Incised/Ripley Triangular). Several of the TL dates may support a fifteenth-century occupation of Thomas/Luckey and extend the temporal ranges for some pottery types (e.g., Levanna Cord-on-Cord and possibly Carpenter Brook Cord-on-Cord), but the large standard deviations render the dates relatively useless for chronological discussions of the site and do not aid in refining the existing Iroquoian pottery typologies.

To summarize, multiple lines of evidence, including pottery types, AMS dates, and TL dates, were obtained to explore the chronological placement of Structure 2 at Thomas/Luckey. Although typologies and TL dates were ambiguous, the statistically significant similarity between the AMS dates suggests at least a fifteenth-century occupation for this portion of the site. Sites dating to this time, temporally equivalent to the Iroquoian period Chance phase, known best from the core area, are recognized as regionally varied. However, most researchers agree that by A.D. 1350 the "basic form and function of the later Iroquoian longhouse was fully developed" (Snow 1994:29; see also Ritchie 1980:314; Ritchie and Funk 1973). This "basic form and function" was characterized by paired cubicles (compartments) along each side of the structure. Within the structure resided a matrilocal and matrilineal descent group. Nuclear families occupying compartments on opposite sides of the dwelling shared a central hearth (Snow 1994:40–46; Warrick 1996:11–12). Fifteenth-century villages, for the most part, are said to be palisaded and situated in defensible locations. In addition pottery types, while considered to be more variable than house structure, are said to have incised decoration on a smoothed surface. These "typical" Chance phase

Table 4.5. Thermoluminescence Dates from the Thomas/Luckey Site, Area in and Adjacent to Structure 2

Feature Number	Location in Relation to Structure 2	Feature Type	AMS Date	Pottery Type	Expected Pottery Ages (A.D.)	TL Lab no.	Uncorrected Age (A.D.), 1σ	Corrected Age (A.D.), 1σ	Age (A.D.), 2σ
117	outside, to the south	storage	1326(1421)1450	Carpenter Brook Cord-on-Cord	900–1100	UW 702	1302±185		1032–1572
171	inside, eastern portion	storage	1223(1288)1393	Levanna Cord-on-Cord	900–1100	UW 706	1188±67		1054–1322
188	outside, to the south	storage	1275 (1318, 1352, 1388) 1437	Kelso Corded	1200–1300	UW 703	1418±56	943±202	539–1347
119	outside, to the south	storage	1281(1302, 1369, 1382) 1408	Oak Hill Corded	1200–1400	UW 707	1392±57	1202±99	1004–1400
175	inside, eastern portion	hearth	1435(1481)1640	Richmond Incised/ Cayuga Horizontal or Lawson Incised/ Ripley Triangular	1250/1350–1650	UW 705	1667±58	1510±166	1178–1842
134	inside, western portion	small non-cooking	1420(1449)1627	Lawson Incised/ Ripley Triangular	1250–1650	UW 704	1384±50		1284–1484

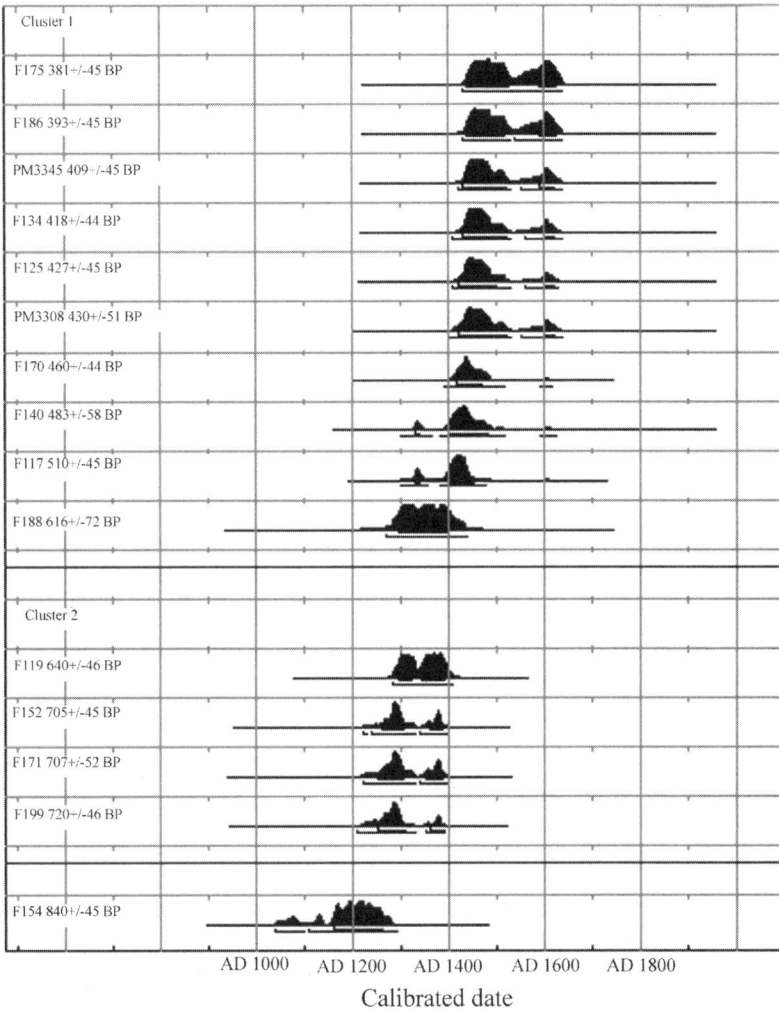

Fig. 4.3. AMS dates from the Thomas/Luckey site, in and adjacent to Structure 2 (OxCal 3.3)

characteristics are absent at Thomas/Luckey, and this deviation may have implications for understanding social and political organization.

Spatial Analysis

One approach to understanding the political economy of a group uses structures, associated features, and artifacts to identify activity areas (Bernardini 2000; Ferring 1984:116–117; Flannery and Winter 1976:34;

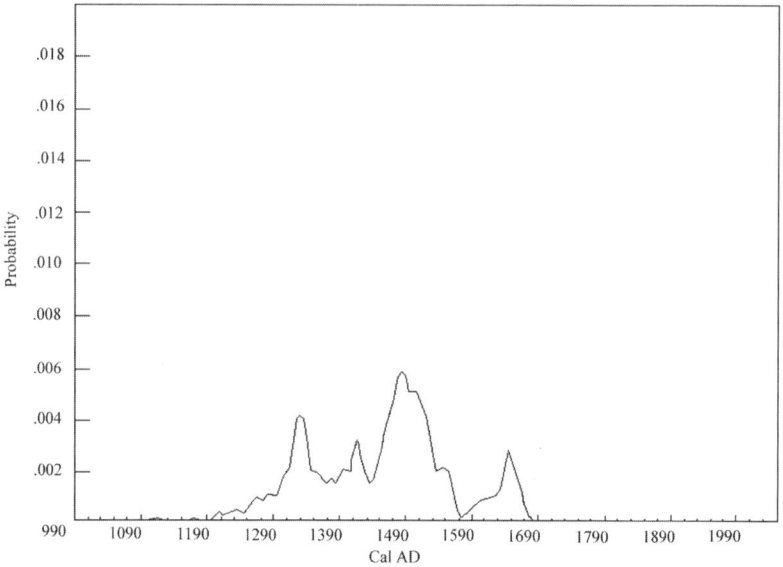

Fig. 4.4. Probability graph, fifteen AMS dates, Thomas/Luckey site, Structure 2 (3 standard deviations, Calib 4.1)

Gnivecki 1987; Hodder 1987:442; Lightfoot 1994; Newell 1987; Pauketat 1994; Prentice 1985; Seymour and Schiffer 1987; Yerkes 1989; see Fogt and Ramsden 1996 and Prezzano 1992 for local-level analyses of Iroquoian sites). Past research has successfully shown that activity-area analysis can be used as an entry point for identifying households and the activities of groups and/or individuals within or outside of particular structures.

The research entailed defining activities—those tasks that leave behind clusters of archaeological materials—based on spatially differentiated artifacts and features within a given horizon (Ferring 1984:116–117; see also Hodder 1987:442; Newell 1987). Activities are often, but not always, clustered in bounded locations called activity areas (Ferring 1984:117). Activity areas are "spatially restricted areas where a specific task or set of related tasks has been carried on, and they are generally characterized by a scatter of tools, waste products, and/or raw materials; a feature, or set of features, may also be present" (Flannery and Winter 1976:34). Mapping the locations and distributions of activities provides data to define the degree of their spatial segregation.

A household's spatial configuration should provide insight into the nature of its occupation and its economic, social, and political organization (Kapches 1979; Layne 1987; Nass and Yerkes 1995; Oswald 1987:296). Different distributions of artifacts and features within and between structures could reveal differences in function or identify changing social relations. Differences in the use of space may be depicted in the types or amounts of artifacts and/or features within a structure or between structures. An understanding of the social organization of the Thomas/Luckey site is aided by the use of artifact and feature types and their contexts to identify potential activity areas (Miroff 2002a).

The process by which a household can be recognized archaeologically starts with identifying spatially discrete sets of activities. It is assumed that a household performs a basic set of activities, yet it is possible that the extent to which each household participates in these particular activities may differ (Kramer 1982). A household level of analysis begins with studying the artifact distributions that are the material correlates of households in order to understand what households do and ultimately the practices of the people who comprised them (Costin and Wright 1998; Tringham 1991). It is expected that if each household performs the same set of activities, this will be manifested in redundant artifact clusters within and around each dwelling (Lightfoot 1994:120). If each household cooperates in communal activities and performs different tasks, this will be exhibited by different artifact clusters within and around each dwelling (Lightfoot 1994:120). Additionally, comparing activity areas within a structure may suggest whether one dwelling consisted of more than one household.

To examine the spatial distribution of artifacts, and thus of activities, associated with Structure 2, artifact densities (count or weight per volume investigated) were calculated to standardize differences between excavated areas. Using isopleth maps, densities were plotted by type and compared to determine if there was overlap that might relate to tool kits and/or activities. Only artifacts identified solely in the unplowed A2 soil horizon were plotted. The A2 horizon lies immediately below the plow zone and overlies the sterile B horizon in which features were identified.

Feature types and their associated artifacts were also examined as they may represent activities that occurred adjacent to the feature. In addition feature types and associated artifacts were compared to artifacts recovered from adjacent areas as another potential line of evidence for delineating activity areas. The distribution of features themselves informs on site activities and structure function. For example, the movement of individuals in longhouses was "directed, and in some cases hampered," by the location of features and posts (Knight 1989:290).

Isopleth maps for individual artifact types from the A2 horizon were first created and examined.[9] Clustering of artifacts across the site was visible in these maps. To determine if this clustering was significant, a variance/mean ratio was calculated for each artifact type using artifact density (Hodder and Orton 1976:34–35). All artifact types had variance/mean values greater than 1, indicating artifact clustering (Miroff 2002a). Artifact types that may have been part of similar activities or represent tool kits were then compared.

Within the structure artifacts clustered in three areas, leaving the center relatively devoid of material (Figure 4.5). In the northwestern portion of Structure 2, there were numerous chipped-stone artifact types, rough stone flakes, ceramics, faunal and floral material, and a sherd with carbon residue. Features included one earth oven, one hearth, and two small noncooking pits containing several artifact types. In addition to being a location in which occupants stored artifacts, this area of the structure was also used for processing and possibly cooking food. Chipped- and rough-stone artifacts, floral remains, and pottery with carbon residue were recovered from the south-central portion of the structure, near cooking features (earth oven and hearth) and the clusters of small post molds, suggesting that this portion of the structure was used for cooking food. Another storage or curation area was present in the northeastern portion of the structure where storage pits and artifacts clustered. In addition occupants manufactured rough- or ground-stone and chipped-stone tools in this location.

Most external activities appear to have been conducted at some distance south of the structure. Artifacts were densest in the southeastern and southwestern portions of the excavation, near cooking features in the east and storage features in the west. In the southwest occupants clearly used several large storage features for floral materials, including maize and beans, but also processed these materials. The southeastern area, near two hearths and an earth oven, was a location for processing plants and animals. In this area occupants also produced chipped and in particular ground/rough stone tools. A third exterior activity area was located to the north of Structure 2 (near the eastern end) adjacent to hearth features. The concentration of faunal and floral materials, pottery, and chipped stone tools suggests that occupants prepared and processed food in this portion of the site. Two additional external activity areas were refuse locations directly to the east and west of Structure 2 where a high density and diversity of artifacts were present.

The artifact concentration to the east of the structure is intriguing in that the eastern posts had an average depth at least 5.5 cm shallower than the posts of the other three walls, suggesting that this end, possibly in the summer, remained open. It also may indicate the intention to expand the

Fig. 4.5. Activity areas associated with Structure 2, Thomas/Luckey site

structure (Snow 1994:44; see also Latta 1985). Furthermore the density of posts in the eastern end was greater than that in the other walls. This may support the hypothesis that this end was repeatedly opened and closed over the use life of the structure.

In terms of density and diversity, most artifacts were concentrated in and around Structure 2 and just east of the structure. Within the structure they tended to be located in the western portion, an area virtually devoid of features. Hearths were also located within the western section and the south-central portion (Figure 4.6). Similarly earth ovens identified within the structure were located in the western region. The density and diversity of artifacts and the presence of cooking/heating features in the western portion of the structure suggest that this section served as a residential area. All storage features identified in Structure 2 clustered in the structure's eastern section. When in use, these pits would have been covered with bark and/or earth (Kapches 1994:260). Conducting activities over the features may have been impossible and would have, at least during the activity, restricted access to the contents. Thus the two "halves" of the structure served different functions: dwelling in the west and storage in the east. The central portion of the structure had a lighter density of artifacts, possibly indicating that this high-traffic area was periodically cleaned. Activities within the structure included artifact storage/curation, processing and cooking food, and chipped, rough, and ground stone-tool manufacture. Activities conducted outside Structure 2 included preparing and processing wild and domesticated plants and animals, storing floral materials, stone tool manufacture, and refuse deposition. Evidence suggests several other activities engaged in by site occupants, including bone- , antler- , and hide-working, facility construction, pottery manufacture, and trade. However, these activities were not clustered in specific areas of the site.

Storage of food—and possibly seed—occurred in two main areas, the eastern portion of Structure 2 and south of the structure (see Figures 4.5 and 4.6). Storage within the structure may represent household-controlled and household-owned remains. The location of goods concealed within pits inside the structure would have meant that nonhousehold members could not quantify the contents, and thus an image of equality may have been perpetuated (DeBoer 1988; Prezzano 1992). Food stored outside may have been held in common among more than one household. Communally stored resources may have been used for particular events or ritual occasions. The external storage area contained a higher density of food remains than that within the structure. Thus an ethic of sharing may have prevailed, but individual households may have held onto a small portion of their food/seed. Although we must be careful not to project the historical record onto the past uncritically, historically women were the primary producers of horticultural goods and controlled their distribution. Storage within the dwelling may have been controlled by women who used these goods as an avenue for prestige and power, providing surplus for winter consumption, for feasting, or for provisioning raids (Prezzano 1997, 1998; Prezzano and Rieth 2001). The household was a dynamic setting in which the choices of individuals, in this case women, were pivotal in the reproduction and transformation of their culture. Alternatively internal and external storage facilities may have been maintained for use in the summer versus winter seasons, and all stores were held in common by at least one household.

The lack of recurrent artifact patterning within the structure argues for a single household (Costin and Wright 1998; Kramer 1982; Lightfoot 1994:120; Tringham 1991). Thus a household at Thomas/Luckey was composed of at least the individuals dwelling within a single structure. Data suggest that Structures 1 and 2 at the site may have acted as separate households (Miroff 2002a).[10]

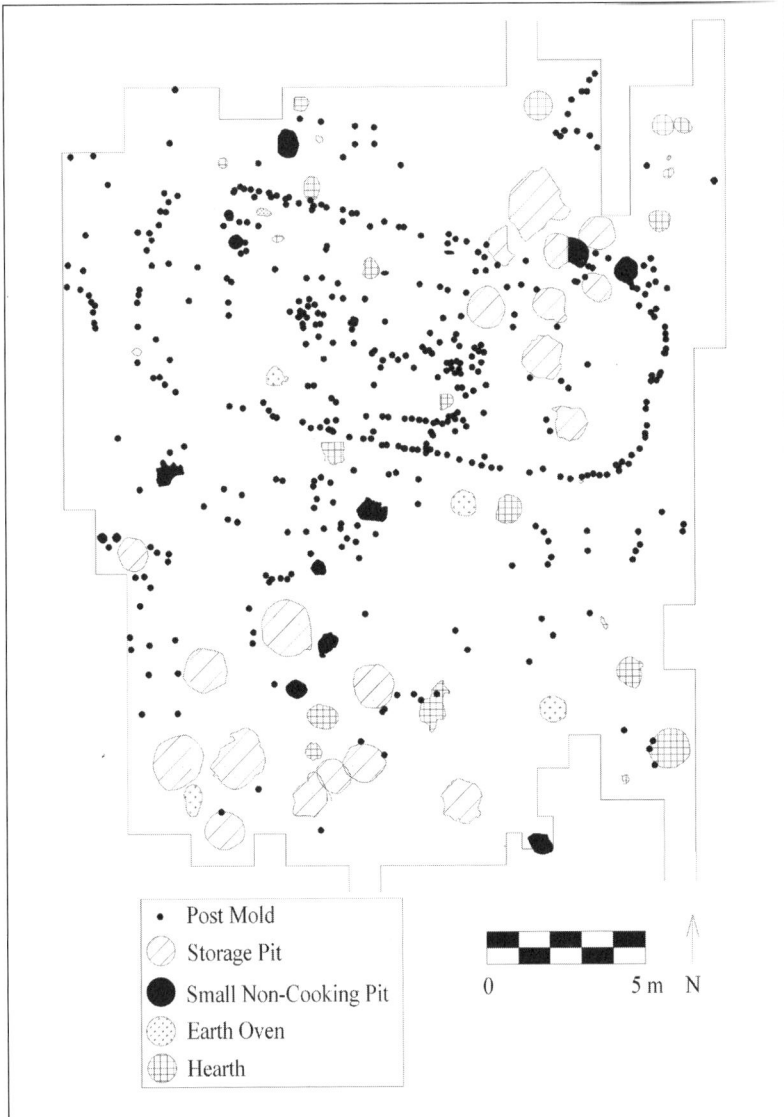

Post Mold

Storage Pit

Small Non-Cooking Pit

Earth Oven

Hearth

0   5 m   N

Fig. 4.6. Feature types in and adjacent to Structure 2, Thomas/Luckey site

The household in this context can be characterized as a group of individuals, likely related, possibly sets of nuclear families, living within a single structure and cooperating together in daily activities, such as food processing and tool manufacture. Botanical remains suggest that the site was occupied at least in the late summer and fall and likely in the late spring and early summer (Asch Sidell 2001b). Although the site may have flooded in the spring, occupants may not have had to abandon the village.[11] Winter occupation was also likely as many of the fruits, nuts, and crops could have been stored for winter use. However, it is probable that not all Thomas/Luckey occupants remained within the village year round, making it critical to examine the temporal and spatial context of the household (Kent 1987).

At least some occupants left the village for a day or more to hunt; trade; tend remote horticultural fields; procure/process edible plants and other raw materials; conduct hide-working, wood-working, and/or meat-processing activities; or engage in rituals, warfare, or diplomacy (Miroff 2002a, 2002b, 2002c; see also Perrelli, this volume). Men and women, of the same or different households, may have left their village together to conduct extra-village activities while elders remained to care for infants or small children. Group composition away from the village may have depended on the specific task—groups may have been composed of all women, all men, both women and men, and individuals of the same or different ages, with or without children. It is possible that outside the village household composition changed. Individuals may have defined themselves, on occasion, as a member of more than one household or may have thought of themselves as a member of a different household as they joined other households in subsistence or ritual activities away from the village proper (Wilk and Miller 1997; Wilk and Netting 1984:2). The composition of the household, then, was not static but fluid and must be defined for each spatial (village, camp, etc.) and temporal (daily, seasonally, etc.) context.

Social Reproduction and Transformation

Thomas/Luckey is unlike typical sites dating to the fifteenth century in that it is not situated on a defensible landform and to date no palisade has been identified. In addition at least one structure at the site does not conform to the basic form of a fifteenth-century longhouse (Snow 1994:29; see also Ritchie 1980:314; Ritchie and Funk 1973), and this departure may further imply that social and political organization also varied from the expected. Although a bench may have been present, no cubicles or midline hearths were identified. The artifact and feature distributions suggest that a single household occupied Structure 2. Pottery data demonstrate that while expected types for the fifteenth century (tall collars with incised decoration on smoothed surfaces) were present, typically "earlier types" (e.g., Carpenter Brook Cord-on-Cord, Levanna Cord-on-Cord, etc.) continued to be used.

Combining local-level analysis at Thomas/Luckey with regional studies demonstrates that the traditional model of the Iroquoian household as
a homogeneous unit, uniform over time and space, is inaccurate. Viewing
households as static and unchanging or as merely adapting to the environment denies their variability (Hendon 1996). Although households
may share certain characteristics, they may have differed in terms of
production, social reproduction, consumption, and socialization, both
between cultures and within a given culture (Cobb 2000; Netting et al.
1984:xxvi). In addition households changed over the course of their lives.
If a homogeneous definition of the household is abandoned, then there
can be no "basic form and function" of the longhouse. A household, then,
cannot be viewed as a permanent and unchanging entity, but must be
seen as an active decision-making unit as demonstrated by the analysis
of Structure 2 at Thomas/Luckey (Pauketat 1996:220).

The persistence of earlier patterns at Thomas/Luckey may indicate
that, for social, political, and/or economic reasons, groups in some
regions chose not to nucleate into regional clusters as was occurring in
other areas, particularly in the Five Nations core area. The continuance
of what might be referred to as traditional forms, including pottery, house
patterns, and household organization, suggests that important choices
regarding social organization were being made. Outside the core area,
quite different local and regional issues resulted in people organizing,
resisting change, and living lives unlike those in other areas (Lightfoot
2001; Pauketat 2001; see also Emerson and McElrath 2001; Sassaman
2001a, 2001b). While ties with groups to the north are evidenced in the
tall-collared pottery, proximity and social ties of Thomas/Luckey occupants with southern groups (evidenced by pottery types and lithic raw
materials) might have been stronger than those with northern groups.
Inhabitants of the Chemung Valley possibly chose to remain in their
homeland, continuing many practices and incorporating new ones.

The presence of a substantial habitation at Thomas/Luckey dating
to the fifteenth century refutes claims that the Susquehanna Valley, and
possibly the nearby Chemung Valley, was abandoned from the fourteenth
to eighteenth centuries (Rippeteau 1978). Not only did occupants not
move north to join the villages located there, they remained in the valley and maintained their established lifeways, living on the floodplain
in their homeland.

Analysis of the use and organization of space at the Thomas/Luckey
site supports the claim that inhabitants continued to live in the valley.
The actions of individuals there served to reproduce and transform their
culture on a daily basis (Lightfoot 2001). Households are a locus in

which social reproduction and transformation occurs and are situated in a particular historical context within which both male and female individuals act. Cultural reproduction and transformation result from the actions and interactions of individuals who may possess different degrees and types of power and may at times represent different interest groups (Brumfiel 1992; Cobb 1993; McGuire 1992; Meillassoux 1972; Miller and Tilley 1984:5; Saitta 1994:202; Trigger 1976, 1985). It is here that the multiscalar nature of human experience is apparent.

At Thomas/Luckey, issues of power were played out at different scales. First, occupants demonstrated their power by resisting the influences of Iroquoian groups to the north. Second, the decision to adopt particular cultural traits and reject others was played out at the level of the household, possibly along gender lines. Although males are frequently portrayed as active agents in ethnohistorical accounts of the Iroquois, women and the household were not passive (Prezzano 1997:97). Women's influence extended to household issues, including the dwelling, the village, and the fields. If these were their typical locales, then their power was key to the reproduction and transformation of all Iroquoian aspects of life. In addition, though women are typically portrayed as staying in and around the village, their power might have extended to external arenas, such as warfare and politics, and in this case the choice as to whether to adopt or resist adoption of particular cultural traits (Prezzano 1997:97; see also Claassen 1997; Hendon 1996; Knapp 2000, this volume; Latta 1991; Sassaman 1992; Versaggi 1996a; Versaggi et al. 2001; Watson and Kennedy 1991; Williams and Bendremer 1997).

While cultural reproduction and transformation have long been described as "punctuated equilibrium" where long periods of stasis are followed by dramatic change, in reality these processes are on-going (Lightfoot 2001:239). Cultural traditions are negotiated based on the interests and needs of individuals and groups (Pauketat 2001:2; see also Lightfoot 2001:238). Thus traditions are maintained and/or redefined within the current context. Their maintenance is often seen as the result of isolation. However, the introduction of history into cultural studies focuses attention on the connections between groups (Stahl 1993). Interactions may influence the reproduction of tradition. Instead of one group dominating another with the end result being the adoption of the dominant culture by the submissive one, groups of equal or unequal power may come together and each maintain their respective traditions as either a means of resistance or as "identity marking related to alliance formations, trade ties, and religious movements, as well as facilitating the identity of friend or foe" (Lightfoot 2001:247; see also Emerson and McElrath 2001; Sassaman 2001b).

At Thomas/Luckey both resistance and identity marking took place. As more dominant groups coalesced to the north, those in the Chemung Valley maintained their traditions as a means of resisting the influence of their northern neighbors. As individuals at Thomas/Luckey interacted with people further south, their traditions acted as boundary markers, materially and ideologically separating them from the groups with whom they interacted (Sassaman 2001a, 2001b). This does not mean that there was no cultural transformation. Instead the traditions of the occupants incorporated those of groups from the south, including their material culture.

Though not far from the heartland, the distance between the two areas and the geographic barriers between them allowed the occupants at Thomas/Luckey the ability to choose whether to adopt new cultural traits and practices into their community. Though still identified as clearly Iroquoian, occupants persisted in their community patterns (Alt 2001). The presence of tall-collared ceramics affirms that occupants knew that cultural changes were occurring to the north, but they negotiated which of these transformations to incorporate into their regional cultural patterns. Occupants may have felt little pressure to alter those practices, such as household organization, that directly affected social relations (Alt 2001). Thus inhabitants at Thomas/Luckey were able to maintain a superficial connection with more northern Iroquoian groups while maintaining their social relations. Cultural reproduction and transformation at Thomas/Luckey resulted in its unique character, differentiating it from contemporary northern and southern groups. This unique character, manifested in part by the persistence of earlier patterns, expresses issues of identity, power, and agency. Local-level analysis of other sites within the Chemung Drainage is necessary to understand better the nature of this regional variation during the fifteenth century.

Conclusion

The multiple lines of data derived from AMS dates, thermoluminescence dates, pottery types, and spatial analyses at Thomas/Luckey highlight regional variability and have demonstrated the potential of thinking beyond established paradigms. Analysis of household spatial organization and associated activity areas has made it possible to address the social organization of a particular group in a specific spatial and temporal context and illuminate the everyday actions of individuals who impacted and were impacted by panregional Iroquoian cultural transformations.

At a larger scale household analysis and extensive dating at the site have provided data to challenge the traditional understanding of the Late Woodland period as it relates to the Chemung Valley and Southern Tier of New York. A growing number of studies suggest that established cultural taxa are too unidirectional and do not always fit all physiographic and cultural contexts (Hart and Brumbach 2003; Miroff 2002a; Versaggi 1999b; Versaggi and Knapp 2000). New dates are refining this culture history and have even redefined as multicomponent some sites once thought to be single-component (Hart 1999, 2000; Hart and Brumbach 2003; Hart and Scarry 1999; Hart et al. 2003; Schulenberg 2002). Hart and Brumbach (2003) have already demonstrated that the existing cultural-historic framework is not suitable for the early portion of the Late Woodland and have proclaimed the "death of Owasco." Breaking free of the standard taxa has allowed researchers to recognize diversity and regional complexity, resulting in more innovative interpretations and allowing engagement in the social and political interpretations that these new data permit (Applegate and Mainfort 2005; Bousman et al. 2002; Sassaman 1995, 2001a, 2001b; Versaggi 1999; Versaggi and Knapp 2000; Versaggi and Miroff 2004). Placing a site within an established phase is thus problematic and self-replicating, constraining interpretations. As has been suggested by other researchers, by the end of the Owasco period, regional cultural variants developed; with this in mind, "wide-spread common pottery types" are not valid indicators of phases (Snow 1994:34; see Hart 1999 for a similar argument concerning Clemson's Island; see also Sassaman 2001a). However, we still tend to fall back into using phase names and associated traits (a holdover from the culture-historic period) mainly for ease of communication.

Research at Thomas/Luckey adds to the work of others arguing that we should "throw off the straightjacket" of culture-historic taxa and explore a richer, more complex understanding of the past that considers multiple pathways (see Hart 2000; Hart and Brumbach 2003; Snow 1994). Period and phase names imply internal homogeneity and mask diversity (Sassaman 2001a:107). Sites located outside the heartland (and even within) do not necessarily fit into the traditional culture history (Snow 1994). This may be even more true of sites dating after A.D. 1350. However, the general Late Woodland culture history is frequently referred to by researchers who forget the potential variability between regions at any given time. Thus a Chance phase site, regardless of its historical context, is expected to possess the "typical" characteristics for a site of this age. Thomas/Luckey is a clear example of regional variability among Iroquoian sites. This variability can not be expressed if the lockstep phases continue to be employed. Analysis of Structure 2 at the Thomas/Luckey site has demonstrated the fundamental importance of a local-level analysis for providing insights into social dynamics that are frequently overlooked when analysis is solely focused on larger temporal and spatial scales. Furthermore, appreciating the dialectical nature of these scales has helped to refine our understanding of both.

Notes

1. I would like to thank Roland Thomas for generously allowing us to excavate at the site, his support, and his invaluable dedication to the project. I would also like to thank the students of the 1996–1998 Binghamton University Field Schools, the participants of the Community Archaeology Program at Binghamton University, and all the volunteers for their hard work and enthusiasm that made this project a success. Specialized analyses for this research were funded by a National Science Foundation Dissertation Improvement Grant (Award #0001997). The grant provided funds for AMS and thermoluminescence dating and for botanical and use-wear analysis. Nina Versaggi and the Public Archaeology Facility graciously processed flotation samples. I would like to thank Nancy Asch Sidell for conducting the botanical analysis, Melody Pope for her microwear analysis, and James Feathers at the University of Washington Luminescence Dating Laboratory. I also thank Albert Dekin, Jr., Nina Versaggi, Sean Rafferty, Tim Knapp, Dean Snow, David Smith, and the two reviewers for providing comments on an earlier version of this paper. All errors and omissions are mine alone.

2. A third longhouse structure was possibly identified north of Structures 1 and 2 during limited excavation in 2001.

3. Nutshell included acorn (*Quercus* sp.), bitternut hickory (*Carya cordiformus*), black walnut (*Juglans nigra*), black walnut/butternut (*Juglans nigra/Juglans cinerea*), butternut (*Juglans cinerea*), butternut/black walnut/hickory (*Juglandaceae*), and hickory (*Carya* sp.). Grass seeds included big bluestem (*Andropogon gerardii*), grass family (*Poaceae*), and wild rye (*Elymus* spp.). Medicinal/beverage plants included bedstraw (*Galium* spp.), pokeberry (*Phytolacca americana*), smartweed (*Polygonum* spp.), sumac (*Rhus* spp.), and dock (*Rumex* spp.). Fleshy fruits included hawthorn (*Crataegus* spp.), huckleberry (*Gaylussacia* spp.), bramble

(*Rubus* spp.), elderberry (*Sambucus* spp.), and blueberry (*Vaccinium* spp.). Economic/weed seeds identified were goosefoot (*Chenopodium* spp.).

4. The same is true of Pennsylvania's pottery chronologies, which are based on sites in the West Branch and Lower Susquehanna areas (Heisey 1971; Heisey and Witmer 1971; Witthoft 1971; Witthoft and Farver 1971).

5. Sackett Corded pottery is typically said to date from A.D. 900 to 1350. AMS dating of residues from the interior of pottery place the starting point as early as the seventh century A.D. (Hart and Brumbach 2003; Hart et al. 2003; Schulenberg 2002; see also Snow 1996).

6. As with Sackett Corded, AMS dating of residues from the interior of pottery dates the type Carpenter Brook Cord-on-Cord to as early as the seventh century A.D. (Hart and Brumbach 2003; Hart et al. 2003; Schulenberg 2002; see also Snow 1996).

7. Dates in both Clusters 1 and 2 were obtained from features/post molds located across the excavation area, both within and outside of Structure 2.

8. The traditional age range for Carpenter Brook Cord-on-Cord has been expanded to A.D. 1200 or 1300 by some researchers (Niemczycki 1984:135) and Levanna Cord-on-Cord has been expanded to A.D. 1350 (Niemczycki 1984:135; Prezzano 1992:144).

9. Artifact categories plotted included ceramic pipes, chipped stone tools, triangular projectile points, utilized and nonutilized bifaces, utilized and non-utilized cores, debitage, utilized flakes, heat treated/burned flakes, pottery, rim sherds, fire-cracked rock, ground stone tools, net weights, pitted stones, and rough stone flakes.

10. A comparison of AMS dates from Structures 1 and 2, coupled with cross-mended sherds and spatial patterning of features, demonstrates that the two structures may have been contemporaneous and that the occupants were in some way associated (Miroff 2002a). The similarity in artifact and feature types and a similar distribution of features suggests the possibility that the structures acted as separate households.

11. The location of the structures on a ridge, the character of the river at the time (David Cremeens, GAI Consultants, personal communication, 1999), and the absence of the dams (presently located to the west and channel flood waters down to this section of the river instead of allowing the water to spread out before it reaches the site) may have meant that occupants could have remained at the site year round.

5

An Unbounded Future?
Ceramic Types, "Cultures," and Scale in Late Prehistoric Research

Timothy D. Knapp

Models of Late Prehistoric interaction are crucial for understanding the dramatic social transformations that occurred in the Northeast during the millennium and a half before the arrival of Europeans (A.D. 0–1500).[1] Prior to A.D. 500, native groups were organized in small mobile bands that moved about the landscape in a seasonal round, revisiting favored hunting, fishing, and collecting spots where they targeted seasonally abundant and concentrated wild food resources (Custer 1996:234–261; Finlayson 1977; Funk 1993:268–269, 289–290, 317; Ritchie 1980:241–246; Ritchie and Funk 1973:117–122, 352–354; Snow 1995c:64; Spence et al. 1990; Tuck 1978:324; Versaggi 1996a). Settlement models suggest that, for most portions of the Northeast, residential group size fluctuated seasonally. In the late winter or early spring a number of nuclear families coalesced at camps along major waterways or lakes, where they formed multifamily residential groups that remained together through the summer and fall. Families shared in productive tasks during these seasons of relative resource abundance. An important subsistence pursuit in which families likely cooperated was harvesting and processing rich seasonal runs of migrating fish, as well as, quite likely, wild-rice harvesting (Hart et al. 2003; Spence et al. 1990). While many of the sites of this period tended to be small multifamily camps located along major waterways or lakes, or even smaller nuclear family upland fall-winter hunting camps, there is also evidence for larger semipermanent camps that appear to have been occupied nearly year-round, such as Kipp Island in the northern Finger Lakes region and sites in the Rice Lake area of southern Ontario (Ritchie and Funk 1973:353; Spence et al. 1990). These sites, marked by the presence of structures and extensive middens, occur infrequently, are located exclusively on the Ontario Lake Plain, and are notably absent from the glaciated portion of the Appalachian Plateau. Although structural data for this period are scarce, it appears that small houses occupied by a single extended family were in use (Ritchie and Funk 1973:353; Snow 1980:275).

The subsistence-settlement system and form of social organization in place immediately prior to A.D. 500 stands in stark contrast to seventeenth-century Northern Iroquoian lifeways. These were centered on a subsistence economy focused primarily on the growing of crops, supplemented by animal foods and, to a lesser degree, gathered plants, and involved living in fortified year-round villages (Fenton 1978; Heidenreich 1971; Morgan 1962 [1851]; Parker 1968c [1916]; Ramsden 1990; Snow 1994a; Tuck 1978). Although beans, squash, and sunflower thrived in Northern Iroquoian fields, the focal crop was maize. Wild plant foods continued to be collected during the early Historic period; however, their role may have shifted largely to that of famine food (Heidenreich 1971:161). Central to Iroquoian life during the historic period was the longhouse—elongated structures that lodged several related families (Morgan 1962 [1851]). Ethnohistoric research demonstrates that the normal practice among Northern Iroquoian groups was for these long-houses to shelter a single matrilineal-matrilocal descent group made up of a core of mother, sisters, and daughters (Fenton 1978; Trigger 1985). Although other site types rounded out the historic Iroquoian settlement system, the central element was the village, which typically consisted of tightly clustered longhouses enclosed by palisade walls. These villages tended to be located on easily defendable landforms and/or at a distance from waterways, indicating that a heightened level of intergroup hostilities affected decisions on site locations.

Clearly the lifeways of Native Americans a millennium and a half before European arrival differed radically from those of the Historic period. Current archaeological explanations for these changes take two basic forms. The first is an in situ explanation that stresses continuity and argues that change is a local process (Crawford and Smith 1996; Dincauze and Hasenstab 1989; Dodd, et al. 1990; Fox 1990; Hart 2001; Hasenstab 1987; Niemczycki 1984, 1986, 1988; Ritchie 1980; Ritchie and Funk 1973; Smith 1990; Starna and Funk 1994; Williamson 1990). In this view indigenous peoples participated, wittingly or unwittingly, in fundamental shifts in lifeways. These changes may have resulted from perceived social, demographic, and/or environmental pressures and were undoubtedly connected to larger-scale trends in the Eastern Woodlands. The second is a migration explanation that models an expansion of horticultural populations into the Northeast replacing and/or incorporating local populations (Snow 1994a, 1995c, 1996a, 2001a). Snow (1995c:794), the primary proponent of a migration explanation, argues that for New York the initial population influx occurred by at least A.D. 900 and possibly as early as the seventh century A.D.

Although evidence from the critical period between A.D. 600 and 900 is spotty, emerging data from this span and from later times make it clear that many components of historic Northern Iroquoian lifeways developed at different times (Hart and Brumbach 2003). Tightly nucleated and heavily palisaded villages located on easily defended landforms, one hallmark of historic Iroquoian life, have a clear developmental history over the millennium before European arrival. The earliest Late Prehistoric hamlets and/or villages tend to be located on relatively unprotected floodplain locations (Prezzano and Rieth 2001; Snow 1995c). Only rarely are these communities palisaded. However, it is unclear if these functioned as defensive features or as symbolic boundary markers separating village from field/forest (Ritchie 1980:281). This stands in stark contrast to the sixteenth and seventeenth centuries, when villages in the Five Nations heartland areas tended to be perched on steep-sided elevated landforms that facilitated defense. Similarly palisades appear to have been more clearly focused on defense as is witnessed by a dramatic increase in the frequency of palisades at seventeenth- and eighteenth-century sites, as well as the addition of secondary and tertiary palisades (see Engelbrecht, this volume). These data on site location, structure density, and palisades clearly indicate that significant social changes marked Late Prehistoric times.

In a similar vein, recent botanical evidence has dismissed the idea that the Iroquoian Three Sisters of maize, squash, and beans—a supposedly quintessential feature—entered the Northeast as an intact horticultural package. Rather, emerging data indicate that each of these crops may have a different history of introduction into the Northeast. An intensive program of AMS dating of potentially early beans in the Northeast suggests that this cultigen was not introduced until circa A.D. 1300 (Hart and Brumbach 2003; Hart and Scarry 1999). The history of squash (*Cucurbita pepo*) in the Northeast is less well understood. The only direct evidence in New York is from Roundtop, where squash seeds have been dated to around A.D. 1350 (Hart 1999, 2000; Hart and Brumbach 2003). However, squash phytoliths identified from Kipp Island, Hunters Home, and Wickham have been dated to the seventh and eighth centuries A.D.

(Hart et al. 2003). Our understanding of the timing of the introduction of maize into the Northeast has been revolutionized by the increasingly common practice of direct AMS dating of maize remains. In the late 1990s Crawford, Smith, and Bowyer (1997) rocked the archaeological community with the publication of the results of a suite of AMS dates from southwestern Ontario that indicate that maize was introduced to at least one area of the Northeast sometime between the third and seventh centuries A.D. More recently Hart and colleagues have reported AMS dates on carbon residue adhering to the inside of pottery vessels from sites in the upper Finger Lakes region that suggest that maize may have been present as early as the seventh century in central New York (Hart et al. 2003). Maize from Deposit Airport I, located in Delaware County, New York, was submitted for direct AMS dating and returned an uncalibrated radiocarbon age of 1210 B. P. ± 40. When calibrated, this maize has a one sigma range of cal A.D. 770 to 890, indicating that this crop had been introduced to the Upper Delaware Valley possibly as early as the eighth century A.D. (Knapp 2003). Together these data on squash, beans, and maize indicate a complex and varied history for these crops in the Northeast.

Similarly recent radiocarbon dates question the antiquity of the long-house, a classic hallmark within Iroquoia (Hart 2000). Through a critical review of published New York dates, coupled with 15 new radiocarbon and AMS dates, Hart (2000) argues that existing evidence suggests that longhouses did not appear on New York sites until the thirteenth century. Present data suggest that structures dating earlier than the thirteenth century were relatively small structures, which implies a different form of social organization than is associated with longhouses. This trend from small dwellings to longhouses indicates that Late Prehistoric structures in the Northeast have a dynamic history, which likely correlates with significant social transformations as indigenous groups shifted their lifeways from relatively mobile hunter/gatherers prior to A.D. 500 to village-based agriculturalists by historic times.

From the compelling site location, plant, and structure data, it is clear that a fully developed Northern Iroquoian package never entered the Northeast and that in fact there was considerable in situ change/development of Iroquoian subsistence, settlement, and social relations from at least A.D. 800 on and possibly even earlier. This does not mean that migration had no role during the late prehistory of the Northeast. While there were undoubtedly sporadic influxes of people and ideas, the transformations that marked the Northeast Late Prehistoric period were primarily the result of the history of local populations.

Clearly the Late Prehistoric period in the Northeast was incredibly dynamic. Central to modeling this dynamic social history is a focus on people and the forms of social interactions they practiced. One form of interaction materialized in the ceramic wares from two Late Prehistoric sites in southern New York State. Analytic scale can mask important variability, and thus it is important to consider multiple analytic scales. Implicit analytic scales embedded in our traditional cultural and pottery typologies at times have led to the automatic (and largely unexamined) creation of the category of "foreign pottery." The identification of "foreign pottery" has led to uncritical arguments for the presence of captured women, often with no supportive data suggesting internecine warfare. Using ceramic data from the Thomas/Luckey site, located on the Chemung River, and the Deposit Airport I site, situated on the West Branch of the Delaware River, one can suggest that the cooccurrence of distinct pottery traditions at a single site may reflect interaction in the form of intermarriage between Late Prehistoric communities.

Cultural Taxons, Boundaries, and Pottery Types

As archaeological investigations in North America intensified during the middle of the twentieth century, researchers developed classification systems to facilitate organizing the rapidly growing prehistoric database. The Midwestern Taxonomic System and its later modifications provided mechanisms for classifying archaeological sites into progressively more inclusive taxonomic groupings based on shared traits (McKern 1939; Phillips and Willey 1953; Willey and Philips 2001). Using these systems, William Ritchie (1944, 1946, 1951, 1980) created the regional taxonomic blueprint largely still in use today. In his last synthesis, Ritchie (1980:xxviii) defined a phase "as a recurring complex of distinctive archaeological traits, sufficiently different from any other complex to suggest that it represents the product of *a single cultural group,* pertaining to a limited territory and to a relatively brief period of time" (emphasis added). On the next rung of his classificatory scale, Ritchie (1980:xxviii) defined a culture as "the particular strain of social heredity of a group of individuals larger than that represented by the phase, and united by sharing of a common tradition or traditions." Explicit in each of these definitions is the notion that phases and cultures represent social groups. However, a number of researchers have reminded us that our taxonomic units were originally defined as sets of spatially and temporally limited artifacts and features and do not necessarily identify any past social group (for recent Northeastern statements, see papers in Williamson and Watts 1999). Despite these warnings, archaeologists have repeatedly proceeded as if phases, and the more inclusive cultures, were social realities. Thus archaeologists have written about Late Prehistoric Owasco, Clemson Island, and Shenks Ferry "peoples" as if these represented real social groups who shared a common identity; this invokes images of closed and bounded systems. Modeling cultures as bounded systems privileges the regional scale while obscuring local-scale variation. This filtering mutes community-level variability and ultimately suppresses dynamic interpretations.

Intimately linked to assumptions of group boundedness are assumptions implicit in ceramic typologies. The taxonomies of native northeastern pottery were originally established as tools for refining temporal and spatial relationships between archaeological sites (MacNeish 1952; Ritchie and MacNeish 1949). However, in practice, pottery types and cultures are often conflated to the point where specific pottery types have come to symbolize entire cultures, with specific styles taking on a quasi-ethnic identity (see Morrow 1999 for a similar argument for point styles). So linked are ceramics and cultures that many Late Prehistoric pottery types include cultural designations in their names (e.g., Owasco Corded Horizontal, Shenks Ferry Incised, and Clemson Island Platted Horizontal). This one-to-one mapping of pottery and culture likely imposes inappropriate boundary conditions on pottery distributions. This insistence on ceramic style boundaries creates tensions between local- and regional-scale views, which ultimately compels archaeologists to identify some vessels as "local" and others as "foreign."

Typically one of the first concerns for archaeologists working at the scale of an individual site is establishing the site's cultural affiliation— that is, they attempt to place their site within existing cultural taxonomies. Spence (1999) argues that our archaeological taxonomies begin at the scale of the palisade walls and work outward, with individual sites forming taxonomically indivisible blocks. It is the tension between taxonomically indivisible sites and bounded cultures that presents a dilemma when a number of stylistically distinct ceramics are recovered in clear association at a single site. Central to the act of assigning cultural affiliation to a site is the nearly automatic, and almost always uncritical, segregation of pottery into "local" and "nonlocal" types. Criteria used to identify local vessels typically include a site's geographic location and/ or proportions of ceramic types present. Vessel types occurring in relatively low numbers, and seemingly outside of their typical cultural range, are classified as foreign without any further corroborative evidence.

Although a number of explanations could account for these so-called foreign pots, the bounded-culture model implicit in most Late Prehistoric research leads to the interpretation of these pots as material markers of captive women—what has been dubbed the "Captured Bride Syndrome." This arises from the implied hard-and-fast nature of group boundaries, which are so impenetrable that the movement of people between groups requires violent force (Figure 5.1). Varying our analytic scales allows us to imagine other possibilities distinct from the "Captured Bride Syndrome," thereby opening up more nuanced and dynamic interpretations of early Late Prehistoric interaction.

The Sites

Focusing on recent excavations at two early Late Prehistoric sites—one in the Upper Susquehanna drainage (Thomas/Luckey) and the other in the Upper Delaware watershed (Deposit Airport I; Figure 5.2)—highlights the impacts of analytic scale. These sites were chosen because their pottery assemblages include vessels that would traditionally be identified as "foreign." Researchers working in the Susquehanna Valley have defined Owasco, Clemson Island, and Shenks Ferry as spatially and temporally bounded early Late Prehistoric traditions (Funk 1993; Graybill 1989; Hay et al. 1987; Heisey 1971; Heisey and Witmer 1971; Kinsey and Graybill 1971; Kinsey et al. 1971; Ritchie 1980; Ritchie and Funk 1973; Stewart 1990, 1994; Witthoft and Farver 1971). The Owasco tradition dates between A.D. 900 and 1350 and is found in central New York and northern Pennsylvania. Clemson Island sites date between A.D. 800 and 1250 and are most common in central Pennsylvania (Stewart 1990:80–81; Turnbaugh 1977: 209–210). The Stewart Phase, a northern early Shenks Ferry variant, begins around A.D. 1250 and terminates about A.D. 1400, and is distributed along the Susquehanna's west and main branches (Graybill 1989). At Thomas/Luckey, Owasco and Shenks Ferry tradition vessels are found together repeatedly in feature contexts. Deposit Airport I provides evidence for the association of Owasco and Clemson Island tradition wares. Therefore these two sites are ideal for exploring the impact of analytic scale and interaction.

Thomas/Luckey

Thomas/Luckey (SUBi-888) is a Late Prehistoric village located on the relatively flat floodplain of the Chemung River, a New York State tributary of the Susquehanna River which lies to the south of the historic heartland of Iroquoia, in an area historically known as the Iroquois Southern Door (Figure 5.2). The site's location places it along one of the main avenues of travel and trade between the Susquehanna River and western and central New York State (Bradley 1987; Wallace 1993:46–48). The Chemung flows through a steep-sided, U-shaped valley typical of the glaciated portion of the Appalachian Plateau. At approximately 24 km downstream from Thomas/Luckey, the Chemung joins the Susquehanna at Tioga Point. The site is located approximately 300 m from the current river channel. The Public Archaeology Facility (PAF), Binghamton University Field School, and PAF Community Archaeology Program excavated at the site between 1994 and 2001. Two longhouse structures have been completely excavated and a possible third longhouse was tentatively identified during limited work in 2001 (Knapp 1996a; Miroff 2002a, this volume). The focus here is on the 1994 excavations of Structure 1, a longhouse which was 32 m long and 6.5 m wide (Figure 5.3; Knapp 1996a, 1996b, 2002b). The presence of a curved line of posts within the western half of Structure 1 indicates that when initially constructed, this house was 19.5 m long. This suggests that during the uselife of the longhouse, the residential group felt a need to expand their enclosed structural space, as was common during the Late Prehistoric period. This may have resulted from the growth of the coresident group. Excavations also revealed 72 features, including hearths, earth ovens, large and small storage pits, and a single smudge pit. Fourteen flotation samples from seven features have been analyzed to date (Knapp 1996a, 1996b, 2002b). Botanical data indicate that the residents of Thomas/Luckey grew maize, beans, and possibly sunflowers in their fields. Noncrop seeds are dominated by grasses and economic weeds. All the grass seeds were recovered from features interpreted as storage pits and likely represent the remains of grass pit linings intended to retard mold. Residents collected economic weed seeds, including chenopod, sunflower, and possibly knotweed. Seeds from the fleshy fruits of hawthorn and elderberry were also recovered. Collected fall nut masts included hickory, butternut, and acorns.

Classifying ceramic vessels according to traditional pottery types indicates that a diversity of ceramic types is located within and around Structure 1 (Table 5.1). Pottery types identified in feature contexts include Carpenter Brook Cord-on-Cord, Levanna Cord-on-Cord, Sackett Corded, Kelso Corded Collar, Oak Hill Corded, and Shenks Ferry Incised. Taken individually these types appear to represent the entire range of the early Late Prehistoric period (ca. A.D. 900–1400). However, the relative proportions of ceramic types point to a period of occupation

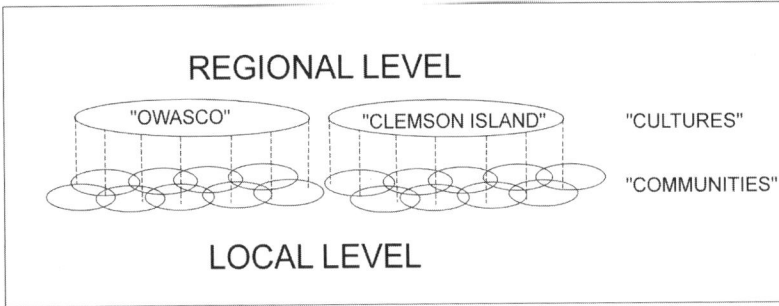

Fig. 5.1. Bounded model of Late Prehistoric interaction

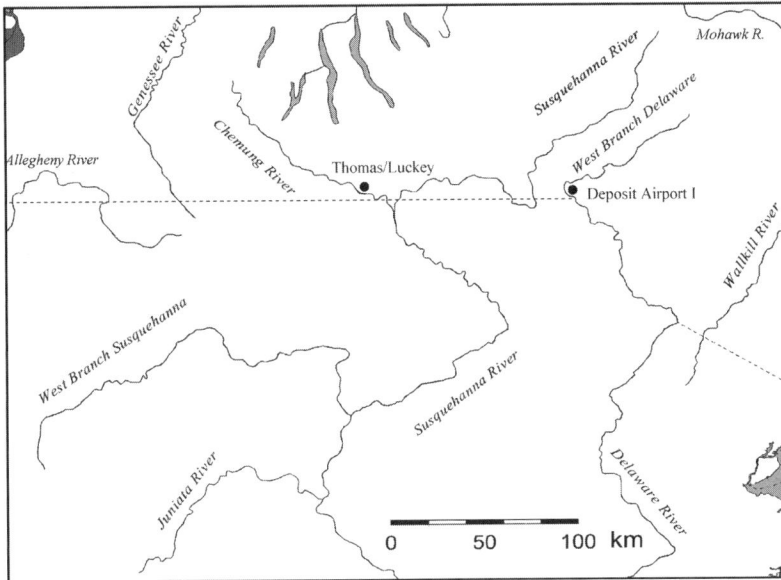

Fig. 5.2. Location of Thomas/Luckey and Deposit Airport I sites

traditionally referred to as Late Owasco or Castle Creek phase (ca. A.D. 1200–1300). By way of comparison, the ceramic frequencies differ only slightly from the Castle Creek type site (Knapp 1996a:Table 23). Based on this ceramic evidence, the initial site report suggested that the longhouse and its associated features date between A.D. 1250 and 1325 (Knapp 1996a).

A total of nine radiocarbon dates, five conventional and four AMS dates, are associated with features in and around Structure 1 (Table 5.2; Knapp 1996a, 2002b). Initial radiocarbon dating during the data recovery excavations relied solely on the standard radiometric dating of five

Table 5.1. Pottery Types from Features Associated with Structure 1 at Thomas/Luckey

Pottery Type	Count	Percent
Carpenter Brook Cord-on-Cord	15	12.4
Levanna Cord-on-Cord	8	6.6
Sackett Corded	56	46.3
Kelso Corded Collar	19	15.7
Shenks Ferry Incised	22	18.2
Oak Hill Corded	1	0.8
Total	121	100.0

wood-charcoal samples that provided mixed results (Knapp 1996a). The maximum 2σ range for these samples spanned more than a millennium (A.D. 561 to 1622) and covered a time range that includes dates too early and too late for an early Late Prehistoric site. More recently, AMS dates secured for one bean sample and three maize fragments have clarified the age of Structure 1 and its associated features (Hart and Scarry 1999; Knapp 2002b). The maximum 2σ range for these AMS dates is a much tighter A.D. 1260 to 1483. Radiocarbon dating is a probabilistic technique that tends to disperse dates, often overestimating the duration of site occupation (Asch and Brown 1990; Ottaway 1987; Shott 1992). Therefore, setting aside the problematic wood dates, this would suggest that the area of Thomas/Luckey including Structure 1 dates between A.D. 1300 and 1450. This is slightly later than expected based on the ceramic data; however, our expected ceramic ages rest on relatively few radiocarbon dates secured more than 20 years ago (see Miroff, this volume, for a critique and revaluation of traditional ceramic chronologies vis-à-vis the Chemung Valley). Additionally, recent suites of AMS dates have demonstrated a much greater degree of temporal variability than was once thought to exist (Hart and Brumbach 2003; Miroff 2002a, this volume; Schulenberg 2002).

Table 5.3 presents correlation coefficients for pottery recovered from feature contexts. Several positive correlations of pottery types are highlighted by this table: Carpenter Brook Cord-on-Cord with Levanna Corded; Levanna Corded with Sackett Corded; and Kelso Corded Collar with Shenks Ferry Incised. Interestingly there are no significant negative correlations, suggesting that the pottery types are not mutually exclusive. Of particular importance for the present discussion of interaction is the clear evidence at Thomas/Luckey for the association of Owasco series

Kelso Corded Collar pottery and Shenks Ferry Incised ceramics typically identified as a Pennsylvania pottery type. Exploring this cooccurrence involved examining the association of these two types in features that had at least two distinct vessels. Fifteen features with a minimum of two vessels each contain either Shenks Ferry Incised or Kelso Corded vessels. One of these features contains only Shenks Ferry vessels, while another feature has only Kelso Corded Collar vessels. Of the remaining 13 features, eight (62 percent) contain sherds from both types. As the number of vessels within a feature increases, correlations should become even more obvious. This is in fact the case, with 70 percent of the ten features with a minimum of three vessels having both types. Given the indisputable association of Shenks Ferry Incised and Kelso Corded and the perceived uniqueness of this association, maize from three features containing both vessel types was submitted for AMS dating (Knapp 2002b). These three samples returned virtually identical AMS dates, which, when averaged, produce a calibrated 1σ range of cal A.D. 1406 to 1433 (Table 5.2; 2σ range: cal A.D. 1330–1350 and cal A.D. 1390–1450).[2]

Not only do Kelso Corded and Shenks Ferry Incised cooccur in Thomas/Luckey features, these vessels are quite similar in form and

Fig. 5.3. Structure 1 at Thomas/Luckey

Table 5.2. Thomas/Luckey and Deposit Airport I Radiocarbon Dates

Lab no.	Context	Technique	Material	$^{13}C/^{12}C$	^{14}C Age (BP)	Maximum Calibrated 2σ Range and Intercepts (A.D.)[*]	Source
			Thomas/Luckey				
Beta-82470[***]	Fea. 4	standard	wood	-27.8	1360 ± 70[**]	561 (662) 780	Knapp 1996a
Beta-82471	Fea. 36	standard	wood	-26.3	460 ± 60[**]	1331 (1439) 1622	Knapp 1996a
Beta-82472	Fea. 40A	standard	wood	-28.7	960 ± 60[**]	981 (1034) 1217	Knapp 1996a
Beta-82473	Fea. 57	standard	wood	-28.6	1100 ± 80[**]	723 (904, 910, 976) 1152	Knapp 1996a
Beta-82474	Fea. 75	standard	wood	-26.7	780 ± 60[**]	1159 (1263) 1376	Knapp 1996a
Beta-144728	Fea. 22	AMS	maize	-8.5	480 ± 50[**]	1331 (1434) 1483	Knapp 2002a
Beta-144729	Fea. 21	AMS	maize	-8.7	530 ± 50[**]	1304 (1412) 1446	Knapp 2002a
Beta-144730	Fea. 3	AMS	maize	-8.5	540 ± 50[**]	1302 (1409) 1443	Knapp 2002a
AA29122	Fea. 78	AMS	bean		695 ± 45[**]	1260 (1292) 1392	Hart and Scarry 1999
			Deposit Airport 1				
Beta-168303	Fea. 6	AMS	maize	-9.1	930 ± 60[**]	1000 (1050, 1100, 1140) 1240	this study
Beta-168306	Fea. 29	AMS	wood	-25.0[****]	850 ± 40[**]	1050 (1200) 1270	this study
Beta-168307	Fea. 34	AMS	maize	-9.1	920 ± 40	1020 (1200) 1210	this study

[*] Calibrations done with CALIB 4.3 (Stuiver and Reimer 1993).

[**] Corrected for isotopic fractionation.

[***] Small sample required extended counting time.

[****] Lab estimated.

Table 5.3. Thomas/Luckey Pottery Correlations

	Carpenter Brook Cord-on Cord	Levanna Cord-on-Cord	Sackett Corded	Kelso Corded Collar	Shenks Ferry Incised	Oak Hill Corded
Carpenter Brook Cord-on-Cord	1.00	0.31*	0.15	-0.08	-0.09	0.17
Levanna Cord-on-Cord	0.31*	1.00	0.41*	-0.13	-0.13	-0.04
Sackett Corded	0.15	0.41*	1.00	-0.13	-0.08	0.03
Kelso Corded Collar	-0.08	-0.13	-0.13	1.00	0.60*	0.14
Shenks Ferry Incised	-0.09	-0.13	-0.08	0.60*	1.00	-0.05
Oak Hill Corded	0.17	-0.04	0.03	0.14	-0.05	1.00

*Correlation significant at p=0.05 level.

decoration, despite traditionally being assigned to distinct pottery traditions. Kelso Corded, a type proposed by Lenig (1965), collapses Owasco Corded Collar, Bainbridge Collared Incised, Hummel Corded, Dansville Corded, and horizontally decorated Oak Hill Corded forms. Bodies range from elongated to globular, and vessel necks are constricted with a concave contour that flows up to a pronounced collar (MacNeish 1952; Ritchie and MacNeish 1949). Collars are short to medium in height, often displaying interior channeling, and always have flat lips (Prezzano 1992:145). Bodies exhibit cord-roughened surfaces, while necks and collars have been smoothed to receive decoration by either cord-wrapped sticks or the edge of a cord-wrapped paddle. At Thomas/Luckey collar decoration consists of a band of parallel horizontal lines encircling the collar; collar bases are decorated with oblique cord-impressed lines. On some vessels a second band of horizontal cord-impressed decoration appears on the neck. Kelso Corded vessels date from the Canandaigua phase to the Oak Hill phase, but they are most frequent on Castle Creek sites (Late Owasco) that date between A.D. 1250 and 1350. Kelso Corded vessels have traditionally been associated with Owasco sites with a geographic distribution centered on central New York.

Strikingly similar to Kelso Corded vessels, particularly in form and decorative motif, yet clearly distinctive in both surface treatment and method of applying decoration, are Shenks Ferry Incised pots. These vessels have egg-shaped bodies with rounded bottoms and typically exhibit moderate neck constriction. Vessels have well-defined short to medium collars with flat lips. Bodies are cord-marked, necks are smoothed, and collars display vertically-oriented cord markings. Shenks Ferry Incised pots are decorated with parallel incised lines (Witthoft and Farver 1971). Rims recovered from Thomas/Luckey fall into the multiple-banded subtype (Heisey and Witmer 1971) and are decorated using a combination of uninterrupted bands of horizontal or oblique lines. Collars bear parallel horizontal lines; parallel oblique incised lines begin at the base of the collar and continue to the neck; at the neck is a band of parallel horizontal incised lines. Shenks Ferry Incised is a major ceramic type associated with the Blue Rock and Stewart phases of Pennsylvania (Heisey 1971; Lucy 1971; Witthoft and Farver 1971:454). These geographically separated but contemporary phases date between A.D. 1250 and 1400 (Graybill 1989:54). The clear similarities between short-collared Shenks Ferry Incised and Kelso Corded pots—particularly vessel shape, rim profile, and decorative motif—immediately suggest coparticipation in some larger interaction sphere. Additionally each type appears to mark a temporal transition in their respective heartland regions between uncollared and tall-collared later forms.

To summarize the data from the area of Structure 1 at Thomas/Luckey briefly, these Chemung Valley residents lived in longhouses; occupied the site between A.D. 1300 and 1450; grew corn, beans, and possibly sunflowers; and used pottery that has been assigned by archaeologists to Owasco and Shenks Ferry traditions.

Deposit Airport I

Deposit Airport I is a multicomponent site situated adjacent to the West Branch of the Delaware River (Figure 5.2; Knapp and Versaggi 2002). The site, which includes a Late Prehistoric component, occupies a relatively wide section of floodplain. Upstream and downstream the floodplain narrows considerably. Approximately 17.7 km to the southeast, the West Branch and East Branch converge to form the main trunk of the Delaware River. In the vicinity of the site, the current river channel hugs the western valley wall, thus producing the wide floodplain on the eastern bank. The elevation is remarkably flat at approximately 302 m amsl;

however, the nearby valley walls rise dramatically to well over 518 m. Upland draining creeks feed the river from the west and north. Oquaga Creek and other tributaries entering from the west originate near the drainage divide separating the Delaware and Susquehanna watersheds, and they probably provided an important transportation link between these drainages. At Deposit Airport I, the West Branch of the Delaware is only 15 km east of the main trunk of the Susquehanna River. PAF crews discovered the Deposit Airport I site in 2000 during reconnaissance surveys of two alternates for proposed water and sewer lines (Hohman and Bonner 2000; Knapp 2000b). Both alternates intersected the site and indicated that Deposit Airport I is a large site, covering an area of more than 1.2 hectares. PAF conducted site examination and data recovery excavations at the Deposit Airport I site in 2000 and 2001 along a 3 to 4 m wide linear corridor approximately 660 m long. This corridor is only 12 to 55 m to the west of the current river channel.

The recognition of structural patterns was hindered to a degree by the narrow project area. However, at least five structures have been tentatively identified by post-mold patterns. Four linear post patterns appear to represent the remains of walls likely associated with structures; however, the outline of these structures is unclear given the narrow project limits (Figure 5.4). Structure 2 consists of a relatively straight wall that extends for at least 3 m. Structure 3 includes a curving wall that is at least 2 m long. Structure 4 is identified by two lines of posts that may represent the end and side walls of a single longhouse. If these two lines do intersect, they form a structure that is at least 6 m in one dimension, larger than the small dwellings noted for the Upper Delaware. The line of posts making up Structure 5 is more ambiguous but appears to form a straight wall at least 3 m long. More-extensive exploration of Structure 1 identified what appears to be the end of a longhouse structure (Figure 5.5). This post pattern includes two parallel, and apparently straight, walls, as well as a rounded end connecting the two walls. These walls form a structure approximately 6 m wide, a width typical for Late Prehistoric longhouses (Prezzano 1992:269–270). Numerous features were recovered in and around this structure, including a hearth located along the structure's centerline.

The site examination and data-recovery excavations identified 32 prehistoric features, including hearths, small pits, and large storage pits. A series of three AMS radiocarbon dates supports the presence of an early Late Prehistoric component at Deposit Airport I (Table 5.2). These dates are also statistically identical and, when averaged, result in a

Structure 2

Structure 3

Structure 4

Structure 5

1 meter

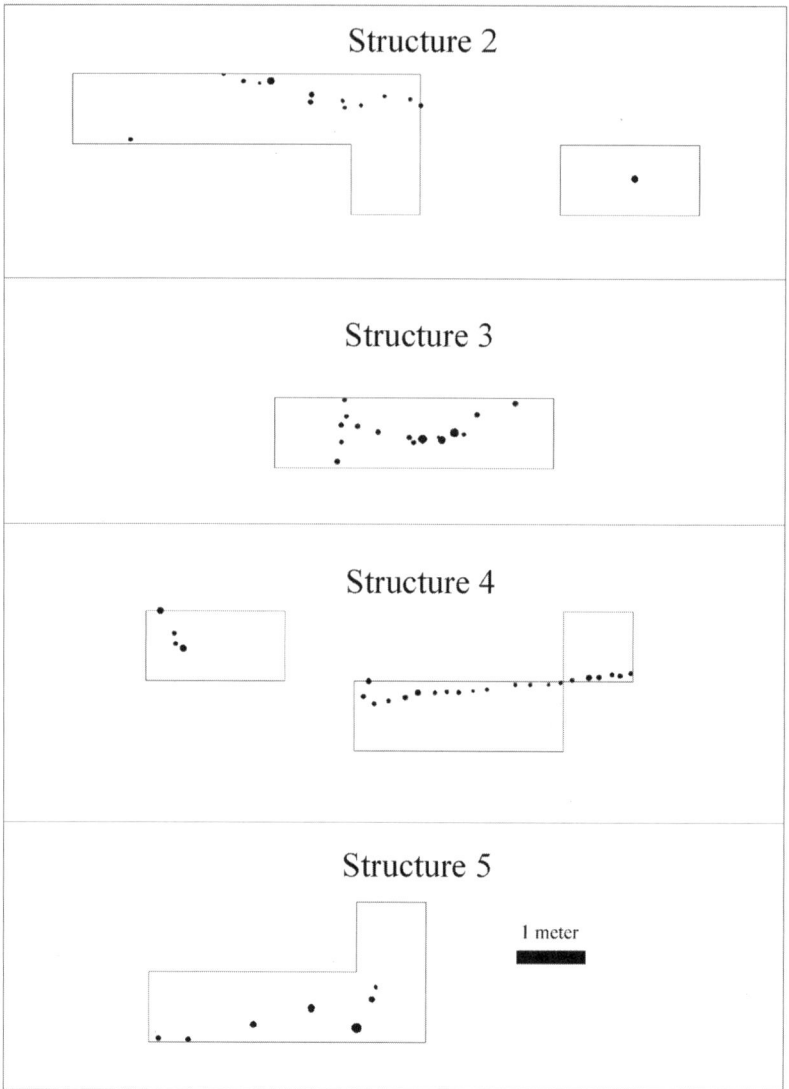

Fig. 5.4. Structures 2–5 at Deposit Airport I

calibrated 2σ range of cal A.D. 1040 to 1220. Thirty-nine flotation samples from 27 features have been analyzed (Knapp and Versaggi 2002;
Knapp 2003). Given the presence of multiple components and the general
lack of diagnostic artifacts in feature contexts, only plant data from
three radiocarbon-dated early Late Prehistoric features are considered
here. The three radiocarbon-dated early Late Prehistoric features con-

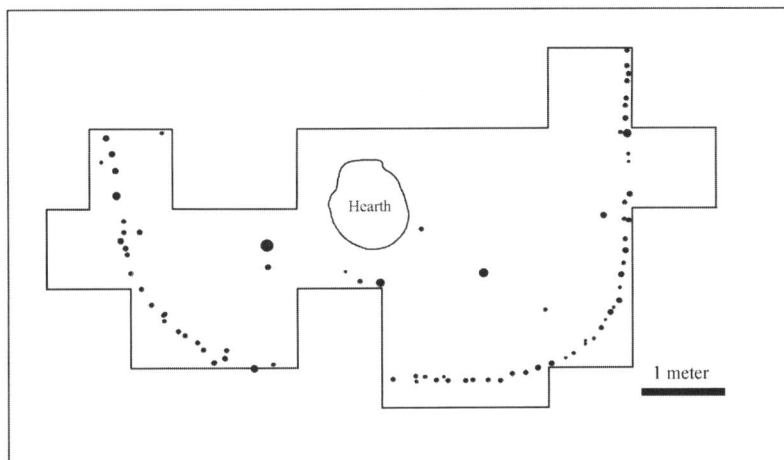

Fig. 5.5. Structure 1 at Deposit Airport I

Table 5.4. Early Late Prehistoric Pottery Types from Deposit Airport I

Pottery Type	Count	Percent
Carpenter Brook Cord-on-Cord	15	28.3
Levanna Cord-on-Cord	5	9.4
Sackett Corded	22	41.5
Wickham Corded Punctate	2	3.8
Clemson Island	9	17.0
Total	53	100.0

tained maize. Feature 34, the central hearth associated with Structure 1, contained one cupule and two kernels. Feature 6, a large storage pit, included two cupules, one glume, and one kernel. Feature 29, a bell-shaped storage pit, contained two cupules, one glume, and two kernels. Nearly 60 percent of this early Late Prehistoric maize consists of cob fragments (cupules and glumes). Such a high frequency of cob fragments suggests that the maize was grown near the site.

The early Late Prehistoric ceramic assemblage includes a mix of Owasco and Clemson Island series ceramics: Sackett Corded; Carpenter Brook Cord-on-Cord; Levanna Cord-on-Cord; Wickham Corded-punctate; and various Clemson Island types (Table 5.4). The association of Clemson Island with Owasco ceramic types is fairly strong with approximately one of every six rims representing a Clemson Island type.

Additional support for the cooccurrence of these types comes from the spatial distribution of pottery types across this large site. Four of the seven spatially distinct clusters producing early Late Prehistoric sherds include both Owasco and Clemson Island ceramic types, indicating that these wares are associated.

Typical Clemson Island vessels are conoidal in shape with somewhat elongated bodies and rounded bottoms (McCann 1971:422; Turnbaugh 1977:235). These pots range from moderately constricted examples to those exhibiting pronounced neck constriction. Rim profiles include straight, flaring, and overhanging forms. Lips are often thickened and are always flattened. Vessel exteriors are either fabric impressed or cord-marked (Jones 1971; Lucy 1971:384; McCann 1971:419). Two techniques of decoration were used on the exterior surfaces of vessels: cord-wrapped paddle impression and/or punctations. Cord-wrapped paddle impressions in the form of horizontal, vertical, herringbone, or plats of vertical or oblique lines appear on the shoulder and neck. These exterior decorations almost invariably occur over a roughened surface. Only occasionally is the surface partially smoothed to accept decoration. Lip interiors are often decorated with parallel oblique lines. Lip surfaces are frequently cord-wrapped paddle impressed in an oblique, transverse, or encircling orientation. Rim exteriors often bear an encircling band of oblique cord-impressed lines below the lip.

The most-diagnostic decorative feature associated with some Clemson Island vessels is distinctive punctation. Punctations may occur on either the interior or the exterior surface and are often so deep that bosses appear on the opposite face. Punctations occur as a row encircling the vessel just below the lip—occasionally two rows of punctations are present. Although the presence of punctations is quite diagnostic of Clemson Island wares, their presence is not requisite. At the type site, Clemson Mound, and the similar Book Mound, punctations are found on only 60 percent of the pots (McCann 1971:419). McCann suggests that the proportion of punctate-decorated vessels may be even less at other Clemson Island sites.

Clemson Island ceramics and Owasco wares have been repeatedly linked in archaeological discussions. Linkages arise from the similarity between these two ceramic traditions. So alike are these wares that when punctations are absent, distinguishing between these two wares is difficult. Given the similarity between these two ceramic series and the difficulties in drawing a boundary between Owasco and Clemson Island distributions, several authors have begun to refer to "Clemson Island/

Owasco" settlements and pottery rather than attempt to distinguish these two wares (e.g., Garrahan 1990; Hatch 1980; Turnbaugh 1977).

Although discrimination between Owasco and Clemson Island wares may be possible in some regions, a relationship between the makers of these wares is clearly indicated by the resemblance. Turnbaugh (1977:228) has argued that whatever the relationship between Owasco and Clemson Island culture, it was limited only to the early portion of the Owasco period. As evidence he points to the scarcity of Middle and Late Owasco ceramics along the West Branch. Stewart (1990) argues that Clemson Island originated as a regional variant of an Owascoid phenomenon that linked the Appalachian Region from New York to Virginia between A.D. 700 and 1000. This geographically expansive Owascoid manifestation is based on a shared core ceramic style—grit-tempered vessels of a similar form, decorated with cord-wrapped stick or dowel impressions. A process of regionalization working on this Owascoid base produced distinctive late Middle Woodland and early Late Woodland styles of decoration. Each of these regional manifestations is thought to represent a "major social territory, perhaps each being the realm of one or more bands that frequently interacted" (Stewart 1990:90). For Stewart, Clemson Island is an expression of one of these regional territories. This regionalization model suggests that late Middle Woodland and early Late Woodland cultures witnessed an in situ genesis from a pre–late Middle Woodland base (Stewart 1990:89). Therefore, similarities between Clemson Island and Owasco ceramics arise from a shared base, as well as from continued interaction among regions. The appearance of punctated Clemson Island vessels at Deposit Airport I, and their occurrence on other Owasco sites, clearly demonstrates some form of social interaction between people living in central Pennsylvania and southern New York.

To summarize the data from Deposit Airport I briefly, these Delaware Valley residents likely lived in longhouses; occupied the site between A.D. 1040 and 1210; grew corn near the site; and used pottery traditionally assigned by archaeologists to Owasco and Clemson Island traditions.

Others

Thomas/Luckey and Deposit Airport I clearly demonstrate interactions between peoples in southern New York and central Pennsylvania, but how extensive is this pattern? A cursory review of archaeological sites from the Susquehanna drainage reveals a number of cases of cooccurring

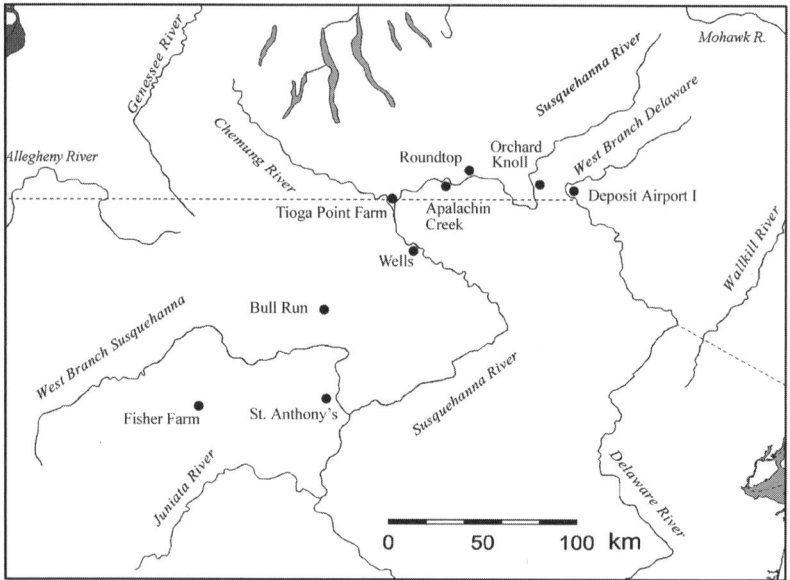

Fig. 5.6. Sites with an association of Clemson Island and Owasco Pottery

"local" and "foreign" pottery. Sites within the traditional Owasco culture area where Clemson Island type pots have been recovered include
Roundtop (Ritchie 1980; Ritchie and Funk 1973), Apalachin Creek
(Rieth 1997), Orchard Knoll (Rieth 1997), and Tioga Point Farm (Figure 5.6; Lucy 1971, 1979; Lucy and Vanderpoel 1979). The traditional
Clemson Island culture area is more difficult to assess, for Ritchie and
MacNeish's (1949) Owasco pottery typology has been used to classify
most of the nonpunctated vessels recovered from sites assigned a Clemson Island affiliation. A small sample of Clemson Island sites containing
Owasco pottery types include Wells (Stewart 1990), Fisher Farm (Hatch
1980), St. Anthony's (Stewart 1990), and Bull Run. At a slightly later
time, a similar pattern of the cooccurrence of Shenks Ferry and Owasco
pottery types is evident at Tioga Point (Lucy 1971), Boland (Prezzano
1992), and Blue Rock (Figure 5.7; Heisey and Witmer 1971). Clearly
the pattern noted at Thomas/Luckey and Deposit Airport I is common
to southern New York and northern Pennsylvania.

A New Model of Late Prehistoric Interaction: An Alternative to the "Captured Bride Syndrome"

These data document a high degree of regional interaction between early
Late Prehistoric communities in the glaciated portion of the Appalachian

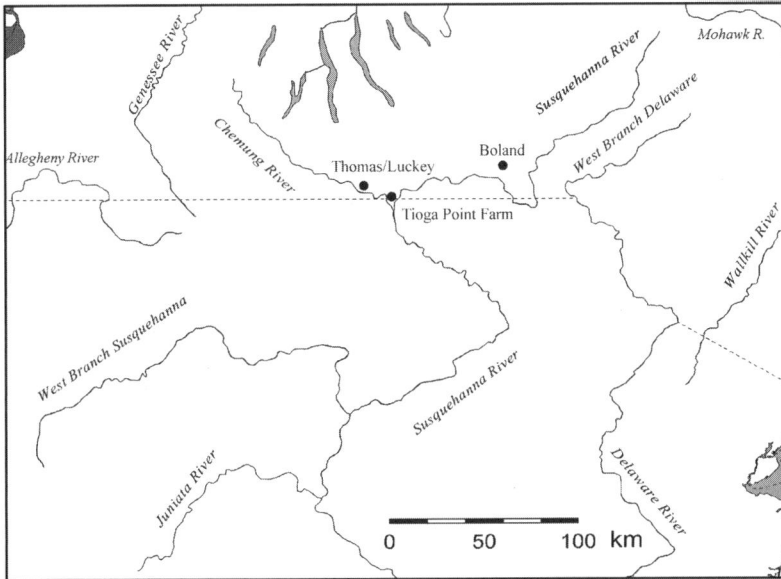

Fig. 5.7. Sites with an association of Shenks Ferry and Owasco Pottery

Plateau. Traditional archaeological narratives interpret the recovery of supposedly foreign vessels at Late Prehistoric horticultural villages as evidence for the presence of captured wives taken during warring raids (Engelbrecht 1972, 1974; Heisey and Witmer 1971:479; MacNeish 1952:7; Snow 1994a; Trigger 1968; Whallon 1968; Witthoft and Farver 1971:428; but see Latta 1991 for an alternative view). These interpretations are based on historical analogy. Seventeenth-century Iroquoian groups are known to have conducted warring raids during which women were captured, brought back to the village, and adopted (Engelbrecht 2003; Richter 1983, 1989, 1992; Snow 1994a; Trigger 1985). However, this explanation does not fit the data from either Thomas/Luckey or Deposit Airport I, where no evidence of warfare has been documented to date. Each site's location on relatively flat floodplains afforded no natural protection. At Thomas/Luckey, where more than 1500 m^2 of the site has been exposed, excavations have failed to encounter a palisade. Rather than assume that foreign vessels indicate the presence of captive women, it is possible that the association of distinct ceramic types documents a peaceful form of interaction among early Late Prehistoric groups and, furthermore, that women took an active role in cultivating this interaction.

At a very basic level there are two ways that so-called foreign pottery styles might have appeared at a site: either they were transported to the site or they were locally produced pottery crafted in a foreign style (Whallon 1968). One mechanism that might bring foreign pots to a site is trade—either pots or their contents may have been bartered along the Susquehanna drainage. Alternatively, people joining a community either through marriage or adoption may have brought a small number of such pots to a site. In contrast locally produced pots may have been executed in a foreign style through local copying of foreign vessels or through local crafting by potters who joined the community through marriage, adoption, or capture.

One way to distinguish locally produced vessels from pots crafted elsewhere is trace element analysis of pottery clays (e.g., Cruz 1996; Kuhn 1985, 1986, 1987; Rieth 1997). Rieth (1997) demonstrated, using X-ray fluorescence, that during the Upper Susquehanna's early Late Prehistoric period, stylistically "foreign" vessels were often locally made. It is therefore reasonable to assume that at least some Kelso Corded and Shenks Ferry Incised pots were made at Thomas/Luckey and that examples of both Owasco and Clemson Island wares at Deposit Airport I were locally crafted.

If we accept that women were the potters, as was the case during the historic period, then we can posit that women at Thomas/Luckey crafted stylistically distinct Shenks Ferry and Owasco pots. Although the majority (82 percent) of the pottery is attributable to Owascan types, nearly one out of five vessels is Shenks Ferry Incised.[3] This association is even more striking when collared vessels only are considered. The Thomas/Luckey Structure 1 assemblage has nearly even numbers of Shenks Ferry Incised and Kelso Corded pots, the only collared types found in and around Structure 1. This would seem to suggest more than just a minor occurrence of a few isolated trade vessels or pots attributable to captured wives—at this site half of the collared pots are made in a foreign style. Also compelling is the early Late Prehistoric Deposit Airport I ceramic assemblage, where one in six vessels are Clemson Island wares more typical of central Pennsylvania. Data from these two sites, along with others, suggest that women at these Late Prehistoric sites were producing two pottery types typically believed to belong to separate ceramic traditions, one based in central Pennsylvania and one in central New York State.

So why were women creating stylistically distinct pots? Assuming fluidity of group membership and rejecting tightly bound communities, then what is reflected in the pottery is possibly alliance building through intermarriage. Members of small Late Prehistoric villages are likely to have sought mates in neighboring communities. In this scenario, women potters who crafted stylistically distinctive pots joined the Thomas/Luckey and Deposit Airport I communities through marriage.

The suggestion that some women shifted residence at marriage may appear at odds with the historical view that Iroquoians practiced matrilocality (Fenton 1978). However, residence patterns are ideals, not straitjackets, and it is probable that residence patterns actually were more variable even among historic Iroquoians (Engelbrecht 1984; Richards 1967; Trigger 1978). If matrilocal residence was an ideal pattern only in the seventeenth century, projecting strict matrilocality back three to five centuries is problematic. Therefore it is plausible that residence patterns during the early Late Prehistoric period were more fluid, with both men and women joining their mates' communities.

Assuming that women were the potters and that on marriage some women moved to their husband's communities, the question becomes, why did these women continue to craft vessels in a style distinct from that of their new community? The answer lies in conceptualizing style as a means for communicating information about group membership (Pollock 1983; Wobst 1977). The repeated and regular association of distinctive ceramic attributes suggests that distinct styles were indeed represented at these sites. Clearly foreign styles are found in relatively large numbers. If style communicates identity, then the data from Thomas/Luckey and Deposit Airport I would seem to indicate that these vessels do not represent captured women. Chilton (1996:124) has argued that the extended time required for cooking maize stew placed pots in a central and highly visible location for long periods and that decorated collars would have been prominent. If pots communicate messages, then it does not seem likely that captured women would have been allowed to broadcast a foreign message in such a conspicuous manner. In a similar vein Sassaman (2001a) has made the case that stylistic variability is, to a degree, inversely proportional to institutional constraints. If this is true, it is hard to comprehend why adopted captives, presumably under strict institutional constraints, would be allowed to produce pottery in a foreign style.

Given these institutional constraints, it seems more likely that these cooccurrences of pottery types reflect alliance building through marriage. Women may have manufactured distinctive pottery styles as a purposeful act of identifying membership with their home community. The distinctions between some of the supposedly foreign and local pottery types are technically minor, yet encode a clear stylistic message. While visually distinctive, these differences are technically simple, and female potters entering a new community would have been able to adapt their pottery easily to the local style. Importantly, these distinctions were likely to have been easily read by community members. For Early Owasco and Clemson Island wares, pots are visually virtually identical, except for the presence of punctations on the latter. For each of these wares, the underlying decorative grammars are indistinct. It is hard to imagine that any differences in motor skills would have prevented potters from embellishing their wares with punctates—equally obvious is the ease with which punctates could have been omitted. Similarly, although there are other clear differences, the most immediate differences between Kelso Corded and Shenks Ferry Incised are surface treatment (smoothed or cord-marked, respectively) and the tool used to apply decoration (cord-wrapped stick or stylus). Again it is unlikely that potters were incapable of altering their method of surface treatment or manner of decorative application. Despite the relative technological ease of adapting their crafting of pots, it is clear that some women chose to continue potting in their natal style.

So, if the differences between Owasco vessels and Clemson Island pots, as well as Kelso Corded and Shenks Ferry Incised ceramics, are not the result of the inability of potters to adapt their style to a local standard, then why is it that women opted to craft visually distinctive wares? It is likely that women chose to craft certain pottery styles as a means of marking group identity and consequently staking future claims for support from their natal communities. One time when group identity may be emphasized is during periods of subsistence stress. All systems of food acquisition are marked by a degree of risk. This is especially the case when subsistence relies on a less diverse range of resources, such as cultivated plants, and when mobility is restricted, as it is likely to be among horticulturalists. An added level of risk is introduced into horticultural economies located in areas where climatic factors are not optimal. Such is the case for the Allegheny Plateau, which "would have been a risky region for growing maize, given that the frost-free period ranges locally from 90 to 170 days and that the growing season required for eight-row northern flint maize—the kind grown prehistorically—was 120 days" (Hasenstab and Johnson 2001:10).

One strategy for mitigating subsistence risk is the fostering of reciprocal exchange relationships (Halstead and O'Shea 1989). By establishing social ties, communities develop a sense of mutual obligation that can be mobilized in times of localized subsistence failure. In this sense exchange may be viewed as social storage (O'Shea 1989:58; Rowley-Conwy and Zvelebil 1989:50). Horticultural communities are certainly not immune to the unpredictable fluctuations of their ecosystem. Occupation of Thomas/Luckey occurred sometime between A.D. 1300 and 1450, approximately the time of the onset of the Little Ice Age, a period of significant cooling (Baerreis and Bryson 1965; Bernabo 1981; Bryson and Wendland 1967). This climatic change may have presented new subsistence challenges. Deposit Airport I, although predating the Little Ice Age, was still likely to have been affected by localized crop failures. One way to ameliorate these risks is by fostering social ties between communities. Late Prehistoric horticulture in the Northeast was particularly susceptible to localized microclimatic variations (Hasenstab and Johnson 2001). Valleys, or even segments of valleys, are likely to have witnessed different microclimatic histories. One year a particular valley may witness an uncharacteristically late frost while the neighboring valley is spared this killing frost; one spring a tributary creek valley may be marked by severe flooding not experienced in other areas; another year an upstream valley segment may be inflicted with a severe hail storm that destroys most of the annual crop. It is the potential for localized microclimatic crop failure that may lead individuals to develop social networks that tie communities from neighboring valleys. At Thomas/Luckey and Deposit Airport I, women may have crafted pottery as a means of marking group identity and consequently staking future claims on subsistence resources at times of localized crisis.

According to Sassaman (1998:94) "the rules and boundaries that define human interactions are forms of power." Women, in the process of crafting pottery, created conduits of interaction that facilitated access to the resources of their natal communities. This risk-reducing access also created avenues for nonlocal women to exert power in their new communities. Spence (1999) questions the role of pottery in interaction and communication between communities given that historically men acted as intermediaries between villages. However, if women were the makers of pots and also held the primary responsibility for horticultural production, it may have been an effective social strategy for women to use potting to assert identities tying them to other communities as a means for ameliorating subsistence risk.

Although the specific examples presented here could be argued to be a border phenomena, associated with communities lying well away from heartlands, this building of strategic alliances through intermarriage and the deliberate marking of at least one aspect of social identity through potting are likely a hallmark of early Late Prehistoric horticultural communities throughout the Northeast. It may be the agricultural marginality of the Northeast that made this a successful social option. With the increased risk inherent in northeastern horticulture, women marrying into new communities and largely responsible for plant food production may have opted to maintain relations with their birth communities in order to ameliorate lean times. These ties are materialized in potting. In this view the act of potting is a statement of identity and simultaneously a marker of obligation.

At "cultural margins" these messages may be easier for archaeologists to read (e.g., Shenks Ferry Incised pottery that is similar to that found in the West Branch of the Susquehanna and Kelso Corded similar to pottery found in the Upper Susquehanna). However, communities located near "archaeological heartlands" likely employed a similar scheme of strategic intermarriage to create a social safety net. In these heartland cases, intermarriage among neighboring villages likely moved men and women into new communities. Potters entering a new community continued to make pottery as they had learned in their natal community. However, these styles were virtually identical to those of the villages into which they married. It is likely that it is this process itself that creates what archaeologists view as "cultures." Through the repeated intermarriage of a number of core communities, a common material culture develops. If this model holds, then identity signaling in ceramic style will manifest itself differently on ceramic heartland sites than it does at border sites. At the border recognizably distinct ceramics cooccur, signaling identity and obligation, while heartland sites have homogenous pottery styles, also marking identity and obligation.

Conclusion

Both the site and culture analytic scales are inadequate for capturing the variability apparent at a number of Upper Susquehanna and Upper Delaware sites. Following Sassaman (1999), a more useful approach is to tack back and forth between a number of analytic scales. In particular we need to focus more on mid-level scales that connect settlement to settlement or individual to individual, rather than relying on large-scale groupings such as phases or cultures that were likely outside the daily experiences of the individual.

By exclusively focusing on either the community (village) or the archaeological culture (Owasco, Clemson Island, or Shenks Ferry), we lose some potentially important information on the social dynamics of the Late Prehistoric period. With a focus on the community scale only, pottery types would be divided into supposed local and foreign types. The latter category has been traditionally interpreted as the material manifestation of captured wives. In contrast research at a larger scale of analysis would strive to place each site into a culture based on the dominant ceramic types found at a site. This results in the marking of hard boundaries encircling groups of sites and fosters a view of minimal interaction between sites of different cultures. Analysis at each of these scales fails to capture a dynamic view of women and men engaged in social strategies during the Late Prehistoric period. Tacking back and forth between local and regional scales reveals patterns apparent in ceramic data, suggesting that women crafted pots in particular styles with the purpose of identifying and marking social obligations that could be mobilized at times of subsistence failure.

A multiscalar approach also highlights the various social scales that enmesh people. Late Prehistoric women in the Northeast were potters, gardeners, mothers, wives, sisters, and lineage, clan, and village members, among many other roles. It is therefore difficult to pick a single analytic scale at which to view women in the past. Each role provides its own set of concerns—concerns that will at times conflict. As but one example, some women at the Late Prehistoric Thomas/Luckey site appear to have been born into communities living along the West Branch of the Susquehanna River. In their natal community, these women were daughters and sisters. On marriage these women joined their husband's community along the Chemung River. Here they held roles as wife, mother, and gardener. During times of crop failure, as provider of crop foods, they might call on the assistance of their natal village. This would be then reciprocated when their natal community was in crisis. However, these various roles, operating at different scales, occasionally came into conflict. If crops failed in a woman's natal and marriage communities in the same year, her obligations would come into conflict. If these roles came into conflict repeatedly over time, this might lead to social changes that would mediate these tensions. In the case of the Late Prehistoric Northeast, a shift from ambilocal residential pattern, where choice of postmarital residence is unconstrained, to a matrilocal residence pattern may have resolved these tensions, at the same time possibly weakening some of the intercommunity ties of early times. A multiscalar approach highlights some of these tensions and may provide important insights into social change.

A multiscalar approach is also necessary, given the integrated nature of local- and regional-level processes. Local-level actions often have regional outcomes, and, at the same time, regional processes affect local behavior. It is likely that regional pottery zones are created at the local level through intercommunity marriages where some wives join their husbands' villages and craft pottery as they were taught by their mothers, aunts, and grandmothers. Over time the intermarriage of neighboring communities is likely to lead to uniformity in regional pottery style. Thus we should heed Spence's (1999) advice that we look inside the palisade walls (or within the local residential community) at the central role of marriage in the creation, maintenance, and potential source of change in our larger taxonomic units.

Bringing a multiscalar approach to bear presents an alternative to the "Captive Bride Syndrome" used to explain the presence of "foreign" pottery on early Late Prehistoric sites in the Northeast. At Thomas/Luckey, Deposit Airport I, and other southern New York and northern Pennsylvania sites, there are no data to suggest that warfare was a major threat. These sites are all located on relatively flat floodplains or slightly elevated terraces, which would have afforded no natural protection. The majority of these sites appear to be unpalisaded. Defense does not appear to have been a concern for these Late Prehistoric peoples. Therefore it would be wrong to assume that supposedly foreign ceramics represent captured women. Additionally the capture of women would have imposed new institutional constraints on these women, and it seems unlikely that potters would have been allowed to craft in their natal styles. Instead it is probable that these ceramics are the material signature of women freely marrying into new communities. Through potting in the style of their natal community, these women were stating identity and marking obligations. By maintaining an identity that tied them to another area, these women were in a position to call on assistance in times of subsistence failure. This ability to enlist aid, in addition to their key role in horticultural production, undoubtedly allowed women to exercise power within their communities. If further evidence bears out this model, we will have to recast our conceptions of local and foreign pottery at these small-scale Late Prehistoric horticultural communities. Much of this pottery may actually be local, while at the same time invoking an identity with another community as part of a series of weblike relations interconnecting a number of communities.

Notes

1. I wish to thank Roland Thomas, to whom I am truly indebted for allowing me repeated and untethered access to the Thomas/Luckey site and who funded, encouraged, and facilitated our research at this site. Research at Deposit Airport I resulted from Cultural Resource Management contracts at the Public Archaeology Facility (PAF) at Binghamton University funded by the Delaware County Planning Department. The staff of PAF and Binghamton University 1994 and 1995 field schools performed the fieldwork at these sites. I truly appreciate the excitement and dedication the crews and students brought to their work at these sites. All laboratory research for these sites was performed by the staff at PAF. I wish to thank Laurie E. Miroff, Nina M. Versaggi, and Laura Knapp, whose comments on early drafts greatly improved this paper. All errors and omissions are my responsibility.

2. All calibrations were calculated using Oxcal 3.10. With a p=0.05.

3. "Owascan" is used in this essay to refer to pottery belonging to any of the Owasco pottery types. This usage is distinct from the term "Owascoid," meaning Owasco-like.

6

The Community and the Microhousehold
Local Scales of Analysis within an Iroquoian Village

Tracy S. Michaud-Stutzman

As researchers study development and change through time among different Iroquois groups and other middle-level tribal societies, there is value in viewing data at multiple scales since domestic life is experienced at various levels. Even within individual communities, local activities are played out at multiple scales (Fogt and Ramsden 1996; Lightfoot et al. 1998).

In archaeology material remains collected from across a community or from a microhousehold level each provide different types of data. The act of analytically segregating and contrasting community and microhousehold enhances understanding of the cultural dynamics of a group. This richness is missed when researchers indiscriminately lump together all local level information from a site.

In Iroquois studies ethnographic accounts have been valuable in filling in the "details" of domestic life. However, a multiscalar analysis of material remains at the local level can also fill in some of these details, thus the focus here is on analyzing archaeological data at two different scales within Parker Farm, a late prehistoric Cayuga Iroquois village site. The research incorporates archaeological data from broad-based community remains as well as data from a microhousehold context. The use of both data sets creates a more holistic view of Cayuga Iroquois domestic activities, reveals variability at the local level, highlights factors affecting the scale at which activities are visible, and provides a strong comparison to the ethnographic record.

In the following, domestic life is broadly defined as all economic and sociopolitical pursuits associated with the inhabitants of the Parker Farm village. Domestic life is therefore represented in the remains of subsistence practices, processing, manufacturing, ritual activities, and external interaction. Analysis at the community level is based on archaeological data collected from shovel test pits and surface collection from across the entire Parker Farm village. This includes information from across various households. Domestic life is also analyzed through a micro-household perspective from contextual archaeological data recovered from the excavation of a single longhouse compartment.

The Cayuga

The Parker Farm site falls within the historic Cayuga Iroquois homeland. Although less is known about the origins and lifeways of the Cayuga than those of other Iroquoian groups (Fenton 1978), recent archaeological research has gathered new data on the Cayuga (Allen 1994, 1998, this volume; Baugher and Clark 1998; Michaud-Stutzman 2001, 2002; Michaud-Stutzman and Allen 1998; Williams-Shuker, this volume; Williams-Shuker and Allen 1998). Between the fourteenth and sixteenth centuries, there were two spatially discrete Cayuga village clusters, one on the east side and one on the west side of Cayuga Lake in upstate New York. Based on spatial proximity and similarity in ceramic styles, it is presumed that the villages on both sides of the lake were part of one coherent tribal system. The Cayuga villages on both sides of the lake proceeded through a sequence of village relocations eventually converging into one village on the east side of the lake during historic times (Niemczycki 1984).

Parker Farm

The Parker Farm site (UB 643) is located on the western side of Cayuga Lake on a small terrace above Taughannock Creek. Two radiocarbon dates were obtained for Parker Farm from Beta Analytic, Inc. Sample 1 returned an uncalibrated date of 450±60 B.P. (Beta-162110),[1] which, when calibrated, has a 2σ range of cal A.D. 1400–1520 and cal A.D. 1580–1630. The uncalibrated date for sample 2 is 340±40 B.P. (Beta-162111).[2] The 2σ calibrated radiocarbon date for sample 2 is cal A.D. 1450–1650. These data support ceramic seriation indicating that Parker Farm is a late prehistoric community (Michaud-Stutzman 2002). Ceramic chronology indicates a specific date of A.D. 1525–1550 (Niemczycki 1984; see also Edmonson 1976) for the occupation of the

Parker Farm village. Parker Farm is one of the last prehistoric Cayuga settlements occupied before significant European contact in Iroquoia.

According to floral analysis, the natural environment during the occupation of the Parker Farm site was a regional climax forest composed of northern hardwoods (Asch Sidell 2001a; Braun 1950). The location of the village offered easy access to water and clay. Today the eastern portion of the site is in a plowed field, and the western portion is in a wooded area. The site is about 1.4 ha in size, which is larger than most other Cayuga villages (Figure 6.1).

The soil stratigraphy at Parker Farm is relatively straightforward in both the plowed and wooded sections of the site. In the plowed portion of the site, there is a 30 to 35 cm deep plow zone on top of lighter subsoil. In the wooded portion of the site, Stratum A is 20 to 25 cm deep. Stratum A is most likely a nonmodern plow zone on top of lighter subsoil. The soil in Stratum A in most excavation units and test pits was characterized as a dark brown loam (Munsell 7.5YR3/2). The subsurface soil (Stratum B) was easily distinguished from the plow zone, being a harder packed yellowish brown clay loam (Munsell 10YR5/6 to 5/8). Based on tree-ring counts from fallen trees at the site, the wooded portion of the site has not been disturbed by farming practices for at least 65 years, and therefore preservation was quite good.

Theoretical Orientation

Community

The community is an important spatial scale since this is the broad arena where domestic activities are conducted (Deagan 1995; Lightfoot et al. 1998). Although the community is one of the more important contexts of social interaction, the concept of the community is typically underdeveloped in archaeological studies. Archaeological sites are generally assumed by researchers to encompass discrete communities. While this is an accurate assessment in some cases, it is important not to assume that the community is a static, closed, and homogenous unit (Canuto and Yeager 2000). Jamieson (1989) argues that prehistoric communities were less static and more complex than is noted in many ethnographic and historic documents, hence the importance of archaeological research at the community level.

Archaeological investigations inside communities, including information from various households, are successful in describing inter- and intrasite relations and showing the dynamic nature of past communities (Fogt and Ramsden 1996). Viewing a community through its people,

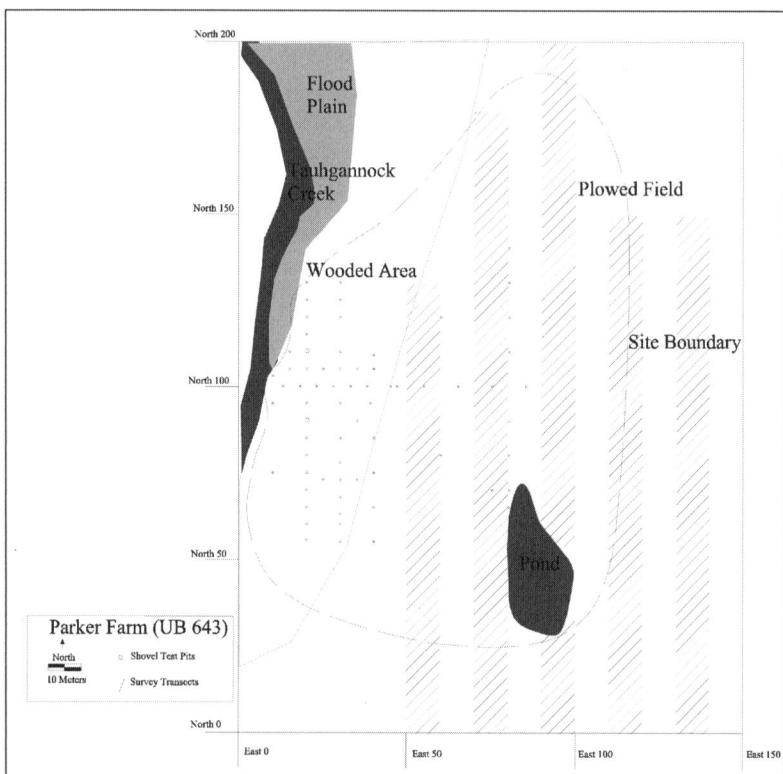

Fig. 6.1. Map of the Parker Farm village boundary, survey transects, and shovel test pits

their interactions, and historical context allows for an in-depth exploration of behaviors and activities that characterize the community. The
late prehistoric New York Iroquoian archaeological sites lend themselves
especially well to community-level exploration since site occupation
tends to be relatively short. This presumably allows a relatively accurate
snapshot of the occupants during a discrete time period. For the purpose
of this discussion, the Parker Farm village site represents the community.
Although smaller outposts associated with the larger Parker Farm village
are likely, none has been identified thus far.

Household

According to Wilk and Rathje (1982), the household is the socioeconomic level at which adaptation can be most directly studied. Material remains associated with the household allow a contextual analysis of

domestic activities and behaviors that represent a set of social relations among the residents. In a household analysis, although studying the structure itself is informative, the use of a variety of evidence, including ceramic remains and other household artifacts, leads to more robust conclusions (Bermann 1996; Hirth 1993). By studying contextual material remains associated with the household, researchers can better identify activities conducted, delimit work areas, and make inferences on the division of labor (Bermann 1996; Hirth 1993; Kapches 1979).

Most Iroquoian researchers consider the longhouse the significant household unit (Brown 1970; Fenton 1978; Heidenreich 1971; Kapches 1990, 1994; Prezzano 1997; Snow 1994b; Tooker 1984, 1991). Historically the longhouse was occupied by the matrilineal extended family (Morgan 1962 [1851]). Within the longhouse smaller nuclear families lived in compartments that formed the larger egalitarian corporate group. Prehistorically each nuclear family is assumed to have completed the same types of tasks while working cooperatively (Hayden 1977; Kapches 1979). However, recent research has brought up questions about what role nuclear families actually played within the larger household, how similar and different these families were, how much autonomy each family had, and if all families worked together on every task (Allen 1992; Martelle 1999).

The archaeological record of New York Iroquois longhouses has shown that compartments are typically delineated from each other and have private storage associated with them. This could indicate that each nuclear family functioned somewhat independently from other nuclear families within the same longhouse (Allen 1994; Snow 1997). Research by Allen (1992) and Martelle (1999) indicates that not every family necessarily completed the same tasks, and that different activities, or differing intensity of activities, might be occurring within each compartment in the longhouse. Therefore a nuclear-family compartment, taken as the spatial manifestation of a microhousehold inside the larger longhouse, is a unit worthy of study. At the very least, a compartment serves as an example of the activities characterizing part of the larger longhouse household.

Multiscalar Data

Community level data in this analysis are compiled from artifacts and features representing activities throughout the Parker Farm village. Community data was recovered from 50 by 50 cm shovel test pits spread over the Parker Farm site and systematic, timed surface collection in 10 m wide transects covering the entire western half of the plowed field. Each transect was collected in 5 by 5 m contiguous units and enabled the delineation of site boundaries of the Parker Farm village (See Figure 6.1). The microhousehold data in this analysis are composed of artifacts and features from a single longhouse compartment, assumed to be a nuclear family compartment. Microhousehold data were recovered through the contextual excavation of 1 by 1 m and 1 by 0.5 m units, as well as through feature excavation (Figure 6.2).

Community Data

In shovel test pits completed over Parker Farm, 18 post molds were uncovered. Posts were recognized from their circular shape and charcoal inclusions. Most post diameters ranged from 4 to 13 cm. The average diameter was 8.17 cm, which is similar in size to other Cayuga site post

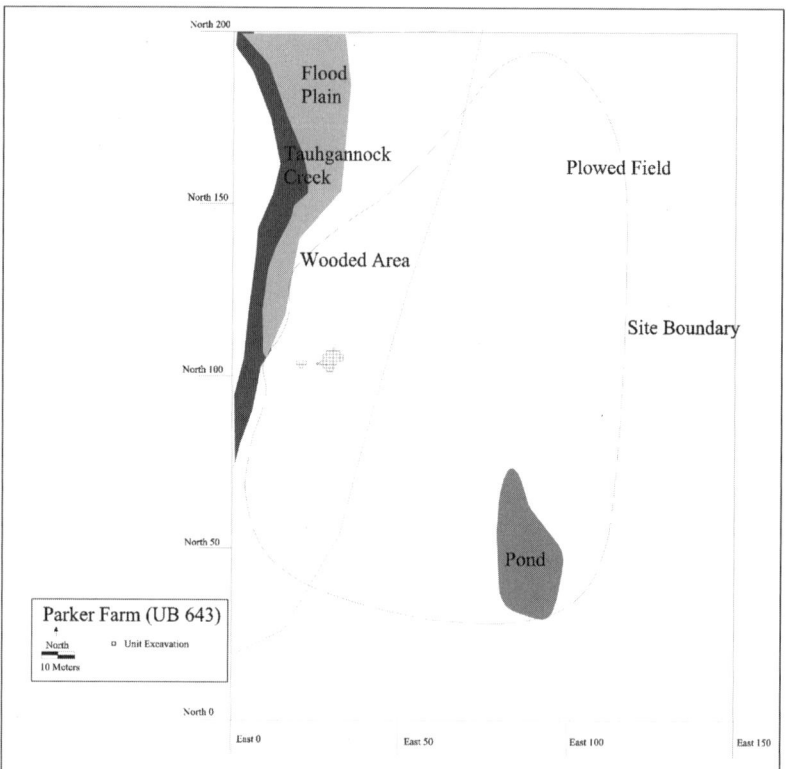

Fig. 6.2. Map of excavation units located in the western wooded portion of Parker Farm

molds (Williams-Shuker and Allen 1998). Posts are assumed to represent structures, such as longhouses, drying racks, sweat baths, or menstrual huts. The distribution of post molds at Parker Farm shows a concentration of structural elements in the western portion of the community. This part of the site is currently wooded. Three posts in the northern part of the wooded area were later discovered to be part of Longhouse 1 at Parker Farm.

Modern plowing of the eastern portion of the village most likely truncated many post molds and features, making them harder to identify. Although many posts and features in the western, wooded portion of the site extended below the level of Stratum A, no posts were recorded in shovel test pits completed in the plowed field. Shovel test pits, though, were spaced further apart in the field, so structures could have been missed in this area. The lack of posts in the plowed field should not be interpreted at this time to indicate that no structures were located in the eastern portion of the site.

Eight features were uncovered in the shovel test pits (Table 6.1). Many features were only partially exposed, and most were not bisected at initial exposure. Hearth, midden, and possible pit features were recognized. These types of features have been identified on other Cayuga Iroquoian sites (Allen, this volume; Baugher and Clark 1998; Williams-Shuker and Allen 1998). Hearths, representing cooking and heating activities, typically can be found in the central corridor of longhouses. Middens are found outside of structures and are composed of the remains of domestic activities that took place both inside and outside of the longhouse (Heidenreich 1978). Pits are used for storage and for waste disposal. Other features found indicate the presence of either a sheet midden or outdoor activity dealing with clay removal.

Household Data

At least one longhouse has been identified and partially excavated at Parker Farm. This longhouse is smaller in width (4.8 m) than most excavated Cayuga longhouses, which fall between 6.1 to 6.45 m (Williams-Shuker and Allen 1998) and could indicate that this longhouse played a different role than a typical residential longhouse. However, the nuclear family compartment (Compartment 1) investigated inside Longhouse 1 at Parker Farm is similar to other Cayuga longhouse compartments in bench width, central corridor layout, compartment partitioning, and internal features, such as hearths and storage pits (Williams-Shuker and Allen 1998). A sweat-bath feature found inside Longhouse 1 at Parker

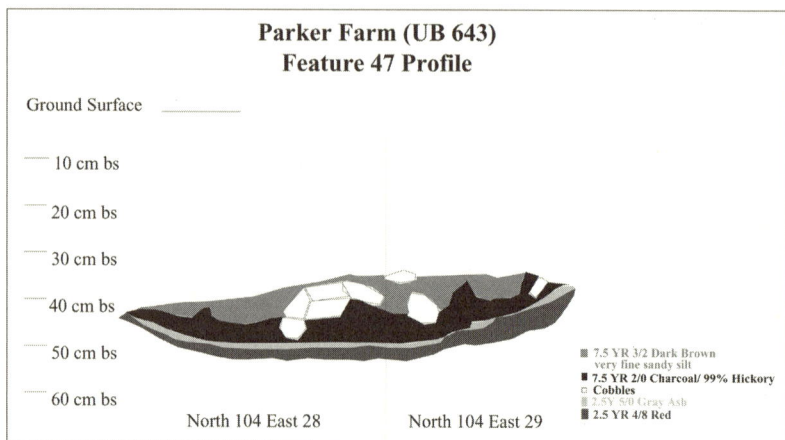

Fig. 6.3. Profile of the sweat bath, Feature 47, in Longhouse No. 1, Compartment No. 1 at Parker Farm

Farm is the first to be identified in any late prehistoric Cayuga longhouse (Figure 6.3; Michaud-Stutzman 2001).

Despite the small width of Longhouse 1, post-mold patterns in Compartment 1 are similar in shape and layout to other Cayuga longhouses. Excavation of the compartment uncovered 188 post molds. These post molds outline a back wall, bench, compartment partitions, and storage area. Five back wall posts, 12 bench posts, nine partition wall posts, four compartment storage-area posts, and 11 central corridor posts were bisected. The average depth of post molds in the compartment is 42 cm below the current ground surface. Posts typically extended over 20 cm below subsoil. The typical post-mold shape was conical with a tapered point at the bottom. Posts at Parker Farm are similar in size to longhouse post molds excavated at the Cayuga Carman site (Williams-Shuker and Allen 1998).

Within the exposed section of the longhouse, a total of 13 features were identified. Ten of these were bisected, screened through 1/8 inch wire mesh, and had floral analysis completed on them. Figure 6.4 is a map of features and post molds inside the household. Most of these features appear to be associated with typical longhouse domestic pursuits as noted ethnographically (Table 6.2). Of the ten bisected features, five are pit features, most likely associated with storage. Features 13 and 32 are cooking features. Feature 35 appears to be a food-processing area, and Feature 47 a sweat bath. Feature 39 is composed of a shallow layer of red soil, and it is not clear what it represents. With the exception of

Table 6.1. Descriptions of Features Uncovered in Shovel Test Pits over the Parker Farm Village Site

Feature Type	Feature Number	Length (cm)	Width (cm)	Depth (cm)	Description
Hearth	13	74	80	50	Fire-reddened soil, ash and charcoal; roughly circular.
Midden	11	50+	50	50+	Multiple dark soil layers.
Possible Storage Pits	2	19	23	unexca-vated	Dark and oblong in plan; characteristic of small storage pit features.
	3	14	11	unexca-vated	
	12	24	12	unexca-vated	
Other	16	50+	50+	unexca-vated	Close proximity to one another; consist of dark charcoal and ash. May be part of a large sheet midden given the concentration of artifacts. Possibly associated with clay removal, ceramic manufacture, or another outdoor activity since features are on top of clay subsoil and the area around them is the only place where clay is close to the surface.
	17	50+	50+	unexca-vated	
	18	27	13	unexca-vated	

the sweat bath, most features inside the household appear to deal with subsistence practices, particularly cooking, storage, and food processing. These types of features were identified at the nearby Carman site as well (Allen 2002, this volume) and are common at other Iroquoian sites (Finlayson 1985; Snow 1995c; Tuck 1971).

Multiscalar Analysis

Proportions of material remains recovered from the community and from the nuclear family longhouse compartment or microhousehold at Parker Farm are compared in bar graphs (Figure 6.5; Table 6.3). These graphs and tables indicate, with a degree of high confidence (95 percent C.L.),

Table 6.2. Descriptions of Features Uncovered in Compartment No. 1, Longhouse No. 1 at the Parker Farm Site

Feature Type	Feature Number	Length (cm)	Width (cm)	Depth (cm)	Description
Hearth	13	75	80	50	Oblong/circular shape with multiple compacted layers of ash, charcoal (includes maize), burned bone, and fire reddened soil. Wood charcoal from this feature was composed of maple, birch, beech, ash, and poplar (Asch-Sidell 2001).
	32	105	30	47	Long linear feature with alternating layers of ash, charcoal, and fire reddened soil. Feature is directly north of the hearth and appears to be a place where waste ash and charcoal from the hearth was brushed.
Food processing	35	98	99	75	Largest subsurface feature of Compartment No. 1. Shallow bowl shape, dark in color with charcoal chunks throughout. Faunal remains dominate, with a small amount of lithic debitage and ceramics. High amount of maize. Only ground stone artifact in the household was found next to feature.
Pits	55	27	25	62	Straight sides and curved bottoms. Artifacts recovered include lithic tools, ceramics, debitage, maize, and seeds. Unburned and burned bone comprise the largest material remain class. Nonutilitarian shell and bone artifacts recovered in F26, 40, 41.
	50	28	23	43	
	26	19	17	60	
	40	22	29	50	
	41	35	27	47	

Table 6.2. continued

Feature Type	Feature Number	Length (cm)	Width (cm)	Depth (cm)	Description
Sweat bath	47	98	98	39	Circular bowl-shaped feature. Distinct 4 cm layer of red ocherlike substance at bottom, a 0.5 cm noncontinuous layer of ash above it, a 6 cm charcoal layer, and a layer of cobbles on top. Surrounded by a circle of post molds forming a 2 m wide structure. Forty-six fire-cracked rocks—highest amount from any feature. Wood is 99 percent hickory; hickory not found within hearth (F13); some maize remains also recovered. (Asch Sidell 2001).
Other	39	52	192	38	Located under bench; shallow layer of red ocherlike soil on top of subsoil.
	52	9	25	unex	Dark colored soil. Unknown use.
	53	29	28	unex	Dark colored soil. Unknown use.
	58	34	70	unex	Dark colored soil. Unknown use.

Unex=unexcavated.

that there are significant differences between the community and microhousehold artifact assemblages. The economic activities (subsistence,
processing, manufacturing, cooking, storage) and sociopolitical activities
(ritual, external contact) represented by these two artifact assemblages
are discussed below.

Economic Activities

In viewing the general patterns at the site from both the community
and the microhousehold, the artifacts and features associated with economic pursuits at Parker Farm seem to be similar to general patterns
found at other Cayuga sites. The high percentage of cultivated maize
remains (as compared with other floral remains) found at the Parker
Farm site supports historical accounts that note the reliance of this group
on cultivated maize (Asch Sidell 2001a). The large quantity of faunal

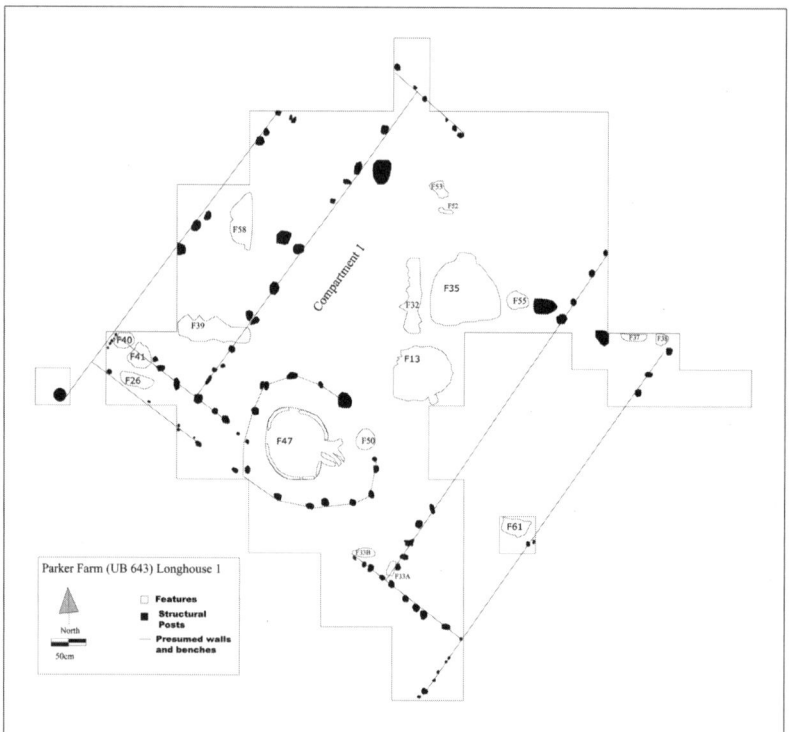

Fig. 6.4. Map of structural posts and features located in Longhouse No. 1, Compartment No. 1
at Parker Farm. Note: Only excavated units that had posts associated with Longhouse No. 1 are
shown

remains recovered (7,236 out of 13,905 total material remains) is also a pattern supported in ethnographic accounts (Fenton 1978) and found on other Cayuga sites (Allen 1994; Williams-Shuker, this volume). The archaeological record shows that hunting and consumption of animals were a large part of Cayuga Iroquois subsistence, and this tendency may distinguish the Cayuga from other Iroquoian groups.

The Cayuga were "known as great hunters" (Fenton 1978:298), and White et al. (1978) suggest that the Cayuga relied more on hunting than did other New York Iroquois groups because of the abundance of deer in the region. The dominance of deer found in the faunal assemblage at Parker Farm supports the suggestion that the Cayuga relied to a great extent on deer for their subsistence needs (Fenton 1978:298; White et al. 1978).

However, when analyzing the data collected from the community and microhousehold levels separately, more nuanced patterns emerge. For instance, faunal remains are represented in higher quantities in the microhousehold than in the community as a whole. Although burned bone comprises similar proportions at each level (29 percent in the community and 31 percent in the household), unburned bone in the microhousehold (28 percent) occurs at more than twice the proportion found throughout the community (12 percent). Likewise ceramics form a higher proportion of the artifact assemblage in the microhousehold (18 percent) as compared to the community (13 percent).

The longhouse compartment investigated at Parker Farm seems to be a place where food preparation, cooking, and consumption activities occurred as these are associated with high quantities of faunal and ceramic remains. These data complement ethnographic accounts indicating that much subsistence-related activity took place inside the longhouse structure (Brown 1970; Fenton 1978; Heidenreich 1971; Morgan 1962 [1851]; Tooker 1991).

Lithic tools viewed at different scales also provide insight into the economic pursuits of this group. At Parker Farm lithic tools are not as abundant in the microhousehold as compared to the rest of the community (Figure 6.6; Table 6.3). Projectile points or hunting tools make up the smallest percentage of all tool types inside the microhousehold (5 percent) and form a smaller percentage when compared to the community assemblage (12.2 percent; Table 6.4). Although the animals (indicated by unburned and burned bone) obtained from hunting activities are strongly associated with the microhousehold, hunting activities themselves (indicated by projectile points and hunting tools) are not. This is to

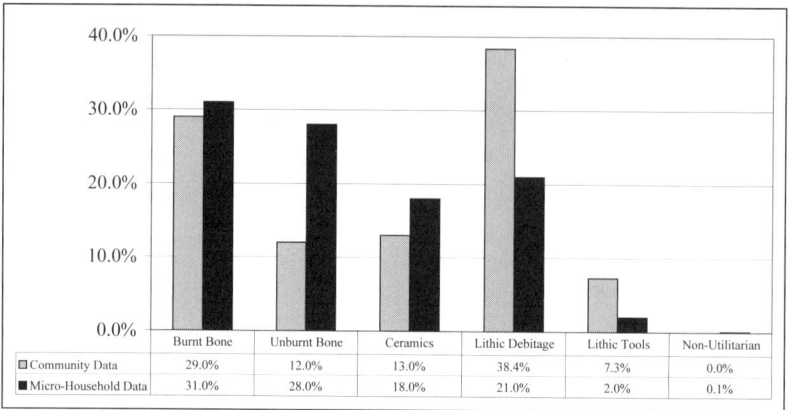

	Burnt Bone	Unburnt Bone	Ceramics	Lithic Debitage	Lithic Tools	Non-Utilitarian
☐ Community Data	29.0%	12.0%	13.0%	38.4%	7.3%	0.0%
■ Micro-Household Data	31.0%	28.0%	18.0%	21.0%	2.0%	0.1%

Fig. 6.5. Bar graphs comparing proportions of material remains from the microhousehold assemblage and from the community assemblage at the Parker Farm site

Table 6.3. Community and Microhousehold Artifact Assemblage Frequency, Proportion, and 95% Confidence Level

Type	Community Data Frequency	Proportion and 95% Confidence	Microhousehold Data Frequency	Proportion and 95% Confidence
Burned bone	1,608	29%±1.2%	2,617	31%±0.9%
Unburned bone	650	12%±0.8%	2,361	28%±0.9%
Ceramics	713	13% ±0.8%	1,558	18%±0.59%
Lithic debitage	2,102	38.4%±1.3%	1,746	21%±0.9%
Lithic tools	401	7.3% ±0.7%	141	2%±0.3%
Non-utilitarian	0	0	8	0.1%±0.05%
Total	5,474		8,431	

be expected since hunting activities are assumed to have taken place outside the household and village (Brown 1970; Fenton 1978; Heidenreich 1971; Morgan 1962 [1851]; Tooker 1991).

Additionally certain lithic tools at Parker Farm directly represent processing activities, such as the scraping and cutting of meat, hide, and plants. These activities are clearly important to the domestic life at Parker Farm as scraping and cutting tools are seen in abundance at both levels. The higher overall proportion of processing tools (scrapers and knives) throughout the community (37.2 percent), however, indicates that although processing activities were a major part of what defines domestic life, they were not as visible in the particular microhousehold investigated (25 percent), perhaps because these activities occurred in another part of the longhouse, in another longhouse altogether, or outside.

Other manufacturing tools are also seen in differing quantities in each data set at Parker Farm. While lithic tools such as drills, gravers, and spoke shavers (used to create wood, bone, and antler utensils, as well as other items) are found in a higher proportion within the micro-household (13 percent as compared to 4.7 percent in the community), lithic tool manufacturing, represented by debitage, is more predominant at the community level (38.4 percent as compared to 21 percent in the microhousehold).

Expedient tools, or informal tools, by far dominate both the community and household lithic assemblages (46 percent and 57 percent, respectively). Expedient tools are used for a variety of pursuits, including processing and manufacturing activities. Parry and Kelly (1987) argue that a high amount of expedient tools in an assemblage indicates increased sedentism. Historical documents and settlement research in Iroquoia point to the sedentary nature of the late prehistoric Iroquois who lived in year-round villages (Niemczycki 1984; Tuck 1971).

Expedient tools also occur in places where there is a relative abundance of raw material (Andrefsky 1994). Onondaga chert is a local raw material used for lithic tools at Parker Farm and in Iroquoia. This material is easily found in abundance in small glacial cobbles throughout the region, and it perhaps accounts for the high amount of expedient tools in both assemblages. Expedient tools have been linked to female labor (Sassaman 1992a), and in fact there is a higher proportion of expedient tools in the Parker Farm microhousehold. This supports ethnographic accounts that more female activities took place inside longhouses as compared to male activities.

Sociopolitical Activities

Although there are abundant ethnographic descriptions of the ritual activities of the Iroquois, the only archaeological evidence linked to ritual activity at Parker Farm is found inside the longhouse. All the nonutilitarian items recovered at Parker Farm, including shell and bone beads, a drilled shell pendant, and a drilled and polished bear tooth,

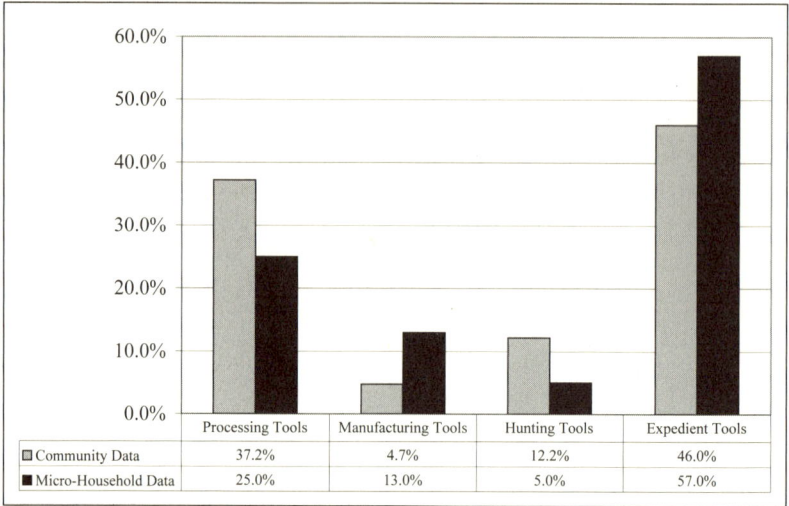

Fig. 6.6. Bar graphs comparing proportions of lithic tool types from the microhousehold assemblage and from the community assemblage at the Parker Farm site

came from storage pits near a sweat-bath feature inside the longhouse compartment, the first to be identified in any late prehistoric Cayuga longhouse. Although nonutilitarian remains recovered at Parker Farm were found in small quantities, this does not mean that ritual practices were not an important part of Iroquois sociopolitical activities. On the contrary the sweat bath feature located on the edge of Compartment 1 and the central corridor inside Longhouse 1 at Parker Farm indicates important ritual practices took place inside the longhouse. Historically, Native American sweat bathing has been used for ritual purposes.

The sweat-bath feature at Parker Farm is distinct in shape and content from other interior features (Michaud-Stutzman 2001). This feature is relatively shallow and holds 46 igneous stones. The wood charcoal from this feature is 99 percent hickory (Asch Sidell 2001a). In the hearth feature the wood charcoal is much more varied (Asch Sidell 2001a). The sweat bath was surrounded by a 2 m diameter circle of post molds, presumably enclosing it.

Shaman have used sweat bathing as a means to contact the spirit world. Researchers argue that Iroquoian sweat bathing also played an important social role in integrating people into the household, especially unrelated men living inside the matrilineal longhouse (MacDonald 1988; Tyyska 1972; Warrick 2001). The presence of a sweat-bath feature inside the Parker Farm compartment indicates that ritual practices were a

Table 6.4. Community and Microhousehold Lithic Tool Assemblage
Frequency, Proportion, and 95% Confidence Level

Type	Community Data		Microhousehold Data	
	Frequency	Proportion and 95% Confidence	Frequency	Proportion and 95% Confidence
Processing tools (scrapers, knives, groundstone*)	149	37.2%±4.7%	35	25%±7.2%
Manufacturing tools (gravers, drills, spokeshavers)	19	4.7%±2.1%	19	13%±5.6%
Hunting tools (projectile points)	49	12.2%±3.2%	7	5%±3.6%
Expedient tools	184	46%±4.8%	80	57%±8.2%
Total	401		141	

*No groundstone was recovered from outside the microhousehold.

distinct part of sociopolitical activities making up domestic life at the microhousehold level.

External interaction is another activity influencing domestic life. It is visible at Parker Farm in both the microhousehold and community data sets through the presence of nonlocal ceramic styles and raw materials. Most nonlocal ceramic styles at Parker Farm can be associated with neighboring tribes. The introduction of these nonlocal pottery styles could come from a variety of contact mechanisms, including trading, feasting, warfare, or marriage practices (Allen 1988; Engelbrecht 1972; Knapp 2002b, this volume). The dominance of local styles and raw materials at Parker Farm, however, is typical of other Cayuga sites and indicates that although the Cayuga had contact with other groups, they still appear to have had a strong local domestic focus (Allen 1998; Baugher and Clark 1998).

Factors of Scale

Differences in the types of artifacts and the intensity of domestic activities within the broad community and within the microhousehold are apparent at Parker Farm, demonstrating the utility of viewing data at different local scales. Various factors influence why certain activities might be strongly associated with and/or visible at the microhousehold or community level. The factors listed below are not assumed to be mutually exclusive. More than one factor likely influenced past domestic activities and their present visibility in the archaeological record.

Microhousehold Variability

The first factor with potential to create a difference between the microhousehold and the community artifact assemblages at Parker Farm is microhousehold variability as represented by individual compartments inside the longhouse. The microhousehold data represent activities in a single longhouse compartment, and the community level represents data from numerous compartments and longhouses throughout the village. Recent research into ceramic production indicates that different types or amounts of activities might have taken place within each compartment of a longhouse (Allen 1992; Martelle 1999).

Compartment partitions along the edge of the excavated Parker Farm compartment are similar to those seen in other New York Iroquois longhouses (Snow 1997). These divisions suggest some autonomy of nuclear-family compartments. Most of the subsistence-related activities (hearth, food-processing features, and storage features) in the Parker Farm household are located in the central corridor, which is the more public realm within the house. However, small storage pits were also found under the bench and along the back wall of the compartment, indicating private storage, and hence some autonomy, by nuclear families. Therefore the differences in the microhousehold and the community material remains at Parker Farm could represent different social and economic pursuits taking place within different longhouses.

Waste Disposal

Waste-disposal practices can also have an effect on the visibility of certain activities inside the longhouse (Maholy-Nagy 1990). Sedentary groups such as the Iroquois are less likely to leave debris in primary context or in an area of high traffic (Hayden and Cannon 1983). Cleaning practices include the sweeping of debris out of the way. A high concentration of artifacts was found under the bench area in Compartment 1 at Parker Farm and could be partially a result of these waste-disposal practices.

However, remains such as debitage, which are sharp and abundant, were probably removed from inside Iroquois longhouses altogether. Comparing the data sets, lithic debitage composes a smaller amount of the material remains in the microhousehold than in the community. Outdoor midden features at Parker Farm have a higher percentage of lithics than features inside the household. This pattern could be accounted for by waste disposal practices.

Seasonality

Differences in artifact proportions between the microhousehold and the broader community are influenced by seasonal pursuits that would be completed inside or outside the longhouse depending on the time of year. Community data from Parker Farm include remains of activities completed both inside and outside of longhouses, whereas the microhousehold data only reveal the remains of activities taking place inside. Summer and fall pursuits might be an important part of domestic life but are less represented inside a household and seen better at the community scale of analysis since many of the activities during this time of year took place outside (Allen 2002; Heidenreich 1978).

It has been noted ethnographically that initial maize processing was done outside the longhouse in the summer and fall (Parker 1968c [1916]). However, floral data obtained at other Iroquois sites indicate that initial processing of maize took place within the structure (Asch Sidell 2001a). Floral analysis of Parker Farm features within Compartment 1 appears to corroborate some ethnographic accounts of initial processing of maize taking place outside (Asch Sidell 2001a), although it is possible that it took place in another part of the structure. In addition winter and spring activities, such as the manufacturing of clothes and other items (Heidenreich 1978), are noted ethnographically to be completed inside the longhouse. The percentage of manufacturing tools in the household at Parker Farm supports these accounts as they comprised a higher proportion than at the community level.

Division of Labor

The division of labor can leave distinct patterns of material remains within a household as compared to the broader community if males and females complete their tasks in different parts of the village or longhouse. In ethnographic accounts Iroquois females are more frequently associated with the longhouse than males (Heidenreich 1978; Morgan 1962 [1851]; Snow 1994b). In addition hunting and diplomacy practices, typically associated with male labor, take place away from the village. Therefore it is reasonable to assume that more remains associated with female activities would be found inside a longhouse.

In the research completed at Parker Farm, although burned and un-burned bone are found in large quantities and strongly associated with the microhousehold, the hunting tools used to obtain these animals are not. A higher proportion of projectile points is found at the community level and could be the result of males not spending as much time in the longhouse compartment. It could also indicate that the initial removal of projectile points from hunted animals took place outside the household. Historic accounts note that Iroquois women would accompany males on hunts to do initial processing of animals before bringing them back to the household for further processing and cooking (Fenton 1978).

Higher quantities of ceramics and expedient tools in the microhouse-hold data set as compared to the community might also be attributed to the division of labor. Expedient tools are typically associated with female pursuits (Sassaman 1992a), and most ethnographic accounts link ceramic making and use to females (Brown 1970; Fenton 1978; Tooker 1984).

Data-Recovery Techniques

Data-recovery techniques may have influenced the visibility of domestic pursuits at each level investigated in this research. Data recovered from shovel test pits and surface collection throughout the Parker Farm village produced a good view of the range of domestic activities occurring over the whole community, while contextual excavation of a microhousehold compartment inside a longhouse provided a more meaningful context for the analysis of specific activities represented by features and material remains. For example, knowing the placement of the sweat-bath feature inside the longhouse and its association with other features and nonutilitarian material remains enabled the uncovering of specific information on the sociopolitical aspects of the Cayuga by showing the integration of ritual and economic activities within the microhousehold. Also the lack of maize cupules and glumes from features located inside the longhouse compartment indicated that initial processing of maize took place outside of this compartment. In other Iroquoian longhouses the remains of initial maize processing have appeared within the structure (Asch Sidell 2001a). These microviews of domestic life would have been missed if data were collected and analyzed only within the broader community context.

Conclusion

Current archaeological research at Parker Farm (Michaud-Stutzman 2001, 2002; Michaud-Stutzman and Allen 1998) has generated new information about the late prehistoric western Cayuga. By analyzing and comparing the data from various local scales at Parker Farm, a more accurate view of the culture and activities associated with domestic life is created. The community and the microhousehold level provide different types of information because of factors such as household variability, waste disposal, seasonality, division of labor, and data-recovery techniques.

Domestic life at Parker Farm is seen in a generalized way through the community data set. Seasonal outdoor pursuits, activities typically assigned to the male division of labor, and those that would be subject to waste removal practices are better represented at this level. The microhousehold investigated at Parker Farm provides a more contextual analysis of domestic life. The Parker Farm data show the microhousehold as a place where female domestic activities such as food preparation, cooking, and consumption dominated. Activities that took place in the winter have a higher representation in this data set than warm weather activities. The microhousehold is where ritual activities (as indicated by a sweat-bath feature predominated by hickory and nonutilitarian items such as a shell pendant and drilled bear tooth) are best interpreted. The location and contextual analysis of the sweat bath (the first to be identified in a late Cayuga Iroquois longhouse) indicates an integration of subsistence and ritual activities inside the longhouse.

In addition to the sweat bath, the microhousehold data reveal other unique variables, including a lack of initial maize processing and a smaller overall longhouse structure. Household variability and other factors that might be responsible for these patterns have thus been identified and warrant further investigation. In conclusion analysis of data recovered at different local scales creates a more in-depth view of domestic life than any single-level analysis alone would have done, and it forms a stronger addition to ethnographic accounts and to research done on other Cayuga sites. Approaching research this way can better inform issues of variability and change through time.

Notes

1. Charred material ($\delta^{13}C$ = -24.1 o/oo).
2. Charred material ($\delta^{13}C$ = -8.7 o/oo).

7

Temporal and Spatial Scales of Activity among the Iroquois
Implications for Understanding Cultural Change

Kathleen M. Sydoriak Allen

The interpenetration of space and time in the archaeological record is well worth exploring.[1] Understanding the dimensions of space and time is a key issue that archaeologists deal with constantly in the course of doing archaeological fieldwork, in interpreting results, and in working on particular research problems. In examining the relationship between these two dimensions, one finds many scales at which they can be addressed.

Identifying temporality has been a cornerstone of archaeological research. The early great methodological advances in archaeology were chronological, including stratigraphy as developed by Kidder and Nelson, seriation as practiced by Kroeber and Ford in the early 1900s, and radiocarbon dating developed by Libby in the mid-1900s (Trigger 1989). Emphasis in most dating techniques has been on time writ large, the macrotemporal scale. Witness the great attention to the development of chronologies common in North America in the mid–twentieth century. In the absence of more-precise dating techniques, less attention has been centered on smaller-scale time units. In fact the argument has often been made that we cannot deal securely or reliably with small-scale units of time, the microscale of time. Our understanding of time, especially at this smaller scale, is often implicit rather than explicit.

In contrast much more effort has been devoted to dealing with space at a variety of scales. In some ways dealing with space seems easier than dealing with time, as space is in some sense external and more readily understood. A large body of analysis and associated vocabulary has grown up around the identification of spatial units. In the spatial dimension, a number of scales have been identified and analyzed. The site is one such basic unit and is characterized in various ways, including by type, size, location, features, artifact content, etc. It is then compared with other sites. It is often further broken down into smaller units based on architecture and activity area in a variety of forms of intrasite analysis. The region is another primary unit of analysis. Sometimes the region is defined on the basis of natural features, such as watersheds or topographic areas; other times the region may be defined somewhat arbitrarily on the basis of size. Techniques for spatial analysis at the regional level have become increasingly common and complex using various statistical techniques and the power of GIS studies, such as predictive site models and viewshed analyses among others (Allen et al. 1990; Maschner 1996; Westcott and Brandon 2000). GIS is also a powerful tool for moving between these spatial scales.

Although issues of temporality are an integral part of archaeological methodology, they have been less well integrated into current research. One problem may be the relative lack of detailed chronological information that allows for attributing site occupation to a narrow time span. Although we can readily document where remains are located and analyze space (given sufficient attention to depositional and formation processes), we have fewer clear indications of where the activities that have gone on can be placed specifically in time. There is always a gap between the remains we observe in their specific locations and their temporality.

This problem has been addressed more recently by a number of archaeological researchers who stressed the importance of examining smaller temporal units as well as large ones (Bailey 1987; Shennan 1993). The *Archaeological Review from Cambridge* (vol. 6, no. 1) devoted an entire issue to time in 1987. Some of this stems from the work of individuals in other disciplines, such as Braudel's (1980, 1981) on time scales, Bourdieu's (1977) on daily practice, and Giddens's (1979) on agency, structure, and change. These approaches opened a window to multiple scales of analysis that can be pursued and are constitutive of social life.

An explicit awareness of the spatial and temporal scales we are examining is important. At the smaller scale, our attention to the contribution of short-term activities that produce archaeological data is essential for more accurate interpretations of archaeological remains. Understanding of specific and diverse strategies occurring at small scales illuminates the contribution of these actions to larger-scale processes. Large-scale change occurs through the actions of many individuals and groups over the long term, and attention paid to the temporality of activities by participants sharpens our focus.

Time

How has time been addressed archaeologically? The emphasis has most often been on what has taken place over the long term. This has been acknowledged as one of the great strengths of archaeology, the ability to examine long-term cycles and trajectories of development and change. This is time at the macroscale. Macroscale research focuses on long-term change, the longue durée, as discussed by Braudel (1980, 1981). In archaeological terms it has often been thought that this is the scale at which we can most readily analyze material remnants of past behavior, because of the relatively poor temporal resolution of our data. Archaeological remains are the result of long-term processes. The archaeological record is a palimpsest of all the activities that have occurred over time at a particular site location or in a region as seen through the filter of the archaeological methods of data recovery, the kinds of waste disposal practices practiced by the group, and postdepositional processes. Each archaeological site may contain the remains of many activities that have occurred over long periods of time and may be examined as a single unit of analysis.

On the other hand, the microscale is also evident in the archaeological record. In many ways this is the scale we come face-to-face with when we excavate a site, whether we are recovering structures, other features, or material remains. The structure that has been built, expanded, repaired, and abandoned reflects the day-to-day activities that are at the core of the microscale. The same applies to the excavation of a pit that may be used for storage over a period of time on a regular basis before its final use as a receptacle for the discarded contents of a cooking pot (Gamble 2001) or other trash from processing and manufacturing activities. The microscale includes especially the activities that occur on a regular basis (daily, periodic) whose remains are most represented in the record. Again this is seen through the filter of waste disposal practices as much of the daily waste produced will be disposed of in other locales.

Bourdieu's (1977) practice theory stems from a concern with daily activities and the way they produce the everyday world. In a recursive relationship, the *habitus* (these structured practices) produce history, which in turn structures practice. In other words, "social life is inherently recursive" (Giddens 1979:217). Examinations of repetitive daily activities and of the ways people perform them and organize their space are fruitful areas of research for understanding how people structure and make sense of their lives (Lightfoot et al. 1998). In fact it has been argued that the archaeological record is ideally suited to the analysis of daily practice (Lightfoot 2001; Lightfoot et al. 1998; Shennan 1993). Shennan (1993:55) describes the archaeological record as being "the residue of practices" that can occur at two levels: those associated with important events, and those resulting from routine activities at the microscale. Rather than focusing on the extremes, we must be cognizant of the continuum between them as well, for this is how cultural traditions and behavior are constructed.

A number of levels within the microscale of time, as a continuum, can be identified, as both activities that occur on a regular daily basis as well as those that occur more irregularly but on a periodic basis are considered. Daily activities include, among others, food preparation, eating, childcare, sleeping, and other maintenance tasks. For other tasks the specific components may change on a seasonal basis, but participation in a category of activity is continual. For example, subsistence activities (i.e., acquiring and processing food) must be carried out on a daily basis, but the specific component tasks will vary from season to season. Some of the features present on a site result from activities that occurred on a short time frame; others from activities occurring at several time scales, including those occurring daily, seasonally, or even more intermittently. The accumulation of material culture associated with these activities creates the archaeological record that we use to examine long-term cycles or trajectories of development. Incorporating an understanding of both the shorter- and longer-term activities that are responsible for all of the material remains present on a site will allow us to more carefully track social components and the ways in which change develops from the micro- to the macroscale.

Practice theory and the microscale of daily activities have been addressed in the literature on gender, as gendered divisions of labor can be usefully studied at this level (Dobres 1995; Picazo 1997). The temporality inherent in these daily activities is different than that involved in annual subsistence activities or in longer-term cycles as day-to-day activities operate in a shorter time frame than those in other domains of social life (Picazo 1997). Maintenance activities, those numerous tasks that are associated with the reproduction of the family and household, are most often performed by women and include the daily activities of cooking, eating, and childcare, among others (Picazo 1997). Recognition of the temporal frequency of activities may be a better way of identifying their differential contribution to one's cultural experiences and practices than focusing on activities based on their products. Examining these products of activity without considering the frequency of occurrence of the activities responsible for them provides only a coarse measure of their differential contribution to social life. Attention must be paid to developing potentially feasible temporal frameworks for prehistoric groups using different criteria depending on the arena of activity discussed. Attention to the "multiple readings of temporal meanings" (Picazo 1997:64) allows for a more comprehensive understanding of the impact of microscale activities on the development of macroscale temporal patterns of change.

Integrating these levels is not an easy task. There are a number of confounding factors including the length of time sites are occupied and the time depth of the research focus. Often research focused on times closer to the present are more likely to use a notion of time that Bailey (1981, 1987) refers to as "time perspectivism." Time perspectivism stems from a belief that various aspects of behavior are "brought into focus" by different scales of time that employ different kinds of explanatory principles (Bailey 1981:103). Processes occurring at one time scale are not necessarily visible at others. He stresses that most of the archaeological record indicates average tendencies of behavior over long periods of time. However, he suggests these time scales need to be analyzed in their own right to see the ways they intermesh and identify which scales are most suited to different kinds of studies (Bailey 1981,1987). Though his work emphasizes long-term trends that originate in Paleolithic times, the attention to time scales he calls for is also needed in shorter-term events that combine to produce long-term cycles. Attention to scale in space as well as time is also required.

Time and Space

Time and space are intimately related to each other. In some ways activities that occur over time create place and landscape (Gamble 2001). When we examine regional patterns of settlement, there is an element of time embodied in that concept. Each settlement was occupied for a particular length of time; some of these overlap with other settlements. The distributional patterns of sites stem from human activities that occur over time. Each site also has a temporal component to it. A special purpose site may be the location of a short-term occupation that takes place repeatedly over long periods of time. A village site represents longer-term occupation at a particular location. Each structure has a temporal aspect as well. Over time houses are built and may be repaired, extended, and eventually abandoned. Structures may be enlarged or added on to, space rearranged, and pits (features) dug, used for storage, and later filled in. Areas between structures may be used for other purposes, including food processing (butchering, preliminary processing of maize), producing stone tools, making pottery, preparing deer hides (scraping and drying) for use in clothing, and cooking (roasting large game, etc.). Each of the areas we identify has specific kinds of temporality associated with it. In addition each of the objects that form a part of activities has temporality. For example, the pot whose contents are being dumped (an act of short duration, although it may occur a number of times) has a longer time span associated with its use life, one that may extend over a number of years. The pit into which the contents are dumped may have been dug for some other purpose and later abandoned. The tools used for butchering activities at one particular moment may have a long use life as they are maintained or curated and used both for that purpose and for other purposes. One of the aims in archaeological excavation is to identify both activities, as well as the temporalities associated with them.

In addition much economic activity that takes place at different temporal and spatial scales is gendered. Though each specific case must be examined to ensure that we are not assuming stereotypical gendered tasks, some patterns occur frequently. Women are often associated with the household (the local level) and the activities most associated with it including daily tasks, although they may also participate in the public arena (Nelson 1997). Archaeologically we can see daily practice expressed through the organization of space, how everyday domestic tasks were done, how garbage was disposed of, and the routine actions that often dominated, and often still do, life (Lightfoot et al. 1998:201). It is these activities that are usually best represented in the archaeological record, and Iroquois women had a major role in the performance of these tasks. Men were often associated with activities that take place away from the household, although they may also have engaged in daily household as well as seasonal and longer-term labor. Examining activities on the microscale at the local level provides information on the interplay between subsistence needs and coordination of men's and women's work.

Just as with space, smaller units are embedded within larger ones, so also for time. The temporal microscale is embedded and enclosed within the macroscale. Daily practice both constitutes and reflects the broader organizational principles of society and can be examined for insight into macroscale issues of organization as well as change over longer periods of time. Changes in daily practice can be used to identify local factors for change. These can be examined at a number of scales to discern the effect of local and daily microscale processes on long-term change in a region. The embeddedness of the microscale within the macroscale occurs for both space and time, and analysis at several scales has the potential for providing a broader understanding of change. Variability within and between households and structures on a site can be problematized and examined with both scales in sight.

Application to the Iroquois

The Iroquoians of eastern North America have been intensively studied, both ethnographically and archaeologically, providing information about some aspects of these temporal and spatial scale differences, as investigations have been done at many scales (Ellis and Ferris 1990; Engelbrecht 1994; Fenton 1978, 1998; Morgan 1962 [1851]; Prezzano and Steponaitis 1990; Ritchie 1954,1980; Ritchie and Funk 1973; Sempowski and Saunders 2001; Snow 1995b; Wray et al. 1987, 1991; Wright 1974; and many others). This section will consider some of this research at both macro- and microscale levels in the context of Iroquois activities as well as examine the insights gained from a microscale analysis.

By considering some Iroquoian notions of time as reported ethnographically, we see the temporal dimension from a more emic perspective. For the Iroquois a number of time scales can be identified that hold some importance. Four cycles have been noted and are primarily tied to ecology (Fenton 1978). These include the daily (diurnal) round, the yearly (seasonal) round, the two-decade village-movement cycle, and the lifetime of activities of an individual. The yearly cycle is the one most emphasized and is exemplified by the names of months (Snow 1994b) and ceremonies that were practiced (Fenton 1978; Wallace 1969) as shown in Figure 7.1. Nine of the 12 months refer to seasonal subsistence activities; the other three are identified by reference to the weather and the annual midwinter thanksgiving festival. The breakdown of the primary activities engaged in during the year by gender is shown in Figure 7.2 (following Spector 1983). This figure does not reflect the complexity of gendered seasonal activities, but provides an overview. Women were active in subsistence tasks associated with horticulture and the gathering of wild plant foods; men were involved with hunting and external contact such as trade, councils, and war. Winter was a time for manufacture and maintenance of material culture and for storytelling.

The spatial component of these seasonal activities is identified by considering where they take place (Figure 7.3). The places noted correspond to divisions that the Iroquois considered important and that appear in some of their major traditions (Engelbrecht 2003; Fenton 1998; Foster 1985; Hamell 1987). These include the clearing (which encompasses the village and possibly horticultural field areas, depending on their proximity to the village), the wood's edge, and the forest. Sea-

MONTH	NEW MOON NAME AND CEREMONIES
February	Midwinter
March	Sugar, Thanks to Maple
April	Fishing
May	Planting
June	Strawberry
July	Blueberry
August	Green Corn
September	Freshness
October	Harvest
November	Hunting
December	Cold
January	Very Cold

Fig. 7.1. Month, moon names, and ceremonies (Fenton 1978; Snow 1994:108; Wallace 1969)

sonal activities for women took place mostly in the village and the field with some movement further afield for gathering wild resources. Note that while both men and women engaged in activities in a number of different areas relative to the village, women were more likely to be close to the village than men. An additional category for "beyond" is added for men's activities as they may have occurred some distance away.

Finally, at the daily and periodic temporal scales, other kinds of activities that are part of the diurnal cycle and not tied to any particular season are identified (Figure 7.4). In the Iroquois world, daily practice that occurred within the village was dominated by the work of women. These daily activities revolved around food preparation, childcare, and movements in and out of the village in search of needed subsistence and technological resources. The frequency of movement varied by season although men were always more likely to leave, travel further, and spend more than one day away. Women's activities were intensive in and around the village. Daily activities that involve food preparation and childcare were more likely to take place in the village, although whether they occurred inside or outside of the longhouse may have depended in part on the season (Kapches 1979) and the specific weather on that day, and not solely on a narrow requirement that the activity take place inside or outside the longhouse.

Cycles of time identified as most critical to the Iroquois include longer-term (two-decade village movement) time spans, as well as seasonal and diurnal rounds. When we move to archaeological research and macroscale analysis, the kinds of problems that frequently are investigated include the origins of tribal organization, the origin of the Confederacy, and tracking ethnic identity through both ceramic analysis and settlement pattern studies tracing village (population) movements over time and space (Bamann et al. 1992). Studies at this macroscale level often focus on particular categories of material culture or on sites as units. For example, the tracing of village movements over time and space has focused on tracking populations through comparisons of longhouse structures and other items of material culture, most often pottery (as in Tuck 1971). European goods have been useful for identifying village sequences, as the temporality can be more tightly controlled (Wray and Schoff 1953, Wray et al. 1991).

When analyzing material at this scale, the village is considered as a single unit, although a number of studies have looked at smaller scales by examining houses within the village (see Tuck 1971 and others). As Iroquois villages are believed to have been occupied for about 15 to

20 years, at least as we approach European contact, the archaeological record at a site is the accumulation of the remains of activities that took place over this time span. When making comparisons at the macroscale, information from the site is compiled, and the village is characterized on the basis of the sum total of material recovered. The sites are characterized by tables summarizing the total percentage of ceramics types, lithic tools and debitage, and bone counts, along with the number of structures. This may suit the purpose of a broader regional investigation but results in the loss of variability. Drawing comparisons between tribal

MONTH	WOMEN'S ACTIVITIES	MEN'S ACTIVITIES
February	Midwinter Ceremony	
March	gather firewood	deer hunting
		fishing
April	maple sap ----------------	
May	burning over fields ------	clear fields
	collecting greens	
		war/trade/defense
	planting	
June	fields -	(summer fish, odd jobs,
	strawberries	some fieldwork,
	hoeing	bark work)
July	tending	
	blueberries	
August		
	gathering berries, indian hemp	
September	harvesting	
	drying	return from war and trade
	nut gathering	
October	storing	
		some fishing, hunting
		mass hunts
November		
		councils, war
	All in village	
December	weaving mats	manufacture fishnets
	maintenance tasks	
	feasting, stories	
January		some ice fishing and trading

Based on: Waugh 1916, Heidenreich 1971, Parker 1968, Fenton 1978, Herrick 1995, and Engelbrecht 2003.

Fig. 7.2. Primary seasonal activities by gender

areas is primarily done at the macroscale, which is the 20-year village movement cycle and longer term cycles of the group and its evolution. These studies have been crucial in providing the broad chronological and spatial frameworks within which Iroquoian cultures developed.

Smaller scales in both time and space have also been investigated. The temporal microscale can be approached through focusing on the village occupation as a period of time with a duration of 15 to 20 years. It is at the microscale that the most detailed and substantial archaeological

SPATIAL COMPONENT OF MEN'S ACTIVITIES				
SEASON	VILLAGE	FIELD	EDGE	FOREST
Spring			gather firewood	
				maple sap
		burning	collecting greens	
		planting	collecting berries	
Summer				
		hoeing	collecting berries	
	drying berries			
		tending		
			gathering berries, indian hemp	
Fall		harvesting		
	drying crops		nut gathering	
	storing			
				hunting
	councils			councils
Winter	manufacturing: weaving mats tool maintenance feasting and socializing			

SPATIAL COMPONENT OF MEN'S ACTIVITIES				
SEASON	VILLAGE	FIELD	FOREST	BEYOND
Spring			fishing	
			maple sap	
		clearing		
				war and trade
Summer	defense bark work - houses, utensils		peel bark some fishing	
Fall	return from war and trade			
			fishing mass hunts	
	councils			councils war
Winter	most residents here manufacturing feasting and socializing		some ice fishing some trade	

Fig. 7.3. Spatial components of women's and men's activities

DAILY ACTIVITIES	PERIODIC ACTIVITIES
VILLAGE	MOSTLY VILLAGE AREA
rise with sun	manufacturing:
	pottery wood bowls
keep fire going	mats beads
	baskets ornamentation
cooking	hide processing
	bone awls
eating	stone tools
	bark containers
childcare	
	village maintenance:
cleaning utensils	replacing wall posts
	replacing bark walls
carrying water	building new structures
	strengthen palisade
chopping wood	
	process food for storage:
garbage disposal	dry berries, crops
	clean fish
sleeping	butcher animals

Fig. 7.4. Diurnal cycle of activities done primarily by women

information exists. In actuality that 20-year occupation is made up of a variety of different kinds of activities that take place over differing lengths of time. It is this level that is highly visible at the archaeological site. A segment of the site's temporality is investigated when the long-house structure is examined in terms of its architectural components and the evidence for repair (common in those houses occupied for longer periods of time). Studies of the complexity of village organization and longhouse construction, additions, and repairs have been conducted at a number of sites, including the Fonger (Warrick 1984), Draper (Finlayson 1985), Ball (Knight 1987, 1989), and Benson (Fogt and Ramsden 1996) sites among others (see also Dodd 1984). Kapches (1979, 1990, 1993) has dealt with the complexity associated with the longhouse structure as well as how we can track changes in structure and organization over time and interpret them in social terms. Paleo-ethnobotanical studies have also made comparisons between and within villages (Monckton 1992). Most of these studies deal with several temporal scales ranging from the two-decade village movement to annual cycles.

It is the microscale as well that is represented in many of the other features found at a site, although they are associated with a temporality that corresponds more closely to the seasonal or daily cycle. Hearths were used on a daily basis, while pits may have been used seasonally for food storage, and eventually their use terminated, as they were filled with refuse (Moeller 1992). Hearths and pits may have been cleared out and reused a number of times, such that identifying each separate occasion of its use may not be possible. However, we can often identify that a feature was continually reused and can document the last several uses of the feature. Pits that were used for storage may not have any evidence for that use but were often filled with refuse after the fact, as they deteriorated and became more liable to pest infestations (Dickens 1985). Features may thus result from continual use and reuse as well as from single use. The material remains that they contain may result from a number of uses or from the last use of the feature (Moeller 1992).

In addition to considering the different temporalities that are associated with the village and longhouse, the spatial microscale is also important because this is where we can observe most clearly the operation of the smallest time scales. Within the longhouse the smallest spatial scale that is socially meaningful is the compartment. If the household is defined as the economic, productive, reproductive, and cultural unit (Wilk and Rathje 1982), where habits, practices, identity, and ethnicity in some sense were maintained and passed on, then the compartment is the unit at the smallest spatial level that may function in one or several of those ways. The compartment is centered around the hearth. This is the central symbol of the longhouse, associated with all of the daily kinds of maintenance activities done by women. The hearth was the center of the activities that go on at the smallest temporal and spatial levels. It was where the day began and ended. The daily acts of practice and sustenance were centered around the hearth; it is associated with maintenance activities "including food preparation, distribution and consumption, refuse deposition, and food storage" (Picazo 1997:60). Women were the primary agents in these maintenance and nurturing activities. The hearth is enclosed within the longhouse, which consists of a series of central hearths flanked by compartments on either side. The organization of space at this level and the daily kinds of refuse activities that take place within and outside the longhouse can be examined and compared with other households and structures for an understanding of the overall organizing principles of Iroquois society as exemplified at this community level. Once the microscale is better understood, comparisons can be made between several different communities and the impetus for change associated with contact or other factors will be better understood.

Specific Example from the Cayuga Iroquois

In the group of villages located on the west side of Lake Cayuga in central New York State, there are four village sites that have been studied, although several more are known from the area (Figure 7.5). These four village sites include Klinko, Indian Fort Road, Parker Farm, and Carman and were identified as a village sequence by Marian E. White (n.d.) in the early 1970s. According to the classic Iroquoian model, these villages are believed to represent successive occupations of a population moving from north to south in this region (Niemczycki 1984).

These four villages are generally recognized as one segment of the Cayuga tribe. The Cayuga shared the heavy reliance on horticulture common to the Iroquois but were noted to be good hunters (Fenton 1978) and to rely more on hunting than the other tribes (White et al. 1978). The main population was located on the east side of Lake Cayuga, but this small population on the west side of the lake was in the area for a period of only about 150 years from about A.D. 1450 to the late 1500s (Nelson 1977; Niemczycki 1984). There is little evidence for village sites prior to this time in this area, and after the late 1500s there is little evidence for a population remaining in this region. Rather it is thought that the population moved back to the east side of the lake, probably after the occupation of the Carman site (Niemczycki 1984).

This area west of Lake Cayuga has good agricultural land (Hasenstab 1996), although it is more marginal for several optimal soil characteristics than the Seneca region (Allen 2000). The presence of these villages in this area raises several questions both about subsistence strategies as well as the social relationships that existed between this population and others in the region. First, are subsistence strategies the same for this group and for others located closer to the lake plain or are they different? If they rely more on hunting, what are the implications for the scheduling and organization of activities and for the associated gendered tasks? Second, where did this population come from and what happened to it after the end of the 1500s? Relationships between this population and other Cayuga east of the lake, as well as those in the Seneca area to the west, the Mohawk in the far east, and the Susquehannock to the south have been noted based on the presence of pottery styles from these groups (Niemczycki 1984; Sempowski and Saunders 2001). What are the social and political implications of these similarities?

These questions stem from macroscale issues but can more effectively be examined at the microscale in order to reach a clear understanding of the impact of local processes on regional patterns and of the way daily

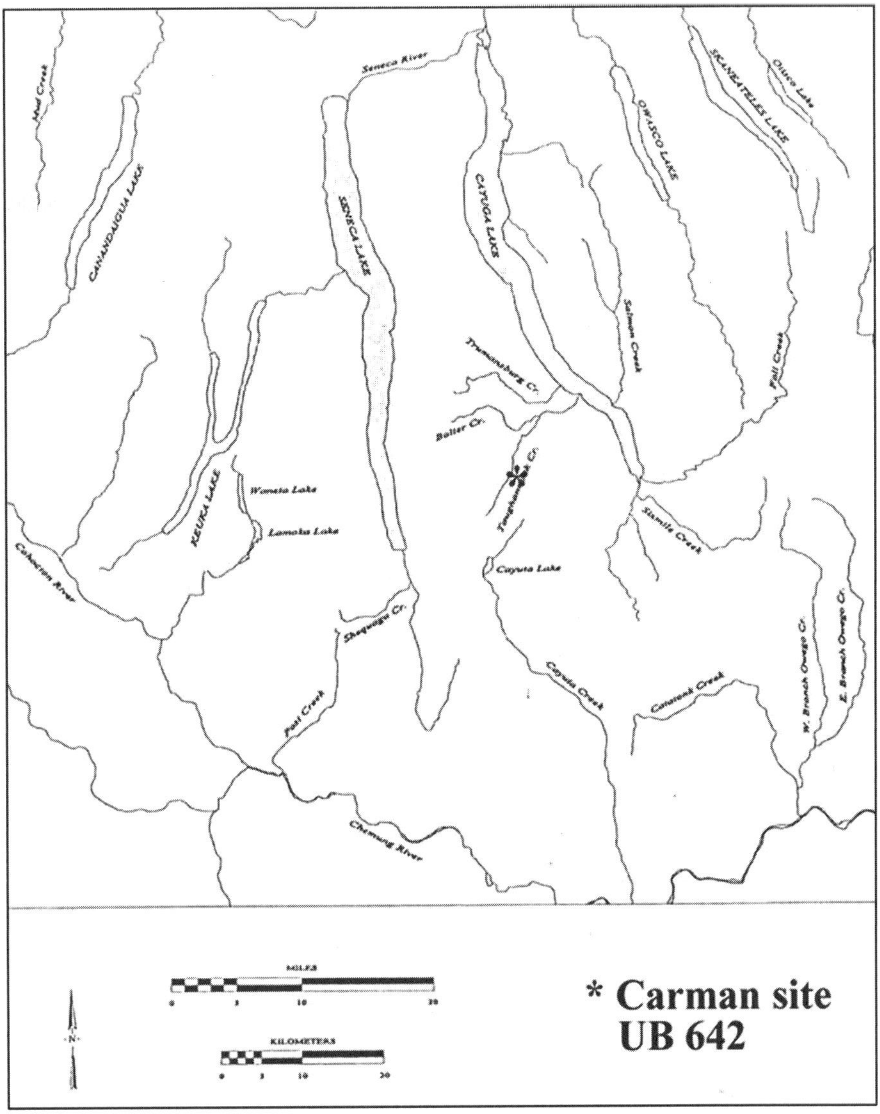

Fig. 7.5. Finger Lakes region, central New York State, with one (Carman) of the four villages on the west side of Cayuga Lake indicated

practice can be altered to accommodate changed circumstances, thus resulting in long-term change. Dealing with these kinds of questions necessitates looking at the data at a variety of scales (both temporal and spatial). At the micro-temporal scale, the content of one feature, a refuse pit, from one site can illuminate broader issues of time, labor, and space.

Excavations have taken place at the Carman site (UB642), the southernmost village site of the group of those located west of Lake Cayuga. This 1 ha site was occupied in the late 1500s (Niemczycki 1984) and is believed to be the last village in the sequence. The site is in an agricultural field, and the plow zone, ca. 30 cm deep, was removed to locate cultural features. Nearly 40 features have been identified, although only five have been analyzed for paleobotanical material. Three longhouses have been identified on this site (Figure 7.6), and a number of features were found both inside and outside of these structures.

At the north end of Longhouse 1, just outside the door, there is a large oblong refuse pit (Feature 18) that exhibits several distinct strata. This feature is the largest and most complex feature found at the site to date. Based on its close proximity to the house, this feature may contain the remains of daily or seasonal refuse from domestic activities that took place inside the longhouse as well as debris associated with a variety of kinds of manufacturing and processing work that took place outside. Analysis of a sample of lithic debitage from the site showed close similarities between the debris from this feature and that present

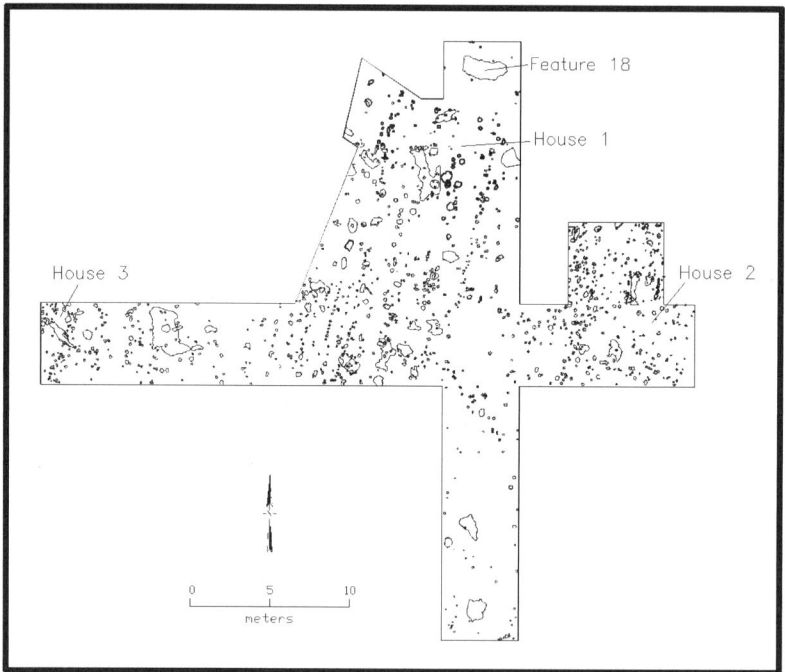

Fig. 7.6. Map of Carman site with Longhouse 1 and Feature 18 indicated

in the hillside midden (Knight 1996). The feature has clear evidence for different depositional episodes, and examination of the differences between these levels helps identification of the kinds of domestic activities evidenced by refuse dumped outside, but in close proximity to the house, and consideration of the gendered nature of these tasks. Do the feature contents represent the steady accumulation of refuse over longer periods of time or the quick infilling of a pit? Does the material indicate a variety of activities were taking place or a more limited range? Are the contents most clearly identified with women's activities occurring inside and in the vicinity of the longhouse?

Certainly other features located within the longhouse compartment may have been utilized on a daily or on a more intermittent basis. Features that are located close to the hearths and the central corridor may be associated with processing or cooking activities while those located under benches and in private storage areas may be individual or family private storage (Snow 1995b). On the other hand, the contents of refuse pits may be the results of daily or periodic disposal activities associated with processing, manufacturing, cooking, and subsequent cleanup activities.

Feature 18, a refuse pit located outside the longhouse, is explored with these questions in mind. The feature is roughly 3 m by 1 m in size, 80 cm deep, and is irregularly shaped, with a basin-shaped profile along the east-west axis (Figure 7.7) and a V-shaped profile along the north-south axis. It appears to be a natural depression, possibly a tree fall, that was filled in with refuse. In the bisected profile three distinct depositional episodes are apparent. The lowest layer (Level III) was a greasy black silt loam while the upper layer of this feature was a dark brown silt (Level I). These two layers were separated by a layer of yellowish-brown silt loam (Level II). During excavation, several distinctions were made within each of these three layers as they became apparent in the wall profile; the contents of these six layers from the northern half of the feature are examined here.

A total of 2,611 items were recovered from this portion of the feature. The material recovered from these levels falls into a number of categories, including lithics (236 pieces), pottery (779 sherds), and faunal material (1,596 fragments). Floral remains (180 pieces) were recovered from three of the levels, including the top one (Level I) and lower two (Levels IIIA and IIIB).

One level, Level IIA, contained a slightly greater amount of pottery than bone (Figure 7.8), while the most plentiful material recovered from the other five of the six levels was faunal. The lowest two levels (Levels

IIIA and IIIB) contained slightly higher proportions of ceramics relative to faunal material than the other levels. There are some differences between depositional episodes, although the large amount of animal bone suggests that activities associated with hunting and processing fauna are primary. Although only a small segment of the faunal material has been identified, most of the bone is deer with some bird, fish, turkey, dog, and squirrel bones also present.

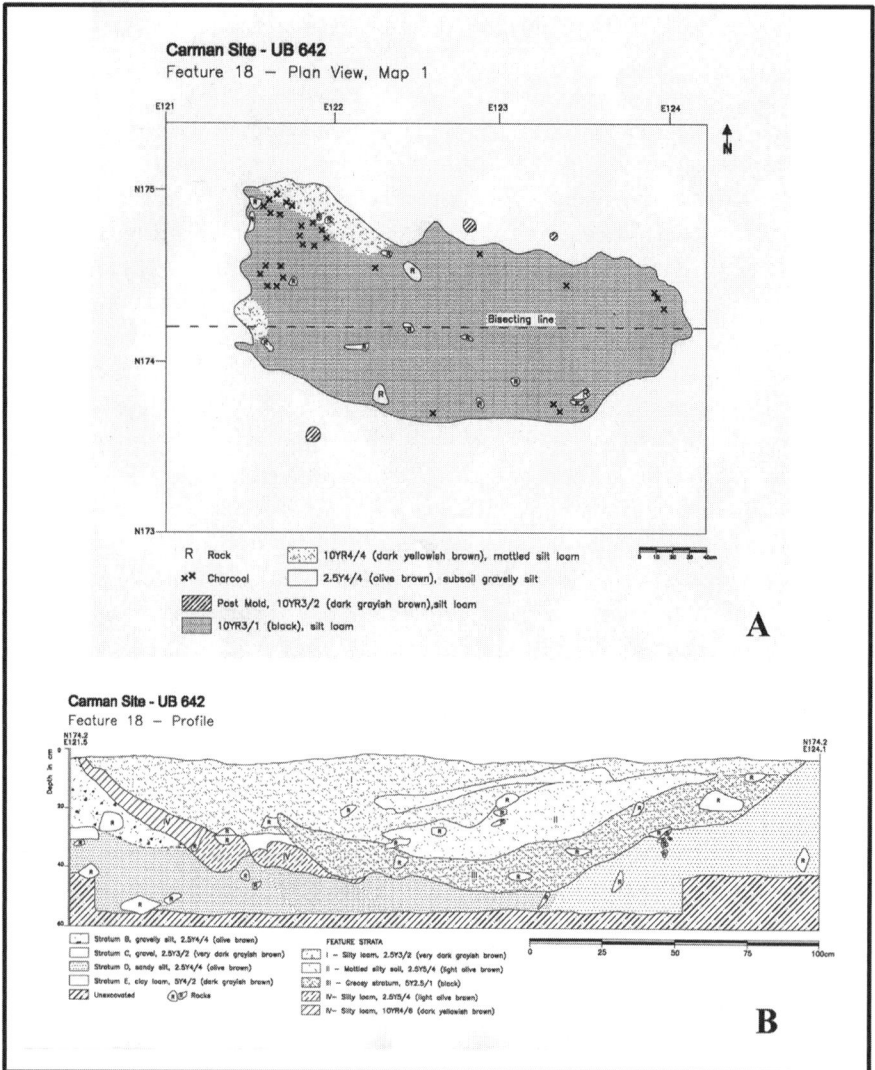

Fig. 7.7. Feature 18, plan view (A) and profile (B)

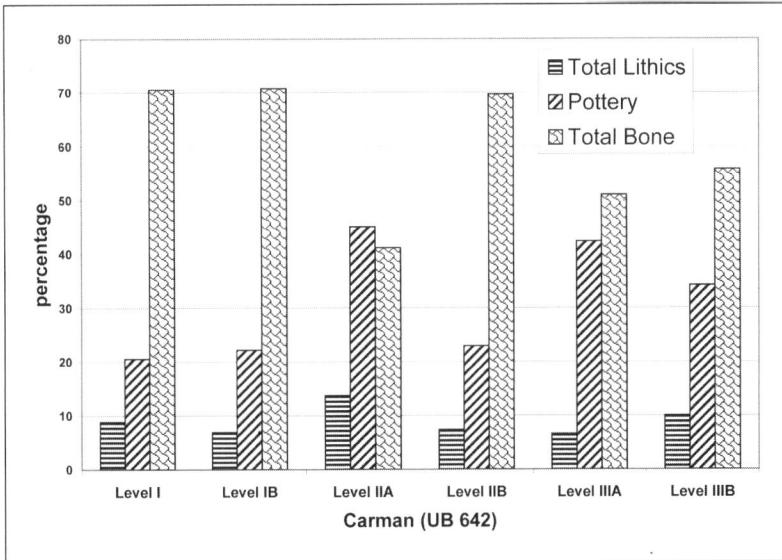

Fig. 7.8. Lithic, pottery, and bone proportions by level, Feature 18

In order to differentiate the kinds of activities represented by the animal bone, proportions of unburned and calcined bone were examined (Figure 7.9). There were 1,099 fragments of unburned bone and 489 of calcined bone in this half of the feature. Unburned bone dominates in five of the six levels although the relative proportion varies. Three levels (Levels I, IIB, and IIIB) have proportions of unburned bone of about 70 percent, while three levels have proportions of unburned bone that are slightly lower and range from the upper 40s to close to 60 percent (Levels IB, IIA, and IIIA). Unburned bone is the product of hunting, processing, and, perhaps, cooking activities, while calcined bone is indicative of cooking activities primarily even if bone was calcined after the primary cooking event (Moeller 1992).

Floral remains were recovered from flotation samples analyzed from four levels of the feature. Fifty percent of the carbonized seed and 11 percent of the carbonized nut fragments recovered from the site so far were found here (Asmussen 1998). One of the four levels, Level IIA, contained two items; the others contained larger quantities, including the upper level of the feature, Level I, and the lower two, Levels IIIA and IIIB (Figure 7.10). The paleobotanical remains from the three levels all contain maize (*Zea mays*), blackberry/raspberry (*Rubus* sp.), and nut fragments (mostly hickory) but exhibit quite different patterns. Level

I shows a high proportion of carbonized nut shells (72 percent), Level IIIA shows a high proportion of blackberry/raspberry seeds (68 percent), and Level IIIB shows a more balanced proportion of maize (21 percent), blackberry/raspberry (43 percent), and nut fragments (35 percent).

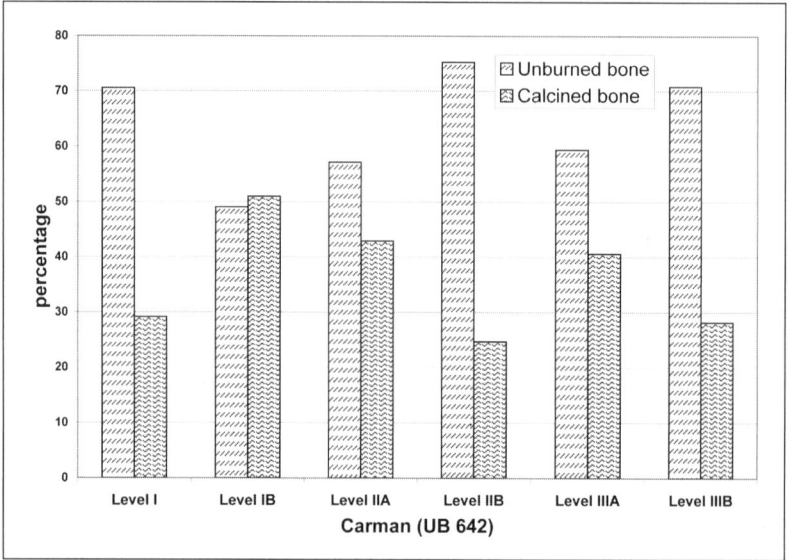

Fig. 7.9. Faunal material proportions by level, Feature 18

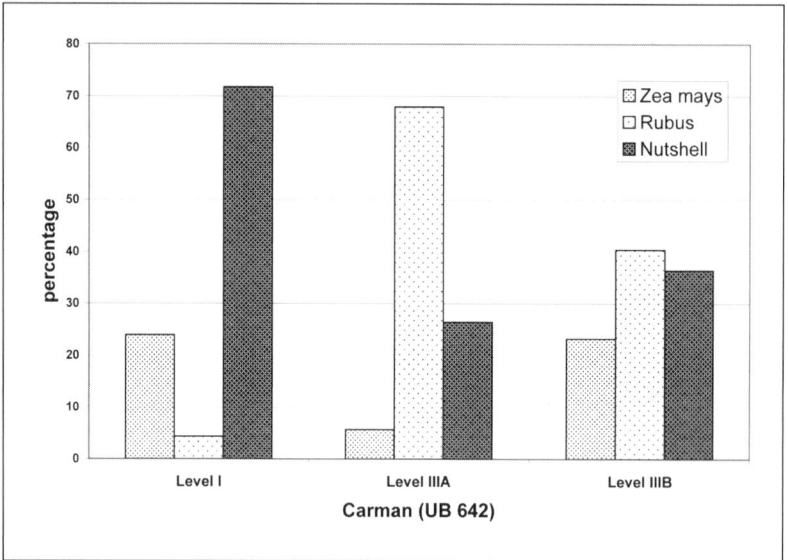

Fig. 7.10. Carbonized floral material by level, Feature 18

The lithic, pottery, and faunal materials were grouped into two categories based on whether the remains can be interpreted as the result of cooking or of processing and lithic manufacturing activities. Pottery and calcined bone are most closely associated with cooking activities as Iroquoian pots are primarily utilitarian cooking vessels and calcined bone suggests cooking or at least its presence near a hearth. The lithic debitage is similar to that recovered from the midden area as it contains a high proportion of shaping and primary reduction flakes (Knight 1996) which likely result primarily from tool manufacture. Lithics in conjunction with fragmentary, unburned faunal material (some of which exhibit cut marks) is indicative of faunal processing and tool manufacturing activities. When the material is grouped in this way (Figure 7.11), two levels show a higher proportion of processing and/or manufacturing activities (Levels I and IIB), three levels show a higher proportion of cooking activities (Levels IB, IIA, and IIIA), and one shows a roughly equal proportion of both (Level IIIB).

Discussion

The remains from this feature appear to be a combination of food waste and other cultural material. These include faunal and floral remains as well as broken pottery and lithic debitage. The pottery, calcined bone, and carbonized seeds and nuts suggest cooking activities, while the unburned bone and lithic debitage are more likely associated with food processing and preparation. The proportions of maize, berry, and nut remains indicate the importance of wild foods in the diet along with cultivated ones, and this is a pattern similar to that obtained for the Huron (Monckton 1992). It appears that the feature contents are the result of both general refuse disposal as well as some cleaning out of hearths as both calcined bone and wood charcoal were present and fire-cracked rock was found in the lowest level. This refuse pit contains material associated primarily with daily activities such as cooking, processing, and clearing out of hearth areas, tasks typically done by Iroquois women.

In order to discern better the pattern of disposal represented by this feature, the three levels with the most material were compared further. It is not clear if each of these levels result from single or multiple refuse dumping episodes, although there are some differences between them (Figure 7.12). Bone accounted for 71 percent of all material from Level I. It also contained the largest proportion of lithics relative to pottery (30 percent to 70 percent) and more nut fragments than any other level. Levels IIIA and IIIB contained roughly 50 percent faunal remains. Level

IIIA had the most pottery relative to lithics of any level (87 percent to 13 percent) and a large amount of berry remains. Level IIIB had a more even distribution of all three primary kinds of floral remains and a proportion of pottery to lithic of 77 percent to 23 percent.

Seasonal differences may be responsible for these patterns, but it is not entirely clear. All of the floral remains could have been dried, stored, and eaten at different times during the year. They are also carbonized, which suggests that they may have been incidentally burned as processing occurred at the hearth. However, this does not negate an attempt to identify seasonality. The differences seen between the three levels are subtle. They appear to be the remains of different specific activities although all are associated with food preparation and cooking. Level I is most distinct as it contains more bone (most of it unburned) than the others, and has the highest proportion of nut fragments, both of which suggest processing activities. Both of these categories of material culture are indicative of late fall activities (Parker 1968b [1916]; Waugh 1916). The other two levels may also result from relatively short-term work. Given its interpretation as a natural feature rather than a constructed storage pit and its location in the village outside the end of a longhouse, it is likely that it was filled in a short period. Level IIIA has the most evidence for cooking activities in the form of pottery along with berry remains. Level IIIB, the first depositional episode, contains the most even distribution of floral material and has slightly more lithics and less pottery than Level IIIA.

The contents of the three levels appear to contain remnants of early to late fall or late fall through late winter refuse disposal episodes. The large quantity of animal bone suggests that hunting activities were ongoing at the time of pit infilling. Large-scale hunts among the Huron were typically conducted in the late fall (mid- or late October) and late winter (March) (Heidenreich 1971). Nut harvesting would occur after fall frosts and black raspberries ripen in August and September (Waugh 1916). This would also be the season for maize harvesting. Although in a different context, Dickens (1985:43) has hypothesized that storage pits are more likely to be abandoned and filled with garbage in the fall and early winter than at other times. Although this pit does not appear to have served as a storage pit at any time, given its irregular shape, the relatively low frequency of rodent gnawing suggests quick infilling, and the many small bone fragments suggest extensive processing and perhaps trampling (Lewandowski 2002). Thus the material may have come from inside the longhouse or some other heavily traveled area. At

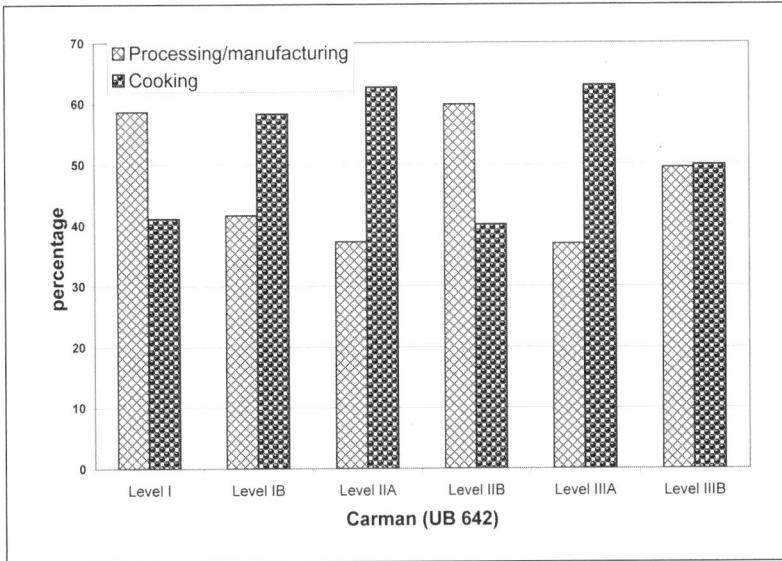

Fig. 7.11. Processing/manufacturing and cooking activities represented by levels, Feature 18

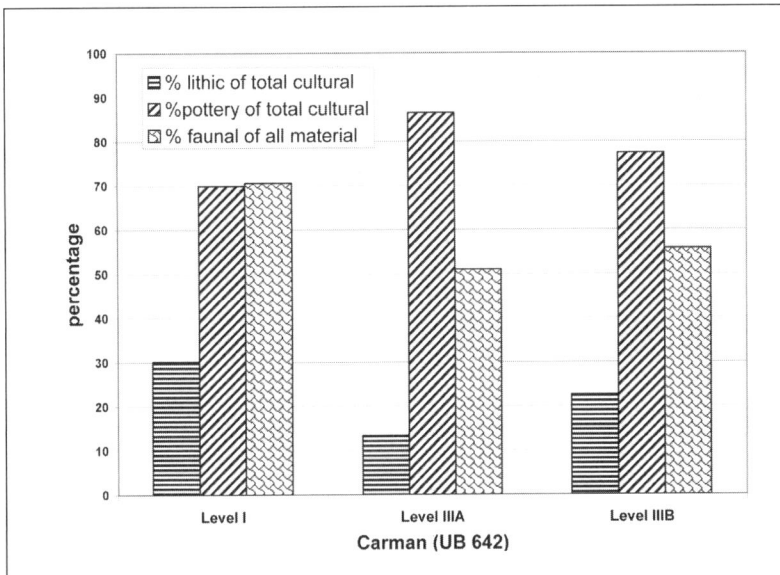

Fig. 7.12. Comparison of lithic, pottery, and faunal material in three levels, Feature 18

any rate the feature most likely was filled in a period of no more than a few months' duration in the fall or early winter.

Although this conclusion seems likely, other evidence may be brought to bear. Comparisons between this feature and other features, both within and outside the longhouse, as well as the hillside midden can further illuminate the refuse disposal activities that take place on short and longer time scales at this site and their relationship to seasonal subsistence practices. Clearly the contents of the pit primarily reflect the processing and cooking activities that occur on a daily basis, most likely carried out by women.

Conclusions

This study is a small-scale study using archaeological data to inform on daily practice. Normally these remains might be considered to be a palimpsest of the village occupation without the possibility of recovering a short-term event. Here the short-term event seems clear. Although this detailed analysis of the depositional episodes in a single feature has focused on the microscale, several larger-scale questions are apparent. Some of these are methodological and center on the need for more-detailed feature comparisons; some are broader and concern the organization of activities and the ongoing compromises and negotiations that must have taken place between men and women as the seasons progress. If the Cayuga did rely more heavily on hunting than other groups, can we see evidence for this difference in comparison with other Iroquois groups? Is the location of these villages in an upland setting related? Did the organization of women's activities change in order to accommodate the greater efforts that had to be devoted to deer processing? Were there other alterations in the organization of space and refuse disposal that accompanied these changes?

These questions stem from the detailed consideration of a short-term disposal pattern and its relationship to the broader cycle of site occupation. In reality there is a continuum as we examine the remnants of activities taking place within the household at the compartment level, within the longhouse between compartments, between longhouses, between neighboring villages, and within and between tribal areas over space and time. The process is quite complex as we move back and forth between the microscale and macroscale levels of analysis. The macroscale level puts activities occurring on the microscale into better focus so we do not assume that tasks occurring at a village are done in isolation from the larger social networks on the landscape. Attention to the microscale reminds us of the importance of social action on the part of individuals and groups. Microscale approaches get us closer to an understanding of life as lived by these people, to a more intimate understanding of daily practices and everyday life; macroscale approaches help in charting change that occurs over time. Moving back and forth through multiple scales of analysis allows each to inform on the other and provides needed perspective on both micro and macro change.

Note

1. Thanks go to all of the field-workers who participated in fieldwork at the Carman site and especially to Ellen Cowie, Christopher Pool, Heidi Fieldsa Asmussen, and Rachel Brinkman for their work excavating and documenting this complex feature. Heidi Asmussen analyzed the paleobotanical material, which played an important role in the interpretation. Several students in my laboratory class worked on portions of this feature and the material from it. They include Michael Baltusavich, Terri Pogozelski, Emily Bender, Michael Lewandowski, Laura Quinn, Oliver Mueller-Heubach, Angela Heberle, Marcy Megella, Mark Michalski, Jesse Kelly, Yvette Magistro, and Benjamin Goldblatt. Maps were made by Greg Smith, Chris Hill, Kimberly Williams, Catie Daquilla, and Denise Schaan and prepared for publication with the assistance of Mark Mooney. I greatly appreciate comments on a draft of this essay from Christine Beaule, Nicole Constable, Mark Mooney, Kimberly Williams, David Smith, Dean Snow, and especially Laurie E. Miroff and Timothy D. Knapp, the editors of this volume, who also graciously invited my participation. Despite all this assistance, any errors remain mine.

8

Defense in an Iroquois Village

William Engelbrecht

Iroquois oral tradition states that fighting was once common.[1] According to Parker (1968a:17 [1916]), "Feuds with outer nations, feuds with brother nations, feuds of sister towns and feuds of families and of clans made every warrior a stealthy man who liked to kill." Assuming this to have been the case, fighting involved social and political units of variable scale. Therefore it is not surprising that an Iroquois concern with defense can be inferred archaeologically at both the regional and village level. Regionally the development of Iroquois nations is reflected in the location of contemporaneous villages near one another (Engelbrecht 2003:112–126). It is assumed that members of these villages came to one another's defense in the event of an attack. The development of large palisaded hilltop communities typical of the sixteenth-century Iroquois is commonly interpreted as a defensive response to endemic warfare. Thus it is likely that a concern with defense is also reflected at smaller spatial scales.

A feature can be considered to have a defensive property if it serves to restrict physical access. The location of many Iroquois sites on a hilltop or point of land with a steep bank on one or more sides provides well-known examples. A palisade typically protected accessible routes of entry, channeling movement through a narrow passageway. This palisade was the first and most important line of defense, but on occasion enemies still gained entry to a village.

Palisaded Villages

When Europeans first encountered Iroquois palisaded villages, they referred to them as "castles." This may strike us as a quaint misnomer, but there were similarities. First, a village on a hill surrounded by a 20 or 30 ft (6.1 or 9.1 m) high palisade would have appeared imposing even if it were not made of stone in the fashion of a walled European castle. Second, both European medieval castles and Iroquois palisaded villages were built for defense and restricted access to the interior. Third, a large number of people lived in both.

Iroquois palisades evolved over time, becoming increasingly effective as defensive structures (Keener 1999:782). Though the diameter of palisade post molds varies within sites, over time there is an increase in size (Prezzano 1992:242; Ritchie and Funk 1973:363). There may have been considerable variation in palisade height, even around the same community, but it is thought that the majority of palisades were somewhere between 4 and 10 m in height (Prezzano 1992:248). Champlain observed that the palisade around the Iroquois village he attacked in 1615 was some 30 ft (9.1 m) high, while he estimated a triple palisade around a Huron village at 35 ft (10.7 m; Grant 1959:283, 292 [1907]).

In some cases a ditch was dug in front of the palisade, with the dirt piled at the base, creating what today is known as an earth ring. Gabriel Sagard (1939:91–95 [1632]) observed large tree trunks laid along the base of a palisade to strengthen it, and he noted branches and saplings woven between the upright posts to create a wall 8 or 9 ft (2.4 or 2.7 m) high. These palisades must have involved a great deal of labor to construct. Palisades may have had secondary functions as snow fences or windbreaks or served various symbolic functions, but their sturdiness and the obvious effort involved in their construction suggest that defense was their primary function.

Palisades with more than three rows of posts are sometimes encountered in excavation (Figure 8.1). There are no ethnographic descriptions of such palisades, and a palisade of four or five rows of posts would seem unnecessary. Gary A. Warrick (1988) has suggested that village duration might be inferred from the number of post molds observed along a longhouse wall; many post molds suggest decay of the original posts and repairs using new posts. In similar fashion, the presence of more than three rows of palisade posts suggests rebuilding. This is a different situation from that of multiple palisade rows resulting from village expansion or contraction.

There were generally only one or two gateways in a palisade. These were often passageways created by overlapping palisade lines that required people to walk single file. These could be easily closed off. Such an entryway was described for the Huron (Sagard 1939:91–95 [1632]), and examples have been recovered archaeologically from a number of

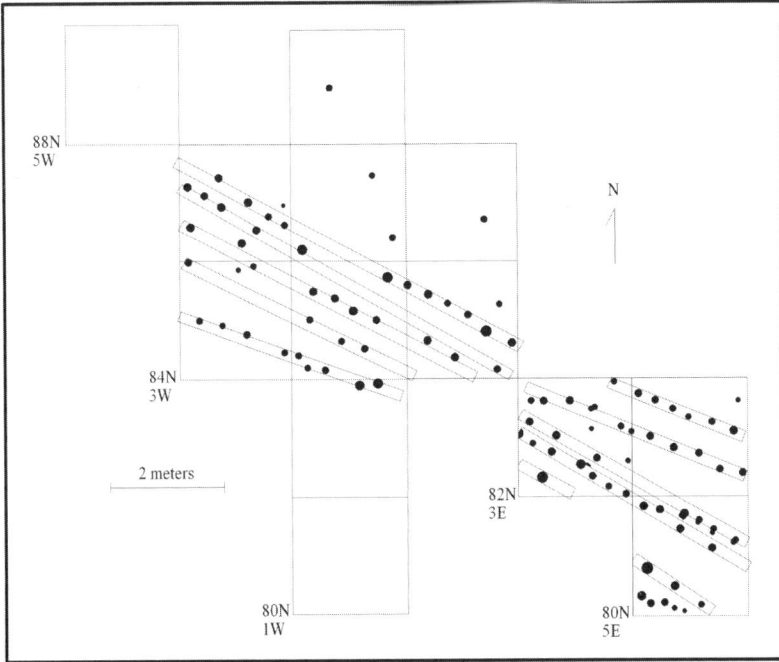

Fig. 8.1. Five row palisade at the Eaton site, West Seneca, New York. The function of the sixth line of posts in the southwest portion of 80N 5E is unknown

sites. In 1634 Van den Bogaert observed a relatively wide main entryway of 3.5 ft (1.1 m) into an Oneida village, but a second entryway was only 2 ft (0.6 m) across (Gehring and Starna 1988:12). The Iroquois appear to have borrowed the concept of gates from Europeans, for during the winter of 1692–1693 Frontenac encountered Mohawk towns "closed with gates" (O'Callaghan 1858:IX:550; see also Abler 1970:28).

Village Structure

While palisades served as the first line of a village's defense, they were not always successful. Even with a sturdy palisade, there was always the possibility that the enemy might gain entry into an Iroquois village in a surprise attack. *The Jesuit Relations* (Thwaites 1896–1901:29:253) of 1646 contains an account of two Huron sentries who fell asleep and were killed by Iroquois warriors. Abler (1970:28) notes that there are numerous accounts in *The Jesuit Relations and Allied Documents* of enemy warriors gaining entry into villages. For the Huron a warrior gained great prestige if he successfully entered an enemy village at night and captured or killed someone (Finlayson 1998:19). "While the Iroquoians seem to have gone to much trouble to build these palisades, to the modern reader it seems almost useless because of their reluctance to use sentries at night" (Abler 1970:28). In situations when an enemy was within the village, secondary interior defenses would have become critical.

The plans that we have from excavated palisaded villages suggest that houses were often located close to one another. Arranging houses close together would have minimized the effort required to construct a palisade. The restricted area of many hilltop village locations would have encouraged community nucleation. It is also possible that placement of houses within a village was motivated by considerations of defense. Sagard (1939:92 [1632]) stated that an open space was left between the palisade and Huron longhouses to facilitate defense. William D. Finlayson (1985:407, 1998:20) argues that at the Draper site in Ontario, houses were placed so as to create defensible corridors and reduce access to the center of the village in the event that the palisade was breached. The excavation plan of the Nodwell site, also in Ontario, exhibits lines of posts linking longhouses to palisades (Figure 8.2; Wright 1974:5; see also Finlayson 1998:20). These lines presumably acted as cordons to restrict access. The late Dr. Robert E. Funk recently produced a new plan of the houses at the Garoga site (Figure 8.3; also Engelbrecht 2003:94). While the arrangement of houses maximized the available space (Funk 1967:81), the position of the middle longhouses would also have presented barriers to an enemy attempting to move across the village.

The Longhouse

A number of authors have discussed the advantages and disadvantages of longhouse life. In addition to construction efficiency, there are advantages to having a household with many members. Iroquois patterns of hunting, fishing, trading, and warfare took men far from the village for extended periods, leaving women, children, and old people behind to carry out other activities, a situation encouraging the formation of both matrilocal residence and extended families (Harris 1979:97; Pasternak et al. 1976; Trigger 1978). In an extended household, many individuals can cooperate in a task, or a variety of tasks can be performed at the same time as needed (Coupland and Banning 1996:2–3; Wilk and Rathje 1982). Groups of related women cooperated in planting, harvesting, processing, and storing the crops in their longhouses (Parker 1968b:34 [1910]; Quain 1961:250). In particular large quantities of seasonally available foodstuffs (crops, fish, and venison) were stored within the longhouses. As Lisa Rankin (2000:44) observes, "rectilinear houses are the easiest to expand when populations increase or more storage area is required." However, as Keener (1995:101) and others have suggested, sedentary villages with large stores of food are potential targets for others wanting these resources.

Despite the economic and social advantages longhouses provided, from a Western perspective a longhouse sacrifices both privacy and ease

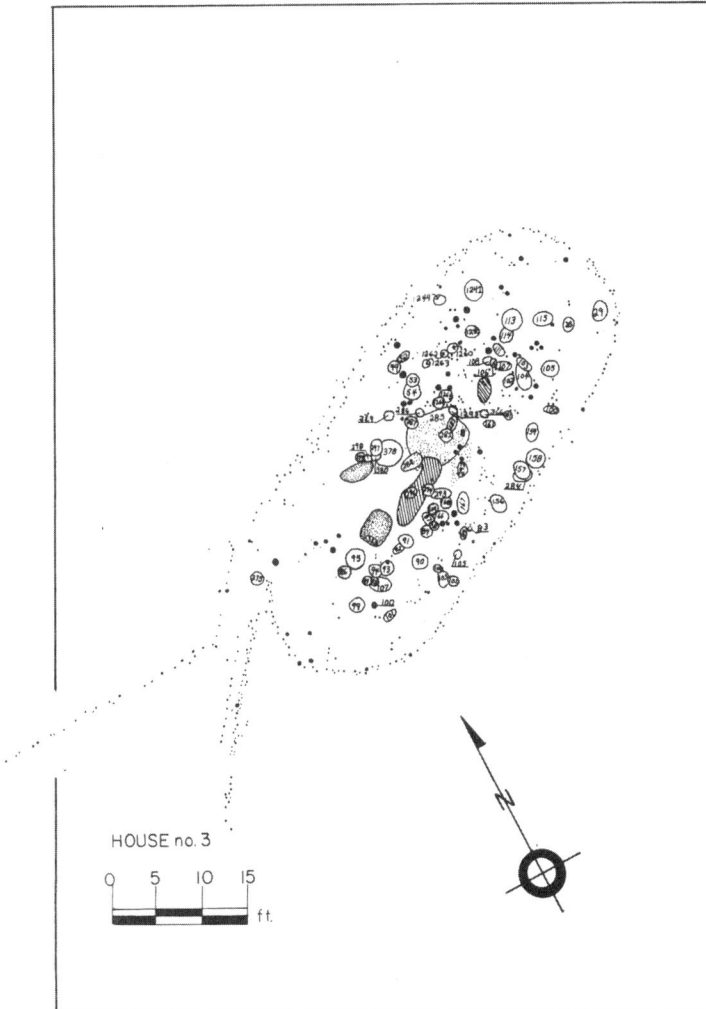

HOUSE no. 3

0   5   10   15

ft.

N

Fig. 8.2. Longhouse with associated lines of posts from the Nodwell site, Port Elgin, Ontario (Image © Canadian Museum of Civilization, Mercury Series, paper no. 22, The Nodwell Site, by J. V. Wright, Ottawa, 1974, Figure 10, page 26, image no. 73-25852)

of use (Blanton 1994:32). The existence of a door at either end creates limited access to the interior. Individuals living toward the center of a longhouse had to regularly pass by other families living closer to a door. Yet more doorways could have been incorporated easily into longhouse design, and some longer examples did have side entrances. Having more doorways would not have negated the economic or social advantages of longhouse life.

There are three potential advantages to having limited access to long-houses. First, it restricts access to food stored there. However, if this were the critical factor, one would expect food to be stored in the center of a longhouse, not in storage compartments at the ends. Second, a limited number of doorways would have reduced drafts in winter. Initial entry to a longhouse was into an unheated storage area, which would have served a secondary insulation function. One then entered another doorway to the living area. This arrangement makes sense in winter. Third, there is a defensive advantage for a number of families to move together into a single house with limited access (Rowlands 1972:456).

Warrick (1996:19) considered the possibility that longhouses might be related to defense, but his emphasis is on correlating longhouse length with warfare intensity. After reviewing the evidence, he concludes that "change in Iroquoian house size in prehistory is independent of warfare

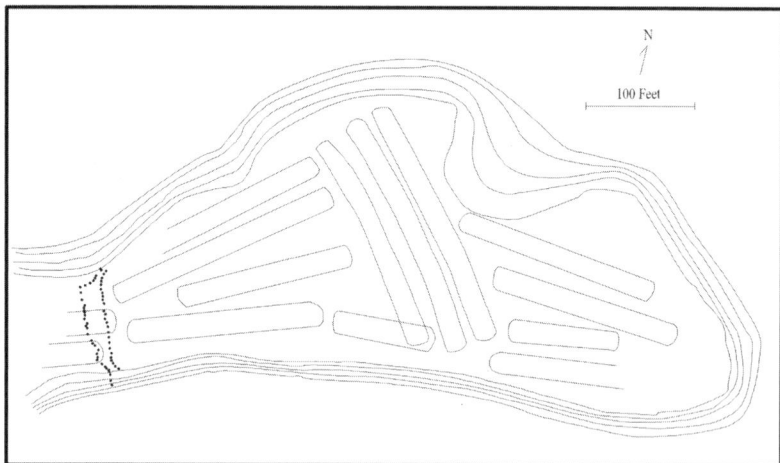

Fig. 8.3. The Garoga site, Fulton County, New York. This illustration is based on a map drawn by the late Robert Funk (see Funk and Kuhn 2003: 84). The dimensions of some longhouses are esti-mates. The overlapping of some houses with the palisade and with one another suggests rebuilding during occupation of the village. A few 1 ft contour intervals are sketched to indicate the hilltop location. The slope falls off steeply to a creek approximately 150 ft below.

intensity" (Warrick 1996:19). The argument presented here emphasizes longhouse form rather than length in defensive considerations.

Iroquois men were typically absent from the village for long periods of time—hunting, fishing, trading, and waging war. If Iroquois peoples had lived in nuclear-family dwellings, many houses would have lacked an adult male member for much of the year. Even if longhouse residents were warned of intruders by barking dogs, it is unlikely that women, children, and old people could have put up an effective defense against enemy warriors. However, with many families living together, a few men positioned at either longhouse door could defend many families. To get inside a longhouse, enemy warriors would have to enter the outer door, get through the outer storage compartment or vestibule, and then enter the inner door. Once inside they would still be faced with a series of living compartments. The primary reason for these compartments was no doubt privacy, but they would also have served to restrict movement.

There is security in numbers as well. Individuals probably felt safer living with an extended family than living in a nuclear family or alone. The security a longhouse afforded its inhabitants is reflected in the following oral tradition: "At night none dared leave their doorways lest they be struck down by an enemy's war club. Such was the condition when there was no Great Law" (Parker 1968a:17 [1916]).

Lafitau (1977:22 [1724]), a Jesuit missionary stationed along the St. Lawrence at the Mohawk settlement of Caughnawaga (1712–17), describes traditional longhouse doors as follows: "The doors of the lodges are movable sheets of bark hung from above, with neither key nor lock. In the past, nothing was closed in Indian houses. When they were gone a long time on a campaign, they contented themselves with fastening their doors with wooden bars to protect them from the village dogs."

Lafitau (1977:22 [1724]) then noted changes that had occurred in the historic period: "Others strengthen their lodges at the gables with grossly made planks and install in them wooden doors with bolts bought from the Europeans." He attributes these changes to the thieving of nearby Europeans, but these changes can also be interpreted as relating to increased security from attack. Such changes were not new for the Mohawk. In 1634 Van den Bogaert observed interior longhouse doors made of split planks with iron hinges (Gehring and Starna 1988:4, 31). Van den Bogaert also observed iron chains and bolts in these longhouses, though he does not state explicitly that they were used in connection with the doors (Gehring and Starna 1988:4, 30–31). Kurt A. Jordan (2002, this volume) has suggested that historic period longhouses may be thought of as a hybrid artifact form, and the evidence suggests that early changes were in the direction of greater security. Some six or seven years after Van den Bogaert's observation, the Jesuits found the Neutral fastening their doors against them (Thwaites 1896–1901:21:219; see also Abler 1970:30).

> Indeed, they no sooner approached a village, than from all sides was screamed: "These are the Agwa who are coming" (this is the name they give to their greatest enemies) "fasten your doors;" so that the Fathers coming to cabins in order to enter them, according to the rule and custom of the country, found there generally only closed doors; for they were looked upon as sorcerers who carried death and misfortunes everywhere. (Thwaites 1896–1901:21:21)

In 1646 three Hurons set out to avenge the death of the two sentries mentioned earlier and found the doors to the houses in a Seneca village closed. "After twenty day's march, they arrive at Sonnontouans, the most populous of the hostile villages; finding these the cabins closed, they break into one of them at the side, and enter it in the silence and darkness of the night" (Thwaites 1896–1901:29:253). Chopping through a palisade or the side of a longhouse was probably made easier by the introduction of the metal axe (Keener 1999:785).

Following the epidemic of 1634, longhouses decrease in length (Snow 1994b:111). This trend continues through the century as the Iroquois lose population to disease, warfare, and out-migration (Guldenzopf 1984:83). Lineages and clan segments responded to these losses by adopting captives and taking in refugees. As a consequence, Snow (1995b:304, 362) argues, the residents of longhouses increasingly formed ad hoc social units. For example, at Caughnawaga in the Mohawk Valley, longhouses are of standardized lengths, suggesting that houses defined the social units, rather than the opposite (Snow 1995b:363, 430). The form remained, but the composition changed (Snow 1995b:363). Building on this observation, it is likely that the defensive advantage of longhouse life was a consideration in retaining the traditional form. During the mid–eighteenth century, Moravian missionaries visiting a Seneca village were told by a chief that his house was the largest in town, serving as "the meeting place for the Council as well as their fortress" (Beauchamp 1916:74).

Finally, ancient metaphors may contain wisdom that has been lost. The League was described by the metaphor of the longhouse, with the Seneca and Mohawk being the "Keepers of the Western and Eastern Doors," respectively. If the presence of only two longhouse doors was related to defensive concerns, then the title of doorkeeper takes on a military dimension that is generally overlooked.

Conclusions

Iroquoian village structure and longhouse form evolved in a cultural context in which hostile encounters with individuals of other groups were common. It should not be surprising, therefore, that an examination of Iroquois villages at varying scales reveals defensive features. An enemy warrior seeking to enter a longhouse within an Iroquois village would have found his access restricted at a number of junctures once inside the palisade. The placement of structures within some villages would have channeled the movement of enemy warriors through restricted spaces, providing a second line of defense. The absence of windows and the existence of only two doors in a longhouse served to restrict access to the interior providing a third line of defense. An inner door would have provided a fourth point of restricted access, and interior partitions within a longhouse provided still more restrictions to physical movement.

Houses in a palisaded Iroquois village were set close together to minimize the circumference of the palisade and maximize the use of defensible terrain. The social, political, and economic functions of longhouses have long been noted and are not disputed here. Though defensive concerns are not the sole explanation for Iroquois village structure and longhouse form, the defensive advantages of these are suggested by looking at restricted access at multiple scales.

Note

1. Thanks go to Kurt A. Jordan, Craig Keener, Timothy D. Knapp, Laurie E. Miroff, and Keith Otterbein for commenting on an early draft of this paper.

9

"Bottom-Up" Perspectives of the Contact Period

A View from the Rogers Farm Site

Kimberly Williams-Shuker

The effects of European interaction as experienced at the household level of social organization have not received a great deal of explicit attention in the body of literature dealing with Iroquoian groups during the Contact period.[1] It is far more common for historical studies to tackle broad-scale[2] themes, emphasizing issues such as demography and epidemiology, political and military affairs, the fur trade, and ideology (e.g., Graymont 1981; Hamell 1987; Jennings 1975, 1984; Richter 1992; Tooker 1981; Trelease 1960; Trigger 1985). Archaeological investigations of the period also tend to implement larger-scale approaches, focusing on the acculturation process, the selective incorporation of European goods into the material culture inventory, or changes in the orientation of trade routes (e.g., Allen 1990; Bradley 1987; Chapdelaine 1996; Moreau 1996, 1998). Given the nature of these research questions, the geographic scope of these works is correspondingly large, ranging from the regional to the intercontinental. Likewise the levels of social integration that are the object of these studies are also of a broad scale; most often they discuss the activities of society, tribe, nation—or all Native Americans as a group.

Archaeological research at finer scales of analysis, such as the household, can complement these lines of investigation. Household membership is a fundamental element of any individual's social identity. The household is the primary unit of social and economic organization of a society (Hirth 1993:21). It is intermeshed with all aspects of society and both reflects and contributes to larger processes of societal development (Yanagisako 1979). Therefore, by reconstructing the organization of domestic activities, the archaeology of Contact period Iroquois households can be expected to reveal information about the social and economic processes involved in interaction with the European newcomers and shed light on daily life during this period of cultural flux. By viewing the Contact period from the "bottom up," such research should enable a fuller understanding of the ramifications of interaction with European newcomers among Iroquoian groups.

This perspective can also address local issues that larger-scale studies of the Contact period may fail to see. For example, several studies have explored the impact of European contact on the social relations that defined Iroquoian household membership (e.g., Engelbrecht 1985; Hayden 1977; Richards 1967, 1969; Smith 1970; Warrick 1996). By focusing on the internal, rather than external, workings of Iroquois society, research at the household scale can help create a more comprehensive view of the period.

Ethnohistoric and ethnographic accounts provide an overview of "traditional," precontact domestic organization and activities (Fenton 1978; Morgan 1962 [1851]; Parker 1968c [1916]; Tooker 1984, 1991). Although there is danger in the uncritical use of these sources due to their cultural biases and potential unreliability, they remain an invaluable store of information about Iroquoian lifeways. The household was closely tied to the longhouse, residential structures, which were inhabited by matrilineally related extended families that made up the elemental socioeconomic units of Iroquoian society. Matrilocal rules of postmarital residence were ideally followed (Kapches 1994; Morgan 1962 [1851]; Trigger 1978). The families within a longhouse served as a corporate kinship group, sharing productive duties and economic risk as well as social obligations. By pooling labor, the extended families of the longhouse undertook a diversity of tasks—including agriculture, manufacturing, child rearing, trading, hunting, gathering, and warfare—that could not be accomplished by a nuclear family alone (Heidenreich 1971:114, 123; Kapches 1979:25; Warrick 1984). Social reproduction, warfare, and ceremonial events were rooted in the household and demonstrate the integration of the matrilineage of a longhouse with suprahousehold spheres of activity (see Yanagisako 1979:191).

It is worth assessing the ways in which Iroquois households conformed to, or deviated from, this model of traditional household composition and activity within the context of the historical processes and societal changes occurring during the Contact period. Archaeological research was undertaken at the Rogers Farm site, a Cayuga Iroquois village dating from the 1660s to 1680s, located in Savannah, New York.

Archaeological evidence of the site's households can be evaluated in comparison with domestic-sphere remains from both prehistoric and contemporaneous Iroquois settlements in light of the historic record. The Rogers Farm site dates to a period when the Cayuga had already experienced contact with Europeans for more than 50 years. By the time of the site's occupation, the community had previously suffered the effects of European-born epidemics, had engaged in the escalating warfare between the League Iroquois and other neighboring tribes, and was increasingly abandoning Native technologies in favor of European trade goods. Furthermore Rogers Farm is believed to have been the site of the mission of St. René. As the Cayuga community witnessed the arrival of Jesuit missionaries into Iroquois territory and hosted the priests in the village, the frequency and intensity of face-to-face interaction with Europeans increased. Investigations of the site were aimed at gathering domestic-context archaeological data that would provide a "bottom-up" view of the historical events occurring during the period and generate a fuller understanding of the day-to-day lives of the members of the community.

The Cayuga Iroquois during the Seventeenth Century

The seventeenth century was a time of flux for the Cayuga and all Iroquoian societies. The historical narrative of Iroquois lands during this period points to a range of large-scale events with the potential to play out in the realm of the household. Perhaps the two most powerful forces of change introduced by the newcomers were pathogens and a desire for beaver peltry. An exploration of the historical contingencies stemming from these factors provides a context for the consideration of the Contact period from the household scale of analysis.

European-introduced epidemics brought about widespread depopulation. Smallpox outbreaks occurred in 1634 and 1662, drastically reducing the populations of Iroquois communities across New York State (Snow and Lanphear 1988). Disease spread rapidly through the crowded shelters of the Iroquois. By the 1640s the population of the Five Nations Iroquois was halved, to an estimated total of 10,000; by 1670, the figure may have been as low as 8,600 (Richter 1992:59, 114). Among the Cayuga, population fell from 4,000 in 1630 to 2,000 in 1640. In 1680 there were 1,200 members of the nation, increasing to 1,280 by 1690 (Snow 1994b:Table 7.1).

The mid-1600s also represented several decades of intense bloodshed and war. The initiation of the fur trade brought not only profit but warfare to the Iroquois. During the so-called Beaver Wars, Iroquois traders raided neighboring groups for rights to their hunting territories or to steal pelts. The use of firearms, beginning in the 1640s, made the conflicts even more deadly, further contributing to population loss (Jennings 1975, 1984; Richter 1992; Snow 1994b).

Wars of revenge and mourning were another dimension of the violent conflict and may have been equal to the pursuit of beaver furs in motivating warfare, adding to the cycle of population decline. Throughout the seventeenth century, death took a heavier toll than usual, and Iroquois warriors frequently sought foreign captives to replace family members lost to disease or to wars (Jennings 1975, 1984; Richter 1992; Snow 1994b). Although the influx of adoptees into local communities may have offset local population loss, the presence of foreigners may have placed stress on the solidarity of the Iroquois host lineages (Engelbrecht 1987; Richter 1992). In the Requickening Ceremony, after the hostage was tested by physical ordeal, the captive was adopted into the matrilineage and given the name of the deceased. Though this rite signified the social death of the captive and his or her rebirth as the lost member of a matrilineage, few totally assimilated into Iroquois society (Richter 1992). Furthermore early accounts suggest that Iroquois males may have preferred refugee brides as a means of avoiding or lessening obligations to their new household (Richards 1967; Trigger 1978).

The arrival of Jesuit missionaries to Five Nations territory in the mid–seventeenth century was another consequence of the military conflicts and large-scale adoption of foreign captives, and this also potentially contributed to changes in the traditional social relations within households. Jesuits came to Iroquois villages in part to minister to the many Huron adoptees who were Christian converts (Richter 1992:108; Stewart 1970:46). For the Iroquois, missions were also a means of ensuring peace with the French, the priests in their territory a guarantee against hostilities (Richter 1992:111).

Jesuit-Cayuga relations in the seventeenth century were quite unstable and generally defined on Iroquois terms. In 1656 the first Jesuit mission to the League Iroquois, Ste. Marie, was established in Onondaga territory. From this chapel Fr. René Menard went into Cayuga lands and founded the mission of St. Joseph, but he was turned away within two months. In 1658 the French priests were ousted from all Five Nations territory. During the 1660s war was raging between the Susquehannock and the League Iroquois. In 1664 the Cayuga requested the return of the Jesuits. In 1668 St. Joseph was reestablished, and permanent chapels were founded at St. Steven and St. René (Rogers Farm). By this time the Jesuit presence was seen as a source of strength against the Susquehannock. Opposition to the Jesuits was prevalent, however. By 1682 the

Iroquois had defeated the Susquehannock, relations with the French had deteriorated, and the missionaries were once again expelled from Native territory (Metz 1995; Richter 1992; Stewart 1970; White et al. 1978).

Many Iroquois viewed the Jesuits with heavy suspicion and rightly blamed them for the spread of disease and imminent threats to their culture. The onslaught of disease had led to an upsurge in Native cere- monialism as shaman attempted to cure the ill and protect the com- munity. The shaman who was unable to restore the health of the ailing may have lost some degree of prestige, but French priests who failed to heal the sick were treated with outright hostility, their rites of prayer and baptism seen as sorcery. Others, however, found in Christianity new spiritual answers to the societal problems induced by European contact. Conversion also meant material benefits from the priests as well as trad- ing rights (Richter 1992; Trigger 1985). Moreover during the epidemics the loss of a community's elders, who were repositories of traditional religious knowledge, made Iroquoian groups "less able at a theological level to resist the attacks of the Jesuits" (Trigger 1985:250).

Converts often found themselves persecuted by their non-Christian Iroquois brethren. They were subject to verbal abuse and physical assault and denied traditional rights and titles. At the same time, they were also strongly encouraged by the Jesuits to abandon traditional practices perceived as inimical to Christianity, such as belief in dreams, divorce, curing rituals, and indulgence in feasts (Bonvillain 1986; Richter 1992; Trigger 1985). As a result traditionalist and Christian factions emerged within Iroquois communities. These were often also politically aligned, with converts favoring the French. By the mid-1670s, the new English government at Albany began to foster relations with the Five Nations, laying the foundations of the Covenant Chain and creating an anglo- phile faction as well. Since matters of conflict were settled by consensus among the Iroquois, the primary means of dealing with such religious and political dissension was by relocating. Some Christian converts left the area completely, moving to mission villages north of Lake Ontario and becoming known as the Iroquois du Nord (Jennings 1984; Richter 1992).

Accompanying this chain of events was a reorientation of Iroquois trade relations and a shift in patterns of consumption and production of durable goods. Throughout the seventeenth century, the trade of beaver pelts with Europeans made the Iroquois participants in the emerging world-market economy and initiated sweeping changes in the Native material culture inventory. By the mid–seventeenth century, European traders were supplying Indian groups with a complement of items produced in North America and Europe specifically for the Native market, such as woolen cloth, wampum, copper kettles, and hatchets. In return for this array of objects, the Iroquois traded only one item—fur. The exchange was also unequal in terms of time, as it took far longer for the Natives to hunt and prepare peltry than it did the Europeans to produce their trade items (Delâge 1993; Jennings 1975; Richter 1992).

Typically the earliest Contact period sites show a preference for European items with functional equivalents in indigenous artifact typologies, such as beads, copper items, and cutting tools. European artifacts were often treated as raw material: iron axes were chipped, and scrap metal from copper kettles was reworked into projectile points, cutting edges, and awls. Later, artifacts that did not have Native equivalents became incorporated into the material culture inventory. Textiles, metal containers, and iron axes replaced their Native-made counterparts, and after several generations Native manufacture of pottery and lithic tools for utilitarian items ceased. Dependence on European suppliers for the tools used in everyday affairs ensued (Bradley 1987; Mandzy 1992, 1994; Richter 1992). Reliance on European sources for durable goods was also a result of the loss of many expert Native artisans who passed away during the epidemics before they were able to teach their skills to younger members of their communities (Trigger 1985:250).

Mandzy (1992, 1994) has documented a similar sequence of adoption of European artifacts for historic Cayuga sites. By the time of the historic occupation of the Rogers Farm site, there was a proliferation of European-made objects at Cayuga settlements. Although nonutilitarian objects continued to be made from traditional materials, the manufacture of pottery and lithic tools had been abandoned. The increase in European-manufactured items at mid-seventeenth-century Iroquois sites may be partially caused by the institution of the Covenant Chain in the late 1670s, which assured entry into the markets of Albany, where prices for beaver pelts were better than those previously offered by the French. It is also likely that the appearance of Jesuit missions at this time contributed to the increase. With Frenchmen within the midst of the villages, more individuals—particularly Christian converts—had access to European materials (Jennings 1984; Richter 1992).

Rogers Farm Site Investigations

The Rogers Farm site (NYSM 2502) is located in the Hunter's Home area near Savannah, Wayne County, New York, at the northern end of

Cayuga Lake. It is situated in a plowed field on a small terrace above Montezuma Marsh, to the west of the Seneca River and to the north of Crusoe Creek. The site is on lands owned by the New York State Department of Environmental Conservation and is currently under the stewardship of that agency as part of the Montezuma Wetlands preserve (Figure 9.1).

Hunter's Home is a region rich in archaeological resources, heavily dotted with sites dating from the Paleoindian through Late Woodland/Owasco periods. Occupants of these sites utilized the resources

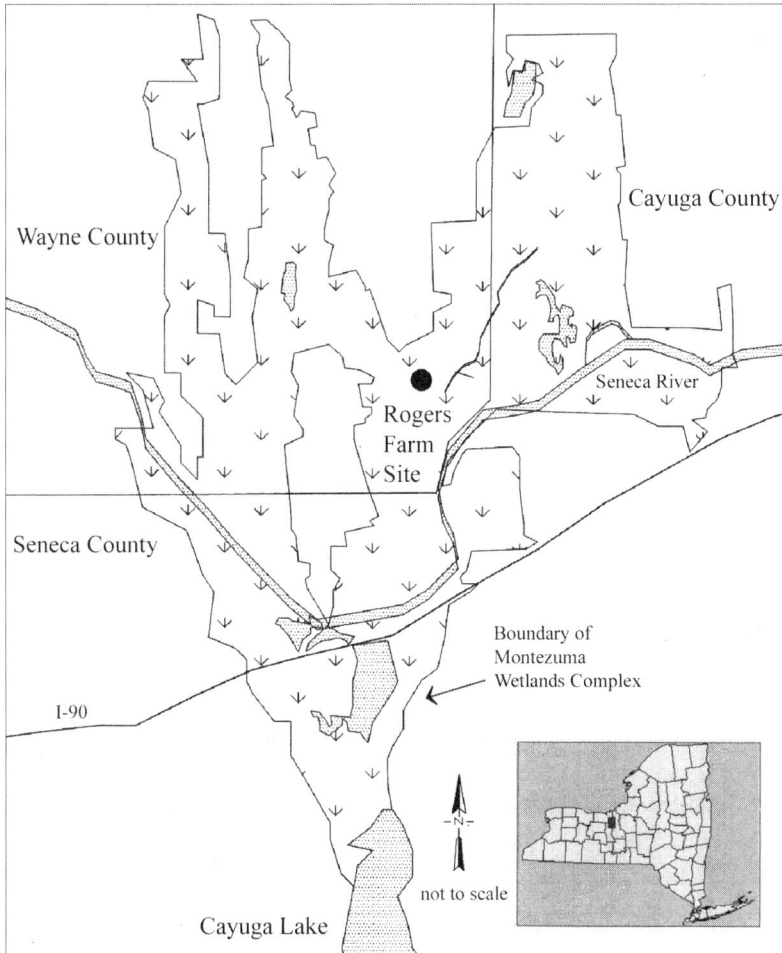

Fig. 9.1. Location of the Rogers Farm site and the Montezuma Wetlands Complex

provided by the cattail marsh and wooded swamps prominent in the area. Prehistoric occupation of Hunter's Home, however, dropped off with the development of classic Iroquois groups throughout central New York. While it is possible that local Iroquois groups continued to use the Hunter's Home area for hunting, there are no permanent settlements in the area, and no artifactual remains from this period have been identified there. However, after abandoning Hunter's Home for about 400 years, in the mid–seventeenth century the Cayuga Iroquois established a village, called Onontaré, at the Rogers Farm site (Mandzy 1990; Secor 1987). Onontaré is generally believed to have been the location of St. René, one of the three Jesuit missions established in Cayuga territory in 1668 (Mandzy 1990).

The site has been collected since its identification in the 1880s and has been plowed for over a century (Mandzy 1990). Today about half of the site has been built over by Morgan Road, several farm buildings, and a gravel parking lot at the eastern end of the area (Figure 9.2). On the basis of observations of surface scatter of historic artifacts prior to the construction of the parking lot, the seventeenth-century occupation consisted of a small village area, about 0.4 ha in extent, and it does not appear to have been palisaded (Harold Secor, personal communication, 1998). The location of the site and its lack of palisades contrast with precontact Iroquoian settlement patterns, which after A.D. 1400 were commonly sited in defensible upland locales and surrounded by stockades (Snow 1994b; Tuck 1971).

Three outlying cemetery areas are associated with the site. Two are located to the southwest of the main village area, with the third toward the eastern border of the site (Figure 9.2). These were excavated by the Rochester Museum and Science Center (RMSC) in the 1930s and by local avocational archaeologist Harold Secor in the 1980s; assemblages from these excavations are curated at the RMSC. Mandzy (1990) analyzed materials from the RMSC Rogers Farm collections, including Christianization rings, religious medals, crucifixes, a gun lock, knives, pipes, and glass beads, which he used to date the site's occupation from approximately the 1660s to the 1680s.

Archaeological excavations sponsored by the University of Pittsburgh were conducted at the Rogers Farm site during the summer of 2000. This fieldwork represents the first systematic investigations of the site. Research began with a surface collection to refine estimation of the site's boundaries and locate areas with the densest concentrations of historic materials. Provenience was assigned in 5 by 5 m collection units. Several concentrations of historic remains were noted: north of Morgan Road at the east end of the field, along the western and southern boundaries of the site, and to the extreme west of the field (Figure 9.3). The artifact cluster at the western end consisted largely of more-recent materials associated with a barn in the vicinity that was torn down several years ago.

Excavation focused on the eastern concentration of historic materials (see Figure 9.2). Initially 141 by 1 m test units were staggered across an east-west axis in 10 m intervals. Units were excavated down to sterile subsoil, which underlay the plowzone. Plowzone deposits were taken out as a single stratum and typically reached a depth of about 30 cm below surface. Possible alignments of post molds visible at the top of the subsoil were noted in several of the test units placed just north of Morgan Road. A larger area was opened around these excavations to clarify these patterns and determine if they were associated with housing remains. Ultimately a total of 40 m² of the subsurface was exposed in this location (see Figure 9.2). Excavation here also uncovered evidence of the prehistoric occupation of the site; in the following analysis, only remains pertaining to the historic village are discussed.[3]

The horizontal clearing revealed an array of postholes defining the footprint of the end of a longhouse (Figure 9.4). The longhouse end measured 6.70 m in width and an alignment of posts was apparent on the side walls, indicating sleeping benches averaging 1.55 m in depth. A storage cubicle area at the end of the house was indicated by an alignment of posts as well. A feature surrounded by reddened soil was identified at the centerline of the structure and interpreted as a hearth area. A total of about 36 m² of the house was exposed.

Deposits in the area above the longhouse contained substantial amounts of prehistoric artifacts and materials of unattributable age, including pottery fragments, lithic objects, and faunal remains. The assemblage of historic artifacts was smaller and included metal, kaolin (white ball clay), glass, and ceramic (European) remains. Artifacts that were found in this area of excavation, as well as artifacts collected in the 5 by 5 m surface collection units in the area of the horizontal excavation, are listed in Table 9.1. Also available for analysis was an assemblage of items surface-collected by Harold Secor from the same area as the horizontal excavation. Figure 9.5 illustrates the distribution of the historic artifacts across the block excavation.

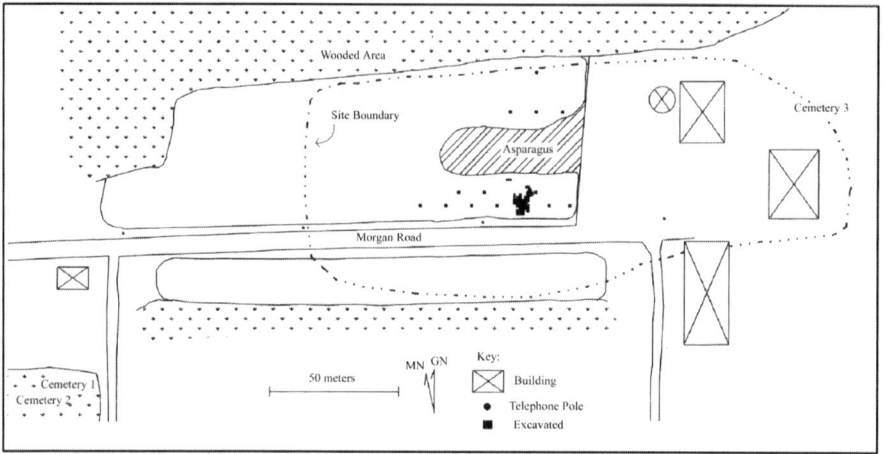

Fig. 9.2. Rogers Farm site environs, showing location of excavated areas

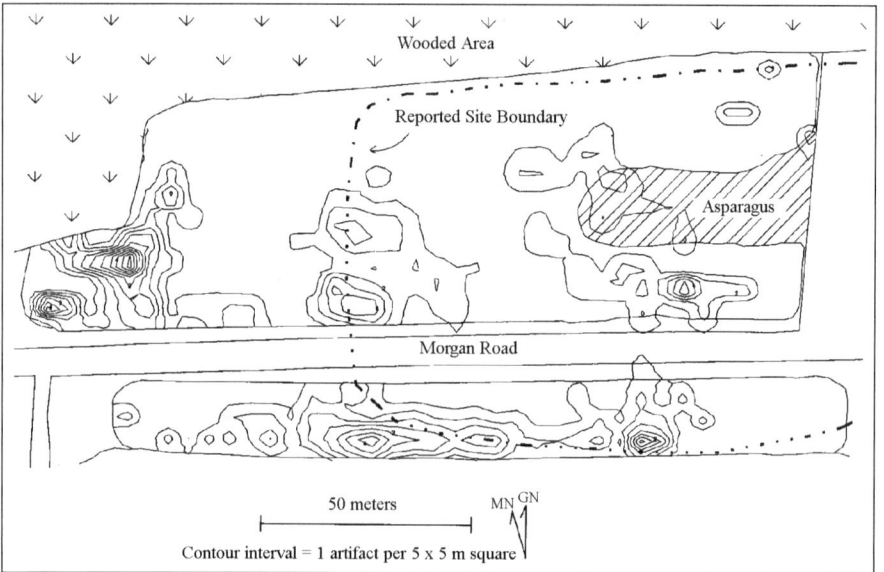

Fig. 9.3. Surface distribution of historic artifacts

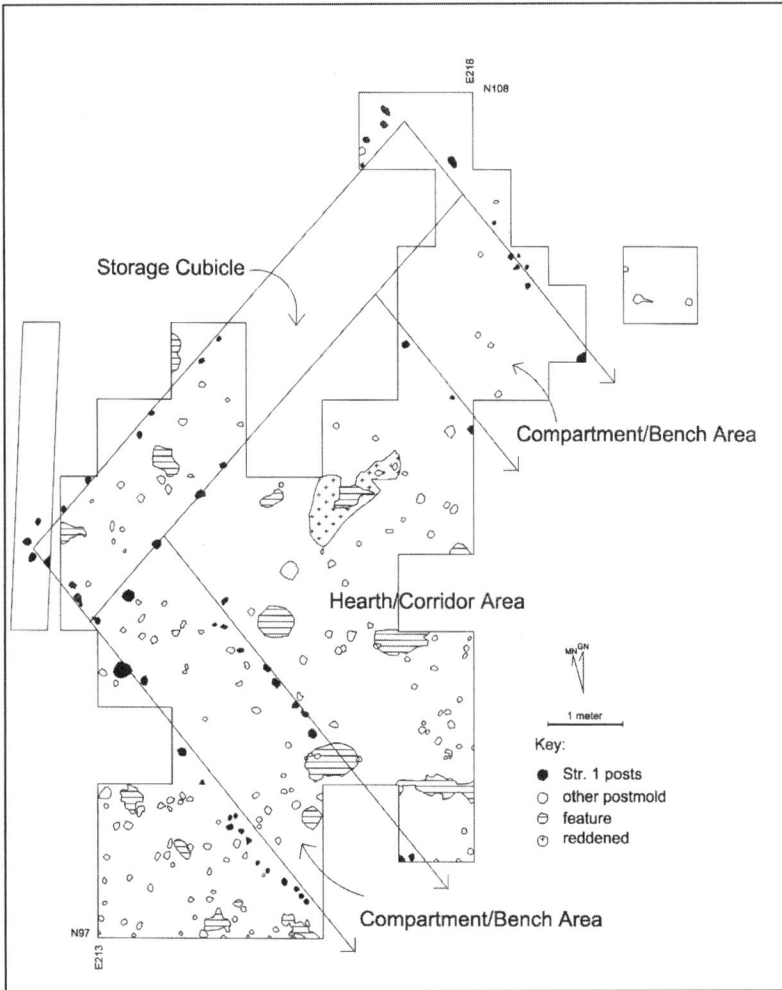

Fig. 9.4. Floor plan and interpretation of Rogers Farm longhouse end

Analyses and Discussion

House Size

Based on the site's topography, it is estimated that the house extended no farther than a total of 25 m; following the orientation of the house, there is a drop in grade to the south that was likely not built on. This would give the house a total area of approximately 167.5 m². A house of these dimensions would likely have had three or four central hearths and hosted a total of six to eight families, assuming a hearth spacing of

Table 9.1. Artifact Inventory from Longhouse Vicinity

Materials		Excavation Units	Surface Collection	Secor Collection	Totals N	%
Historic Artifacts						
Glass beads		27	1	7	35	13.9
Iron	Fragments	15	1	59	75	
	Nails	5	0	4	9	
	Knife blades	0	0	2	2	
	Gun lock	0	0	1	1	
	Chisels	0	0	2	2	
	Total	20	1	68	89	35.3
Copper/ Brass	Fragments	35	0	38	73	
	Projectile point	1	0	0	1	
	Kettle lug	0	0	1	1	
	Awl	0	0	1	1	
	Beads	0	0	2	2	
	Bangles	0	0	2	2	
	Ring	0	0	1	1	
	Bracelet	0	0	1	1	
	Total	36	0	46	82	32.5
Lead	Fragments	0	0	3	3	
	Musket balls	2	0	6	8	
	Total	2	0	9	11	4.4
Ceramic (European) Fragments		17	2	0	19	7.5
Gunflints (European)		2	0	0	2	0.8
Kaolin (white ball clay)	Fragments	8	0	0	8	
	Pipestems	0	0	6	6	
	Total	8	0	6	14	5.6
Historic Totals		112	4	136	252	100.0
Prehistoric/Unattributable Artifacts						
Lithics	Debitage	2508	70	0	2578	
	Tools	83	6	1	90	
	Fire-cracked rock	17	0	0	17	
	Groundstone	2	0	0	2	
	Total	2610	76	1	2687	43.4

Materials		Excava-tion Units	Surface Collection	Secor Collection	Totals	
					N	%
Pottery	Sherds	2117	9	0	2126	
	Pipe fragments	6	0	3	9	
	Total	2123	9	3	2135	34.5
Faunal remains	Burned bone	1135	51	0	1186	
	Unburned bone	147	0	0	147	
	Teeth	28	0	0	28	
	Modified bone	7	0	0	7	
	Shell	2	0	0	2	
	Total	1319	51	0	1370	22.1
Prehistoric/unattributable Totals		6052	136	4	6192	100.0

about 6 m based on Snow's (1997:81) reading of ethnohistoric records and observations of Mohawk houses indicating that compartments along the sides of a longhouse tended to be as long as the house was wide, with hearths placed centrally within compartments.

There are no longhouse data from contemporary historic Cayuga sites against which to compare the estimated size of the Rogers Farm longhouse, nor do available data for partially excavated precontact Cayuga houses permit assessment of total house size (see below). However, the house does seem to be similar in size to longhouses uncovered at other Contact period sites, such as at the late-seventeenth-century Mohawk site of Caughnawaga (Grassman 1969; Grumet 1995:366; Snow 1989), as well as on historic sites in Ontario, such as Ball (Knight 1989) and Le Caron (Johnston and Jackson 1980). Historical houses in these areas show a general decrease in house size when compared to precontact longhouses (Dodd 1984; Snow 1989; Warrick 1996).

These smaller longhouses and correspondingly smaller households are a reflection of the sheer demographic decline across Iroquoia. When the residents of Rogers Farm constructed new houses, they built them to accommodate households that were reduced in size by the earlier epidemics and other sources of population loss. Additionally population decline may have resulted in a shortage of labor, which would have been further compounded by the increased amount of time that males, who were responsible for building longhouses, spent away from the village for trading, military, and diplomatic missions (Richards 1967, 1969; Tooker 1984; Trigger 1985). The use of smaller longhouses would have helped reduce the amount of labor needed for construction and maintenance.

Longhouse Structural Attributes

Although data on house size are incomplete, longhouse remains from precontact Cayuga sites enable other comparisons of structural attributes. In order to assess the degree of change in traditional household organization and domestic material culture, the Rogers Farm longhouse was compared to floor plans of six Late Prehistoric and Protohistoric period houses. Data for two partially excavated longhouses at the Klinko site and three partially excavated longhouses at the Carman site were available for analysis (Kathleen Allen, personal communication, 2000). A small segment of a longhouse wall and interior was also identified at the Indian Fort Road site (Baugher and Clark 1998:46). All three sites are located southwest of Cayuga Lake; the Klinko and Indian Fort Road sites date to the late fifteenth to early sixteenth centuries, and Carman dates to the mid–sixteenth to early seventeenth centuries (Baugher and Clark 1998; Niemczycki 1984:73–74). Though the sample of excavated longhouses in the area is meager in comparison to those in the Huron, Neutral, and Mohawk areas, regional variations in longhouse construction have been noted (e.g., Allen and Williams-Shuker 1998; Dodd 1984; Kapches 1994; Snow 1997), making structural comparisons with Cayuga houses more desirable when possible. Measurements of house width, average bench width, wall post-mold density, interior post-mold density, and feature density were taken and compared with these attributes of the Contact period house at Rogers Farm (Table 9.2; Figure 9.6). Summary statistics and 95 percent confidence intervals were computed for the earlier houses (Table 10.3).

In most aspects the longhouse at Rogers Farm differs little from the structures at the earlier sites. The depth of the benches is consistent with the approximate 1.5 m standard size seen across Iroquoia, showing that the Native unit of measurement noted by Kapches (1993), the *ten*, was still expressed by residential architecture. Furthermore, while demographic decline and the death of a community's artisans may have led to the loss of Native technologies such as ceramic and lithic manufacture (Trigger 1985), traditional architectonic principles continued to be practiced. Like the precontact Cayuga houses, the Rogers Farm longhouse features a central hearth, sleeping platforms, and end storage area.

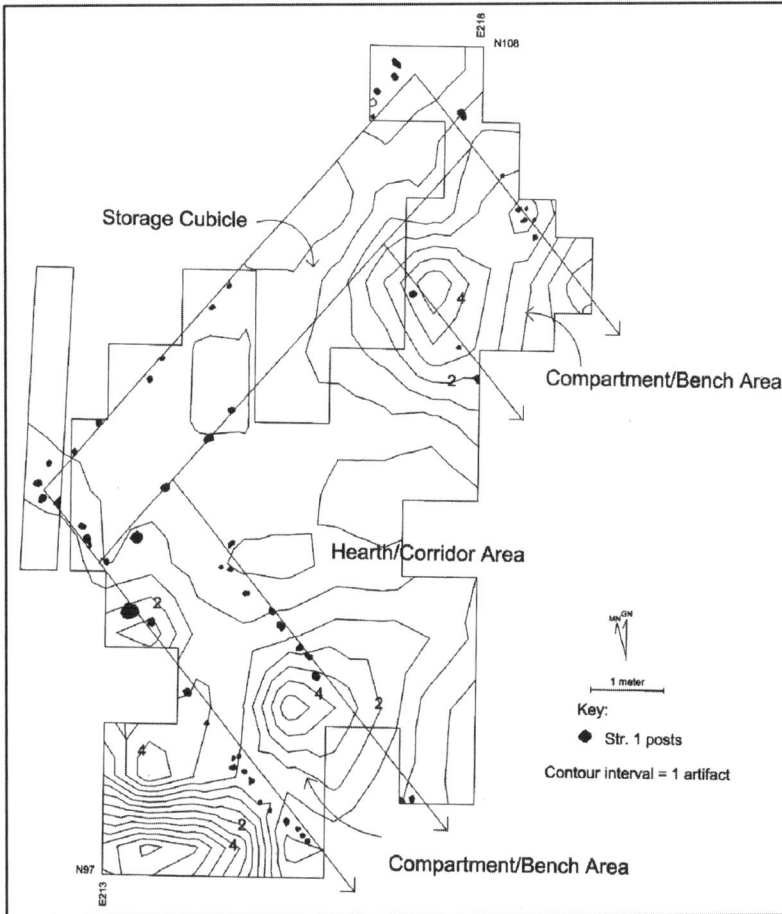

Fig. 9.5. Distribution of historic artifacts within longhouse

Additionally, by maintaining the traditional longhouse layout, the Rogers Farm structure demonstrates a continuation in the amount of privacy afforded to its inhabitants. Often domestic architecture is divided into public and private zones, either physically or conceptually, with back areas of a house sheltering private activities such as sleep, sexual intimacy, or food preparation (Sanders 1990:68). In a longhouse these activities would have taken place within spatially delineated locales, the facing compartments of the families sharing a hearth. However, any privacy these areas offered would be quickly and easily violated as they were within view of any person walking through the central corridor of the house. Given the redundant "railroad car" layout of the living spaces within a longhouse, such foot traffic would have been frequent and unavoidable. The openness of Iroquoian living compartments mirrors that of present-day Dayak longhouses in Borneo; of these Helliwell (1992) argues that permeability within structures reinforces community relationships and serves as a means of social control. Such architectural features underscore the social and economic obligations of the occupants of an Iroquoian household and suggest that the cooperative endeavors of household membership persisted into the late seventeenth century despite the social stresses associated with the period.

Similarities in interior post density and feature density indicate that the household members were utilizing the space within the house as intensively during the Contact period as before. Although the households and their homes may have been reduced in size, the remaining populations appear to have been carrying out household activities with the same frequency. This may also have resulted from sustaining household membership by the inclusion of foreign captives and refugees. At Rogers Farm the presence of a possible ossuary—identified during the 1930s excavation of the cemetery area to the southwest of the main

Table 9.2. Comparison of Longhouse Attributes at Precontact Cayuga Sites and at the Rogers Farm Site

Longhouse	Width (m)	Bench Depth (m)	Wall Density (posts/m)	Interior Post Density (posts/m²)	Feature Density (features/m²)
Klinko House 1	5.50	1.46	2.20	0.57	0.05
Klinko House 2	5.30	1.45	2.26	0.92	0.06
Carman House 1	6.10	1.50	2.60	1.80	0.16
Carman House 2	6.40	1.40	2.70	2.40	0.20
Carman House 3	—	—	3.79	2.65	—
Indian Fort Road longhouse	—	—	2.50	1.05	—
Rogers Farm longhouse	6.70	1.55	2.18	2.40	0.19

village area—indicates that Huron groups may have resided at the site (Mandzy 1990). This is tentatively suggested by the width of the house as well. Among the Cayuga longhouses examined, the one at Rogers Farm is the widest, surpassing the upper limit of the 95 percent confidence interval, making the 6.7 m width somewhat unusual compared to the earlier houses (see Table 9.3). If the population of historic longhouses has the same average width and variability as shown in the precontact sample, the observed value from Rogers Farm would be considered a rare occurrence. Although at 0.5 m the difference between the width of the Rogers Farm house and the widths of the earlier Cayuga structures is not an especially strong one, it is a highly significant one given the range of variability. Wide houses are associated in particular with the Huron; a sample of 125 longhouses examined by Dodd (1984:408) produced an average width of 7.2 m. If this observation is in fact the result of Huron influence on longhouse construction, it represents an interesting example of sociocultural expression through domestic architecture.

The Rogers Farm longhouse departs from the precontact data in one other suggestive way. Among the earlier houses, there are strong, positive significant correlations among the wall-post, interior-post, and feature density variables (Table 9.4). In the Rogers Farm structure, however, wall-post density did not increase with interior-post density. A regression

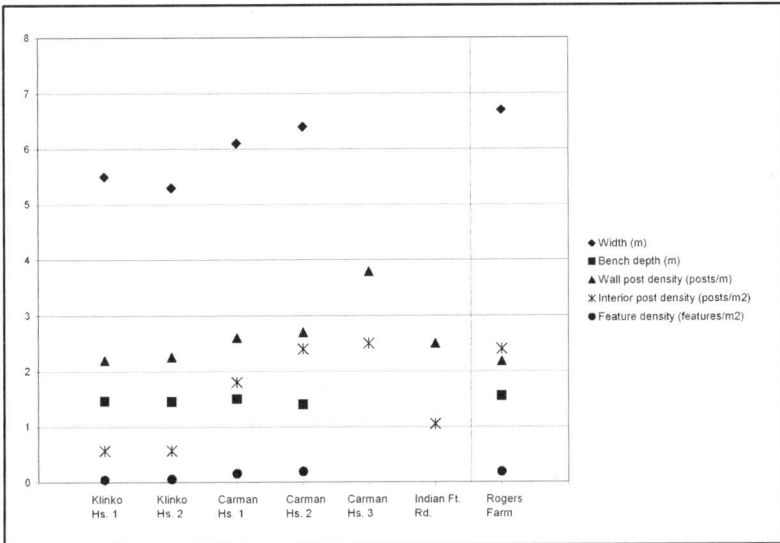

Fig. 9.6. Comparison of longhouse attributes at precontact Cayuga sites and at the Rogers Farm site

Table 9.3. Summary Statistics of Longhouse Attributes from Precontact Cayuga Sites

Statistic	Width (m)	Bench Depth (m)	Wall Post Density (posts/m)	Interior Post Density (posts/m²)	Feature Density (features/m²)
Mean	5.83	1.45	2.68	1.57	0.12
St. dev.	0.51	0.04	0.58	0.85	0.07
St. error	0.26	0.02	0.24	0.35	0.04
95% Confidence interval	5.01 – 6.64	1.38 – 1.52	2.07 – 3.28	0.67 – 2.46	0.00 – 0.24

of these factors in the precontact houses predicts that the Rogers Farm house should have 3.15 wall post molds per meter of perimeter wall ($r = .831, p = .040, Y = 1.787 + .567X$). The observed value of 2.18 posts per meter shows that, given the intensity of use, there were fewer repair episodes to the wall than expected. This may reflect several aspects about the longhouse's residents. As mentioned previously, it is generally reported that males during the Contact period spent an increased amount of time away from their communities (Richards 1967, 1969; Trigger 1985); their absence may have resulted in less attention to the maintenance of a village's longhouses. Alternatively the presence of iron nails in the artifact assemblage from the longhouse vicinity may indicate the use of building technologies that made the house walls more durable than all-bark construction. The use of iron hinges was noted by Harmen van den Bogaert while traveling through a Mohawk village in 1634 (Gehring and Starna 1988:4), demonstrating the household-level use of European hardware for traditional forms of material culture.

Spatial Organization

Another question that can be explored with the domestic material from Rogers Farm is the question of household membership. Ceramic analysis has been used to reconstruct the kinship relations structuring Iroquoian communities (e.g., Allen 1988; Engelbrecht 1974; Whallon 1968). This approach is not possible at the Rogers Farm site, as pottery was no longer manufactured at the village (De Orio 1978; Mandzy 1990, 1992, 1994). Instead an analysis of the organization of space within the structures was conducted, following Kapches's (1990) spatial

Table 9.4. Correlation Coefficients of Longhouse Variables

		Wall Post Density	Interior Post Density	Feature Density
Wall post density	Pearson correlation	1.000	.831	.997
	Significance	—	.040	.003
	N	6	6	4
Interior post density	Pearson correlation	.831	1.000	.990
	Significance	.040	—	.010
	N	6	6	4
Feature density	Pearson correlation	.997	.990	1.000
	Significance	.003	.010	—
	N	4	4	6

dynamics model. This model suggests that a correlation exists between the amount of organized space within a structure and matrilineal orientation of household membership. Four of the longhouses in the sample were believed to have been excavated sufficiently to be representative of the entire structure. The proportion of the total excavated house area devoted to permanent and semipermanent features (sleeping benches, storage cubicles, and hearths) was calculated (Table 9.5). At Rogers Farm the amount of organized space is less than that of the precontact longhouses, suggesting that definition of longhouse membership on the basis of matrilineal relationship was less structured. Kapches (1990:63) also noted a decrease in organized space at the historic Ball site, which she has suggested may partially have resulted from the societal stresses caused by European interaction.

The impact of European contact on the social structure of Iroquoian groups has received a fair amount of attention. Richards (1967, 1969) contends that matrilocal postmarital rules of residence were a product of the Contact period, resulting from the increased duration and frequency of male absences from the village. Rothenberg (1979) likewise argues that women's control over agricultural resources, and the power connected with this authority, was augmented by the absence of males. Others have argued that involvement in the fur trade and warfare strengthened the economic importance and prestige of males at the expense of the clan matrons, who had previously governed household matters. As traders and warriors challenged hereditary chiefs, their authority and the matrilineal ties binding households eroded (Hayden 1977; Hayden and Cannon 1982; Smith 1970).

It is posited here that the matrilineage and matrilocal residence rules became less important in defining household membership, but for a different set of reasons. The loss of family members in the course of the population decline endured by Iroquoian groups in the seventeenth century meant the fragmentation of lineages (Warrick 1996). It is likely that there were no longer enough members of a matrilineal household to undertake necessary tasks of food and craft production and that household membership was therefore defined by criteria other than the matriliny. It is also possible that the social mechanisms for maintaining traditional household organization became overwhelmed by the sheer numbers of nonlocal people living in the Iroquois communities. The strategy of literally replacing population may have broken down, and lineage solidarity could no longer be sustained (Engelbrecht 1985; Richter 1992; Snow 1994b). Factionalism across religious and political lines would have further contributed to the fragmentation of lineage solidarity. Intrahousehold dissent may have prompted some to move to other households with common views and religious practices, forcing a more flexible pattern of household definition. Two of the seventeenth-century ethnohistoric cases presented by Richards (1967) describe ad hoc living arrangements among the Huron after epidemics swept the region. Additionally Snow (1989:298) suggests that the small, standardized longhouses at Caughnawaga represent the repackaging of surviving members of kinship groups. While not enough of the Rogers Farm

Table 9.5. Organization of Space in Select Cayuga Longhouses

Long-house	Total Excavated Area (m²)	Bench Area (m²)	Storage Cubicle Area (m²)	Hearth Area (m²)	Total Organized Space	
					m²	%*
Klinko House 1	64.89	29.72	12.00	2.10	43.82	67.5
Klinko House 2	53.06	24.86	10.99	1.40	37.25	70.2
Carman House 1	112.84	47.22	20.33	5.20	72.75	64.5
Rogers Farm long-house	36.55	10.66	10.50	0.60	21.76	59.5

*Summary statistics of percent organized space for precontact sites: mean = 67.4%; st. dev. = 2.87; st. error = 1.66; 95% confidence interval = 60.22%–74.88%; n = 3.

community plan is known to conclude that the houses were of standard size, the household evidence does point to population reduction, presence of foreigners, and reduction in matrilineal control over structures, supporting this interpretation of events.

Historic Artifact Assemblage

The historic artifacts found in association with the longhouse demonstrate that household patterns of consumption and production of durable goods had changed in the seventeenth century. Based on analysis of burial materials from the Rogers Farm site, it was previously demonstrated that the production of lithic and ceramic items had dropped off (De Orio 1978; Mandzy 1990, 1992, 1994). These were activities traditionally undertaken within the context of the household (Allen 1992). The excavation of the longhouse did yield quantities of pottery and lithic artifacts, but the pottery and projectile points can be associated with the prehistoric occupations of the area. The majority of the lithic remains, as well as the faunal remains, are not attributable to either period, however. Nevertheless the assemblage does show changes in the household material culture inventory and technology.

Although Native technology of pottery had declined, this did not spell the end of household-based manufacture of goods for both utilitarian and nonutilitarian purposes. European-made materials are present both in modified and unmodified form. Examples of unmodified items include iron knives, lead shot, a portion of a gunlock mechanism, and glass trade beads. Modified items include iron scraps apparently sharpened into chisels, a projectile point, beads, awl point, and items of personal adornment fashioned out of copper/brass fragments, presumably cut from kettles (see Table 9.1). Interestingly, analysis of burial data from Rogers Farm by Mandzy (1992, 1994) indicates quantities of nonutilitarian objects made of native materials. With the exception of a broken slate gorget recovered near the house, which may predate the village, no such items were present in the longhouse excavations.

The incorporation of these new materials for many of the daily tasks undertaken by the household is evident. Many activities associated with the historic artifacts are similar to what would be seen at a prehistoric longhouse (Table 9.6). The majority of the household-associated artifacts represent mundane activities such as food preparation and craft manufacture. Materials related to cooking, eating, and food storage include ceramic fragments and a copper/brass kettle lug. Craft production

Table 9.6. Household Activities Represented by Artifact Assemblage

Mundane Activities		Warfare/ Hunting		Nonutilitarian		
Item	No.	Item	No.	Item	No.	Total
Iron knife blades	2	Gun lock mechanism	1	Glass beads	35	
Iron chisels	2	Copper/brass point	1	Kaolin pipestems and fragments	14	
Iron nails	9	Lead musket balls and fragments	11	Copper/brass jewelry	6	
Copper/brass kettle lug	1	Gunflints	2			
Copper/brass awl	1					
Ceramic fragments	19					
Iron fragments	75					
Copper/brass fragments	73					
Total mundane	182	Total warfare/ hunting	15	Total nonutilitarian	55	252
Percent of total assemblage	72	Percent of total assemblage	6	Percent of total assemblage	22	

is indicated by implements such as knife blades, chisels, awls, and nails, as well as by iron and copper/brass fragments that are byproducts of manufacturing activities. Also present in the assemblage are artifacts associated with warfare and hunting, including the gunlock mechanism, lead musket balls, and the copper/brass projectile point, emphasizing the role of the household in organizing military and hunting parties. Jennings (1975:88–89) also notes the extensive labor and skill required by the household and village in supporting trading activities, describing the preparation of pelts for trade as a cottage industry. A relatively high frequency of nonutilitarian items, which are typically quite rare on precontact sites, appears in the Rogers Farm household assemblage. Artifacts representing nonutilitarian functions include glass trade beads, copper/brass jewelry (e.g., bangles and tubular beads), and kaolin pipestems and fragments. Their prevalence is likely indicative of the increase in ceremonialism taking place within the context of the household as an aftereffect of the epidemics (Trigger 1985:250). Additionally the site shows a proliferation in European objects over earlier Cayuga sites (Mandzy 1992, 1994), and the ready availability of the materials may have influenced patterns of curation. Trade, warfare, and ritual were all activities conducted in the traditional household (Heidenreich 1971:114); the historical processes of the Contact period likely resulted in an intensification of these practices, rather than a complete overhaul of their organization.

The distribution of artifacts within the longhouse suggests that traditional notions of shared social and economic obligations within the household persisted at the time of Rogers Farm's occupation. Three clusters of historic artifacts appear in the house segment; denser concentrations appear under both benches, with a third, smaller concentration along the south wall (see Figure 9.5). The impression is that one family did not seem to control significantly more resources than another. The presence of the end storage cubicle further indicates the communal economy of the longhouse. Well into the eighteenth century, based on the observations of European travelers in Iroquois lands, it appears that "the vast majority of Iroquois continued to operate in a traditional native nexus of reciprocity and redistribution" (Richter 1992:263). The mechanisms of the fur trade followed Iroquoian rites of gift giving, generosity, and reciprocity (Richter 1992; Trigger 1985). In addition cooperative work groups of women continued to be responsible for horticultural production and the bulk of the community's food reserves (Brown 1970; Rothenberg 1979). Participation in a capitalist economy and the emerging world market via the fur trade does not seem to have led to a loss of the ethos of reciprocity and corporate nature of the household (Delâge 1993; Richter 1992).

Conclusions

From a reading of the broad-scale processes described in the historical literature concerned with European contact, one may expect the tumult of the period to have left the organization and activities of Iroquois households in a state far different from the state of affairs prior to the Contact period. Household-scale analysis of the Rogers Farm site tempers such a view. In some ways the large-scale processes—those affecting the nation, tribe, all indigenous peoples—are reflected in the household, but in other ways they are not. The evidence from the Rogers Farm site indicates that many features of the traditional Iroquois household endured in the face of the Contact period. The household adapted to the various forces of population decline by shrinking the longhouse to fit the downsized groups, but they still occupied their homes as intensively and still utilized distinctively Iroquoian architecture. The household began using new, European-supplied materials and developed new ways to work them, but carried on many of the same activities. The various historical events associated with the Contact period meant that household membership may no longer have been strictly matrilineal and became more flexible, but the household still functioned as a cooperative whole.

The "bottom-up" perspective permits a more nuanced view of the Iroquois during the Contact period. It is clear that micro- and macro-scale approaches to the period complement and inform each other. Interpretation of the household-scale evidence was guided by the broader historical narrative; in turn the information of local-level processes can deepen the overall understanding of the period. By considering the period from multiple perspectives, we can hope to create a richer picture of a period and its legacy, which remain important, politically charged areas of study.

Notes

1. I would like to express my appreciation to Laurie E. Miroff and Timothy D. Knapp for their efforts in putting together this volume and for their invitation to participate. Thanks are owed to Kathleen Allen, Laurie E. Miroff, and Timothy D. Knapp for their suggestions on draft versions of this paper and to this chapter's two reviewers for their comments. I am grateful to Harold Secor for sharing his time and knowledge of the area's archaeological resources, as well as for granting access to his personal collections from the Rogers Farm site. The project was sponsored by the University of Pittsburgh's Department of Anthropology in conjunction with its summer archaeological field school program. I am especially thankful to Kathleen Allen, Tracy Michaud Stutzman, and Kurt Jordan for contributing their expertise during fieldwork, as well as for the hard work and dedication of the field school's students. Several individuals were instrumental in helping me organize the project and get it off the ground, including Penelope Drooker, Charles Vandrei, Philip Lord, David Odell, and David Woodruff—their assistance is deeply appreciated. I am also grateful to Michael Shuker for lending his insight into the data, and for his support and encouragement as I worked on this essay. Any errors or omissions in the text, of course, are purely my own doing.

2. In discussing scale here, I utilize a colloquial interpretation of the word *scale* rather than the geographer's definition. That is, I refer to the region or nation as a broad- or large-scale area and to the community or household as fine- or small-scale area.

3. Materials related to the prehistoric components at Rogers Farm were mixed with the seventeenth-century assemblage throughout the site. Prehistoric features encountered in the block excavation included two basin-shaped pits containing Point Peninsula pottery types as well as several shallow pits of indeterminate age; all were truncated by plowing activity. In addition post molds outlining a small oblong structure, presumably predating the historic longhouse, were identified. A complete report of the excavations at the Rogers Farm site can be found in Williams-Shuker 2005.

10

Regional Diversity and Colonialism in Eighteenth-Century Iroquoia

Kurt A. Jordan

Examinations of regional variation are a staple of the archaeological literature on the Precolumbian and protohistoric Northeast (e.g., Kuhn and Sempowski 2001; Niemczycki 1984; Sempowski 1994; Versaggi 1999a).[1] However, in Postcolumbian periods of the Iroquois sequence there has been surprisingly little consideration of differences in cultural and economic practices among the Five (and, after 1722, Six) Nations. Lack of systematic comparison is particularly evident in studies of eighteenth-century Iroquois peoples. Scholarly works have concentrated either on diplomatic and military affairs at the scale of the Confederacy (e.g., Aquila 1997; Fenton 1998; Parmenter 1999; Richter 1992) or have remained rooted in National or local concerns (Guldenzopf 1986; Kuhn and Funk 2000; Snow 1995b; Wallace 1969; Wray 1973). Although it is widely recognized that individual Iroquois Nations had different sorts of alliances and animosities with the European and Native powers on their borders, the impact of such differences on local political economic processes have not been addressed.

Archaeology remains an important source of local-level data, and the poorly developed nature of eighteenth-century Iroquois archaeology has inhibited comparative treatments both within Iroquoia and with better-known areas outside the region. Iroquois sites from this era rarely have been subject to sustained archaeological research; excavations of domestic areas have been particularly sparse and much of the data remain unpublished (Jordan 2002:33–56). Mohawk sites have been the most systematically explored (Guldenzopf 1986; Hagerty 1985; Kuhn and Funk 2000; Moody and Fisher 1989; Rick 1991; Snow 1995b), but new data and reanalysis of existing information from the Seneca region (Jordan 2002, 2003, 2004) now permit more detailed comparison to take place.

Archaeological and documentary evidence reveals significantly different cultural and economic practices in the Seneca and Mohawk areas during the eighteenth century, divergences so great that they represent forms of local political economy different not by degree but in kind. The apparent "Europeanization" seen among the Mohawks that is often taken to be the norm for all of the Six Nations is in fact atypical. Comparison helps to expose the key causative role European territorial encroachment played in forcing so-called acculturative changes in the Mohawk Valley and also helps to highlight the significant political-economic innovation that took place in the more autonomous Seneca region.

This study makes use of previously published documentary and excavation data from the Mohawk region, focusing mainly on the principal Mohawk sites of Fort Hunter and Indian Castle (Figure 10.1). In addition to revisiting published sources, analysis of the Seneca region draws on data from the Townley-Read site (Jordan 2002). Townley-Read (occupied circa 1715–54) was a "neighborhood" within the first dispersed community in the Postcolumbian Seneca sequence (Jordan 2004). Many of the political-economic patterns established at Townley-Read were maintained at later Seneca sites such as Kanadesaga and Genesee Castle. The comparative examination of locally specific evidence from the Mohawk and Seneca regions dating to the 1710–79 period reveals markedly divergent practices in terms of subsistence, settlement, and social relations.

Evidence for Regional Divergence, 1710–1779

Housing

Eighteenth-century Iroquois residences can be classified as being built in Iroquoian, European frame or masonry, European log, or intercultural styles (Jordan 2002:383–440). The Mohawk region provides evidence both for the use of a wide variety of house forms and the construction of true European-style houses at an early date. Using post-Revolutionary Mohawk war claims for compensation for property abandoned in 1777, Guldenzopf (1986) determined that two classes of Mohawk houses—which he terms "elite" and "common"—existed by the time of the Revolution. Although the war claims inventories should not be used uncritically, as they were recorded and paid at a time when British officials sought to carry favor with Mohawk leader Joseph Brant (Taylor 2006:254–255), they were checked for accuracy by colonial officials opposed to Brant and are likely to accurately measure the scale of differences among Mohawk houses and property holdings (Guldenzopf 1986:191–195).

Elite dwellings were often elaborate houses built in European styles, evidenced by (1) a 1750 documentary reference to an obviously European-style two-story dwelling at Fort Hunter (Doblin and Starna 1994:35); (2) the archaeologically-recovered traces of the stone foundation, Dutch-style Brant House dwelling at Indian Castle, occupied circa 1754–77 (Guldenzopf 1986); (3) the remains of the stone-foundation Enders House at Fort Hunter, built circa 1760 (Moody and Fisher 1989; Snow 1995b; and (4) a 1773 documentary description of a village fire at Fort Hunter relating that two Mohawk-owned frame structures had burned down (Sullivan et al. 1921–1965:8:753). Common structures in the Mohawk Valley from 1710 to 1779 are poorly understood; none has been fully excavated. Hagerty's (1985:275–283) description of the remains of a mid-eighteenth-century Mohawk "cabin" on Oak Hill does not mention any attempt to locate subplowzone features that might have provided information on the methods used to construct the dwelling. Documentary descriptions are too cursory to determine in what style or styles nonelite houses were built, although some were definitely constructed with logs (Lord 1996).[2] Scholars' reconstructions of nonelite Mohawk housing patterns (e.g., Snow 2001b:23; Snow and Guldenzopf 1998:36) therefore should be treated as models to be tested rather

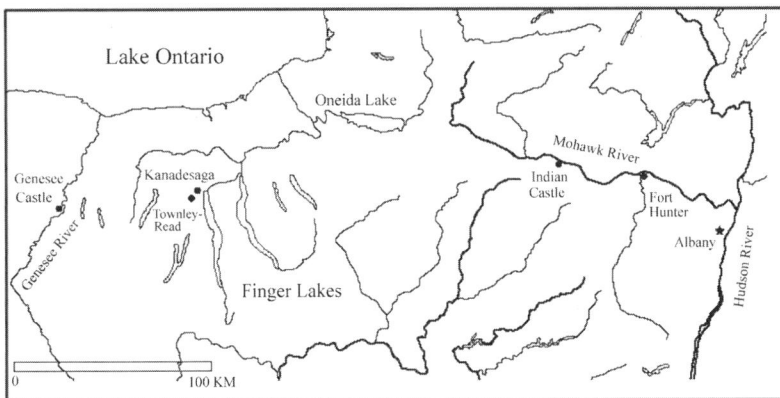

Fig. 10.1. Location of Mohawk and Seneca sites mentioned in the text; Albany is provided as a reference point. Base map adapted from Premier USA Map Collection, Map Resources, Lambertville, NJ, 2002 edition

than fully supported conclusions. The Mohawk war-claims inventories indicate that outbuildings, including barns, were common on both elite and nonelite houselots by 1777 (Guldenzopf 1986).

The structures used by Senecas offer a dramatic contrast. At the 1715–54 Townley-Read site, the floorplan of a short longhouse dwelling (*sensu* Kapches 1984) was recovered (Jordan 2003). This structure clearly has an Iroquoian floorplan with four weight-bearing interior support posts, meaning it likely contained a central hearth and two sleeping platforms. Based on the presence of a significant number of iron nails, the limited use of large and square posts in exterior walls, and the decreased frequency of wall posts as compared to earlier structures, we can interpret the Townley-Read structure as an "intercultural/creolized" dwelling. It was built using a core set of Iroquoian architectural principles, while its builders at the same time made significant use of European tools and hardware and substituted more rigid log, pole, or plank siding for traditional bark (Jordan 2003).

Documents from the 1779 American Sullivan expedition into Seneca territory (Conover 1887; Division of Archives and History 1929) suggest that such intercultural dwellings may have made up the majority of the Seneca housing stock at later sites, including Kanadesaga and Genesee Castle (Jordan 2002:421–424). Although expedition members described most Seneca houses as "cabins" sided with whole or split logs or planks, the American soldiers' journals also make frequent reference to traditional Iroquoian features such as sleeping compartments, gable-end doors, end storage compartments, bark roofing and possibly siding, and smoke holes. Many of these architectural details are incompatible with European forms of log construction, making 1779-era Seneca "cabins" likely more akin to the Townley-Read short longhouse than European notched-log dwellings.

Definite European-style houses—which expedition members called "Tory houses," "buildings of English construction," or "frame" houses— also were found in Seneca territory. However, they were rare, being mentioned at only seven of the 17 Seneca sites destroyed by the Sullivan expedition, and for the most part relatively new, as they were predominantly located at sites settled in the 1760s or after (Jordan 2004:42–43). The builders and occupants of these European-style structures cannot be determined with certitude, although loyalists lived in the vicinity of several of the settlements with "Tory houses" (Hayden 1901:92; Murray 1908:118–119).[3] The European-style houses in the Seneca region were in no way as elaborate as the examples from the Mohawk Valley, and the overall impression of Revolutionary-era Seneca housing is one of rough equality, in contrast to clear Mohawk residential stratification. There is no mention of Seneca stone foundation or multiple-story dwellings or barns in any of the Sullivan journals.

Use of Domesticated Animals

Kuhn and Funk (2000) indicate that the combined eighteenth-century Mohawk mammalian faunal deposits recovered from the Fort Hunter and Indian Castle sites contained 53.6 percent European domesticated animals, including pig, cow, sheep or goat, horse, and cat remains. The lower stratum at the Enders House site, dating to 1750–60 and thus overlapping in part with the end of the occupation at Townley-Read, contained 57.2 percent European domesticates (Rick 1991).[4] European chicken, rat, and house mouse remains also were recovered from these Mohawk sites. The 1777-era Mohawk war claims document the ownership of pigs, cattle, horses, sheep, and oxen (including "milk cows" and "fatning hogs") in small numbers by most Mohawk households (Guldenzopf 1986:195–208). All of these data are consistent with household use of domesticated animals for meat, dairy products, wool, transportation, traction, and hides. The frequent mention of barns in the war claims indicates that some of these animals resided on Mohawk farms for at least part of the year.

In contrast mammalian remains recovered from the Townley-Read site contained only 2.6 percent European domesticates, consisting of 2.3 percent pig and 0.3 percent cow remains (Adam Watson, personal communication, 2007).[5] Seneca use of European domesticated animals increased slightly subsequent to the occupation at Townley-Read but still remained at low levels in the 1779 villages described by Sullivan expedition members and captives (Conover 1887; Division of Archives and History 1929; Merrifield 1915) and even on Seneca Reservations in the 1790s (Lantz 1980; Wallace 1969:191).[6] Additionally there is no evidence for animal-related outbuildings at any pre-Reservation Seneca settlement.

Participation in the Fur Trade

Primary production for the beaver trade does not seem to have received much emphasis in either the Mohawk or Seneca regions during the eighteenth century. Beaver remains made up only 4.6 percent of the mammalian number of identified specimens (NISP) at Fort Hunter, 0.4 percent of mammalian NISP at Indian Castle, and 3.1 percent at Townley-Read

(Kuhn and Funk 2000:Table 4; Adam Watson, personal communication, 2007). Even accounting for the fact that the bones of beavers procured from far-off hunting territories would be unlikely to be deposited in homeland villages, the percentage of beaver at all these eighteenth-century Iroquois sites represents a substantial decrease from the 7.7 percent level seen at the 1657–79 Mohawk Jackson-Everson site (Kuhn and Funk 2000:Table 4; occupation dates from Snow 1995b:403).

The faunal data show that the Mohawks and the Senecas responded differently to eighteenth-century changes in the fur trade. Mohawks largely turned away from primary production in the fur trade, although they continued to play an important role as middlemen in the illegal fur trade between Albany merchants and direct producers in the St. Lawrence Valley (Parmenter 2001). In the Seneca region, hunters concentrated on primary production of deerskins. At Townley-Read 79.7 percent of mammalian NISP consisted of white-tailed deer remains (Adam Watson, personal communication, 2007); deer made up 59–86 percent of identified vertebrate specimens in each of the six eighteenth-century excavation loci at Townley-Read. Both the high proportion of deer remains—a level not seen in the Mohawk Valley since Precolumbian times (Kuhn and Funk 2000:Table 3)—and the fact that they occurred at a site in which a good portion of clothing would have been made from European cloth rather than deer hides suggest that subsistence deer hunting had been supplemented by commercial deer hunting. Remains of a number of other pelt-bearing animals, including raccoon, black bear, gray fox, muskrat, pine marten, fisher, and red fox, also were recovered at Townley-Read, evidencing a diverse pelt procurement strategy.

Farming Practices

Textual sources indicate that Seneca agriculture remained centered on the extensive cultivation of maize, beans, and squash through the American Revolution (Conover 1887; Division of Archives and History 1929). Documents also demonstrate that some non-Mohawk Iroquois adopted select European plants during the eighteenth century, including tree crops such as apples and peaches and garden crops such as watermelons, potatoes, cucumbers, cabbage, turnips, and peas (Bartram 1966 [1751]:42; Conover 1887; Division of Archives and History 1929; Halsey 1989:132–133).

At Townley-Read, surface survey and excavation indicate that houses were located 60–80 meters apart in a line along a stream. Houses were placed adjacent to a basin of floodplain soil likely used as an outfield; the distance between houses at the site allowed plenty of space for infields and work areas. Although this form of community organization also would have provided ample room for European plants—which were used contemporaneously by Onondagas (Bartram 1966 [1751]:42) and neighboring Senecas at Kenedaia (Conover 1887:46)—no European plant remains were found among over sixteen thousand botanical specimens recovered at Townley-Read (Jack Rossen, personal communication 2006). Instead, the botanical assemblage looks overwhelmingly traditional: it includes maize kernels and cupules, beans, squash seeds, gourd rind, butternut and hickory nutshell fragments, and sumac and blackberry or raspberry seeds (Jack Rossen, personal communication 2006). Bodner (1999) also documents sunflower achenes found in a brass kettle plowed out of a grave at the site. The archaeological record at Townley-Read contains no evidence of intensive agriculture such as fences, harness tackle, or plow fragments.[7]

By 1779, documents show that many Seneca communities had adopted the use of European-derived apple and peach trees (Conover 1887; Division of Archives and History 1929); however, no garden plants were reported by American soldiers. It appears that Revolutionary-era Senecas not only expanded their plant use through the adoption of European species, but also transformed their agriculture through the creation of an infield-outfield orchard system, which coupled together intensively managed and monitored infields, floodplain outfields planted with maize, beans, and squash, orchards of fruit and nut trees, and gathered plants. This diversified, creolized agricultural system likely allowed an expanded repertoire of plants to be grown, including fragile and labor-intensive ones that would not have survived in distant outfields.

In contrast it appears that many Mohawks adopted intensive agriculture—the permanent cultivation of plowed, fenced fields. Snow (2001b:24) posits an eighteenth-century Mohawk system of "intensive river-flat horticulture."[8] At least as early as the 1750s, colonial officials such as William Johnson actively encouraged Mohawks to adopt European-style farming and land tenure practices by plowing their fields and giving them boards for house and fence construction (Guldenzopf 1986:71–75). Plows commonly are listed in the Mohawk war-claims inventories detailing property abandoned in 1777 (Guldenzopf 1986:195–208). The adoption of intensive agriculture also can be inferred from the Mohawk reliance on domesticated animals. Widespread stock raising is in main part incompatible with northeastern extensive agriculture, primarily because domesticated animals (especially pigs, cattle, and horses) invade unfenced fields and devour crops (Cronon

1983:130–132).[9] The heavy labor demands of building and maintaining fences encouraged greater commitment to, and possibly eventual permanent cultivation of, particular fields.

It is highly likely that Mohawk intensive agriculture also had a creolized character. Documentary sources dating to as late as 1750–76 (e.g., Snow et al. 1996:241, 244, 259, 284) suggest that Mohawks continued to use slash-and-burn techniques, that farming took place in locations (such as relatively inaccessible islands) that precluded intensive practices, and that women remained in control of some Mohawk agriculture. The degree to which these practices were typical remains an open question. The weight of the evidence favors widespread Mohawk adoption of permanent-field agriculture, indicating that a major transformation away from the traditional system of extensive farming had taken place.

Frontier Exchange Economy

No later than the 1650s, Mohawks traded subsistence products such as venison, fish, crabs, and wild fowl to Europeans in Albany and Schenectady (Rothschild 2003:158–159). By the mid–eighteenth century, Mohawk women and men also produced craft goods to trade with Europeans, including wooden trays, bowls, spoons, shovels, rakes, baskets, brooms, shoes, and stockings (Rothschild 2003:131–132; Snow and Guldenzopf 1998:36). These transactions provided Mohawks with another way to access European goods outside the fur trade and diplomatic interactions. The intercultural market in subsistence and craft goods can be described as a "frontier exchange economy" analogous to that described by Usner (1992, 1998) in the lower Mississippi Valley.

Documents record isolated instances where Senecas provided food to Europeans. French agent Louis-Thomas Chabert de Joncaire acquired 900 bushels of maize for the garrison at Fort Michilimackinac from the Senecas in 1715 (Kent 1974:87), and Senecas reportedly supplied the French garrison at Niagara with "fresh meat" (O'Callaghan 1853–87:X:85). However, the very small populations of Europeans residing in and near Seneca territory and poorly developed transportation networks (Beauchamp 1916:68) did not permit the growth of a major "frontier exchange economy" in foodstuffs or craft goods in the Seneca region prior to the post-Revolutionary reservation period.

Land Allocation and Property Definition

The Mohawk war claims data tabulated by Guldenzopf (1986:83–87, 191–208) document that private ownership of land was almost universal among the Mohawks by the time of the Revolution. In addition the war claims demonstrate that substantial economic inequality had arisen within the Mohawk population: total house and barn values ranged from 15 to more than 250 New York pounds, and 11 of the 58 Mohawks filing claims owned 64 percent of the total private acreage (Guldenzopf 1986:84). Mohawk men frequently were named as property owners, in contrast to traditional conceptions of property ownership by women. Snow and Guldenzopf (1998:36) mention that Mohawks held land in a mix of communal and private holdings at Indian Castle in 1763, suggesting that the transition to full private ownership may have taken place at a late date.

Evidence regarding property ownership from the Seneca region is scarce, which may in itself be telling.[10] Continuities in Seneca housing, animal use, and farming practices all suggest that Seneca land likely continued to be allocated communally. This contention receives documentary support from other regions of Iroquoia. At Onondaga in 1750 the Moravian missionary Cammerhoff observed, "a large company of 33 women, who were hoeing corn" (Beauchamp 1916:46), probably a communal work party. Joseph Bloomfield's 1776 comment that the residents of Oneida Castle "have only one Very large cleared Field in which all their Horses & Cattle graise promiscusly" (Lender and Martin 1982:66) suggests that communal regulation of land access may have continued to be practiced.

Community Structure

Mohawks and Senecas both appear to have adopted dispersed community plans in the early part of the eighteenth century. Archaeological survey data from the Townley-Read site (Jordan 2004) and interpretations of Mohawk site structure (particularly at Indian Castle) based on archaeological, cartographic, and documentary information (Lenig 2003; Lord 1996; Snow 2001b:23–24; Snow and Guldenzopf 1998:32, 43) suggest that communities in both regions were "fully dispersed" in that they featured substantial distances between houses and were aligned linearly along watercourses (see Jordan 2004 for definitions and discussion of Iroquois site structure).

Despite the similarity in outcome, separate motivations may have caused residential dispersal in the two regions. It seems likely that Mohawk communities dispersed primarily to secure land access in the face of European territorial encroachment, while Senecas dispersed primarily for reasons of economic opportunism. Mohawk and Seneca community structure therefore may provide a classic example of equifinality, given that the same end result was produced by different processes. Despite different causes, dispersed settlements may have provided some of the same labor-saving and ecological benefits in both regions (see Jordan 2002:376–380 for Seneca data).

Locally Specific Political-Economic Factors

Important questions remain to be answered about the timing and pace of eighteenth-century change and the degree of homogeneity or heterogeneity within and between villages in both the Seneca and Mohawk regions. Archaeological deposits from the first half of the eighteenth century—particularly in the Mohawk Valley—need to be targeted for excavation so data can be acquired to address these issues. However, the evidence indicates a clear-cut divergence between the Seneca and Mohawk regions by 1750.

It would be easy to conclude that these regional contrasts in the Iroquois adoption of European lifeways were the product of differential acculturation and that the Mohawks were the most "Europeanized" due to their greater degree of interaction with Europeans. However, analysis of the Seneca evidence suggests a more complicated picture. The Senecas did adopt a significant amount of European technology, plants, and animals. But they did so selectively, adopting only those aspects of European culture that fit within their own system of extensive agriculture, hunting, gathering, and communal property ownership. This selectivity is absent from the Mohawk evidence; they adopted European technology and subsistence practices, if the phrase can be permitted, "whole hog."

Why were the Senecas selective while the Mohawks apparently were not? Arguments based on differences in the amount of contact with Europeans are inadequate. The Senecas had decades of knowledge about European crops, animals, and building practices. Reports from the 1687 Denonville expedition state that the Senecas had obtained pigs (O'Callaghan 1849–51:1:239; Olds 1930:38), but they had not adopted them in significant numbers even 100 years later. Savo-Karelian Finns introduced notched-log construction to the Delaware Valley by the 1640s (Jordan and Kaups 1989), and numbers of Senecas and other Iroquois peoples settled in close proximity to notched-log cabin builders in Pennsylvania starting in the 1690s (Kent 1993; McConnell 1992). Yet there is little evidence for Iroquois adoption of European-style log cabins in the absence of directed culture change even up to the American Revolution (Jordan 2002:444–457). It is likely that the Senecas did not adopt these and other aspects of European lifeways, because they had a choice. The Mohawks, on the other hand, did not.

The European presence in Seneca territory was slight; there were never more than a handful of traders, diplomats, soldiers, smiths, and missionaries in the Seneca region at any given time, and permanent European outposts (such as those at Niagara and Oswego) were distant from Seneca villages. The innovative use of and experimentation with European technology and subsistence practices seen in the Seneca region was made possible by the Senecas' control of their land base and their continued ability to make significant decisions about the conduct of their daily lives themselves. Their relationship with Europeans can be considered to be a continuation of what had persisted throughout the Postcolumbian period—a relationship of cultural *entanglement* (Alexander 1998; Dietler 1998), not outright control.

To the East the Mohawks were faced with not only a greater degree of contact with Europeans, but with a different kind of contact. The divergence in cultural patterns between the Mohawk and Seneca regions was initiated by the 1711 English construction of Fort Hunter at the Mohawk Lower Castle. This proved to be a double-edged sword: the fort provided a citadel where Mohawks could flee in the event of attack, but it also protected European settlers from the Mohawks moving into the valley. European encroachment in the Mohawk Valley began immediately on the heels of the fort's construction, when 500 Palatine German refugees settled in the Schoharie area in 1712 (Otterness 2004:119–125); by 1720, 1,000 Palatines lived in the Schoharie Valley (Guldenzopf 1986:52). Palatine population then expanded to the Mohawk Valley, settling at German Flats and Stone Arabia in 1723 (Otterness 2004:142–143). German Flats sat to the west of the Mohawk "castles," meaning that there were European towns both above and below Iroquois communities on the Mohawk River. Other European communities, including Cherry Valley, followed in the 1730s (Tiro 1999:52–53). Settlement was accompanied by purchases of Mohawk land by Dutch and English speculators from Albany, which frequently involved fraud (Nammack 1969); Mohawks began complaining to the Albany Commissioners for Indian Affairs about land transactions by 1730 (Parmenter 1999:60). By 1757 an estimated 650 European houses had been constructed at and between Fort Hunter and German Flats, housing a total population of 2,600 to 4,500 persons (Guldenzopf 1986:55).

Postencroachment ecological changes in the Mohawk Valley undoubtedly paralleled the developments in New England described by Cronon (1983:82–156). European settlement obviously constrained Native American farming, hunting, gathering, and settlement relocation options. The total forest clearance required for European agriculture reduced the "edge area" habitats preferred by deer and turkeys, increased erosion, and made streamflow more erratic as there was less ground cover to retain water. Europeans built roads to transport crops and drive livestock, channeling movement and in the process making certain areas less attractive to wild animals. Wolves and other predators systematically were eradicated, creating a ripple effect within the food chain. Six Nations representatives told the Albany commissioners in 1737 that "wherever the Christians settled . . . hunting was destroyed for the Bever & Deer &c. Fled from the places they disturbed" (quoted in Parmenter 1999:71–72).

Widespread European use of domesticated animals provoked major changes even among Native populations that did not use them. European-owned livestock frequently broke out of their pastures and damaged unenclosed fields (Cronon 1983:130–132; see also Guldenzopf 1986:70); this problem was particularly acute with hogs, as Europeans typically allowed them to run feral for some or all of the year and at times directed them toward unfenced Indian cropland. These pressures eventually forced Native Americans to fence in their fields, a labor-intensive practice unknown in Indian extensive agriculture. Europeans also converted large areas of land into hay meadows, devoting to animals two to ten times the amount of land they tilled for human food crops. Old Indian fields and drained beaver meadows proved easy to convert to pastures, reducing the number of deer and beaver in the process. Cattle competed with deer for forage, and overgrazing by cattle could lead to the replacement of grass species by thorny, inedible bushes.

Politically the occupation of Mohawk lands by Palatines and other Europeans created new forms of competition for land. The Iroquois system of communal landholding—with extensive agriculture done largely by women and with men out of the region for much of the year while warring, trapping, and trading—was unlikely to preserve access to land in the face of European intensive agriculture, stock raising, and highly formalized notions of land tenure. Threats to their land likely forced Mohawk men to stay in the locality for a greater part of the year to protect their desirable floodplain fields. To ensure adequate legal protection in the face of European land grabs, Mohawks needed to have their property defined and their title established. The fact that European legal systems expected males to own land probably encouraged Mohawks to define property ownership, at least in some situations, as male-owned.

Many Mohawks decided that these transformations and the additional labor they required were not worthwhile and migrated to other areas (such as the St. Lawrence Valley) where a subsistence system based on extensive agriculture, hunting, and gathering still could operate. For those that stayed in the Mohawk Valley, the investments of time and labor forced by European encroachment and directed-culture change incentives eventually made it more sensible for Mohawks to adopt smaller households located directly near their fields, more intensive agriculture and stock raising, and male-dominated private property.

Mohawks adopted these practices as a package only when they had been locally overwhelmed both militarily and demographically and their pre-encroachment mode of subsistence had been made ecologically and politically impossible. The historian Richard White (1983, 1991) has called this type of intercultural relationship "dependence," but it would be better termed "colonialism," here defined as a bureaucratic, territorial, and ecological form of expansion and control. In this setting the Mohawk adoption of European lifeways was a rational response to colonialism.[11] The new property relations initiated by permanent houses and fields and the need for secure private title provided the institutional infrastructure necessary for the broad elaboration and expression of political-economic differences seen within Mohawk communities by the time of the Revolution.

Conclusions

The Seneca example illustrates that the processes of "Europeanization" seen in the Mohawk Valley were in no way inevitable products of contact. The changes in the Mohawk Valley happened only after the arrival of a large population of European settlers who were protected by military force. Local European territorial encroachment initiated a total change in Mohawk subsistence, settlement, and property relations. In contrast the Senecas maintained a system of subsistence and settlement, the core of which is easily recognizable as Iroquoian, until after the American Revolution. They also kept control over their territory and their labor allocation—the most effective forms of Native resistance. Quite simply the two cases encapsulate the differences between cultural entanglement and colonialism.

The acculturative changes that many observers posit occurred gradually among Iroquois peoples throughout the eighteenth century were in fact limited to the Mohawk Valley and were the direct products of colonialism. This thesis is substantiated by the striking parallels between the cultural transformations that took place in the Mohawk Valley after 1711 and those that occurred on Iroquois reservations after the American Revolution, when similar Euroamerican territorial encroachment and colonialism spread to the rest of the Iroquois homeland (Jordan

2002:458–467, 503–505). These Reservation-period changes took place quite rapidly, often within a single decade, which may indicate that the earlier Mohawk changes occurred at a similar pace.

Thus eighteenth-century Mohawk archaeology needs to be decoupled from the archaeology of the rest of the Iroquois Confederacy. The Mohawk example provides a poor basis for a normative description of eighteenth-century Iroquois culture, as it was in fact the least typical case. The atypicality of the Mohawk situation should be underscored in local studies of eighteenth-century Mohawk lifeways to preclude inaccurate generalization. Comparative analysis at the scale of local political economy brings sharp contrasts between regions to light, restores agency to Iroquois social actors, and allows better exploration of vital questions regarding the timing and causes of eighteenth-century social change.

Notes

1. I thank Timothy D. Knapp and Laurie E. Miroff for their dedication and labor in their efforts to have this volume published. Although they may not agree with the conclusions presented here, David Guldenzopf, Wayne Lenig, and Dean Snow generously shared their detailed knowledge of the Mohawk region. The editors, Nan A. Rothschild, Jon William Parmenter, Eric Cheyfitz, Gary A. Warrick, Jim Folts, George R. Hamell, and two anonymous reviewers provided helpful comments and leads to sources. Fieldwork at the Townley-Read site was supported by Columbia University, Hobart and William Smith Colleges, the National Science Foundation, and the Early American Industries Association; analysis has been supported by the Department of Anthropology, American Indian Program, and Archaeology Program at Cornell University. Adam S. Watson, Michael West, Nerissa Russell, Kevin McGowan, Jessica Herlich, and Jack Rossen supplied crucial assistance in the identification and interpretation of the Townley-Read faunal and botanical assemblages. Access to Seneca artifact collections at the Rochester Museum and Science Center (Rochester, New York) was aided by a 1995 Arthur C. Parker Graduate Student Fellowship provided by the Rock Foundation. The staff and resources of the Olin Library Map Collection, Cornell University, proved invaluable in the production of the map.

2. The 1776 journal of American soldier Joseph Bloomfield contains a description of the normative Iroquois house as "very small, consisting only of a little cottage" (Lender and Martin 1982:84–85; Snow et al. 1996:285). The rest of the journal indicates that Bloomfield marched near but spent little time in Mohawk villages (Lender and Martin 1982:47, 61). He did stay for several days in Oneida Castle and "visited most of their Huts in quest of Indian

Whampum &c." (Lender and Martin 1982:66). I therefore find it difficult to accept that Bloomfield's "little cottage" specifically describes a Mohawk house. François-Jean de Beauvoir's 1780 journal describes a Mohawk house outside Schenectady that appears to contain many traditional features, such as a central smoke hole and two sleeping platforms (Snow et al. 1996:293–294). This observation was made during the American Revolution after most British-allied Mohawks had abandoned the Mohawk Valley; this structure may therefore have been constructed under duress by a refugee and may not have been typical of the dwellings built under normal circumstances.

3. I am grateful to Jim Folts and George R. Hamell (personal communications, 2004) for information on the prevalence of Europeans in Seneca territory in 1779, which caused me to rethink my previous position that Senecas occupied most of the "Tory houses" (Jordan 2002:425–426, 2004:42–43).

4. For data compatibility purposes, the Enders House site mammalian faunal numbers presented in Rick (1991:Tables 1–2) were slightly modified for this paper. From the 1750–60 strata, the following were not counted: (a) 1 *Rodentia* specimen; (b) 2 *Carnivora* specimens; (c) 45 *Artiodactyla* specimens; (d) 3 *Ungulata* specimens; and (e) 3 moose/cow specimens (although identified as to genus, this classification did not allow separation into the European domesticate or native North American species categories). Elimination of these 54 specimens left 283 specimens identified at the genus or species level, of which 162 (57.2 percent) were European domesticates.

5. Watson is in the process of comprehensively analyzing and reporting on the Townley-Read faunal assemblage; he currently reports 350 mammalian specimens identified to the genus or species level (personal communication, 2007). This information supplants the faunal numbers reported elsewhere (e.g., Jordan 2002; Watson 2000; West 2001).

6. The alleged 1765 narrative of colonial official Ezra Buell, published in 1903 by Augustus C. Buell, states of the Senecas at Kanadesaga in 1765 that they "have a good many horses and a few cattle. But cattle need too much care and feeding in winter to suit the Indians. Besides, they have plenty of wild meat, and as they do not wish for milk, they have little need of cattle" (Buell 1903:238). Historian Milton W. Hamilton (1953, 1956, 1976) documents errors and forgeries in a number of Augustus C. Buell's works, and he considers the alleged 1765 narrative to be a twentieth-century "concoction" by Augustus Buell (see Jordan 2004:43–44). Information from the Buell narrative should be treated with extreme care; I have cited the narrative only in the notes section to reflect its problematic nature as a source.

7. Agricultural tools and hardware have been recovered from other Seneca sites of this era. An iron hoe was found in a grave at the Snyder-McClure site (circa 1688–1710/1715); hoes from unknown context have also been recovered

from the Huntoon site (circa 1710/1715–40). Use of iron hoes is entirely consistent with extensive agriculture. Iron animal shoes, including specimens identified by the collection catalogue as "ox shoes," have been recovered from Snyder-McClure and the White Springs site (circa 1688–1715), but all of these examples were surface-collected and may derive from post-1788 Euroamerican intensive farming of the land. These types of artifacts have not been recovered at Townley-Read. All of the artifacts described here are part of the collections of the Rochester Museum and Science Center in Rochester, New York.

8. This contention seems to be substantiated by Lenig's (2003) analysis of the Swart collection, which has revealed five previously unregistered eighteenth-century Mohawk sites. The sites are 0.8 ha or less in area, and all are located on either the floodplain or immediately adjacent terraces of the Mohawk River or Schoharie Creek. These sites presumably represent the remains of dispersed Mohawk farmsteads and may offer excellent opportunities for obtaining data on nonelite Mohawk households.

9. There is some evidence for the coexistence of large-scale stock raising and extensive agriculture in the Southeast. Perdue (1998:121–123) describes Cherokee stock raising in the 1800–10 period based on free-ranging cattle and pigs inhabiting what had previously been deer-hunting territories; Carson (1997) and White (1983) discuss Choctaw herding. The exact articulation between herding and agriculture among these groups remains underexplored, although it likely involved the transport of livestock away from agricultural fields during the growing season. Differences in population density, the size of European settler populations, the availability of winter fodder, and the distribution of herding-conducive environments (including prairies and canebrakes, which are lacking in the Northeast) suggest that the types of herding practiced in the Southeast may not have been viable in the Northeast (see also Jordan 1993).

10. The problematic Ezra Buell narrative (see note 5) states of the 1765 Kanadesaga Senecas that "cleared land is tilled in common, each family getting its share of the whole product" (Buell 1903:238).

11. In a scenario that has interesting implications for the Mohawk case, Sider (1994:111) has suggested that some Native American communities in the Southeast that were surrounded by Euroamerican settlers maintained a certain autonomy in their "social 'invisibility' [which was] based on copying the outward appearance and economic activities of small Euro-American hamlets."

References Cited

ABEL, TIMOTHY J.
2002   The Plus Site: An Iroquoian Remote Camp in Upland Tompkins
        County, New York. *North American Archaeologist* 21:181–215.

ABLER, THOMAS S.
1970   Longhouse and Palisade: Northeastern Iroquoian Villages of the
        Seventeenth Century. *Ontario History* LXII:17–40.

ALEXANDER, RANI T.
1998   Afterword: Toward an Archaeological Theory of Culture Contact. In
        Studies in Culture Contact, edited by James G. Cusick, pp. 476–495.
        Occasional Paper No. 25. Center for Archaeological Investigations,
        Southern Illinois University, Carbondale.

ALLEN, KATHLEEN M. SYDORIAK
1988   Ceramic Style and Social Continuity in an Iroquoian Tribe. Ph.D.
        dissertation, Department of Anthropology, State University of New
        York at Buffalo, Buffalo.
1990   Modelling Early Historic Trade in the Eastern Great Lakes Using
        Geographic Information Systems. In *Interpreting Space: GIS and
        Archaeology*, edited by Kathleen M. Sydoriak Allen, Stanton W.
        Green, and Ezra B. W. Zubrow, pp. 319–329. Taylor and Francis,
        London.
1992   Iroquois Ceramic Production: A Case of Household-Level Organ-
        ization. In *Ceramic Distribution: An Integrated Approach*, edited by
        George J. Bey III and Christopher A. Pool, pp. 133–154. Westview
        Press, Boulder.
1994   Recent Investigations at the Carman Site, a Cayuga Iroquois Village.
        Paper presented at the Eastern States Archaeological Association
        Federation, Albany, New York.
1998   Archaeology in the Cayuga Lake Region. Paper presented at the
        Cayuga Museum Northeast Archaeological Symposium, Auburn,
        New York.
2000   Considerations of Scale in Modeling Settlement Patterns Using
        GIS: An Iroquois Example. In *Practical Applications of GIS for*

Archaeologists, edited by Konnie L. Westcott and R. Joe Brandon, pp. 101–112. Taylor & Francis, Philadelphia.

2002   Temporal and Spatial Scales of Activity among the Iroquois: Implications for Understanding Cultural Change. Paper presented at the 67th Annual Meeting of the Society for American Archaeology, Denver.

ALLEN, KATHLEEN M. SYDORIAK, STANTON W. GREEN, AND EZRA B.W. ZUBROW (EDITORS)

1990   *Interpreting Space: GIS and Archaeology.* Taylor & Francis, New York.

ALLEN, KATHLEEN M. SYDORIAK, AND KIMBERLY WILLIAMS-SHUKER

1998   Longhouse Remains at the Carman Site. Paper presented at the Cayuga Museum Northeast Archaeological Symposium, Auburn, New York.

ALLISON, PENELOPE M.

1999   Introduction. In *The Archaeology of Household Activities,* edited by Penelope Allison, pp. 1–18. Routledge, New York.

ALT, SUSAN

2001   Cahokian Change and the Authority of Tradition. In *The Archaeology of Traditions: Agency and History before and after Columbus,* edited by Timothy R. Pauketat, pp. 141–156. University Press of Florida, Gainesville.

ANDREFSKY, WILLIAM, JR.

1994   Raw Material Availability and the Organization of Technology. *American Antiquity* 59:21–34.

APPLEGATE, DARLENE, AND ROBERT C. MAINFORT, JR. (EDITORS)

2005   *Woodland Period Systematics in the Middle Ohio Valley.* The University of Alabama Press, Tuscaloosa.

AQUILA, RICHARD

1997   *The Iroquois Restoration: Iroquois Diplomacy on the Colonial Frontier, 1701–1754.* Reprinted with new introduction. University of Nebraska Press, Lincoln. Originally published 1983, Wayne State University Press, Detroit.

ARCHAEOLOGIX INC.

2001   *Archaeological Assessment (Stage 4) Preliminary Report on the Tillsonburg Village (AfHe-38), Town of Tillsonburg, Oxford County, Ontario.* Submitted to the Ontario Ministry of Culture, Toronto.

2002   *Archaeological Assessment (Stage 4) Final Report on the Tillsonburg Village (AfHe-38), Town of Tillsonburg, Oxford County, Ontario.* Submitted to the Ontario Ministry of Culture, Toronto.

ARNOLD, DEAN E.

1991   *Ceramic Theory and Cultural Process.* Cambridge University Press, Cambridge.

ASCH, DAVID L., AND JAMES A. BROWN

1990   Stratigraphy and Site Chronology. In *The Oak Forest Site: Invest-igations into Oneota Subsistence-Settlement in the Cal-Sag Area of Cook County, Illinois,* edited by James Brown, pp. 174–185. At the Edge of Prehistory: Huber Phase Archaeology in the Chicago Area, Part II, James A. Brown and Patricia J. O'Brien, general editors. Center for America Archaeology, Kampsville, Illinois.

ASCH SIDELL, NANCY

2001a   Parker Farm Site Floral Remains. Manuscript on file, University of Pittsburgh, Pittsburgh.

2001b   Thomas/Luckey Site Floral Remains. Manuscript on file, Public Archaeology Facility, Binghamton University, Binghamton, New York.

ASCHER, ROBERT

1961   Analogy in Archaeological Interpretation. *Southwestern Journal of Anthropology* 17:317–325.

ASHMORE, WENDY, AND RICHARD WILK

1988   Household and Community in the Mesoamerican Past. In *House-hold and Community in the Mesoamerican Past,* edited by Richard Wilk and Wendy Ashmore, pp. 1–27. University of New Mexico Press, Albuquerque.

ASMUSSEN, HEIDI

1998   Toward an Understanding of Iroquois Plant Use: Archaeobotanical Material from the Carman Site, a Cayuga Village in Central New York. B.A. honors thesis, Department of Anthropology, University of Pittsburgh, Pittsburgh.

BAILEY, GEOFF

1981   Concepts, Time-Scales and Explanations in Economic Prehistory. In *Economic Archaeology: Towards an Integration of Ecological and Social Approaches,* edited by Allison Sheridan and Geoff Bailey, pp. 97–117. BAR International Series 96. British Archaeological Reports, Oxford.

1987   Breaking the Time Barrier. *Archaeological Review from Cambridge* 6(1):5–20.

BAMANN, SUSAN, ROBERT KUHN, JAMES MOLNAR, AND DEAN R. SNOW

1992   Iroquoian Archaeology. *Annual Review of Anthropology* 21:435–460.

BARNES, RUTH CAROL
1980   Feature Analysis: A Neglected Tool in Archaeological Survey and Interpretation. *Man in the Northeast* 20:101–113.

BARTRAM, JOHN
1966   [1751] *Observations on the Inhabitants, Climate, Soil, Rivers, Productions, Animals, and Other Matters Worthy of Notice made by Mr. John Bartram in his Travels from Pensilvania to Onondago, Oswego, and the Lake Ontario, in Canada.* J. Whiston and B. White, London. 1966 facsimile edition. March of America Series No. 41. University Microfilms, Ann Arbor.

BAUGHER, SHERENE, AND SARA CLARK
1998   *An Archaeological Investigation of the Indian Fort Road Site, Trumansburg, New York.* Cornell University, Ithaca.

BEAUCHAMP, WILLIAM M.
1900   Iroquois Women. *Journal of American Folklore* 49(13):81–91.
1916   *Moravian Journals Relating to Central New York, 1745–66.* Dehler Press, Syracuse, New York.

BEISAW, APRIL
1998   Differential Preservation and Recovery: Taphonomy of Bone Preservation at the Thomas/Luckey Site, Ashland, NY. Master's thesis, Department of Anthropology, Binghamton University, Binghamton, New York.

BERKHOFER, ROBERT F., JR.
1965   Faith and Factionalism among the Senecas: Theory and Ethnohistory. *Ethnohistory* 12:99–112.

BERMANN, MARC
1996   Domestic Life and Vertical Integration in the Tiwanaku Heartland. *Latin American Antiquity* 8:93–112.

BERNARDINI, WESLEY
2000   Kiln Firing Groups: Inter-Household Economic Collaboration and Social Organization in the Northern American Southwest. *American Antiquity* 65:365–377.

BINFORD, LEWIS R.
1982   The Archaeology of Place. *Journal of Anthropological Archaeology* 1:5–31.

BINTLIFF, JOHN L., PHIL HOWARD, AND ANTHONY SNODGRASS
1999   The Hidden Landscape of Prehistoric Greece. *Journal of Mediterranean Archaeology* 12:139–168.

BLANTON, RICHARD E.
1994   *Houses and Households: A Comparative Study.* Plenum, New York.

BODNER, CONNIE COX
1999   Sunflower in the Seneca Iroquois Region of Western New York. In *Current Northeast Paleobotany*, edited by John P. Hart, pp. 27–45. New York State Museum Bulletin 494. University of the State of New York, State Education Department, Albany.

BONVILLAIN, NANCY
1986   The Iroquois and the Jesuits: Strategies of Influence and Resistance. *American Indian Cultural Research* 10(1):29–42.

BOURDIEU, PIERRE
1977   *Outline of a Theory of Practice.* Cambridge University Press, New York.
1984   *Distinction: A Social Critique of the Judgement of Taste.* Routledge and Keagan Paul, Cambridge, Massachusetts.

BOUSMAN, C. BRITT, MICHAEL B. COLLINS, PAUL GOLDBERG, THOMAS STAFFORD, JAN GUY, BARRY W. BAKER, D. GENTRY STEELE, MARVIN KAY, ANNE KERR, GLEN FREDLUND, PHIL DERING, VANCE HOLLIDAY, DIANE WILSON, WULF GOSE, SUSAN DIAL, PAUL TAKAC, ROBIN BALINSKY, MARILYN MASSON, AND JOSEPH POWELL
2002   Paleoindian-Archaic Transition in North America: New Evidence from Texas. *Antiquity* 76:980–990.

BRADLEY, JAMES W.
1987   *Evolution of the Onondaga Iroquois: Accommodating Change, 1500–1655.* Syracuse University Press, Syracuse, New York.

BRAUDEL, FERNAND
1980   *On History.* University of Chicago Press, Chicago.
1981   *Civilization and Capitalism, 15th–18th Century,* Vol. 1. *The Structures of Everyday Life: The Limits of the Possible.* Translated by Sian Reynolds. Harper & Row, New York.

BRAUN, LUCY E.
1950   *Deciduous Forests of Eastern North America.* The Blakiston Co., Philadelphia.

BROWN, JUDITH K.
1970   Economic Organization and the Position of Women among the Iroquois. *Ethnohistory* 17:151–167.

BRUMFIEL, ELIZABETH
1992   Breaking and Entering the Ecosystem—Gender, Class, and Faction Steal the Show. *American Anthropologist* 94(3):551–569.

BUELL, AUGUSTUS C.
1903   *Sir William Johnson.* D. Appleton, New York.

BUTLER, EVA L.
1945   Sweat-Houses in the Southern New England Area. *Massachusetts Archaeological Society Bulletin* 7(1):11–15.

CAMPISI, JACK
1980   Fur Trade and Factionalism on the 18th Century Oneida Indians. In *Studies on Iroquoian Culture*, edited by Nancy Bonvillian, pp. 37–46. Occasional Publications in Northeastern Anthropology No. 6. Department of Anthropology, Franklin Pierce College, Rindge, Hew Hampshire.

CANUTO, MARCELLO A., AND JASON YAEGER (EDITORS)
2000   *The Archaeology of Communities: A New World Perspective.* Routledge, New York.

CARLSON, DAVID
1979   Hunter-Gatherer Mobility Strategies: An Example from the Koster Site in the Lower Illinois Valley. Ph.D. dissertation, Department of Anthropology, Northwestern University, Evanston, Illinois.

CARSON, JAMES TAYLOR
1997   Native Americans, the Market Revolution, and Culture Change: The Choctaw Cattle Economy, 1690–1830. *Agricultural History* 71(1):1–18.

CASTEEL, RICHARD W.
1979   Relationships between Surface Area and Population Size: A Cautionary Note. *American Antiquity* 44:803–807.

CHAMPION, TIMOTHY C. (EDITOR)
1989   *Center and Periphery.* Unwin Hyman, London.

CHANG, CLAUDIA
1992   Archaeological Landscapes: The Ethnoarchaeology of Pastoral Land Use in the Grevena Province of Northern Greece. In *Space, Time, and Archaeological Landscapes*, edited by Jaqueline Rossignol and LuAnn Wandsnider, pp. 65–90. Plenum Press, New York.

CHAPDELAINE, CLAUDE
1995   An Early Late Woodland Pottery Sequence East of Lac Sainte-Pierre: Definition, Chronology, and Cultural Affiliation. *Northeast Anthropology* 49:77–95.

1996   Des "Cornets D'argile" Iroquoiens aux "Pipes de Plâtre" Européens. In *Transferts Culturels et Métissages Amérique/Europe, XVIe–XXe Siècle*, edited by Laurier Turgeon, Denys Delâge, and Réal Ouellet, pp. 189–208. Université Laval, Quebec.

CHAPMAN, L. J., AND D. F. PUTNAM
1984   *The Physiography of Southern Ontario*, Vol. 2. 3rd edition. Ontario Geological Survey Special, Toronto.

CHASE-DUNN, CHRISTOPHER, AND THOMAS D. HALL (EDITORS)
1991   *Core/periphery Relations in Precapitalist Worlds.* Westview Press, Boulder.

CHASE-DUNN, CHRISTOPHER, AND THOMAS D. HALL
1994   The Historical Evolution of World Systems Theory. *Sociological Inquiry* 64:257–280.

CHERRY, JOHN F., JACK L. DAVIS, AND E. MANTZOURANI
1991   *Landscape Archaeology as Long-Term History: Northern Keos in the Cycladic Islands.* Monumenta Archaeologica 16. UCLA Institute of Archaeology, Los Angeles.

CHESTER, DAVID K., AND PETER A. JAMES
1999   Late Pleistocene and Holocene Landscape Development in the Algarve Region, Southern Portugal. *Journal of Mediterranean Archaeology* 12(2):169–196.

CHILTON, ELIZABETH S.
1996   Embodiments of Choice: Native American Ceramic Diversity in the New England Interior. Ph.D. dissertation, Department of Anthropology, University of Massachusetts, Amherst.

CLAASSEN, CHERYL
1997   Changing Venue: Women's Lives in Prehistoric North America. In *Women in Prehistory: North America and Mesoamerica,* edited by Cheryl Claassen and Rosemary Joyce, pp. 65–87. University of Pennsylvania Press, Philadelphia.

COBB, CHARLES R.
1991   Social Reproduction and the "Longue Durée" in the Prehistory of the Midcontinental United States. In *Processual and Postprocessual Archaeologies: Multiple Ways of Knowing the Past,* edited by Robert W. Preucel, pp. 168–182. Occasional Paper 10. Center for Archaeological Investigations, Southern Illinois University, Carbondale.

1993   Archaeological Approaches to the Political Economy of Nonstratified Societies. In *Archaeological Method and Theory,* Vol. 5, edited by Michael B. Schiffer, pp. 43–100. University of Arizona Press, Tucson.

2000   *From Quarry to Cornfield: The Political Economy of Mississippian Hoe Production.* University of Alabama Press, Tuscaloosa.

COBB, CHARLES R., AND PATRICK H. GARROW
1996   Woodstock Culture and the Question of Mississippian Emergence. *American Antiquity* 61:21–37.

COBB, CHARLES R., AND MICHAEL S. NASSANEY
1995   Interaction and Integration in the Late Woodland Southeast. In *Native American Interactions: Multiscalar Analyses and Interpretations in the Eastern Woodlands,* edited by Michael S. Nassaney and Kenneth Sassaman, pp. 205–226. University of Tennessee Press, Knoxville.

CONKEY, MARGARET W., AND JOAN M. GERO
1997 Programme to Practice: Gender and Feminism in Archaeology. *Annual Review of Anthropology* 26:411–437.

CONKEY, MARGARET W., AND JANET SPECTOR
1984 Archaeology and the Study of Gender. In *Advances in Archaeological Method and Theory*, Vol. 7, edited by Michael B. Schiffer, pp. 1–38. Academic Press, New York.

CONOVER, GEORGE S. (EDITOR)
1887 *Journals of the Military Expeditions of Major General John Sullivan against the Six Nations of Indians in 1779*. Knapp, Peck, and Thompson, Auburn, New York.

CONOVER, GEORGE S.
ca. 1889 Kanadesaga and Geneva. Manuscript of 3 bound volumes on file, Archives, Warren Hunting Smith Library, Hobart and William Smith Colleges, Geneva, New York.

CORDELL, LINDA, AND FRED PLOG
1979 Escaping the Confines of Normative Thought: A Reevaluation of Puebloan Prehistory. *American Antiquity* 44: 405–429.

COSTIN, CATHY LYNNE, AND RITA P. WRIGHT (EDITORS)
1998 *Craft and Social Identity*. Archeological Papers of the American Anthropological Association, No. 8. American Anthropological Association, Arlington, Virginia.

COUPLAND, GARY, AND E. B. BANNING
1996 Introduction: The Archaeology of Big Houses. In *People Who Lived in Big Houses: Archaeological Perspectives on Large Domestic Structures*, edited by Gary Coupland and E. B. Banning, pp. 1–9. Monographs in World Archaeology No. 27. Prehistory Press, Madison, Wisconsin.

COWAN, FRANK L., AND DOUGLAS J. PERRELLI
1991 *Stage 1 Archaeological Survey of the Proposed Spaulding Lake Subdivision, Phase 3–6, Town of Clarence, Erie County, New York*. Reports of the Archaeological Survey 23(3). Department of Anthropology, State University of New York at Buffalo.

COWAN, FRANK L., DOUGLAS J. PERRELLI, AND SHANNON M. FIE
1990 *Stage 2 Archaeological Investigations of the Spaulding Lake Site (UB 2497), Town of Clarence, Erie County, New York*. Reports of the Archaeological Survey 22(11). Department of Anthropology, State University of New York at Buffalo.

CRAWFORD, GARY W., AND DAVID G. SMITH
1996 Migration in Prehistory: Princess Point and the Northern Iroquoian Case. *American Antiquity* 61:782–790.

CRAWFORD, GARY W., DAVID G. SMITH, AND VANDY E. BOWYER
1997   Dating the Entry of Corn (*Zea mays*) into the Lower Great Lakes
         Region. *American Antiquity* 62:112–119.

CRONON, WILLIAM
1983   *Changes in the Land: Indians, Colonists, and the Ecology of New
         England.* Hill and Wang, New York.

CRUMLEY, CAROLE L.
1979   Three Locational Models: An Epistemological Assessment for
         Anthropology and Archaeology. In *Advances in Archaeological
         Method and Theory,* Vol. 2, edited by Michael B. Schiffer, pp.
         141–173. Academic Press, New York.

CRUMLEY, CAROLE L., AND WILLIAM H. MARQUARDT
1987   Regional Dynamics in Burgundy. In *Regional Dynamics: Burgund-
         ian Landscapes in Historical Perspective,* edited by Carole L.
         Crumley and William H. Marquardt, pp. 609–623. Academic Press,
         San Diego.

1990   Landscape: A Unifying Concept in Regional Analysis. In *Interpreting
         Space: GIS in Archaeology,* edited by Kathleen M. Sydoriak Allen,
         Stanton W. Green, and Ezra B. W. Zubrow, pp. 73–80. Taylor and
         Francis, London.

CRUZ, MARIA DAS DORES
1996   Ceramic Production in the Banda Area (West-Central Ghana): An
         Ethnoarchaeological Approach. *Nyame Akuma* 45:30–39.

CUSTER, JAY F.
1996   *Prehistoric Cultures of Eastern Pennsylvania.* The Pennsylvania
         Historical and Museum Commission, Harrisburg.

CUTLER, HUGH C., AND LEONARD W. BLAKE
1973   *Plants from Archaeological Sites East of the Rockies.* Missouri
         Botanical Gardens, St. Louis, Missouri.

DANCEY, WILLIAM S.
1981   *Archaeological Field Methods: An Introduction.* Burgess Publishing
         Company, Minneapolis, Minnesota.

DEAGAN, KATHLEEN A.
1995   *Puerto Real: The Archaeology of a Sixteenth-Century Spanish Town
         in Hispaniola.* University Press of Florida, Gainesville.

DEBOER, WARREN R.
1988   Subterranean Storage and the Organization of Surplus: The View
         from Eastern North America. *Southeastern Archaeology* 7:1–20.

DELÂGE, DENYS
1993   *Bitter Feast: Amerindians and Europeans in Northeastern North
         America.* Translated by Jane Brierly. UBC Press, Vancouver.

DE ORIO, ROBERT N.
1978   A Preliminary Sequence of the Historic Cayuga Nation within
        the Traditional Area, 1600–1740. *New York State Archaeological
        Society Beauchamp Chapter Newsletter* 9(4).

DEWAR, ROBERT E.
1986   Discovering Settlement Systems of the Past in New England. *Man in
        the Northeast* 31:77–88.
1992   Incorporating Variation in Occupation Span in Settlement-Pattern
        Analysis. *American Antiquity* 56:604–620.

DEWAR, ROBERT E., AND KEVIN A. MCBRIDE
1992   Remnant Settlement Patterns. In *Space, Time, and Archaeological
        Landscapes,* edited by Jaqueline Rossignol and LuAnn Wandsnider,
        pp. 227–256. Plenum Press, New York.

DICKENS, ROY S., JR.
1985   The Form, Function, and Formation of Garbage-Filled Pits on South-
        eastern Aboriginal Sites: An Archaeobotanical Analysis. In *Structure
        and Process in Southeast Archaeology,* edited by Roy S. Dickens,
        Jr. and H. Trawick Ward, pp. 34–59. University of Alabama Press,
        Tuscaloosa.

DIETLER, MICHAEL
1998   Consumption, Agency, and Cultural Entanglement: Theoretical
        Implications of a Mediterranean Colonial Encounter. In *Studies
        in Culture Contact,* edited by James G. Cusick, pp. 288–315.
        Occasional Paper No. 25. Center for Archaeological Investigations,
        Southern Illinois University, Carbondale.

DINCAUZE, DENA F., AND ROBERT J. HASENSTAB
1989   Explaining the Iroquois: Tribalization on a Prehistoric Periphery. In
        Centre and Periphery: Comparative Studies in Archaeology, edited
        by Timothy C. Champion, pp. 67–87. Unwin Hyman, London.

DIVISION OF ARCHIVES, AND HISTORY
1929   *The Sullivan-Clinton Campaign in 1779.* University of the State of
        New York, Albany.

DOBLIN, HELGA, AND WILLIAM T. STARNA (EDITORS)
1994   The Journals of Christian Daniel Claus and Conrad Weiser: A Jour-
        ney to Onondaga, 1750. *Transactions of the American Philosophical
        Society* 84(2).

DOBRES, MARCIA-ANNE
1995   Gender and Prehistoric Technology: On the Social Agency of Tech-
        nical Strategies. *World Archaeology* 27(1):25–49.

DOBRES, MARCIA-ANNE, AND CHRISTINE HOFFMAN
1994   Social Agency and the Dynamics of Prehistoric Technology. *Journal
        of Archaeological Method and Theory* 1(3):211–258.

DODD, CHRISTINE F.
1984   *Ontario Iroquois Tradition Longhouses.* Mercury Series, Archae-
        ological Survey of Canada, Paper No. 124:181–437. National
        Museums of Canada, Ottawa.

DODD, CHRISTINE F., DANA R. POULTON, PAUL A LENNOX, DAVID G.
SMITH, AND GARY A. WARRICK
1990   The Middle Ontario Iroquoian Stage. In *The Archaeology of
        Southern Ontario to A.D. 1650,* edited by Chris J. Ellis and Neal
        Ferris, pp. 321–359. Occasional Publication of the London Chapter
        No. 5. Ontario Archaeological Society, London, Ontario.

DONLEY-REID, LINDA
1990   A Structuring Structure: The Swahili House. In *Domestic Arch-
        itecture and the Use of Space,* edited by Susan Kent, pp. 114–126.
        Cambridge University Press, Cambridge.

DRAGOO, DON W.
1976   Prehistoric Iroquoian Culture in the Upper Ohio Valley. In *The Late
        Prehistory of the Lake Erie Drainage Basin: A 1972 Symposium
        Revised,* edited by David S. Brose, pp. 76–88. Cleveland Museum of
        Natural History, Cleveland.

DRAGOO, DON W., AND STANLEY LANTZ
1971   *Archaeological Salvage of Selected Sites in the Allegheny Reservoir
        in Pennsylvania and New York, 1969–1971.* Report to the U.S.
        National Park Service, Project No. 14-10-5-950-28 and 14-10-5-
        950-48. Carnegie Museum, Pittsburgh.

DUNGAN, J. L., J. N. PERRY, M. R. T. DALE, P. LEGENDRE, S. CITRON-
POUSTY, M. J. FORTIN, A. JAKOMULSKA, M. MIRITI, AND M. S.
ROSENBERG
2002   A Balanced View of Scale in Spatial Statistical Analysis. *Ecography*
        25:626–640.

DUNNELL, ROBERT C.
1992   The Notion Site. In *Space, Time, and Archaeological Landscapes,*
        edited by Jaqueline Rossignol and LuAnn Wandsnider, pp. 21–42.
        Plenum Press, New York.
1995   What Is It That Actually Evolves? In *Evolutionary Archaeology:
        Methodological Issues,* edited by Patrice A. Teltser, pp. 33–50.
        University of Arizona Press, Tucson.

DUNNELL, ROBERT C., AND WILLIAM DANCEY
1983   The Siteless Survey: A Regional Scale Data Collection Strategy. In
        Advances in Archaeological Method and Theory, Vol. 6, edited by
        Michael B. Schiffer, pp. 267–287. Academic Press, New York.

EBERT, JAMES
1992   *Distributional Archaeology.* University of Utah Press, Salt Lake City.

EDMONDSON, PAUL
1976   Parker Farm and Indian Fort Road Sites: A Report on Two Late
        Prehistoric Settlements in the Vicinity of Trumansburg, New York.
        Honors thesis, Cornell University, Ithaca.

ELLIS, CHRIS J., AND NEAL FERRIS (EDITORS)
1990   *The Archaeology of Southern Ontario to A.D. 1650.* Occasional
        Publication of the London Chapter No. 5. Ontario Archaeological
        Society, London, Ontario.

EMERSON, THOMAS E., AND DALE L. McELRATH
2001   Interpreting Discontinuity and Historical Process in Midcontinental
        Late Archaic and Early Woodland Societies. In *The Archaeology of
        Traditions: Agency and History before and after Columbus,* edited
        by Timothy R. Pauketat, pp. 195–217. University Press of Florida,
        Gainesville.

ENGELBRECHT, WILLIAM
1972   The Reflection of Patterned Behavior in Iroquois Pottery Deco-
        ration. *Pennsylvania Archaeologist* 42(1–2):1–15.

1974   The Iroquois: Archaeological Patterning on the Tribal Level. *World
        Archaeology* 6:52–65.

1984   The Kleis Site Ceramics: An Interpretive Approach. In *Extending the
        Rafters: Interdisciplinary Approaches to Iroquoian Studies,* edited
        by Michael K. Foster, Jack Campisi, and Marianne Mithun, pp.
        325–339. State University of New York Press, Albany.

1985   New York Iroquois Political Development. In *Cultures in Contact:
        The Impact of European Contacts on Native American Cultural
        Institutions, A.D. 1000–1800,* edited by William W. Fitzhugh, pp.
        163–186. Smithsonian Institution, Washington, D.C.

1987   Factors Maintaining Low Population Density among the Prehistoric
        New York Iroquois. *American Antiquity* 52:13–27.

1994   The Eaton Site: Preliminary Analysis of the Iroquoian Component.
        *The Bulletin: Journal of the New York State Archaeological Asso-
        ciation* 107:1–8.

2003   *Iroquoia: The Development of a Native World.* Syracuse University
        Press, Syracuse.

FEATHERS, JAMES
2002   Luminescence Dating of Pottery from the Thomas/Luckey Site,
        Chemung County, New York. Manuscript on file, Public Archae-
        ology Facility, Binghamton, New York.

FEINMAN, GARY M.
1997   Thoughts on New Approaches to Combining the Archaeological
        and Historical Records. *Journal of Archaeological Method and
        Theory* 4(3/4):367–377.

FENTON, WILLIAM N.

1949   Collecting Materials for a Political History of the Six Nations. *Proceedings of the American Philosophical Society* 93:233–238.

1951   Locality as a Basic Factor in the Development of Iroquois Social Structure. In *Symposuim on Local Diversity in Iroquois Culture,* edited by William N. Fenton, pp. 35-54. Smithsonian Institution Press, Washington, D.C.

1952   The Training of Historical Ethnologists in America. *American Anthropologist* 54:328–339.

1955   Factionalism in American Indian Society. *Acts of the Fourth International Congress of Anthropological and Ethnological Sciences* 2:330–340

1968   Introduction. In *Parker on the Iroquois,* edited by William N. Fenton, pp. 1–47. Syracuse University Press, Syracuse, New York.

1978   Northern Iroquoian Cultural Patterns. In *Northeast,* edited by Bruce G. Trigger, pp. 296–321. Handbook of North American Indians, Vol. 15, William C. Sturtevant, general editor. Smithsonian Institution, Washington, D.C.

1998   *The Great Law and the Longhouse: A Political History of the Iroquois Confederacy.* University of Oklahoma Press, Norman.

FERRING, C. REID

1984   Intrasite Spatial Patterning: Its Role in Settlement-Subsistence Systems Analysis. In *Intrasite Spatial Analysis in Archaeology,* edited by Harold J. Hietala, pp. 116–126. Cambridge University Press, New York.

FINLAYSON, WILLIAM D.

1977   *The Saugeen Culture: A Middle Woodland Manifestation in South-western Ontario.* Mercury Series, Archaeological Survey of Canada, Paper No. 61. National Museums of Canada, Ottawa.

1985   *The 1975 and 1978 Rescue Excavations at the Draper Site: Intro-duction and Settlement Patterns.* Mercury Series, Archaeological Survey of Canada, Paper No. 130. National Museums of Canada, Ottawa.

1998   Iroquoian Peoples of the Land of Rocks and Water, A.D. 1000–1650: A Study in Settlement Archaeology. Special Publication 1. London Museum of Archaeology, London, Ontario.

FLANNERY, KENT V., AND MARCUS WINTER

1976   Analyzing Household Activities. In *The Early Mesoamerican Village,* edited by Kent V. Flannery, pp. 34–47. Academic Press, New York.

FOGT, LISA, AND PETER RAMSDEN

1996   From Timepiece to Time Machine: Scale and Complexity in Iro-quoian Archaeology. In *Debating Complexity: Proceedings of the*

Twenty-Sixth Annual Chacmool Conference, edited by Daniel A. Meyer, Peter C. Dawson, and Donald T. Hanna, pp. 39–45. Archaeological Association of the University of Calgary, Calgary.

FORT PLAIN MUSEUM

2002   Smith Farm, Smith Farm II, and Osterhout 54 Sites. Manuscript on file at the Fort Plain Museum, Fort Plain, New York.

FOSTER, MICHAEL K.

1985   Another Look at the Function of Wampum in Iroquois-White Councils. In *The History and Culture of Iroquois Diplomacy*, edited by Francis Jennings, William N. Fenton, Mary A. Druke, and David R. Miller, pp. 99–114. Syracuse University Press, Syracuse, New York.

FOX, WILLIAM A.

1990   The Middle to Late Woodland Transition. In *The Archaeology of Southern Ontario to* A.D. *1650*, edited by Chris J. Ellis and Neal Ferris, pp. 171–188. Occasional Publication of the London Chapter No. 5. Ontario Archaeological Society, London, Ontario.

FUNK, ROBERT E.

1967   Garoga: A Late Prehistoric Iroquois Village in the Mohawk Valley. In *Iroquois Culture, History, and Prehistory: Proceedings of the 1965 Conference on Iroquois Research*, edited by Elizabeth Tooker, pp. 81–84. New York State Museum and Science Service, Albany.

1993   *Archaeological Investigations in the Upper Susquehanna Valley, New York State*, Vol. 1. Persimmon Press Monographs in Archaeology, Buffalo, New York.

GAMBLE, CLIVE

2001   *Archaeology: The Basics*. Routledge, New York.

GARRAD CHARLES, AND CONRAD E. HEIDENREICH

1978   Petun. In *Northeast*, edited by Bruce G. Trigger, pp. 394–397. Handbook of North American Indians, Vol. 15, William C. Sturtevant, general editor. Smithsonian Institution, Washington, D.C.

GARRAHAN, FRANCIS D.

1990   Airport II Site: A Clemson Island/Owasco Settlement on the North Branch of the Susquehanna River. *Pennsylvania Archaeologist* 60(1):1–31.

GEHRING, CHARLES T., AND WILLIAM A. STARNA (TRANSLATORS AND EDITORS)

1988   *A Journey into Mohawk and Oneida Country, 1634–1635: The Journal of Harmen Meyndertsz van den Bogaert*. Syracuse University Press, Syracuse, New York.

GERO, JOAN M., AND MARGARET W. CONKEY

1991   *Engendering Archaeology: Women and Prehistory*. Basil Blackwell, Oxford England.

GETTE, CHRISTOPHER I.
2000   Collectors, Williard Yager, and the Susquehanna River: A Proven-
       ience Analysis of the Upper Susquehanna Collection. Master's thesis,
       Department of Anthropology, Binghamton University, Binghamton,
       New York.

GIDDENS, ANTHONY
1979   *Central Problems in Social Theory: Action, Structure and Contra-
       diction in Social Analysis.* Macmillan, London.
1984   *The Constitution of Society: Outline of the Theory of Structuration.*
       Polity Press, Cambridge.

GNIVECKI, PERRY L.
1987   On the Quantitative Derivation of Household Spatial Organization
       from Archaeological Residues in Ancient Mesopotamia. In *Method
       and Theory for Activity Area Research: An Ethnoarchaeological
       Approach,* edited by Susan Kent, pp. 176–235. Columbia University
       Press, New York.

GOLDENWEISER, ALEXANDER A.
1914   Functions of Women in Iroquois Society. In *Iroquois Women: An
       Anthology,* edited by William Guy Spittal, pp. 51-52. Iroqrafts
       Limited, Iroquois Publications, Ontario, Canada.

GOULD, RICHARD A., AND PATTY JO WATSON
1982   A Dialogue on the Meaning and Use of Analogy in Ethnoarchae-
       ological Reasoning. *Journal of Anthropological Archaeology*
       1(4):355-381.

GRANT, W. L.
1959   *Voyages of Samuel De Champlain: 1604–1618.* Barnes and Noble,
       New York. Originally published 1907, Scribner's, New York.

GRASSMAN, THOMAS
1969   *The Mohawk Indians and Their Valley.* J. S. Lischynsky, Schenec-
       tady, New York.

GRAYBILL, JEFFERY R.
1989   The Shenks Ferry Complex Revisited. In *New Approaches to Other
       Pasts,* edited by W. Fred Kinsey and Roger W. Moeller, pp. 51–59.
       Archaeological Services, Bethlehem, Connecticut.

GRAYMONT, BARBARA
1981   The Six Nations Indians in the Revolutionary War. In *The Iroquois
       in the American Revolution: 1976 Conference Proceedings,* edited
       by Charles F. Hayes III, pp. 25–36. Research Records No. 14.
       Rochester Museum and Science Center, Rochester, New York.

GREEN, WILLIAM, AND LYNN P. SULLIVAN
1997   Pits and Pitfalls: An Analysis of Pit Features and Site Function at the
       Ripley Site. *Northeast Anthropology* 53:1–22.

GRIFFIN, JAMES B. (EDITOR)

1952 *Archaeology of Eastern United States.* University of Chicago Press, Chicago.

GRUMET, ROBERT S.

1995 *Historic Contact: Indian People and Colonists in Today's Northeastern United States in the Sixteenth to Eighteenth Centuries.* University of Oklahoma Press, Norman.

GULDENZOPF, DAVID

1984 Frontier Demography and Settlement Patterns of the Mohawk Iroquois. *Man in the Northeast* 27:79–94.

1986 The Colonial Transformation of Mohawk Iroquois Society. Ph.D. dissertation, State University of New York at Albany. University Microfilms, Ann Arbor.

HAGERTY, GILBERT W.

1985 *Wampum, War and Trade Goods West of the Hudson.* Heart of the Lakes Publishing, Interlaken, New York.

HALSEY, FRANCIS W.

1989 *A Tour of the Hudson, the Mohawk, the Susquehanna, and the Delaware in 1769.* Reprinted. Purple Mountain Press, Fleischmanns, New York. Originally published 1906, Scribner's, New York.

HALSTEAD, PAUL, AND JOHN O'SHEA (EDITORS)

1989 *Bad Year Economics: Cultural Responses to Risk and Uncertainty.* Cambridge University Press, Cambridge.

HAMELL, GEORGE R.

1987 Mythical Realities and European Contact in the Northeast during the Sixteenth and Seventeenth Centuries. *Man in the Northeast* 33:63–87.

HAMILTON, MILTON W.

1953 Myths and Legends of Sir William Johnson. *New York History* 38:18–28.

1956 Augustus C. Buell: Fraudulent Historian. *Pennsylvania Magazine of History and Biography* 80:478–492.

1976 *Sir William Johnson: Colonial American, 1715–1763.* Kennikat Press, Port Washington, New York.

HARRIS, MARVIN

1979 *Cultural Materialism: The Struggle for a Science of Culture.* Random House, New York.

HART, JOHN P.

1999 Dating Roundtop's Domesticates: Implications for Northeastern Late Prehistory. In *Current Northeast Paleoethnobotany,* edited by John P. Hart, pp. 47–68. New York State Museum Bulletin 494.

University of the State of New York, State Education Department, Albany.

2000   New Dates from Classic New York State Sites: Just How Old Are Those Longhouses? *Northeast Anthropology* 60:1–22.

2001   Maize, Matrilocality, Migration, and Iroquois Evolution. *Journal of Archaeological Method and Theory* 8(2):151–182.

HART, JOHN P., AND HETTY JO BRUMBACH
2003   The Death of Owasco. *American Antiquity* 68:737–752.

HART, JOHN P., AND CHRISTINA B. RIETH (EDITORS)
2002   *Northeast Subsistence-Settlement Change: A.D. 700–1300.* New York State Museum Bulletin 496. University of the State of New York, State Education Department, Albany.

HART, JOHN P., AND C. MARGARET SCARRY
1999   The Age of Common Beans (*Phaseolus vulgaris*) in the Northeast United States. *American Antiquity* 64:653–658.

HART, JOHN P., ROBERT G. THOMPSON, AND HETTY JO BRUMBACH
2003   Phytolith Evidence for Early Maize (*Zea mays*) in the Northern Finger Lakes Region of New York. *American Antiquity* 68:619–640.

HASENSTAB, ROBERT J.
1987   Canoes, Caches, and Carrying Places: Territorial Boundaries and Tribalization in Late Woodland Western New York. *The Bulletin: Journal of the New York State Archaeological Association* 95:39–49.

1996   Settlement as Adaptation: Variability in Iroquois Village Site Selection as Inferred through GIS. In *New Methods, Old Problems: Geographic Information Systems in Modern Archaeological Research,* edited by G. Maschner, pp. 223–241. Occasional Paper No. 23. Center for Archaeological Investigations, Southern Illinois University, Carbondale.

HASENSTAB, ROBERT J., AND WILLIAM C. JOHNSON
2001   Hilltops of the Allegheny Plateau: A Preferred Microenvironment for Late Prehistoric Horticulturalists. In *Archaeology of the Appalachian Highlands,* edited by Lynne P. Sullivan and Susan C. Prezzano, pp. 3–18. University of Tennessee Press, Knoxville.

HASSAN, FEKRI A.
1981   *Demographic Archaeology.* Academic Press, New York.

HATCH, JAMES W. (EDITOR)
1980   *The Fisher Farm Site: A Late Woodland Hamlet in Context.* The Archaeology of Central Pennsylvania, Vol. 1. Occasional Papers No. 12. Pennsylvania State University, Department of Anthropology, University Park, Pennsylvania.

HAY, CONRAN, JAMES HATCH, AND JANET SUTTON
1987   *A Management Plan for Clemson Island Archaeological Resources in the Commonwealth of Pennsylvania.* Pennsylvania Historical and Museum Commission, Bureau for Historic Preservation, Harrisburg, Pennsylvania.

HAYDEN, BRIAN
1973   *Settlement Patterns of the Draper and White Sites: 1973 Excavations.* Publication No. 6. Department of Archaeology, Simon Fraser University, Burnaby, British Columbia.

1977   Corporate Groups and the Late Ontario Iroquoian Longhouse. *Ontario Archaeology* 28:3–11.

HAYDEN, BRIAN, AND AUBREY CANNON
1982   The Corporate Group as an Archaeological Unit. *Journal of Anthropological Archaeology* 1:132–158.

1983   Where the Garbage Goes: Refuse Disposal in the Maya Highlands. *Journal of Anthropological Archaeology* 2:117–163.

HAYDEN, HORACE EDWIN
1901   Echoes of the Massacre of Wyoming. *Proceedings and Collections of the Wyoming Historical and Geological Society* 7:78–105.

HEIDENREICH, CONRAD
1971   *Huronia: A History and Geography of the Huron Indians, 1600–1650.* McClelland and Stewart, Toronto.

1978   Huron. In *Northeast*, edited by Bruce G. Trigger, pp. 368–388. Handbook of North American Indians, Vol. 15, William C. Sturtevant, general editor. Smithsonian Institution, Washington, D.C.

HEISEY, HENRY W.
1971   An Interpretation of Shenks Ferry Ceramics. *Pennsylvania Archaeologist* 41(4):44–70.

HEISEY, HENRY W., AND J. PAUL WITMER
1971   The Shenk's Ferry People: A Site and Some Generalities. In *Foundations of Pennsylvania Prehistory,* edited by Barry C. Kent, Ira F. Smith III, and Catherine McCann, pp. 477–507. Pennsylvania Historical Commission, Harrisburg.

HELLIWELL, CHRISTINE
1992   Good Walls Make Bad Neighbours: The Dayak Longhouse as a Community of Voices. *Oceania* 62(3):179–93.

HENDON, JULIA A.
1996   Archaeological Approaches to the Organization of Domestic Labor: Household Practice and Domestic Relations. *Annual Review of Anthropology* 25:46–61.

HERRICK, JAMES W.
1995   *Iroquois Medical Botany.* Edited by Dean R. Snow. Syracuse
        University Press, Syracuse, New York.

HIRTH, KENNETH
1993   The Household as an Analytical Unit: Problems in Method and
        Theory. In *Prehispanic Domestic Units in Western Mesoamerica:
        Studies of the Household, Compound, and Residence,* edited by
        Robert S. Santley and Kenneth G. Hirth, pp. 21–36. CRC Press,
        Boca Raton, Florida.

HODDER, IAN
1987   The Meaning of Discard: Ash and Domestic Space in Baringo. In
        *Method and Theory for Activity Area Research: An Ethnoarchae-
        ological Approach,* edited by Susan Kent, pp. 424–448. Columbia
        University Press, New York.

HODDER, IAN, AND CLIVE ORTON
1976   *Spatial Analysis in Archaeology.* Cambridge University Press,
        Cambridge.

HOHMAN, CHRISTOPHER D., AND JENNIFER L. BONNER
2000   *Cultural Resource Management Survey, Stage 1 Archaeological
        Reconnaissance, Deposit Water/Sewer Project, Village of Deposit
        and Town of Deposit, Delaware County, New York.* Public
        Archaeology Facility, Binghamton University, Binghamton, New
        York.

HOLL, AUGUSTIN
1993   Late Neolithic Cultural Landscape in Southeastern Mauritania: An
        Essay in Spatiometrics. In *Spatial Boundaries and Social Dynamics
        Case Studies in Food-Producing Societies,* edited by Augustin Holl
        and Thomas E. Levy, pp. 95–133. Ethnoarchaeological Series 2.
        International Monographs in Prehistory, Ann Arbor, Michigan.

JAMIESON, SUSAN M.
1989   Precepts and Percepts of Northern Iroquoian Households and
        Communities: The Changing Past. In *Households and Communi-
        ties: Proceedings of the Twenty-first Annual Conference,* edited by
        Scott MacEachern, David J. W. Archer, and Richard D. Garvin, pp.
        307–314. Archaeological Association of the University of Calgary,
        Calgary.

JENNINGS, FRANCES
1975   *The Invasion of America: Indians, Colonialism and the Cant of
        Conquest.* W. W. Norton, New York.
1984   *The Ambiguous Iroquois Empire.* W. W. Norton, New York.

JOHNSTON, RICHARD B., AND L. J. JACKSON
1980   Settlement Patterns at the Le Caron Site, a 17th Century Huron
        Village. *Journal of Field Archaeology* 7:173–99.

JONES, GEORGE T., AND CHARLOTTE BECK
1992   Chronological Resolution in Distributional Archaeology. In *Space,
        Time, and Archaeological Landscapes,* edited by Jaqueline Rossignol
        and LuAnn Wandsnider, pp. 167–192. Plenum Press, New York.

JONES, ROBERT W.
1971   Excavations in Dauphin and Juniata Counties, 1929. In *Foundations
        of Pennsylvania Prehistory,* edited by Barry C. Kent, Ira F. Smith III,
        and Catherine McCann, pp. 393–418. Pennsylvania Historical and
        Museum Commission, Harrisburg.

JORDAN, KURT A.
2002   The Archaeology of the Iroquois Restoration: Settlement, Housing,
        and Economy at a Dispersed Seneca Community, ca. A.D. 1715–
        1754. Ph.D. dissertation, Columbia University, New York. University
        Microfilms, Ann Arbor.

2003   An Eighteenth Century Seneca Iroquois Short Longhouse from the
        Townley-Read Site, c. A.D. 1715–1754. *The Bulletin: Journal of the
        New York State Archaeological Association* 119:43–63.

2004   Seneca Iroquois Settlement Pattern, Community Structure, and
        Housing, 1677–1779. *Northeast Anthropology* 67:23–60.

JORDAN, TERRY G.
1993   *North American Cattle-Ranching Frontiers: Origins, Diffusion, and
        Differentiation.* University of New Mexico Press, Albuquerque.

JORDAN, TERRY G., AND MATTI KAUPS
1989   *The American Backwoods Frontier: An Ethnic and Ecological
        Interpretation.* Johns Hopkins University Press, Baltimore.

JUSTICE, NOEL D.
1987   *Stone Age Spear and Arrow Points of the Midcontinental and
        Eastern United States: A Modern Survey and Reference.* Indiana
        University Press, Bloomington.

KAPCHES, MIMA
1979   Intra-Longhouse Spatial Analysis. *Pennsylvania Archaeologist*
        49(4):24–29.

1980   Wall Trenches on Iroquoian Sites. *Archaeology of Eastern North
        America* 8:98–105.

1984   Cabins on Ontario Iroquois Sites. *North American Archaeologist*
        5(1):63–71.

1990   The Spatial Dynamics of Ontario Iroquoian Longhouses. *American
        Antiquity* 55:49–67.

1993   The Identification of an Iroquoian Unit of Measurement: Architecture and Social/Cultural Implications for the Longhouse. *Archaeology of Eastern North America* 21:137–162.

1994a   The Iroquoian Longhouse: Architectural and Cultural Identity. In *Meaningful Architecture: Social Interpretations of Buildings*, edited by Martin Locock, pp. 253–270. Aldershot, Brookfield, Vermont.

1994b   The Hill Site: A Possible Late Early Iroquoian Ceramic Firing Site in South-Central Ontario. *Northeast Anthropology* 48:91–102.

KEENER, CRAIG S.

1995   Warfare as the Evolutionary Mechanism for Iroquoian Tribalization. In *Origins of the People of the Longhouse*, edited by André Bekerman and Gary A. Warrick, pp. 97–105. Ontario Archaeological Society, London, Ontario.

1999   An Ethnohistorical Analysis of Iroquois Assault Tactics Used against Fortified Settlements of the Northeast in the Seventeenth Century. *Ethnohistory* 46(4):777–807.

KENT, BARRY C.

1993   *Susquehanna's Indians*. Reprinted with a new preface. Anthropological Series No. 6. Pennsylvania Historical and Museum Commission, Harrisburg.

KENT, DONALD H.

1974   Historical Report on the Niagara River and the Niagara River Strip to 1759. In *Iroquois Indians II*, edited by David Agee Horr, pp. 11–201. Garland Publishing, New York.

KENT, SUSAN

1987   Understanding the Use of Space: An Ethnoarchaeological Approach. In *Method and Theory for Activity Area Research: An Ethnoarchaeological Approach*, edited by Susan Kent, pp. 1–60. Columbia University Press, New York.

KINSEY, W. FRED, AND JEFFREY R. GRAYBILL

1971   Murry Site and Its Role in Lancaster and Funk Phase of Shenks Ferry Culture. *Pennsylvania Archaeologist* 41(4):7–44.

KINSEY, W. FRED, III, HENRY HEISEY, AND JEFFREY R. GRAYBILL

1971   Shenks Ferry Culture: A View from 1971. *Pennsylvania Archaeologist* 41(4):1–70.

KNAPP, TIMOTHY D.

1996a   *Stage 3 Data Recovery Thomas/Luckey Site (SUBi-888), Town of Ashland, Chemung County, New York*. Public Archaeology Facility, Binghamton University, Binghamton, New York.

1996b   Early Late Woodland Subsistence: A View from the Chemung Valley. Paper presented at the Archaeobotany in the Northeast Symposium sponsored by the New York Natural History Conference IV, Albany, New York.

2000a   Captured Wives or Agents of Interaction? Women and Peaceful Forms of Integration Among Early Iroquoians. Paper presented at the 65th Annual Meeting of the Society for American Archaeology, Philadelphia.

2000b   *Stage 1B Addendum Reconnaissance, Deposit Water/Sewer Project, Town of Deposit, Delaware County, New York and Stage II Site Examination of the Deposit Airport III Site (SUBi-2050), Town of Deposit, Delaware County, New York.* Public Archaeology Facility, Binghamton University, Binghamton, New York.

2002a   Pits, Plants, and Place: Recognizing Late Prehistoric Subsistence and Settlement Diversity in the Upper Susquehanna Drainage. In *Northeast Subsistence-Settlement Change: A.D. 700–1300,* edited by John P. Hart and Christina B. Rieth, pp. 167–192. New York State Museum Bulletin 496. University of the State of New York, State Education Department, Albany.

2002b   An Unbounded Future? Ceramic Types, "Cultures," and Scale in Late Prehistoric Research. Paper presented at the Annual Meeting of the Society for America Archaeology, Denver.

2003   What's up the Delaware? Recent Middle/Late Woodland Excavations in New York's Forgotten Valley. Paper presented at the 70th Annual Meeting of the Eastern States Archaeological Federation, Mount Laurel, New Jersey.

KNAPP, TIMOTHY D., AND NINA M. VERSAGGI

2002   *Data Recovery Investigations of the Deposit Airport I Site (SUBi-2048), Deposit Water/Sewer Project, Town of Deposit, Delaware County, New York.* Public Archaeology Facility, Binghamton University, Binghamton, New York.

KNIGHT, CHARLES

1996   Lithic Distribution at the Carman (Schoolhouse) Site. Master's thesis, Department of Anthropology, University of Pittsburgh, Pittsburgh.

KNIGHT, DEAN

1987   Settlement Patterns at the Ball Site: A 17th Century Huron Village. *Archaeology of Eastern North America* 15:177–188.

1989   Huron Houses: Structures from the Ball Site. In *Households and Communities: Proceedings of the Twenty-first Annual Conference,* edited by Scott MacEachern, David J. W. Archer, and Richard D. Garvin, pp. 287–292. Archaeological Association of the University of Calgary, Calgary.

KNOERL, JOHN J.

1975   PIN 9357.13. In *I-88 Archaeological Project: 1975 Summer Season,* edited by Margaret L. Weide, pp. VI1–VI26. Public Archaeology Facility, State University of New York State, Binghamton.

KOHL, PHILIP L.
1987   The Use and Abuse of World Systems Theory: The Case of the
        Pristine West Asian State. In *Advances in Archaeological Method
        and Theory,* Vol. 11, edited by Michael B. Schiffer, pp. 1–35.
        Academic Press, New York.

KRAMER, CAROL
1982   Ethnographic Households and Archaeological Interpretation:
        A Case from Iranian Kurdistan. *American Behavioral Scientist*
        25(6):663–675.

KUHN, ROBERT D.
1985   Trade and Exchange among the Mohawk-Iroquois: A Trace Element
        Analysis of Ceramic Smoking Pipes. Ph.D. dissertation, Department
        of Anthropology, State University of New York at Albany, Albany.

1986   Interaction Patterns in Eastern New York: A Trace Element Analysis
        of Iroquoian and Algonquian Ceramics. *The Bulletin and Journal of
        Archaeology for New York State* 92:9–21.

1987   A Preliminary Report on the Attribute Analysis of Mohawk
        Ceramics. *The Bulletin and Journal of Archaeology for New York
        State* 94:40–46.

KUHN, ROBERT D., AND ROBERT E. FUNK
2000   Boning Up on the Mohawk: An Overview of Mohawk Faunal
        Assemblages and Subsistence Patterns. *Archaeology of Eastern
        North America* 28:29–62.

KUHN, ROBERT D., AND MARTHA L. SEMPOWSKI
2001   A New Approach to Dating the League of the Iroquois. *American
        Antiquity* 66:301–314.

LAFITAU, FATHER JOSEPH FRANÇOIS
1977   [1724] *Customs of the American Indians Compared with the Cus-
        toms of Primitive Times,* Vol. 2. Edited and translated by William
        Fenton and Elizabeth Moore. Champlain Society, Toronto.

LANTZ, STANLEY W.
1980   Seneca Cabin Site: Historic Component of the Vanatta Site
        (30CA46). *Pennsylvania Archaeologist* 50(1–2):9–41.

LATTA, MARTHA A.
1985   A 17th Century Attigneenongnahac Village: Settlement Patterns at
        the Auger Site (BdGw-3). *Ontario Archaeology* 44:41–54.

1991   The Captive Bride Syndrome: Iroquoian Behavior or Archaeological
        Myth? In *The Archaeology of Gender: Proceedings of the Twenty-
        second Annual Conference,* edited by Dale Walde and Noreen D.
        Willows, pp. 375–382. Archaeological Association of the University
        of Calgary, Calgary.

LAYNE, LINDA L.
1987   Village-Bedouin: Patterns of Change from Mobility to Sedentism in Jordan. In *Method and Theory for Activity Area Research: An Ethnoarchaeological Approach,* edited by Susan Kent, pp. 345–373. Columbia University Press, New York.

LENDER, MARK E., AND JAMES KIRBY MARTIN (EDITORS)
1982   *Citizen Soldier: The Revolutionary War Journal of Joseph Bloomfield.* New Jersey Historical Society, Newark.

LENIG, DONALD
1965   The Oak Hill Horizon and Its Relation to the Development of the Five Nation Iroquois Culture. *Researches and Transactions* 15(1). New York State Archaeological Association, Buffalo.

LENIG, WAYNE
2003   Mohawk Archaeology and the Swart Collection. Paper presented at the Conference on Iroquois Research, Rensselaerville, New York.

LENNOX, PAUL A.
1995   Introduction. In *MTO Contributions to the Archaeology of the Late Woodland Period in Southwestern Ontario: Small Sites Investigations,* edited by Paul A. Lennox, pp. 1–7. Research Report No. 24. London Museum of Archaeology, London, Ontario.

LENNOX, PAUL A., AND WILLIAM R. FITZGERALD
1990   The Culture History and Archaeology of the Neutral Iroquoians. In *The Archaeology of Southern Ontario to A.D. 1650,* edited by Chris J. Ellis and Neal Ferris, pp. 279–290. Occasional Publication of the London Chapter No. 5. Ontario Archaeological Society, London, Ontario.

LENNOX, PAUL A., AND WAYNE P. HAGERTY
1995   A Prehistoric Neutral Hamlet, Waterloo County, Ontario. In *MTO Contributions to the Archaeology of the Late Woodland Period in Southwestern Ontario: Small Sites Investigations,* edited by Paul A. Lennox, pp. 8–76. Research Report No. 24. London Museum of Archaeology, London, Ontario.

LEVEILLEE, ALAN, AND BURR HARRISON
1996   An Archaeological Landscape in Narragansett, Rhode Island: Point Judith Upper Pond. *Bulletin of the Massachusetts Archaeological Society* 57:58–63.

LEWANDOWSKI, MICHAEL
2002   Final Project: Faunal Analysis. Manuscript on file, Department of Anthropology, University of Pittsburgh, Pittsburgh.

LIGHTFOOT, KENT G.
2001   Traditions as Cultural Production: Implications for Contemporary Archaeological Research. In *The Archaeology of Traditions: Agency*

and History before and after Columbus, edited by Timothy R. Pauketat, pp. 237–252. University Press of Florida, Gainesville.

LIGHTFOOT, KENT G., ANTOINETTE MARTINEZ, AND ANN M. SCHIFF
1998   Daily Practice and Material Culture in Pluralistic Social Settings: An Archaeological Study of Culture Change and Persistence from Fort Ross, California. *American Antiquity* 63:199–222.

LIGHTFOOT, RICKY R.
1994   *The Duckfoot Site, Volume Archaeology of the House and Household.* Occasional Paper No. 4. Crow Canyon Archaeological Center, Cortez, Colorado.

LORD, PHILIP, JR.
1996   Taverns, Forts, and Castles: Rediscovering King Hendrick's Village. *Northeast Anthropology* 52:69–94.

LUCY, CHARLES L.
1971   Pottery Types of the Upper Susquehanna. In *Foundations of Pennsylvania Prehistory,* edited by Barry C. Kent, Ira F. Smith III, and Catherine McCann, pp. 381–392. Pennsylvania Historical and Museum Commission, Harrisburg.
1979   The Tioga Point Farm Sites 36BR3 and 36BR52: 1983 Excavations. *Pennsylvania Archaeologist* 49(1–2):1–18.

LUCY, CHARLES L., AND LEROY VANDERPOEL
1979   Tioga Point Farm Site. *Pennsylvania Archaeologist* 49:1–12.

McCANN, CATHERINE
1971   Notes on the Pottery of the Clemson and Book Mounds. In *Foundations of Pennsylvania Prehistory,* edited by Barry C. Kent, Ira F. Smith III, and Catherine McCann, pp. 419–423. Pennsylvania Historical and Museum Commission, Harrisburg.

McCONNELL, MICHAEL N.
1992   *A Country Between: The Upper Ohio Valley and Its Peoples, 1724–1774.* University of Nebraska Press, Lincoln.

MacDONALD, ROBERT I.
1988   Ontario Iroquoian Sweat Lodges. *Ontario Archaeology* 48:17–26.
1992   Ontario Iroquoian Semi-subterranean Sweat Lodges. In *Ancient Images, Ancient Thought: The Archaeology of Ideology: Proceedings of the Twenty-third Annual Chacmool Conference,* edited by A. Sean Goldsmith, Sandra Garvie, David Selin, and Jeannette Smith, pp. 323–330. Archaeological Association of the University of Calgary, Calgary.

McGUIRE, RANDALL
1992   *A Marxist Archaeology.* Academic Press, Orlando.

McKern, W. C.
1939   The Midwestern Taxonomic Method as an Aid to Archaeological
        Culture Study. *American Antiquity* 4:310–313.

MacNeish, Richard S.
1952   *Iroquois Pottery Types: A Technique for the Study of Iroquois Pre-
        history.* Bulletin No. 124, Anthropological Series No. 31. Depart-
        ment of Resources and Development, National Parks Branch, Na-
        tional Museum of Canada, Ottawa.

Mandzy, Adrian
1990   The Rogers Farm Site: A Seventeenth-Century Cayuga Site. *The
        Bulletin: Journal of the New York State Archaeological Association*
        100:18–25.
1992   History of Cayuga Acculturation: An Examination of the 17th
        Century Cayuga Iroquois Archaeological Data. M.A. thesis,
        Department of Anthropology, Michigan State University, Lansing.
1994   The Results of Interaction: Change in Cayuga Society during the
        Seventeenth Century. In *Proceedings of the 1992 People to People
        Conference,* edited by Charles F. Hayes II, pp. 133–156. Research
        Records No. 23. Rochester Museum and Science Center, Rochester,
        New York.

Marquardt, William H.
1985   Complexity and Scale in the Study of Fisher-Gatherer-Hunters:
        An Example from the Eastern United States. In *Prehistoric Hunter-
        Gatherers: The Emergence of Cultural Complexity,* edited by T.
        Douglas Price and James A. Brown, pp. 59–98. Academic Press,
        Orlando.
1992   Dialectical Archaeology. In *Archaeological Method and Theory,* Vol.
        4, edited by Michael B. Schiffer, pp. 101–140. University of Arizona
        Press, Tucson.

Marquardt, William H., and Carole L. Crumley
1987   Theoretical Issues in the Analysis of Spatial Patterning. In *Regional
        Dynamics: Burgundian Landscapes in Historical Perspective,*
        edited by Carole L. Crumley and William H. Marquardt, pp. 1–18.
        Academic Press, San Diego.

Martelle, Holly
1999   Redefining Craft Specialization: Women's Labor and Pottery
        Production—An Iroquoian Example. In *From the Ground Up:
        Beyond Gender Theory in Archaeology,* edited by Nancy L. Wicker
        and Bettina Arnold, pp. 133–142. BAR International Series 812.
        Archaeopress, Oxford.

Maschner, Herbert D. G.
1996   *New Methods, Old Problems: Geographic Information Systems
        in Modern Archaeological Research.* Occasional Paper No. 23.

Center for Archaeological Investigations Southern Illinois University, Carbondale.

MEILLASSOUX, CLAUDE
1972   From Reproduction to Production. *Economy and Society* 1:93–105.

MERRIFIELD, EDWARD
1915   *The Story of the Captivity and Rescue from the Indians of Luke Swetland*. Publisher not indicated, Scranton, Pennsylvania.

METZ, ELIZABETH
1995   *Ste. Marie among the Iroquois*. Friends of Historic Onondaga Lake, Liverpool, New York.

MICHAUD-STUTZMAN, TRACY S.
2001   Economy and Ritual in a Late Prehistoric Cayuga Iroquois Longhouse. Paper presented at the Annual Meeting of the Society for America Archaeology, New Orleans.

2002   Multi-Scalar Analysis of Domestic Activities at Parker Farm: A Late Prehistoric Cayuga Iroquois Village. Ph.D. dissertation, Department of Anthropology, University of Pittsburgh, Pittsburgh.

MICHAUD-STUTZMAN, TRACY S., AND KATHLEEN M. SYDORIAK ALLEN
1998   Recent Investigations at Parker Farm: A Late Prehistoric Cayuga Iroquois Village. Paper presented at the Cayuga Museum Northeast Archaeological Symposium, Auburn, New York.

MILLER, DANIEL, AND CHRISTOPHER TILLEY (EDITORS)
1984   *Ideology, Power and Prehistory*. Cambridge University Press, Cambridge.

MILLER, NORTON G.
1973   *Late Glacial and Postglacial Vegetation Change in Southwestern New York State*. New York State Museum Bulletin 20. University of the State of New York, State Education Department, Albany.

MIROFF, LAURIE E.
1997   *Thomas/Luckey Site (SUBi-888), 1996 SUNY-Binghamton Field School Report, Town of Ashland, Chemung County, New York*. Public Archaeology Facility, Binghamton University, Binghamton, New York.

2002a   Building a Village One Household at a Time: Patterning at the Thomas/Luckey Site, New York. Ph.D. dissertation, Department of Anthropology, Binghamton University, Binghamton, New York.

2002b   Upland Land Use Patterns during the Early Late Prehistoric (A.D. 700–1300). In *Northeast Subsistence-Settlement Change: A.D. 700–1300*, edited by John P. Hart and Christina B. Rieth, pp. 193–208. New York State Museum Bulletin 496. University of the State of New York, State Education Department, Albany.

2002c   *Prehistoric Land Use in the Chemung Valley: Data Recovery Investigations of the Multi-Component Lamb Site (SUBi-1643,*

NYSM #10269), PIN 6066.41.122, Town of Ashland, Chemung County, New York, MCD 01501, 96PR1211, with contributions by Nancy Asch Sidell. Public Archaeology Facility, Binghamton University, Binghamton, New York.

MITCHELL, WILLIAM W.

1978   Environmental Setting. In *I-88 Archaeological Report, P.I.N. 9357.08 and P.I.N. 9357.12,* edited by Albert A. Dekin, Jr., pp. 3–6. Public Archaeology Facility, State University of New York, Binghamton.

MOELLER, ROGER W.

1992   *Analyzing and Interpreting Late Woodland Features.* Occasional Publications in Northeastern Anthropology No. 12. Archaeological Services, Bethlehem, Connecticut.

MOHOLY-NAGY, HATTULA

1990   The Misidentification of Mesoamerican Lithic Workshops. *Latin American Antiquity* 1: 268–279.

MONCKTON, STEPHEN G.

1992   *Huron Paleoethnobotany.* Ontario Archaeological Reports 1. Ontario Heritage Foundation, Toronto.

MOODY, KEVIN, AND CHARLES L. FISHER

1989   Archaeological Evidence of the Colonial Occupation at Schoharie Crossing State Historic Site, Montgomery County, New York. *The Bulletin: Journal of the New York State Archaeological Association* 99:1–13.

MOORE, HENRIETTA L.

1992   Households and Gender Relations: The Modelling of the Economy. In *Understanding Economic Process,* edited by Sutti Ortiz and Susan Lees, pp. 131–149. Monographs in Economic Anthropology No. 10. University Press of America, Lanham, Maryland.

MOREAU, JEAN-FRANÇOIS

1996   Indices Archéologiques de Transferts Culturels par la Voie du Québec Central. In *Transferts Culturels et Métissages Amérique/Europe, XVIᵉ–XXᵉ Siècle,* edited by Laurier Turgeon, Denys Delâge, and Réal Ouellet, pp. 209–242. Université Laval, Quebec.

1998   Traditions and Cultural Transformations: European Copper-Based Kettles and Jesuit Rings from 17th Century Amerindian Sites. *North American Archaeologist* 19(1):1–11.

MORGAN, LEWIS H.

1962   [1851] *League of the Iroquois.* Citadel Press, Secaucus, New Jersey.

MORIN, EUGÈNE

2001   Early Late Woodland Social Interaction in the St. Lawrence River Valley. *Archaeology of Eastern North America* 29:66–100.

MORROW, TOBY A.

1999   Continuity and Change in the Lithic Technology of the Precontact Great Lakes Region. In *Taming the Taxonomy: Toward a New Understanding of Great Lakes Archaeology,* edited by Ronald F. Williamson and Christopher M. Watts, pp. 219–236. Eastendbooks, Toronto.

MURRAY, LOUISE WELLES

1908   *A History of Old Tioga Point and Early Athens Pennsylvania.* Raeder Press, Wilkes-Barre, Pennsylvania.

NAMMACK, GEORGIANA C.

1969   *Fraud, Politics, and the Dispossession of the Indians: The Iroquois Land Frontier in the Colonial Period.* University of Oklahoma Press, Norman.

NASS, JOHN P., JR.

1995   An Examination of Social, Economic, and Political Organization at the Throckmorton Site, a Monongahela Community in Greene County, Pennsylvania. *Archaeology of Eastern North America* 23:81–93.

NASS, JOHN P., JR., AND RICHARD YERKES

1995   Social Differentiation in Mississippian and Fort Ancient Societies. In *Mississippian Communities and Households,* edited by J. Daniel Rogers and Bruce D. Smith, pp. 58–80. University of Alabama Press, Tuscaloosa.

NASSANEY, MICHAEL S., AND CHARLES R. COBB

1991   Patterns and Processes of Late Woodland Development in the Greater Southeastern United States. In *Stability, Transformation, and Variation,* edited by Michael S. Nassaney and Charles R. Cobb, pp. 285–322. Plenum Press, New York.

NASSANEY, MICHAEL S., AND KENNETH E. SASSAMAN (EDITORS)

1995   *Native American Interactions: Multiscalar Analyses and Interpretations in the Eastern Woodlands.* University of Tennessee Press, Knoxville.

NEEDS-HOWARTH, SUZANNE J. (CR)

1999   Native Fishing in the Great Lakes—a Multidisciplinary Approach to Zooarchaeological Remains from Precontact Iroquoian Villages near Lake Simcoe, Ontario. Ph.D. dissertation, Groningen Institute for Archaeology, University of Groningen, Netherlands.

NELSON, CAROL R.

1977   The Klinko Site: A Late Woodland Component in Seneca County, New York. Master's thesis, Department of Anthropology, State University of New York at Buffalo.

NELSON, MARGARET C., AND MICHELLE HEGMON

2001 Abandonment Is Not as It Seems: An Approach to the Relationship between Site and Regional Abandonment. *American Antiquity* 66:213–235.

NELSON, SARAH M.

1997 *Gender in Archaeology: Analyzing Power and Prestige.* AltaMira Press, Walnut Creek, California.

NETTING, ROBERT M.

1982 Some Home Truths on Household Size and Wealth. *American Behavioral Scientist* 25(6):641–662.

NETTING, ROBERT M., RICHARD WILK, AND ERIC J. ARNOULD

1984 Introduction. In *Households: Comparative and Historical Studies of the Domestic Group,* edited by Robert McC. Netting, Richard Wilk, and Eric J. Arnould, pp. xiii–xxxviii. University of California Press, Berkeley.

NEWELL, RAYMOND

1987 Reconstruction of the Partitioning and Utilization of Outside Space in a Late Prehistoric/Early Historic Inupiat Village. In *Method and Theory for Activity Area Research: An Ethnoarchaeological Approach,* edited by Susan Kent, pp. 107–175. Columbia University Press, New York.

NEW YORK ARCHAEOLOGICAL COUNCIL

1994 *Standards for Cultural Resources Investigations and the Curation of Archaeological Collections.* New York Archaeological Council, Albany.

NEW YORK STATE MUSEUM SITE FILE

2002 New York State Museum Site 4761, 6590, and 8702. Manuscript on file at the New York State Museum, Division of Research and Collections, Albany, New York.

NIEMCZYCKI, MARY ANN P.

1984 *The Origin and Development of the Seneca and Cayuga Tribes of New York State.* Research Records 17. Rochester Museum and Science Center, Rochester, New York.

1986 The Genesee Connection: The Origins of Iroquois Culture in West-Central New York. *North American Archaeologist* 7(1):15–44.

1988 Seneca Tribalization: An Adaptive Strategy. *Man in the Northeast* 36:77–87.

NOBLE, WILLIAM

1969 Some Social Implications of the Iroquois "In Situ" Theory. *Ontario Archaeology* 13:16–28.

NOON, JOHN A.

1949 *Law and Government of the Grand River Iroquois.* Viking Fund Press, New York.

NORCLIFFE, GLEN, AND CONRAD HEIDENREICH
1974   The Preferred Orientation of Iroquoian Longhouses in Ontario.
        Ontario Archaeology 23:3–30.

O'CALLAGHAN, EDMUND BAILEY (EDITOR)
1849–51 *Documentary History of the State of New York*. 4 vols. Weed,
        Parsons, and Co., Albany, New York.
1853–87 *Documents Relative to the Colonial History of the State of New
        York*. 15 vols. Weed, Parsons, and Co., Albany, New York.

OLDS, NATHANIEL S. (EDITOR)
1930   Journal of the Expedition of the Marquis de Denonville against the
        Iroquois, 1687, by Chevalier de Baugy. *Rochester Historical Society
        Publication Fund* 9:3–56.

ORTNER, SHERRY B.
1984   Theory in Anthropology since the Sixties. *Society for Comparative
        Study of Society and History* 26(1):126-166.

O'SHEA, JOHN
1989   Role of Wild Resources in Small-Scale Agricultural Systems: Tales
        from the Lakes and Plains. In *Bad Year Economics: Cultural
        Responses to Risk and Uncertainty*, edited by Paul Halstead and
        John O'Shea, pp. 57–67. Cambridge University Press, Cambridge.

OSWALD, DANA BETH
1987   The Organization of Space in Residential Buildings: A Cross-
        Cultural Perspective. In *Method and Theory for Activity Area
        Research: An Ethnoarchaeological Approach*, edited by Susan Kent,
        pp. 295–344. Columbia University Press, New York.

OTTAWAY, B. S.
1987   Radiocarbon: Where We Are and Where We Need to Be. *Antiquity*
        61:135–137.

OTTERNESS, PHILIP
2004   *Becoming German: The 1709 Palatine Migration to New York*.
        Cornell University Press, Ithaca, New York.

OTTO, B. A.
1991   The Hathaway Site, Sections 6 and 5, Rocky Nook, Kingston,
        Massachusetts: A Small Late Woodland and Late Archaic Lithic
        Work Site, and a Small Late Archaic Shell Midden. *The Bulletin of
        the Massachusetts Archaeological Society* 52:18–127.

OWENS, DONALD W., WILLIE L. PITTMAN, JOHN P. WULFORST, AND
    WILLIS E. HANNA
1986   *Soil Survey of Erie County, New York*. United States Department of
        Agriculture, Soil Conservation Service. Government Printing Office,
        Washington, D.C.

PARKER, ARTHUR C.

1916   The Origin of the Iroquois as Suggested by Their Archeology. *American Anthropologist* 18(4):479–507.

1968a   [1916] The Constitution of the Five Nations, or the Iroquois Book of the Great Law. In *Parker on the Iroquois,* edited by William Fenton. Syracuse University Press Syracuse, Syracuse, New York.

1968b   [1910] Iroquois Uses of Maize and Other Food Plants. In *Parker on the Iroquois,* edited by William Fenton, pp. 1–119. Syracuse University Press, Syracuse, New York.

1968c   [1916] *Parker on the Iroquois.* Edited by William N. Fenton. Syracuse University Press, Syracuse, New York.

PARMENTER, JON WILLIAM

1999   At the Wood's Edge: Iroquois Foreign Relations, 1727–1768. Ph.D. dissertation, University of Michigan. University Microfilms, Ann Arbor.

2001   The Significance of the "Illegal Fur Trade" to the Eighteenth Century Iroquois. In *Aboriginal People and the Fur Trade: Proceedings of the 8th North American Fur Trade Conference, Akwesasne,* edited by Louise Johnston, pp. 40–47. Akwesasne Notes Publishing, Cornwall, Ontario.

PARRY, WILLIAM J., AND ROBERT L. KELLY

1987   Sedentism in the Organization of Core Technology. In *Organization of Core Technology,* edited by Jay K. Johnson and Carol A. Morrow, pp. 285–304. Westview Press, Boulder, Colorado.

PASTERNAK, BURTON, CAROL R. EMBER, AND MELVIN EMBER

1976   On the Conditions Favoring Extended Family Households. *Journal of Anthropological Research* 32(2):109–123.

PAUKETAT, TIMOTHY R.

1994   *The Ascent of Chiefs: Cahokia and Mississippian Politics in Native North America.* University of Alabama Press, Tuscaloosa.

1996   The Foundations of Inequality within a Simulated Shan Community. *Journal of Anthropological Archaeology* 15:219–236.

2001   A New Tradition in Archaeology. In *The Archaeology of Traditions: Agency and History before and after Columbus,* edited by Timothy R. Pauketat, pp. 1–16. University Press of Florida, Gainesville.

PERDUE, THEDA

1998   *Cherokee Women: Gender and Culture Change, 1700–1835.* University of Nebraska Press, Lincoln.

PEREIRA, GARY M.

2002   A Typology of Spatial and Temporal Scale Relations. *Geographical Analysis* 34(1):21–33.

PERRELLI, DOUGLAS J.

1994   Gender, Mobility and Subsistence in Iroquoian Prehistory: An
        Ethnohistorical Approach to Archaeological Interpretation. Master's
        thesis, Department of Anthropology, State University of New York,
        Buffalo.

1995   *Stage 3 Archaeological Investigation of the Spaulding Lake Site (UB
        2497), Town of Clarence, Erie County, New York*. Reports of the
        Archaeological Survey 27(1). Department of Anthropology, State
        University of New York, Buffalo.

1997   *Stage 3 Archaeological Investigation of the Piestrak Site (UB
        2581), Town of Clarence, Erie County, New York*. Reports of the
        Archaeological Survey 29(9). Department of Anthropology, State
        University of New York, Buffalo.

2001   Gender Roles and Seasonal Site Use in Western New York c. A.D.
        1500: Iroquoian Domestic and Ceremonial Production at the
        Piestrak and Spaulding Lake Sites. Ph.D. dissertation, Department
        of Anthropology, State University of New York at Buffalo.

PERRELLI, DOUGLAS J., AND FRANK L. COWAN

1990   *Stage 1 Archaeological Survey of the Spaulding Lake Subdivision,
        Town of Clarence, Erie County, New York*. Reports of the Archae-
        ological Survey 22(10). Department of Anthropology, State Uni-
        versity of New York, Buffalo.

PHILLIPS, PHILIP, AND GORDON R. WILLEY

1953   Method and Theory in American Archaeology: An Operational
        Basis for Culture-Historical Integration. *American Anthropologist*
        55:615–633.

PICAZO, MARINA

1997   Hearth and Home: The Timing of Maintenance Activities. In *In-
        visible People and Processes*, edited by Jenny Moore and Eleanor
        Scott, pp. 59–67. Leicester University Press, London.

POLLOCK, SUSAN

1983   Style and Information: An Analysis of Susiana Ceramics. *Journal of
        Anthropological Archaeology* 2:354–390.

POPE, MELODY

2002   Microwear Analysis of Chipped Stone Artifacts Recovered from
        Thomas/Luckey. Manuscript on file, Public Archaeology Facility,
        Binghamton, New York.

PRENTICE, GUY

1985   Economic Differentiation among Mississippian Farmsteads. *Mid-
        continental Journal of Archaeology* 10:77–122.

PREZZANO, SUSAN C.

1992 Longhouse, Village, and Palisade: Community Patterns at the Iroquois Southern Door. Ph.D. dissertation, Department of Anthropology, Binghamton University, Binghamton, New York.

1996 Household and Community: The Development of Iroquois Agricultural Village Life. *Journal of Middle Atlantic Archaeology* 12:7–16.

1997 Warfare, Women and Households: The Development of Iroquois Culture. In *Women in Prehistory: North America and Mesoamerica,* edited by Cheryl Claassen and Rosemary A. Joyce, pp. 88–99. University of Pennsylvania Press, Philadelphia.

PREZZANO, SUSAN C., AND CHRISTINA B. RIETH

2001 Late Prehistoric Cultures of the Upper Susquehanna Valley. In *Archaeology of the Appalachian Highlands,* edited by Lynne P. Sullivan and Susan C. Prezzano, pp.168–176. University of Tennessee Press, Knoxville.

PREZZANO, SUSAN C., AND VINCAS P. STEPONAITIS

1990 *Excavations at the Boland Site, 1984–1987.* Research Report 9. Research Laboratories of Anthropology, University of North Carolina, Chapel Hill.

QUAIN, BUELL

1961 The Iroquois. In *Cooperation and Competition among Primitive Peoples,* edited by Margaret Mead, pp. 240–281. Beacon Press, Boston.

RAMSDEN, PETER G.

1977 *A Refinement of Some Aspects of Huron Ceramic Analysis.* Mercury Series, Archaeological Survey of Canada, Paper No. 63. National Museums of Canada, Ottawa.

1990 The Hurons: Archaeology and Culture History. In *The Archaeology of Southern Ontario to A.D. 1650,* edited by Chris J. Ellis and Neal Ferris, pp. 361–384. Occasional Publication of the London Chapter No. 5. Ontario Archaeological Society, London, Ontario.

1996 The Current State of Huron Archaeology. *Northeast Anthropology* 51:101–112.

RANKIN, LISA

2000 *Interpreting Long-term Trends in the Transition to Farming: Reconsidering the Nodwell Site, Ontario Canada.* BAR International Series 830. Archaeopress, Oxford.

REID, GERALD F.

2004 *Kahnawà:Ke: Factionalism, Traditionalism, and Nationalism in a Mohawk Community.* University of Nebraska Press, Lincoln.

RICE, PRUDENCE M.
1987   *Pottery Analysis: A Source Book.* Chicago University Press, Chicago.

RICHARDS, CARA
1967   Huron and Iroquois Residence Patterns, 1600–1650. In *Iroquois Culture, History and Prehistory: Conference on Iroquois Research, Glen Falls, N.Y., 1965,* edited by Elisabeth Tooker, pp. 51–56. New York State Museum and Science Center, Albany.

1969   Matriarchy or Mistake: The Role of Iroquois Women through Time. In *Cultural Stability and Cultural Change,* edited by Verne F. Kay, pp. 36–45. University of Washington Press, Seattle.

RICHTER, DANIEL K.
1983   War and Culture: The Iroquois Experience. *William and Mary Quarterly* 40:528–559.

1985   Iroquois Versus Iroquois: Jesuit Missions and Christianity in Village Politics, 1642–1686. *Ethnohistory* 32:1–16.

1989   War, Peace, and Politics in Seventeenth Century Huronia [Iroquoia]. In *Cultures in Conflict: Current Archaeological Perspectives: Proceedings of the Twentieth Annual Conference,* edited by Diana C. Tkaczak and Brian C. Vivian, pp. 283–289. Archaeological Association of the University of Calgary, Calgary.

1992   *The Ordeal of the Longhouse: The Peoples of the Iroquois League in the Era of European Colonization.* University of North Carolina Press, Chapel Hill.

RICK, ANNE M.
1991   Faunal Remains from the Enders House: An Historic Mohawk Dwelling. Manuscript on file, Zoological Identification Centre, Canadian Museum of Nature, Ottawa.

RIETH, CHRISTINA B.
1996   *Cultural Resources Reconnaissance Survey Report for Route 10, Hamlet of Baird's Corners, Town of Jefferson, Schoharie County, New York (PIN 9095.56.121).* New York State Museum, Albany.

1997   Culture Contact during the Carpenter Brook Phase: A Tripartite Approach to the Study of the Spatial and Temporal Movement of Early Iroquoian Groups throughout the Upper Susquehanna River Valley. Ph.D. dissertation, Department of Anthropology, State University of New York, Albany.

1998   *Cultural Resources Reconnaissance Survey Report for Route 80, Town of Minden, Montgomery County, New York.* New York State Museum, Albany.

2002a   Early Late Prehistoric Subsistence and Settlement Diversity in the Southern Tier of New York. In *Northeast Subsistence-Settlement*

Change: A.D. *700–1300,* edited by John P. Hart and Christina B. Rieth, pp. 209–226. New York State Museum Bulletin No. 496. University of the State of New York, State Education Department at Albany.

2002b   *Cultural Resources Site Examination Report of the Webster and Johnstone Sites for PIN 9111.18.121, Towns of Seward and Sharon, Schoharie County, New York.* New York State Museum, Albany.

RINEHART, NIELS

2000   The Faunal Assemblage from the Engelbert Site, Nichols, New York: An Analysis of Subsistence and Paleoecology. *Northeast Anthropology* 59:1–22.

RIPPETEAU, BRUCE

1978   The Upper Susquehanna Valley Iroquois: An Iroquoian Enigma. In *Essays in Northeastern Anthropology in Memory of Marion E. White,* edited by William E. Englebrecht and Donald K. Grayson, pp. 123–155. Occasional Publications in Northeastern Anthropology No. 5. Department of Anthropology, Franklin Pierce, Rindge, New Hampshire.

RITCHIE, WILLIAM A.

1944   *The Pre-Iroquoian Occupations of New York State.* Memoir 1. Rochester Museum of Arts and Sciences, Rochester, New York.

1946   Archaeological Manifestations and Relative Chronology in the Northeast. In *Man in the Northeast,* edited by Frederick Johnson, pp. 96–105. Papers of the Robert S. Peabody Foundation for Archaeology, Vol. 3. Phillips Academy, Andover, Massachusetts.

1951   A Current Synthesis of New York Prehistory. *American Antiquity* 17:130–136.

1954   *Dutch Hollow, an Early Historic Period Seneca Site in Livingston County, New York.* Research Records No. 10. Rochester Museum of Arts and Sciences, Rochester, New York.

1971   *A Typology and Nomenclature of New York Projectile Points.* New York State Museum Bulletin Number No. 384. University of the State of New York, State Education Department, Albany.

1980   *The Archaeology of New York State.* Revised edition. Harbor Hill Books, Harrison, New York.

RITCHIE, WILLIAM A., AND ROBERT E. FUNK

1973   *Aboriginal Settlement Patterns in the Northeast.* Memoir 20. New York State Museum and Science Service, State Education Department, Albany.

RITCHIE, WILLIAM A., DONALD LENIG, AND P. SCHUYLER MILLER

1953   *An Early Owasco Sequence in Eastern New York.* Circular 32. New York State Museum, Albany.

RITCHIE, WILLIAM A., AND RICHARD S. MACNEISH
1949   The Pre-Iroquoian Pottery of New York State. *American Antiquity*
        15:97–124.

ROGERS, J. DANIEL
1995   The Archaeological Analysis of Domestic Organization. In *Missis-
        sippian Communities and Households,* edited by J. Daniel Rogers
        and Bruce D. Smith, pp. 7–31. University of Alabama Press,
        Tuscaloosa.

ROSEBERRY, WILLIAM
1989   *Anthropologies and Histories.* Rutgers University Press, New
        Brunswick.

ROSSIGNOL, JAQUELINE
1992   Concepts, Methods, and Theory Building: A Landscape Approach.
        In *Space, Time, and Archaeological Landscapes,* edited by Jaqueline
        Rossignol and LuAnn Wandsnider, pp. 3–16. Plenum Press, New
        York.

ROSSIGNOL, JAQUELINE, AND LUANN WANDSNIDER (EDITORS)
1992   *Space, Time, and Archaeological Landscapes.* Plenum Press, New
        York.

ROTH, ERIC ABELLA
1989   The Developmental Cycle of Toposa Agro-Pastoralists Households.
        In *Households and Communities: Proceedings of the Twenty-First
        Annual Conference,* edited by Scott MacEachern, David Archer,
        and Richard Garvin, pp. 45–50. Archaeological Association of the
        University of Calgary, Calgary.

ROTHENBERG, DIANE
1979   The Mothers of the Nation: Seneca Resistance to Quaker Inter-
        vention. In *Women and Colonization: Anthropological Perspectives,*
        edited by Mona Etienne and Eleanor Leacock, pp. 63–87. Praeger,
        New York.

ROTHSCHILD, NAN A.
2003   *Colonial Encounters in a Native American Landscape: The Spanish
        and Dutch in North America.* Smithsonian Institution Press,
        Washington, D.C.

ROWLANDS, MICHAEL J.
1972   Defense: A Factor in the Organization of Settlements. In *Man,
        Settlement and Urbanism,* edited by Peter J. Ucko, Ruth Tringham,
        and G. W. Dimbleby, pp. 447–462. Duckworth, London.

ROWLANDS, MICHAEL J., MOGENS LARSEN, AND KRISTIAN
    KRISTIANSEN (EDITORS)
1987   *Centre and Periphery in the Ancient World.* Cambridge University
        Press, Cambridge.

ROWLEY-CONWY, PETER, AND MAREK ZVELEBIL
1989   Saving It for Later: Storage by Prehistoric Hunter-Gatherers in
        Europe. In *Bad Year Economics: Cultural Responses to Risk and
        Uncertainty,* edited by Paul Halstead and John O'Shea, pp. 40–56.
        Cambridge University Press, Cambridge.

RYE, OWEN S.
1981   *Pottery Technology: Principles and Reconstruction.* Taraxacuum,
        Washington, D.C.

SAGARD, GABRIEL
1939   [1632] *The Long Journey to the Country of the Hurons.* Edited by
        G.M. Wrong. Champlain Society, Toronto.

SAITTA, DEAN
1994   Agency, Class, and Archaeological Interpretation. *Journal of
        Anthropological Archaeology* 13:201–227.

SANDERS, DONALD
1990   Behavioral Conventions and Archaeology: Methods for the Analysis
        of Ancient Architecture. In *Domestic Architecture and the Use of
        Space,* edited by Susan Kent, pp. 43–72. Cambridge University Press,
        New York.

SASSAMAN, KENNETH E.
1992a   Lithic Technology and the Hunter-Gatherer Sexual Division of
        Labor. *North American Archaeologist* 13(3):249–262.
1992b   Gender and Technology at the Archaic-Woodland "Transition." In
        *Exploring Gender through Archaeology: Selected Papers from the
        1991 Boone Conference,* edited by Cheryl Claassen, pp. 71–79.
        Monographs in World Archaeology No.11. Prehistory Press,
        Madison, Wisconsin.
1995   The Cultural Diversity of Interactions among Mid-Holocene
        Societies of the American Southeast. In *Native American Inter-
        actions: Multiscalar Analyses and Interpretations in the Eastern
        Woodlands,* edited by Michael S. Nassaney and Kenneth E.
        Sassaman, pp. 174–204. University of Tennessee Press, Knoxville.
1998   Crafting Cultural Identities in Hunter-Gatherer Economies. In *Craft
        and Social Identity,* edited by Cathy Lynne Costin and Rita P. Wright,
        pp. 93–107. Archeological Papers of the American Anthropological
        Association Number 8. American Anthropological Association,
        Arlington, Virginia.
1999   A Southeastern Perspective on Soapstone Vessel Technology in the
        Northeast. In *The Archaeological Northeast,* edited by Mary Ann
        Levine, Kenneth E. Sassaman, and Michael S. Nassaney, pp.75–95.
        Bergin & Garvey, Westport, Connecticut.
2001a   Articulating Hidden Histories of the Mid-Holocene in the Southern
        Appalachians. In *Archaeology of the Appalachian Highlands,* edited

by Lynne P. Sullivan and Susan C. Prezzano, pp. 103–120. University of Tennessee Press, Knoxville.

2001b   Hunter-Gatherers and Traditions of Resistance. In *The Archaeology of Traditions: Agency and History before and after Columbus*, edited by Timothy R. Pauketat, pp. 218–236. University Press of Florida, Gainesville.

SCHIFFER, MICHAEL B.

1987   *Formation Processes of the Archaeological Record*. University of Utah Press, Salt Lake City.

1995   *Behavioral Archaeology: First Principles*. University of Utah Press, Salt Lake City.

SCHLANGER, SARAH H.

1992   Recognizing Persistent Places in Anasazi Settlement Systems. In *Space, Time, and Archaeological Landscapes*, edited by Jaqueline Rossignol and LuAnn Wandsnider, pp. 91–122. Plenum Press, New York.

SCHNEDIER, JANE

1977   Was There a Pre-Capitalist World System? *Peasant Studies* 6(1):20–29.

SCHOHARIE MUSEUM PROJECT FILE

1999   Osterhout 43 and 57 Sites. Manuscript on file at the Iroquois Indian Museum, Department of Archaeology, Schoharie, New York.

SCHULENBERG, JANET K.

2002   New Dates for Owasco Pots. In *Early Late Prehistoric (A.D. 700 - 1300) Subsistence and Settlement Change in the Northeast*, edited by John P. Hart and Christina B. Rieth, pp. 153–165. New York State Museum Bulletin 496. University of the State of New York, State Education Department, Albany.

SECOR, HAROLD

1987   *Pre-History of the Savannah, New York Area*. Wayne County Historical Society, Lyons, New York.

SEMPOWSKI, MARTHA L.

1994   Early Historic Exchange between the Seneca and the Susque-hannock. In *Proceedings of the 1992 People to People Conference*, edited by Charles F. Hayes III, pp. 51–64. Research Records No. 23. Rochester Museum and Science Center, Rochester, New York.

SEMPOWSKI, MARTHA L., AND LORRAINE P. SAUNDERS

2001   *Dutch Hollow and Factory Hollow: The Advent of Dutch Trade among the Seneca*, 3 Parts. Charles F. Wray Series in Seneca Archaeology, Vol. 3. Research Records No. 24. Rochester Museum and Science Center, Rochester, New York.

SEYMOUR, DENI J., AND MICHAEL B. SCHIFFER
1987   A Preliminary Analysis of Pithouse Assemblages from Snaketown, Arizona. In *Method and Theory for Activity Area Research: An Ethnoarchaeological Approach*, edited by Susan Kent, pp. 549–603. Columbia University Press, New York.

SHAFER, ANN E.
1941   The Status of Iroquois Women. In *Iroquois Women: An Anthology*, edited by W. G. Spittal, pp. 71–135. Iroqrafts Limited, Iroquois Publications, Ontario, Canada.

SHEN, CHEN
2001   *The Lithic Production System of the Princess Point Complex during the Transition to Agriculture in Southwestern Ontario, Canada.* BAR International Series 991. Archaeopress, Oxford.

SHENNAN, STEPHEN
1993   After Social Evolution: A New Archaeological Agenda? In *Archaeological Theory: Who Sets the Agenda?*, edited by Norman Yoffee and Andrew Sherratt, pp. 53–59. Cambridge University Press, New York.

SHOTT, MICHAEL J.
1992   Radiocarbon Dating as a Probabilistic Technique: The Childers Site and Late Woodland Occupation in the Ohio Valley. *American Antiquity* 57:202–230.

SIDER, GERALD
1994   Identity as History: Ethnohistory, Ethnogenesis and Ethnocide in the Southeastern United States. *Identities* 1(1):109–122.

SINOPOLI, CARLA
1988   The Organization of Craft Production at Vijayanagara, South India. *America Anthropologist* 90:580–597.

SLOMA, ROBERT A., AND KATHLEEN E. CALLUM
2002   *Archaeological Predictive Models in Vermont: A Retrospective Sample with Recommendations for Future Model Building.* Occasional Publication No. 02-BR-1. GEOARCH, Inc., Leischester, Vermont.

SMITH, DAVID G.
1990   Iroquoian Societies in Southern Ontario: Introduction and Historic Overview. In *The Archaeology of Southern Ontario to A.D. 1650*, edited by Chris J. Ellis and Neal Ferris, pp. 279–290. Occasional Publication of the London Chapter No. 5. Ontario Archaeological Society, London, Ontario.
1997   Recent Investigations of Late Woodland Occupations at Cootes Paradise, Ontario. *Ontario Archaeology* 63:4–16.

SMITH, IRA F., III

1976   A Functional Interpretation of "Keyhole" Structures in the Northeast. *Pennsylvania Archaeologist* 46(1–2):1–12.

SMITH, WALLIS

1970   A Re-appraisal of the Huron Kinship System. *Anthropologica* 12:191–206.

SNETHKAMP, PANDORA E.

1975   PIN 9357.12. In *I-88 Archaeological Project: 1975 Summer Season,* edited by M. Weide, pp. V1–V73. Public Archaeology Facility, State University of New York, Binghamton.

SNOW, DEAN R.

1980   *Archaeology of New England.* Academic Press, New York.

1989   The Evolution of Mohawk Households A.D. 1400–1800. In *Households and Communities: Proceedings of the Twenty-First Annual Conference,* edited by Scott MacEachern, David J. W. Archer, and Richard D. Garvin, pp. 293–300. Archaeological Association of the University of Calgary, Calgary.

1994a   Paleoecology and the Prehistoric Incursion of Northern Iroquoians into the Lower Great Lakes Region. In *Great Lakes Archaeology and Paleoecology: Exploring Interdisciplinary Initiatives for the Nineties,* edited by Robert I. MacDonald, pp. 283–293. Quaternary Sciences Institute, University of Waterloo.

1994b   *The Iroquois.* Blackwell, Cambridge, Massachusetts.

1995a   Microchronology and Demographic Evidence Relating to the Size of Pre-Columbian North American Indian Populations. *Science* 268:1601–1604.

1995b   *Mohawk Valley Archaeology: The Sites.* Institute for Archaeological Studies, State University of New York at Albany, Albany.

1995c   Migration in Prehistory: The Northern Iroquoian Case. *American Antiquity* 60:57–79.

1996a   More on Migration in Prehistory: Accommodating New Evidence in the Northern Iroquoian Case. *American Antiquity* 61:791–796.

1996b   Mohawk Demography and the Effects of Exogenous Epidemics on American Indian Populations. *Journal of Anthropological Archaeology* 15:160–182.

1997   The Archaeology of Iroquois Longhouses. *Northeast Anthropology* 53:31–84.

2001a   The Lessons of Northern Iroquoian Demography. In *Archaeology of the Appalachian Highlands,* edited by Lynne P. Sullivan and Susan C. Prezzano, pp. 264–277. University of Tennessee Press, Knoxville.

2001b   Evolution of the Mohawk Iroquois. In *Societies in Eclipse: Archae-ology of the Eastern Woodlands Indians*, A.D. *1400–1700*, edited by David S. Brose, C. Wesley Cowan, and Robert C. Mainfort, Jr., pp. 19–25. Smithsonian Institution Press, Washington, D.C.

SNOW, DEAN R., CHARLES T. GEHRING, AND WILLIAM A. STARNA (EDITORS)

1996   *In Mohawk Country: Early Narratives about a Native People.* Syracuse University Press, Syracuse, New York.

SNOW, DEAN R., AND DAVID B. GULDENZOPF

1998   The Mohawk Upper Castle Historic District National Historic Landmark. *The Bulletin: Journal of the New York State Archaeological Association* 114:32–44.

SNOW, DEAN R., AND KIM M. LANPHEAR

1988   European Contact and Indian Depopulation in the Northeast: The Timing of the First Epidemics. *Ethnohistory* 35:15–33.

SNOW, DEAN R., AND WILLIAM STARNA

1989   Sixteenth Century Depopulation: A View from the Mohawk Valley. *American Anthropologist* 91: 142–149.

SPECTOR, JANET D.

1983   Male/Female Task Differentiation among the Hidatsa: Toward the Development of an Archaeological Approach to the Study of Gender. In *The Hidden Half: Studies of Plains Indian Women*, edited by Patricia Albers and Beatrice Medicine, pp. 77–99. University Press of America, Washington, D.C.

1998   What This Awls Means: Feminist Archaeology at a Wahpeton Dakota Village. In *Reader in Gender Archaeology*, edited by Kelly Ann Hays-Gilpin and David S. Whitley, pp 359–364. Routledge, New York.

SPENCE, MICHAEL W.

1999   Comments: The Social Foundations of Archaeological Taxonomy. In *Taming the Taxonomy: Toward a New Understanding of Great Lakes Archaeology*, edited by Ronald F. Williamson and Christopher M. Watts, pp. 275–281. Eastendbooks, Toronto.

SPENCE, MICHAEL W., ROBERT H. PHIL, AND CARL R. MURPHY

1990   Cultural Complexes of the Early and Middle Woodland Periods. In *The Archaeology of Southern Ontario to* A.D. *1650*, edited by Chris J. Ellis and Neal Ferris, pp. 125–169. Occasional Publication of the London Chapter No. 5. Ontario Archaeological Society, London, Ontario.

STAFFORD, C. RUSSELL, AND EDWIN R. HAJIC

1992   Landscape Scale Geoenvironmental Approaches to Prehistoric Settlement Strategies. In *Space, Time, and Archaeological*

Landscapes, edited by Jaqueline Rossignol and LuAnn Wandsnider, pp. 137–161. Plenum Press, New York.

STAHL, ANN
1993 Concepts of Time and Approaches to Analogical Reasoning in Historical Perspective. *American Antiquity* 58:235–260.

STARNA, WILLIAM A., AND ROBERT E. FUNK
1994 The Place of the In Situ Hypothesis in Iroquoian Archaeology. *Northeast Anthropology* 47:45–54.

STEIN, JULIE K.
1993 Scale in Archaeology, Geosciences, and Geoarchaeology. In *Effects of Scale on Archaeological and Geoscientific Perspectives*, edited by Julie K. Stein and Angela R. Linse, pp. 1–10. Special Paper 283. Geological Society of America, Boulder.

STEWART, ALEXANDER M.
1970 *French Pioneers in the Eastern Great Lakes Area, 1609–1791.* Edited by John R. Lee. Occasional Papers No. 3. New York State Archaeological Association, Rochester, New York.

STEWART, FRANCES L.
1991 *The Faunal Remains from the Keffer Site (AkGv-14), A Southern Ontario Iroquois Village.* Research Report No. 21. Museum of Indian Archaeology, University of Western Ontario, London.

STEWART, MARILYN
1977 Pits in the Northeast: A Typological Analysis. In *Current Perspectives in Northeast Archaeology*, edited by Robert Funk and Charles F. Hayes III, pp. 149–164. Researches and Transactions XVII(1). New York State Archaeological Association, Rochester and Albany.

STEWART, R. MICHAEL
1990 Clemson's Island Studies in Pennsylvania: A Perspective. *Pennsylvania Archaeologist* 60(1):79–107.
1994 *Prehistoric Farmers of the Susquehanna Valley.* Occasional Publications in Northeastern Anthropology No. 13. Archaeological Services, Bethlehem, Connecticut.

STUIVER, MINZE, AND GORDON W. PEARSON
1986 High-Precision Calibration of the Radiocarbon Time Scale, A.D. 1950–500 B.C. *Radiocarbon* 28:805–838.

STUIVER, MINZE, AND PAULA J. REIMER
1993 Extended 14C Data Base and Revised CALIB 3.0 14C Age Calibration Program. *Radiocarbon* 35(1):215–230.

STURTEVANT, WILLIAM C.
1984 A Structural Sketch of Iroquois Ritual. In *Extending the Rafters: Interdisciplinary Approaches to Iroquois Studies*, edited by

Michael K. Foster, Jack Campisi, and Marianne Mithun, pp. 133–152. State University of New York Press, Albany, New York.

SULLIVAN, JAMES, ALEXANDER C. FLICK, AND MILTON W. HAMILTON (EDITORS)

1920–65 *The Papers of Sir William Johnson.* 14 vols. University of the State of New York, Albany.

SUTTON, RICHARD E.

1990 *Hidden amidst the Hills: Middle and Late Iroquoian Occupations in Middle Trent Valley.* Occasional Papers in Northeastern Archaeology No. 3. Copetown Press, Dundas, Ontario.

TAYLOR, ALAN

2006 *The Divided Ground: Indians, Settlers, and the Northern Borderland of the American Revolution.* Alfred A Knopf, New York.

THWAITES, REUBEN GOLD (EDITOR)

1896–   *The Jesuit Relations and Allied Documents: Travels and Explor-*
1901   *ations of the Jesuit Missionaries in New France, 1610–1791.* 73 vols. Burrows Brothers, Cleveland.

TIMMINS, PETER A.

1997 *The Calvert Site: An Interpretive Framework for the Early Iroquoian Village.* Mercury Series, Archaeological Survey of Canada, Paper No. 156. National Museums of Canada, Ottawa.

TIRO, KARIM MICHEL

1999 The People of the Standing Stone: The Oneida Indian Nation from Revolution through Removal, 1765–1840. Ph.D. dissertation, University of Pennsylvania, Philadelphia. University Microfilms, Ann Arbor.

TOOKER, ELISABETH

1981 Eighteenth Century Political Affairs and the Iroquois League. In *The Iroquois in the American Revolution: 1976 Conference Proceedings,* edited by Charles F. Hayes III, pp. 1–12. Research Records No. 14. Rochester Museum and Science Center, Rochester, New York.

1984 Women in Iroquoian Society. In *Extending the Rafters: Interdisciplinary Approaches to Iroquoian Studies,* edited by M. Foster, J. Campisi, and M. Mithun, pp. 109–123. State University of New York Press, Albany.

1991 *An Ethnography of the Huron Indians 1615–1649.* Syracuse University Press, Syracuse, New York.

TRELEASE, ALLEN W.

1960 *Indian Affairs in Colonial New York.* Cornell University Press, Ithaca.

TRIGGER, BRUCE G.

1968 The Determinates of Settlement Patterns. In *Settlement Archaeology,* edited by Kwang-chih Chang, pp. 53–78. National Press, Palo Alto.

1976   *The Children of Aataentsic: A History of the Huron People to 1660.*
        McGill-Queen's University Press, Montreal.

1978   Iroquoian Matriliny. *Pennsylvania Archaeologist* 48(1–2):55–65.

1981   Prehistoric Social and Political Organization: An Iroquoian Case
        Study. In *Foundations of Northeastern Archaeology,* edited by
        Dean R. Snow, pp. 1–50. Academic Press, New York.

1985   *Natives and Newcomers: Canada's "Heroic Age" Reconsidered.*
        McGill-Queen's University Press, Kingston.

1989   *A History of Archaeological Thought.* Cambridge University Press,
        New York.

1990   *The Huron Farmers of the North.* Holt, Rinehart and Winston, Fort
        Worth, Texas.

TRINGHAM, RUTH E.
1991   Households with Faces: The Challenge of Gender in Prehistoric
        Architectural Remains. In *Engendering Archaeology: Women and
        Prehistory,* edited by Joan M. Gero and Margaret W. Conkey, pp.
        93–131. Basil Blackwell, Oxford, England.

TUCK, JAMES A.
1971   *Onondaga Iroquois Prehistory: A Study in Settlement Archaeology.*
        Syracuse University Press, Syracuse, New York.

1978   Northern Iroquoian Prehistory. In *Northeast,* edited by Bruce G.
        Trigger, pp. 322–333. Handbook of North American Indians,
        Vol. 15, William C. Sturtevant, general editor. Smithsonian Insti-
        tution, Washington, D.C.

TURNBAUGH, WILLIAM
1977   *Man, Land, and Time: The Cultural Prehistory and Demographic
        Patterns of North-Central Pennsylvania.* Lycoming County His-
        torical Society, Williamsport, Pennsylvania.

TURNER, MONICA G., ROBERT V. O'NEILL, ROBERT H. GARDNER, AND
    BRUCE T. MILNE
1989   Effects of Changing Spatial Scale on the Analysis of Landscape
        Pattern. *Landscape Ecology* 3:153–162.

TYYSKA, ALLEN
1972   Huron Sweat Baths. Paper Presented at the Annual Meeting of the
        Canadian Archaeological Association. St. John's, Newfoundland,
        Canada.

USNER, DANIEL H., JR.
1992   *Indians, Settlers, and Slaves in a Frontier Exchange Economy: The
        Lower Mississippi Valley before 1783.* University of North Carolina
        Press, Chapel Hill.

1998   *American Indians in the Lower Mississippi Valley: Social and Eco-
        nomic Histories.* University of Nebraska Press, Lincoln.

VAILLANCOURT, DANA R.

1990   *A Cultural Resources Survey Report of PIN 9306.45.102/BIN 1004080, Route 7 over Cobleskill Creek, Town of Richmondville, Schoharie County, New York.* New York State Museum, Albany.

VAN DEN BOGAERT, HARMEN MEYNDERTSZ

1988   *A Journey into Mohawk and Oneida Country, 1634–1635.* Translated and edited by Charles T. Gehring and William A. Starna. Syracuse University Press, Syracuse, New York.

VAN DER DONCK, A. C.

1996   Description of New Netherland, 1653. In *In Mohawk Country: Early Narratives about a Native People,* edited by Dean R. Snow, Charles T. Gehring, and William A. Starna, pp. 104–130. Syracuse University Press, Syracuse, New York.

VERSAGGI, NINA M.

1987   Hunter-Gatherer Settlement Models and the Archaeological Record: A Test Case from the Upper Susquehanna Valley of New York. Ph.D. dissertation, Department of Anthropology, State University of New York, Binghamton.

1996a   Prehistoric Hunter-Gatherer Settlement Models: Interpreting the Upper Susquehanna Valley. In *A Golden Chronograph for Robert E. Funk,* edited by Chris Lindner and Edward V. Curtin, pp. 129–140. Occasional Publications in Northeastern Anthropology No. 15. Archaeological Services, Bethlehem, Connecticut.

1996b   Hunter-Gatherer Adaptations in the Upper Susquehanna: Are the Uplands Part of the Picture? Paper presented at the Conference on Integrating Appalachian Highlands Archaeology. New York State Museum, Albany, New York.

1999a   Regional Diversity within the Early Woodland of the Northeast. *Northeast Anthropology* 57:45–56.

1999b   Recent Contributions to the Archaeology of Central New York: Discussion. Paper presented at the 39th Annual Meeting of the Northeastern Anthropological Association, Providence, Rhode Island.

VERSAGGI, NINA M., AND TIMOTHY D. KNAPP

2000   Steatite, Interaction, and Persistence: The Transitional Period of New York's Upper Susquehanna. Paper presented at the 65th Annual Meeting of the Society for American Archaeology, Philadelphia, Pennsylvania.

VERSAGGI, NINA M., AND LAURIE E. MIROFF

2004   The Vestal Phase Revisited: A New Look at the Late Archaic in the Susquehanna Valley of New York. Paper presented at the 69th Annual Meeting of the Society for American Archaeology, Montreal, Canada.

VERSAGGI, NINA M., LOU ANN WURST, T. CREGG MADRIGAL, AND
    ANDREA LAIN
2001   Adding Complexity to Late Archaic Research in the Northeastern
    Appalachians. *Archaeology of the Appalachian Highlands*, edited by
    Lynne P. Sullivan and Susan C. Prezzano, pp. 121–133. University of
    Tennessee Press, Knoxville.

VOLMAR, MICHAEL A., AND SHIRLEY BLANCKE
2002   Landscape Interpretation on the Microscopic Scale: Case Studies
    in Southern New England. In *A Lasting Impression Coastal,
    Lithic, and Ceramic Research in New England Archaeology*,
    edited by Jordan E. Kerber, pp. 125–138. Praeger Press, Westport,
    Connecticut.

WALLACE, ANTHONY F. C.
1969   *The Death and Rebirth of the Seneca*. Vintage Books, New York.

WALLACE, PAUL A. W.
1993   *Indian Paths of Pennsylvania*. Pennsylvania Historical and Museum
    Commission, Harrisburg.

WANDSNIDER, LUANN
1992a   Archaeological Landscape Studies. In *Space, Time, and Archae-
    ological Landscapes*, edited by Jaqueline Rossignol and LuAnn
    Wandsnider, pp. 285–292. Plenum Press, New York.
1992b   The Spatial Dimension of Time. In *Space, Time, and Archaeological
    Landscapes*, edited by Jaqueline Rossignol and LuAnn Wandsnider,
    pp. 257–282. Plenum Press, New York.
1998   Regional Scale Processes and Archaeological Landscape Units. In
    Unit Issues in Archaeology Measuring Time, Space, and Material,
    edited by Ann F. Ramenofsky and Anastsia Steffen, pp. 87–102.
    University of Utah Press, Salt Lake City.

WARRICK, GARY A.
1984   *Reconstructing Ontario Iroquoian Village Organization*. Mercury
    Series, Archaeological Survey of Canada, Paper No. 124:1–180.
    National Museums of Canada, Ottawa.
1988   Estimating Ontario Iroquoian Village Duration. *Man in the
    Northeast* 36:21–60.
1990   A Population History of the Huron-Petun, A.D. 900–1650. Ph.D.
    dissertation, Department of Anthropology, McGill University,
    Montreal.
1996   Evolution of the Iroquoian Longhouse. In *People Who Lived
    in Big Houses: Archaeological Perspectives on Large Domestic
    Structures*, edited by Gary Coupland and E. B. Banning, pp. 11–26.
    Monographs in World Archaeology No. 27. Prehistory Press,
    Madison, Wisconsin.

2000   The Precontact Iroquoian Occupation of Southern Ontario. *Journal of World Prehistory* 14:415–466.

2001   The Causes and Consequences of the Iroquoian Colonization of Ontario. Paper presented at the Annual Meeting of the Society for America Archaeology, New Orleans, Louisiana.

WATSON, ADAM S.

2000   Subsistence and Change at Townley-Read: A Faunal Analysis of a Historic Period Seneca Iroquois Site. Senior honors thesis, Department of Anthropology, Cornell University, Ithaca, New York.

WATSON, PATTY JO, AND MARY KENNEDY

1991   The Development of Horticulture in the Eastern Woodlands of North America: Women's Role. In *Engendering Archaeology: Women and Prehistory,* edited by Joan M. Gero and Margaret W. Conkey, pp. 255–275. Basil Blackwell, Oxford, England.

WAUGH, FREDERICK

1916   *Iroquois Foods and Food Preparation.* Government Printing Bureau, Ottawa, Ontario.

WEBER, J. CYNTHIA

1973   *Report of the I-88 Archaeological Salvage Project for PIN 9357.02 through PIN 9357.14.* Public Archaeology Facility, State University of New York, Binghamton.

WEINS, J. A.

1989   Spatial Scaling in Ecology. *Functional Ecology* 3:385–397.

WEST, MICHAEL C.

2001   Early 18th Century Environment and Trade at Townley-Read: A Seneca Iroquois Site Faunal Analysis. Senior thesis, Archaeology Program, Cornell University, Ithaca, New York.

WESTCOTT, KONNIE L., AND R. JOE BRANDON (EDITORS)

2000   *Practical Applications of GIS for Archaeologists.* Taylor & Francis Inc., Philadelphia, Pennsylvania.

WHALLON, ROBERT, JR.

1968   Investigations of Late Prehistoric Social Organization in New York State. In *New Perspectives in Archaeology,* edited by Sally R. Binford and Lewis R. Binford, pp. 223–244. Aldine Publishing Company, Chicago.

WHITE, MARIAN E.

1978   Neutral and Wenro. In *Northeast,* edited by Bruce G. Trigger, pp. 407–411. Handbook of North American Indians, Vol. 15, William C. Sturtevant, general editor. Smithsonian Institution, Washington, D.C.

n.d.   Field Notebook, Cayuga Archaeological Project. Manuscript on file at the Marian E. White Museum, University at Buffalo, State University of New York.

WHITE, MARIAN E., WILLIAM E. ENGELBRECHT, AND ELISABETH
  TOOKER
1978   Cayuga. In *Northeast*, edited by Bruce G. Trigger, pp. 500–504.
        Handbook of North American Indians, Vol. 15, William C.
        Sturtevant, general editor. Smithsonian Institution, Washington, D.C.

WHITE, RICHARD
1983   *The Roots of Dependency: Subsistence, Environment, and Social
        Change among the Choctaws, Pawnees, and Navajos.* University of
        Nebraska Press, Lincoln.
1991   *The Middle Ground: Indians, Empires, and Republics in the Great
        Lakes Region, 1650–1815.* Cambridge University Press, Cambridge.

WIESSNER, POLLY
1974   A Functional Estimator of Population from Floor Area. *American
        Antiquity* 39:343–350.

WILK, RICHARD R., AND STEPHEN MILLER
1997   Some Methodological Issues in Counting Communities and
        Households. *Human Organization* 56(1):64–70.

WILK, RICHARD R., AND ROBERT McC. NETTING
1984   Households: Changing Form and Function. In *Households:
        Comparative and Historical Studies of the Domestic Group,* edited
        by Robert McC. Netting, Richard Wilk, and Eric J. Arnould, pp.
        1–28. University of California Press, Berkeley.

WILK, RICHARD R., AND WILLIAM L. RATHJE
1982   Household Archaeology. *American Behavioral Scientist*
        25(6):617–639.

WILLEY, GORDON R., AND PHILIP PHILLIPS
2001   *Method and Theory in American Archaeology.* University of
        Alabama Press, Tuscaloosa.

WILLIAMS, MARY BETH, AND JEFFREY BENDREMER
1997   The Archaeology of Maize, Pots, and Seashells: Gender Dynamics
        in Late Woodland and Contact-Period New England. In *Women in
        Prehistory: North America and Mesoamerica,* edited by Cheryl
        Claassen and Rosemary Joyce, pp. 136–149. University of Penn-
        sylvania Press, Philadelphia.

WILLIAMS-SHUKER, KIMBERLY
2005   Cayuga Iroquois Households and Gender Relations during
        the Contact Period: An Investigation of the Rogers Farm Site,
        1660s–1680s. Ph.D. dissertation, Department of Anthropology,
        University of Pittsburgh.

WILLIAMS-SHUKER, KIMBERLY, AND KATHLEEN M. SYDORIAK ALLEN
1998   Longhouse Remains at the Carman Site. Paper presented at the
        Cayuga Museum Northeast Archaeological Symposium, Auburn,
        New York.

WILLIAMSON, RONALD F.

1983   *The Robin Hood Site: A Study in Functional Variability in Late Iroquoian Settlement Patterns.* Monographs in Ontario Archaeology 1. Ontario Archaeological Society, London.

1990   The Early Iroquoian Period of Southern Ontario. In *The Archaeology of Southern Ontario to A.D. 1650,* edited by Chris J. Ellis and Neal Ferris, pp. 291–320. Occasional Publication of the London Chapter No. 5. Ontario Archaeological Society, London, Ontario.

WILLIAMSON, RONALD F., AND CHRISTOPHER M. WATTS (EDITORS)

1999   *Taming the Taxonomy: Toward a New Understanding of Great Lakes Archaeology.* Eastendbooks, Toronto.

WITTHOFT, JOHN

1971   Pottery from the Stewart Site. In *Foundations of Pennsylvania Prehistory,* edited by Barry C. Kent, Ira F. Smith III, and Catherine McCann, pp. 467–475. Pennsylvania Historical and Museum Commission, Harrisburg.

WITTHOFT, JOHN, AND S. S. FARVER

1971   Two Shenk's Ferry Sites in Lebanon County, Pennsylvania. In *Foundations of Pennsylvania Prehistory,* edited by Barry C. Kent, Ira F. Smith III, and Catherine McCann, pp. 425–466. Pennsylvania Historical and Museum Commission, Harrisburg.

WOBST, MARTIN

1977   Stylistic Behavior and Information Exchange. In *For the Director: Research Essays in Honor of J. B. Griffin,* edited by Charles Cleland, pp. 317–342. Anthropological Paper 61. University of Michigan Museum of Anthropology, Ann Arbor.

WOLF, ERIC

1982   *Europe and the People without History.* University of California Press, Berkeley.

WOOLFREY, SANDRA, PRINCE CHITWOOD, AND NORMAN E. WAGNER

1976   Who Made the Pipes? A Study of Decorative Motifs on Middleport Pipe and Pottery Collections. *Ontario Archaeology* 27: 3–12.

WRAY, CHARLES F.

1973   *A Manual for Seneca Iroquois Archeology.* Cultures Primitive, Honeoye Falls, New York.

WRAY, CHARLES F., AND HARRY L. SCHOFF

1953   A Preliminary Report on the Seneca Sequence in Western New York, 1550–1687. *Pennsylvania Archaeologist* 23(2):53–63.

WRAY, CHARLES F., MARTHA L. SEMPOWSKI, AND LORRAINE P. SAUNDERS

1991   *Tram and Cameron: Two Early Contact Era Sites.* Charles F. Wray Series in Seneca Archaeology, Vol. 2. C. F. Hayes III, series editor.

Research Records No. 21. Rochester Museum and Science Center, Rochester, New York.

WRAY, CHARLES F., MARTHA L. SEMPOWSKI, LORRAINE P. SAUNDERS, AND GIAN C. CERVONE

1987   *The Adams and Culbertson Sites.* Charles F. Wray Series in Seneca Archaeology, Vol. 1. Charles F. Hayes III, series editor. Research Records No. 19. Rochester Museum and Science Center, Rochester, New York.

WRIGHT, JAMES V.

1966   *The Ontario Iroquois Tradition.* Bulletin 210, Anthropological Series Number 75. National Museums of Canada, Ottawa.

1974   *The Nodwell Site.* Mercury Series, Archaeological Survey of Canada, Paper No. 22. National Museums of Canada, Ottawa.

WRIGHT, MILTON J.

1986   *The Uren Site AfHd-2: An Analysis and Reappraisal of the Uren Substage Type Site.* Ontario Archaeology Monograph Series No. 1. Ontario Archaeological Society, Toronto.

WU, JIANGUO, AND HARBIN LI

2006   Concepts of Scale and Scaling. In *Scaling and Uncertainty Analysis in Ecology: Methods and Applications,* edited by Jianguo Wu, Bruce Jones, Habin Li, and Orie Loucks, pp. 3–15. Springer, Dordrecht, The Netherlands.

YAEGER, JASON, AND MARCELLO A. CANUTO

2000   Introducing an Archaeology of Communities. In *The Archaeology of Communities: A New World Perspective,* edited by Marcello A. Canuto and Jason Yaeger, pp. 1–15. Routledge, New York.

YANAGISAKO, SYLVIA J.

1979   Family and Household: The Analysis of Domestic Groups. *Annual Review of Anthropology* 8:161–205.

YELLEN, JOHN

1977   *Archaeological Approaches to the Present: Models for Reconstructing the Past.* Academic Press, New York.

YERKES, RICHARD W.

1989   Mississippian Craft Specialization on the American Bottom. *Southeastern Archaeology* 8(2):93–106.

ZVELEBIL, MAREK, STANTON W. GREEN, AND MARK G. MACKLIN

1992   Archaeological Landscapes, Lithic Scatters, and Human Behavior. In *Space, Time, and Archaeological Landscapes,* edited by Jaqueline Rossignol and LuAnn Wandsnider, pp. 193–226. Plenum Press, New York.

Contributors

KATHLEEN M. SYDORIAK ALLEN is a lecturer in the Department of Anthropology at the University of Pittsburgh. Her research interests include household and settlement archaeology in the eastern Great Lakes region and cultural interactions between Native populations and Europeans and their expression in material culture.

WILLIAM ENGELBRECHT is professor emeritus of anthropology at Buffalo State College. He is currently analyzing material from 17 summer archaeological field schools he directed at the Eaton site in West Seneca, New York. He is also serving as president of the New York State Archaeological Association.

KURT A. JORDAN is an assistant professor of anthropology and American Indian studies at Cornell University. His research interests include the archaeology of eighteenth-century Iroquois (Haudenosaunee) communities; political economy; colonialism, cultural entanglement, and indigenous autonomy; and the production and circulation of marine shell, red pipestone, and red slate artifacts in the Northeast.

TIMOTHY D. KNAPP is assistant to the director for prehistoric research at the Public Archaeology Facility, Binghamton University, State University of New York. His primary research interests focus on the social implications of the transition from an extractive subsistence economy to one centered on food production as it unfolded across the Northeast.

TRACY S. MICHAUD-STUTZMAN is an adjunct professor of anthropology at the University of Southern Maine. Her work on prehistoric Iroquois sites was rooted in the concept of scale. Her current research interests revolve around economic development and applied anthropology.

LAURIE E. MIROFF is an adjunct professor of anthropology at Binghamton University and a project director at the Public Archaeology Facility, Binghamton University. Her research interests include Late Prehistoric household and community organization in the Northeast. Recently she has been examining hunter-gatherer diversity in the Upper Susquehanna drainage.

DOUGLAS J. PERRELLI is director of the Archaeological Survey, University at Buffalo. His research interests include Iroquoian studies, the archaeology of gender, and the organization of lithic technology.

CHRISTINA B. RIETH is state archaeologist and director of the Cultural Resource Survey Program at the New York State Museum. Her research interests include prehistoric ceramic analysis, Late Prehistoric settlement and subsistence, interaction and exchange among Northeast populations, and archaeometric analysis of artifacts.

PETER TIMMINS is an assistant professor in the Department of Anthropology at the University of Western Ontario and president of Timmins Martelle Heritage Consultants Inc., a cultural resource management firm located in London, Ontario. His research interests include Iroquoian socio-political development, settlement pattern studies, and collaborative projects with local First Nations.

KIMBERLY WILLIAMS-SHUKER is a research associate in the Department of Anthropology at the University of Pittsburgh. She is also an adjunct faculty member at the Community College of Allegheny County. Her research interests in archaeology include household organization, gender roles, and culture contact and globalization processes.

Index

Page numbers in **boldface** refer to illustrations.

Iroquoian Archaeology and Analytic Scale was designed and typeset on a Macintosh computer system using InDesign software. The body text is set in 10/13 Sabon and display type is set in Century Gothic. This book was designed and typeset by Chad Pelton, and manufactured by Thomson-Shore, Inc.